The United States and
the European Trade Union
Movement, 1944–1951

THE United STATES AND THE EUROPEAN TRADE UNION MOVEMENT, 1944-1951

Federico Romero

TRANSLATED BY HARVEY FERGUSSON II

The University of North Carolina Press • Chapel Hill & London

This publication was made possible through the
cooperation of Biblioteca Italia, a Giovanni Agnelli
Foundation program for the diffusion of Italian culture.
Further support was generously provided by the
National Italian American Foundation.

Originally published by Edizioni Lavoro in 1989. © 1989
Edizioni Lavoro

First published by the University of North Carolina Press
in 1992. © 1992 The University of North Carolina Press

Manufactured in the United States of America

96 95 94 93 92   5 4 3 2 1

Library of Congress Cataloging-in-Publication Data
Romero, Federico.
   [Stati Uniti e il sindacalismo europeo, 1944–1951.
English]
   The United States and the European trade union
movement, 1944–1951 / by Federico Romero ; translated
by Harvey Fergusson II.
     p.   cm.
   Includes bibliographical references and index.
   ISBN 0-8078-2065-2 (cloth : alk. paper)
   1. Trade-unions—Europe—History—20th century.
2. Reconstruction (1939–1951)—Europe. 3. Economic
assistance, American—Europe—History—20th century.
4. Marshall Plan.   I. Title.
   HD6657.R6513   1993
   331.88'094'0904—dc20   92-27645
                                                   CIP

The paper in this book meets the guidelines for permanence
and durability of the Committee on Production Guidelines
for Book Longevity of the Council on Library Resources.

To Dorothea Barrett

CONTENTS

PREFACE

This book originated primarily in my curiosity about all aspects of the international role of the United States at the end of World War II. During the reconstruction of Western Europe, America was not only the strategically dominant power, the giver of aid, and the political model that led many nations toward an Atlantic alignment, it was also the suggestive image of a rich and democratic society, an ideal for many to emulate, but a negative one for others, the source of a culture that was widely diffused in myriad ways, both spiritual and material. America was a force both of powerful attraction and of repulsion for many classes of European society.

As has recently been elucidated by the most current historical writing on "Americanization," the United States, in addition to being a world power with which European governments interacted, was also a social, cultural, and anthropo-logical presence, a "new world" which the old societies, rebuilding their rules, actors, and concepts, had to confront. How much of United States predominance in the postwar period was due not only to American troops and economic aid, but to the projection of the totality of American society as an image and model for the future?

The interminable debate of the 1970s on the origins of the Cold War and the nature of American foreign policy suggests that the economic and social aspects constituted not just the background, but rather a crucial factor in United States influence on postwar Europe. Scholars in Italy and especially in Germany have brought to light important events in which the United States played a crucial role in the political reconstruction of those two countries. Research on the Marshall Plan and the continent's economic recovery extended the perceived reach of American influence from trade and financial flows to ideological propaganda, to the diffusion of the acquisitive and consumer-oriented values of the American way of life, to systems of social organization and models of industrial relations. The multifaceted origin of the ideas that inspired the Truman administration's policies, as well as the bureaucracies that implemented them in Europe, showed the degree to which the institutions of American civil society, from industry to unions and from ethnic representation to mass media, were an active part of United States activities in the international arena. They enriched and articulated those activities with the resources, ideas, and solutions that had grown up during the nation's historical development.

The protagonists of these policies were well aware of this, and historians have begun to concentrate in this direction. With the formula of "the politics of productivity" (which all subsequent historical literature has had to consider), Charles S. Maier tied the hegemony of the United States in the reconstruction of Europe to its capacity to project abroad the model of growth and social integration that had developed in the New Deal and wartime mobilization. The conflict over the Marshall Plan that raged in the political and trade union arenas was connected both to Cold War strategies and to the economic assumptions of American foreign policy. Faced with a range of American activities characterized chiefly by pronounced social complexity, many historians began by investigating, on the one hand, the process of the Marshall Plan's formation and, on the other, its implementation and results. What led the main organized social interests to join in the Marshall Plan and in the political and economic initiatives of the Truman administration in general? What was the origin of the extraordinary international activism of the American unions, which was progressively coordinated with Washington's foreign policy? What contribution did this multiplicity of institutional and social organizations, committed to offering a proposal of reconstruction to Europe, make to American international policy? Most important of all, what was their impact on the character of the Cold War, and what were the consequences for the reconstruction efforts adopted by their European partners?

My research derived from these questions, and this book is an attempt to answer them. Its primary topic is American intervention in postwar European trade union affairs. The field of investigation is the political, cultural, and institutional processes that led typically domestic organizations to take an active part in American foreign policy, to become actors in the Cold War, and to attempt to export to Europe their own models of organization and negotiation. From the final phase of the war to the conclusion of the Marshall Plan, the book covers the increasing interaction with which the government and union bureaucracies drew up and applied a policy for Europe that needed to be most successfully applied in the labor field. The European trade union movement in fact was a crucial crossroads between the issues of economic stabilization, the anti-Communist political conflict, a search for consensus, and the modernization of social processes. For this reason it was the object of conspicuous political attention from the American side, to the point that it became one of the decisive "fronts" of the Cold War.

Finally, with an interpretation of the various consequences of this American policy, and with an evaluation of its successes and failures, the book proceeds to reexamine critically some of the bases of American postwar international policy. By comparing the political goals with the development of reconstruction in Western Europe, it attempts to describe the effective meaning of the "Americanization" phenomenon. The book closes with a discussion of some themes I believe are at the center of a comparative historical analysis, which is possible by now and which has been developed on the trade union models adopted by various Western countries in the postwar period and, more extensively, on the basic outlines of modernization in the West.

American foreign policy thinking, on union issues as on many others, looked on Europe as a united whole, as a continental area more than a group of countries. Its economic objectives included overcoming nationalistic policies in favor of supranational integration. The strategic imperative of the United States was to win the battle for international hegemony in the most industrialized regions of the continent. The historical and conceptual roots of the policy came from solutions to development problems reached in the large American market. They were now proposed again as plans for postwar economic policy in Europe. The historical importance of the Marshall Plan is based largely on this universal and unitary aspect. It is therefore in this light and in the light of its continental ambition—though it was soon limited to the western half of Europe—that American activities are reconstructed and analyzed here.

Europe, however, is composed of nations, and even American policy had to descend from a general and common outlook and extend itself in specific and sometimes different situations. It was especially in the context of individual nations, with their differing economic and political realities, that the implementation of American policy encountered its successes and failures, its accomplishments and frustrations. The individual characteristics and traditions of each nation had not been nullified by the war, and they could not be overcome by the intellectual coherence of a universal program for the regeneration of Europe. This contrast was of fundamental importance. It often brought out the basic abstraction that was built into American planning. It is a contradiction that often faces the historian: the impact of American activities can be studied only in the context of individual nations. Therefore this context cannot be avoided in an interpretation of American policy that is meant to consider results as well as intentions.

For this reason, the description of the European context of American policy, especially the Marshall Plan and the struggle to line up the unions with the West, is accompanied and completed by the analysis of a specific national case—that of

Italy. In addition to the author's personal interest, which is not insignificant, the Italian scene has a variety of general and specific characteristics that are both typical and unique and make Italy an enlightening test case for the whole range of American policy, although it is by no means exhaustive. From the United States's perspective it was Italy, after Germany and France, whose political stabilization was the most urgent and also the most difficult to achieve. Both in the immediate postwar period and at the height of the Cold War, Italy was one of the main countries where American activities achieved clear-cut successes and at the same time encountered stiff resistance, testing in this way both the effectiveness of its power and the impossibility of some of its plans.

Italy was the first country where the American government came face to face with the issues of reconstruction and the political and economic problems that were to characterize the reconstruction of the trade union movement in postwar Europe. Furthermore, the nature of the political confrontation and the presence of a strong Communist party put Italy on the frontier of the Cold War, where one of the symbolic battles of the greatest conflict between East and West was fought, especially between 1947 and 1949. Then, during the Marshall Plan period, Italy provided one of the most extreme examples of the contrasts implicit in American activities between desire for reform and modernization, on the one hand, and the strategic priority of anti-Communist stabilization, on the other. Thus an analysis of the Italian case provides an especially vivid example of the tensions present in American policy, of the interaction between various forces and motives that were behind it, and of the partial incongruity of both its inspirations and the results it achieved. The intervention of the American government in Italian trade union activity is presented as a case study that provides greater depth and concreteness to the analysis of a program conceived and carried out on a continental level.

The study of other national cases would clearly bring out different specific problems. But what we know of the impact of the Marshall Plan in Great Britain, Germany, and France, whose experiences will be discussed as a comparison in the conclusion, confirms the same dilemma brought out by the examination of reconstruction in Italy, even though circumstances differed. The American plans elicited responses and reactions from the countries concerned that coincided only partially with Washington's aims. No European nation presented a blank sheet of paper for experiments in social engineering to be derived from the American experience. The proposal to reestablish Europe and to "Americanize" its social customs drew its political force from the strategic universality of its design and from the degree of American commitment. But its limits were there also, due to the abstraction, and to some extent the incoherence, of a theoretical model that could be applied only partially and was sometimes distorted as it was implemented in the reality of specific historical circumstances.

The debts of gratitude accumulated over years of research are such and so numerous that they cannot effectively be repaid. However, these debts can at least be mentioned, although that does not repay them. I have discussed the entire scope of this research as well as its limits, directions, and results with Gian Giacomo Migone and Alan S. Milward, receiving encouragement and guidance that go well beyond a fruitful professional collaboration, since they have not only enriched this book but also led me on an intellectual and personal journey. I have received invaluable advice and inestimable help in locating numerous sources from Ronald Filippelli, Horst Lademacher, and Margherita Zander. Nicola Tranfaglia, Dora Marucco, James Miller, Ennio Di Nolfo, Mariuccia Salvati, and John Harper have read the manuscript in various stages, providing criticism and suggestions without which it would certainly have been poorer and less clear. From David Montgomery, Joseph La Palombara, Charles S. Maier, Lutz Niethammer, Victor Reuther, and Vincenzo Saba I have received several suggestions that rescued me from circular reasoning and pointed the way to more fruitful fields of endeavor. I would like to thank those without whose work in various archives and libraries this book would have been simply impossible: Jerry N. Hess, Sally M. Marks, David A. Pfeiffer, and John Taylor at the National Archives; Catherine Vogel and Tom Connors at the AFL-CIO archives; Anthony Zito at the archives of the Catholic University of America; Robert Lazar at the archives of the ILGWU; Hank Guzda at the Historical Office of the Department of Labor; Mila Scarlatti at the library of the Centro Studi CISL (Florence); and personnel of the Giulio Pastore Foundation in Rome.

Finally, I would like to thank with particular affection Mark, Phyllis, Jim, and Fynnette, because of whom Washington and the United States are not impersonal fields of study.

This American edition was made possible by the generosity of the Giovanni Agnelli Foundation and the friendly efforts of James Miller and Tom Row, to whom I extend my sincere gratitude.

ABBREVIATIONS USED IN THE TEXT

ACC	Allied Control Commission (later Allied Commission, AC)
ACLI	Associazioni cristiane lavoratori italiani (Christian Associations of Italian Workers)
ACTU	Association of Catholic Trade Unionists
AFL	American Federation of Labor
AMG	Allied Military Government
CDG	Consigli di gestione (Worker-Management Councils)
CGIL	Confederazione generale italiana del lavoro (Italian General Confederation of Labor)
CGL	Confederazione generale del lavoro (General Confederation of Labor)
CGT	Confédération Générale du Travail (General Confederation of Labor)
CIA	Central Intelligence Agency
CIO	Congress of Industrial Organizations
CISL	Confederazione italiana sindacati lavoratori (Italian Confederation of Workers' Unions)
CIT	Confederacion Interamericana de Trabajadores (Interamerican Labor Confederation)
CLN	Comitato di liberazione nazionale (Committee of National Liberation)
CLNAI	Comitato di liberazione nazionale alta Italia (Committee of National Liberation in Northern Italy)
CNP	Comitato nazionale per la produttività (National Productivity Committee)
DC	Democrazia cristiana (Christian Democratic Party)
DGB	Deutscher Gewerkschaftsbund (German Federation of Trade Unions)

ECA	Economic Cooperation Administration
ERP	European Recovery Program
ERP-TUAC	European Recovery Program Trade Union Advisory Committee
FEA	Foreign Economic Administration
FIALC	Free Italian-American Labor Council
FIL	Federazione italiana del lavoro (Italian Labor Federation)
FO	Force Ouvrière (French Labor Federation)
FTUC	Free Trade Union Committee
IALC	Italian-American Labor Council
ICFTU	International Confederation of Free Trade Unions
IFTU	International Federation of Trade Unions
ILGWU	International Ladies' Garment Workers' Union
ILO	International Labour Organization
ITS	International Trade Secretariats
ITWF	International Transport Workers Federation
LCGIL	Libera confederazione generale italiana del lavoro (Free Italian General Confederation of Labor)
MSA	Mutual Security Agency
NATO	North Atlantic Treaty Organization
NSC	National Security Council
OEEC	Organization for European Economic Cooperation
OSS	Office of Strategic Services
PCI	Partito comunista italiano (Italian Communist Party)
PdA	Partito d'azione (Action Party)
PRI	Partito repubblicano italiano (Italian Republican Party)
PSI	Partito socialista italiano (Italian Socialist Party)
PSIUP	Partito socialista italiano di unità proletaria (Italian Socialist Party of Proletarian Unity)
PSLI	Partito socialista lavoratori italiani (Italian Socialist Workers' Party)
PSU	Partito socialista unitario (Unitary Socialist Party)
TUC	Trade Union Congress (British)
UAW	United Automobile Workers
UIL	Unione italiana del lavoro (Italian Workers' Union)
UNRRA	United Nations Relief and Rehabilitation Administration
USWA	United Steel Workers of America
WFTU	World Federation of Trade Unions

Part One

THE POST-WAR

RECONVERSION, 1944–1946

CHAPTER

A Prosperous, Stable,
and Democratic World

Toward the end of World War II, the United States looked on the coming peace with contrasting feelings of faith and dismay. It was confronted with a magnificent historical opportunity and at the same time with problems of immense complexity. From the height of their economic and military supremacy, the American leaders regarded the reorganization of the international system as a not entirely diplomatic problem:

> Our objective in all our relations with other nations is to prevent aggression . . . and to develop those conditions of international life that will make it possible to maintain high levels of productive employment and farm income and steadily rising standards of living for all the American people. . . . Economic warfare, depressions, hunger, poverty and despair—these are the conditions that undermine democracy and block its development, that breed tyrants and aggressors, and that turn nations one against the other. These are conditions that we must fight to master if any international organization is to succeed in preserving peace.[1]

Both the government and the majority of the country's elite found the basis of a peaceful new order in the reestablishment of worldwide economic prosperity: "Peace is possible only if countries work together and prosper together. This is why the economic aspects are no less important than the political aspects of peace."[2]

Several very different factors put the economic basis of peacemaking into high relief: the experience of the Depression and the collapse of the international

economic system in the 1930s; the universalism of Wilson's ideals and the new
awareness of America's potential hegemony; the basic expansive interests that
were an integral part of the U.S. manufacturing sector and the need to rebuild the
rest of the industrialized world; a vision of political stability based on economic
growth; and a universal, urgent, and popular demand for security and prosperity.
These ideas were not merely improvised. From the time of the Open Door policy,
American foreign affairs in general had been governed by essentially expansionist
assumptions. As America competed with the colonial powers toward the turn of
the century, the idea of expansion as the "destiny" of American democracy was
connected to the energy with which the U.S. financial and industrial establishment
advocated free trade and the opening of international markets as the nation's
primary historical interest. Woodrow Wilson's universalism had furnished the
country, which had come into a position of economic primacy during World War
I, with a utopian but coherent doctrine expressed in the Fourteen Points. Here
freedom of markets was wedded to political democracy and the self-determination
of peoples, merging the ambitions of American ideals and interests with a concept
of global peace and stability. In Franklin D. Roosevelt's vision of American war
aims from the Atlantic Charter on, the background of these principles was crucial.
They were brought out again by the policymakers of his administration in the light
of the traumatic collapse of the Peace of Versailles and the role of economic
nationalism in the steady decline from the crisis of 1929 to World War II. The
concern for avoiding the disturbances and mistakes of the recent past and for
preventing another recession in the world economy led to the development of
models which guided the process of postwar reconstruction.[3] Roosevelt's efforts,
including the conduct of war, were directed to constructing a mechanism for
security policy based on the United Nations and guaranteed by agreement among
the Allied powers. The assumption was that peace could be based only on an
unimpeded increase in international trade. The administration, especially Secretary of State Cordell Hull, attributed the emergence of power struggles to the
existence of protected economic spheres and drew up a blueprint for peace marked
by the denial of spheres of influence and the affirmation of a multilateral system of
free trade. This multilateralism went beyond the confines of trade policy and
became a model for all American thinking about the postwar world, a standard to
repair to, a guiding principle, and a criterion for action.[4]

    The revisionist school of history, linking the debate on the origins of the Cold
War to American economic interests, emphasized the imperial cast of the ideology
and politics of multilateralism. Using a substantially Leninist analysis of imperial-
ism, the revisionists gave first importance to the necessity for American capitalism

to export goods and capital freely—and to have access to low-cost raw materials—as the primary way of avoiding the painful choice between a return to depression or a change in the country's socioeconomic equilibrium. The onset of the Cold War was thereby interpreted as the result of United States efforts to do away with the protectionism and spheres of influence of others in order to impose "a global sphere of American influence" made possible by its strategic and commercial supremacy.[5] Subsequent "post-revisionist" studies accepted the contribution of revisionist historiography—the great importance of the economic factor—but gave a contrary interpretation to events. The pressures toward multilateralism indeed originated from economic considerations and from the fear that protectionist areas would rise up again and potentially lead to conflict as they did in the 1930s. But the transformation of these concerns into political options derived not so much from fear of a crisis as from the insecurity that was inherent in the new strategic outlook: "The experience of war had sensitized American leaders to the possibilities of future external threats even before the Soviet Union had emerged as the most obvious postwar adversary. This sense of vulnerability reflected not so much fears of an economic collapse at home as it did a new awareness of the global balance of power and the effect recent developments in the technology of warfare might have on it." These concerns were concentrated in an all-embracing concept of national security that led the Truman administration to use international economic policy as a tool for establishing stability and guaranteeing security. The "lesson of history," enshrined by the government and the media alike, was that of Munich, of appeasement in the face of totalitarianism. From this derived the necessity, in terms of containment, of achieving economic and political stability even before military stability.[6]

In its search for security, the American political and economic establishment looked to the start of economic development and the attainment of at least a minimum standard of living. It was thought that economic uncertainty and poverty, after the experiences of the 1930s, led to instability, revolutionary and totalitarian temptations, aggression, and, in the last analysis, war. The will to establish a lasting peace and prevent other collapses, the goal of replacing defeated Fascist regimes with democratic order, the need to guarantee national security, though this did not yet mean containing Soviet communism—all of these postwar imperatives converged in the interdependence of peace, stability, and prosperity. The best route was that of an expanding world economic cycle, without which all problems could develop into explosive confusion. The tradition of the Open Door policy, American commercial interests, the increased interdependence of the world economy, and the ambition to convert the country's increased influence into supremacy induced American leaders to find in an increasing volume of international trade the driving force for expansion. With credits extended to the Allies, the Bretton Woods Accords, and then the negotiation of a loan for Great Britain, the United States imposed its own conception of a multilateral trade system for furthering growth. Truman summed up the terms of the equation when he said, "A large volume of soundly based international trade is essential if we are to achieve prosperity in the United States, build a durable structure of world economy and attain our goal of world peace and prosperity."[7]

The goal of prosperity was a fundamental aspect of the postwar order and a vital element in securing the peace. But before it became a political goal, it was already present as an irresistible pressure from the American body politic, the result of economic changes and political solutions, of conflicts and compromises, of fears and desires that had grown during the war mobilization of the entire country: "In December 1941 young American men and women had known nothing but Depression. . . . The GI hoped, but scarcely dared to expect, to get home to a more affluent life than he had ever known, a better life as far as he was concerned. His parents, who were enjoying that life during the war for the first time in more than a decade, savored it the more for fear that it would vanish. That hoping and that savoring dominated the public mood in 1944 and 1945. At times the enemy seemed to be no foreign nation but the Depression that the war had dispelled."[8]

Stimulated by a tenfold increase in public spending, the American gross national product grew from $91 billion in 1939 to $166 billion in 1945. Seventeen million new jobs guaranteed full employment and relatively high wages. Industrial production rose by 96 percent in those years, making many more goods available to consumers than before the war. Consumption increased and savings grew even more, raising expectations of high consumption levels in the postwar period, when wartime restrictions would be lifted. The relative prosperity brought about important changes in public opinion. As the memory of the Depression faded, so did hostility to large-scale industry, whose image was newly legitimized by its exceptional productive performance. Corporations had an important role in planning war production, in the name of the efficiency the war demanded. The pressures for reform produced by the New Deal were reined in to avoid any cracks in national unity. In Roosevelt's metaphor, "Doctor New Deal" was replaced by "Doctor Win-the-War." The unions found in this wartime situation the conditions for greatly increasing their power. Although their role in the wartime economic system of control was limited to advisory functions with little or no power, the absence of unemployment and the governmental recognition of the unions' role increased their solidity and power. At the end of the war, union membership had grown from 10 million to 14.5 million. The large industrial unions of the Congress of Industrial Organizations (CIO) had by then taken root in the country's principal industries. The percentage of union membership for the first and last time reached that of the industrialized nations in northern Europe. Union participation with government officials and business leaders in negotiations that were more political than industrial fed hopes for strong union influence in the postwar period if this tripartite cooperation were to be translated into regular neocorporatist negotiations between economic interests on the country's major economic choices. There was no lack of tension, and the unions' increasing dependence on the government's benevolent attitude was undermining these optimistic expectations. But the unions approached the postwar world as one of the protagonists on the economic and institutional scene.[9]

In 1944 President Roosevelt was reelected on a platform that, although with caveats and postponements to the postwar period, portrayed a future of full employment and peace on the social front that was not unlike what the Beveridge Plan portrayed for Great Britain. The second "Bill of Rights" reflected and revived deeply felt aspirations, whose implementation needed a reformist vigor that had slowed down and shrunk during the war years. Postwar prosperity was therefore fraught with contrasting tensions and hopes. Social expectations made a return to the past unthinkable. High levels of employment and social well-being were goals that the war had shown to be achievable, and that many Americans would refuse to renounce. No governmental authority could easily ignore these demands. Even in the worlds of industry and finance, hostility against government intervention had largely evaporated, giving way to a moderately Keynesian recognition of the government's role in supporting growth. The necessity of preventing another depression and of avoiding deflationary pressures was a priority common to many currents of opinion. But while the liberals hoped for a wide use of government expenditures to bring about social reforms, the Keynesian principles of the industrialists gave higher priority to tax cuts that would encourage investment, profits, and private consumption. The Employment Act of 1946 set high employment as a priority goal and recognized the national consensus that had grown up around it. However, contrary to what the liberals had hoped for, it did not bind the government to clear social priorities. Other priorities in the liberal program—an increase in the minimum wage and an extension of Social Security coverage—could not be implemented in view of the political balance, most of all in Congress, which favored raising consumption but was hostile both to extending governmental controls and to social legislation.[10]

The postwar world was thus dawning in the context of rediscovered, and much sought-after, prosperity made possible through the extraordinary productive capacity acquired by U.S. industry and through general agreement on the objective of economic expansion. The transformation of social and political balances in the war years precluded any radical redistribution of income or the development of widespread governmental programs in the social area. The cohesion that developed in the national commitment to winning the war, a chiefly economic and productive commitment, seemed to indicate that growth could mitigate conflict, conciliate divisions, and make possible peaceful and orderly bargaining among various interests: "The recurrent ideas all stressed that by enhancing productive efficiency . . . American society could transcend the class conflicts that arose from scarcity." It was this conviction that, in the eyes of American officials, more or less explicitly justified the stabilizing and peacemaking aspects of an internationally expansive policy geared to increasing trade and avoiding the rigors of recession. The social and political goals of American international economic policy were never separated from the financial and commercial ones. They were the differing and sometimes contrasting factors in a global stabilization plan that derived from the American historical experience, but they were inextricably connected and interdependent:

> United States spokesmen came to emphasize economic productivity as a principle of political settlement in its own right. They did this not merely because of the memory of harsh unemployment, nor simply to veil the thrust of a latter-day "imperialism of free trade," nor even because wartime destruction abroad made recovery of production an urgent objective need. Just as important, the stress on productivity and economic growth arose out of the very terms in which Americans resolved their own organization of economic power. Americans asked foreigners to subordinate their domestic and international conflicts for the sake of higher steel tonnage or kilowatt hours precisely because agreement on production and efficiency had helped bridge deep divisions at home. The emphasis on output and growth emerged as a logical result of New Deal and wartime controversies.[11]

The Unions and the Peace: The CIO

The fear of a postwar depression was especially strong in the trade union movement. Conversion to a peacetime economy under a cloud of recession, with millions unemployed and salaries falling, would have led to the renewal of pervasive labor strife under the worst of conditions for the unions. Their economic and organizational strength, the large number of workers for whom they negotiated contracts, and even the prestige the unions enjoyed with workers, corporations, and public opinion might revert to their former precarious state. An entire historical cycle in the entrenchment of unions in American society that began with the New Deal and was consolidated during wartime mobilization was approaching its moment of truth in the postwar period. Union leaders saw the coming test of their organizations' influence, role, and perhaps even existence.

The fear of a recession was especially intense in the large industrial unions of the CIO, which had arisen barely ten years previously during the crisis of the 1930s. These unions organized workers in the mass production sectors—steel, automobiles, and electric machinery and appliances—that were most exposed to the risks of reconversion to peacetime production and most dependent on the system of price and wage controls that the end of the war was to alter, if not cancel. Since the threefold cooperation between the government, the corporations, and the unions was at the base of the recent consolidation of the CIO, its leaders looked to the postwar world primarily with the hope of continuing and expanding that mechanism. They sought therefore to strengthen forms of cooperation and neocorporatist negotiation that would guarantee smooth and orderly industrial relations, a reconversion based on the goal of full employment, high wages, and perhaps a renewal of the social reformism of the New Deal. Indispensable for these plans was a reaffirmation of a liberal orientation in the United States and the strengthening of both the Democratic party and President Roosevelt. Accordingly, the CIO participated enthusiastically in his 1944 reelection campaign and drew up typically Rooseveltian programs for the postwar world.[12] Uppermost in the minds of its leaders was building a lasting peace backed by the agreement of the Allies, whose collaboration, they believed, must continue after the war. The peace settlement should give independence to colonies and have a solid economic and social foundation. The CIO proposed foreign aid, the breakup of monopolies, economic cooperation in order to expand international trade, and the presence of unions at the peace table and in international organizations. The guiding principle was to continue the international anti-Fascist coalition and the alliance with the USSR. CIO leaders could foresee a future of cooperation, economic growth, and social advancement only in such a framework.[13]

The desire to collaborate with the USSR reflected political balances and program guidelines that were essential to the federation, as well as a reconfirmation of the wartime ideals and alliances that were so important to a good part of the American political establishment throughout most of 1945. The CIO originated in the New

Deal period with no political or ideological biases, but with a Communist-inspired left that, while not numerous, was active in union building and thoroughly entrenched in the federation's local and national structures. Although internal unity nearly broke up in the period from 1939 to 1941 following Stalin's pact with Nazi Germany, it was restored in the atmosphere of the anti-Fascist alliance, when the left firmly advocated productivity as a patriotic cause. But this harmony began to fade in 1944–45. In the influential United Automobile Workers (UAW) union, a controversy was heating up between a leftist coalition and an aggressive, united anti-Communist group led by Walter Reuther, a young and able leader of social democratic views.[14] Signs of anti-Communist pressure were evident outside the UAW as well. In the CIO there was a large contingent of ethnic groups of Eastern European origin who became increasingly sensitive to the anti-Soviet controversy in the last months of the Red Army's advance. Especially strong was the Catholic group, organized around the Association of Catholic Trade Unionists (ACTU), which was very active against the Communists. It was the focal point of the right wing, as well as an efficient pressure group on a union bureaucracy where anti-Communist sentiment, though lukewarm, was very widespread. The ACTU's hostility to the left was of significant assistance to Reuther's battle and exercised increasing influence on several Catholic leaders, beginning with CIO President Philip Murray.[15]

But these signs of a future internal rupture that was to break out at the height of the Cold War did not put the CIO's agreed-on policies in doubt in 1945. The left wanted to pursue the anti-Fascist alliance and the policy of a united front among all the reformist forces. (The American Communist party even dissolved itself temporarily in 1945.) The right, although aggressive in internal polemics, was in full agreement with Roosevelt's international strategy. The Yalta agreements were greeted with enthusiasm by everyone in the CIO as the basis of a postwar world under the banner of international collaboration. The CIO leadership's main concern was to preserve the organization's unity, while that of the reformers was to face the unknowns of peacetime conversion and a possible anti-union reaction on the part of the corporations and in Congress, where there was no lack of temptation to reduce the influence of workers' organizations at the end of the wartime emergency. The strategy of CIO unity was firmly grounded in the federation's main interests, in its New Deal tradition, and in the still-convergent goals of its components.[16]

The economic aspects of the peace were equally as important as the political ones for both the CIO and the unions represented by the American Federation of Labor (AFL). The specter of the Depression and awareness of the enormous productive capacity of American industry led both federations to the axiomatic goal of multilateralism geared to expansion of international trade. The enormous gulf between the production levels in the United States and the backwardness and devastation in other countries reduced concern for protectionism to a minimum. Especially for the CIO, the promotion of exports and the increase of wages and internal consumption seemed the royal road to prosperity: "Several of our basic industries are dependent upon export to sustain their high levels of production. . . . Larger volume means lower costs and opportunity for lower prices in this country to consumers on the farms and in the cities. Thus the value of export as a spur to the whole economy greatly exceeds any measurement based solely on the volume of exports. There seems to be a direct correlation between domestic prosperity and foreign trade."[17] The CIO extolled the Bretton Woods Accords not only in the name of the international stability it seemed to promise but especially for the employment that would flow from efficient international exchange mechanisms: "Five million jobs for U.S. in postwar world trade." The CIO established "jobs for all" as its postwar motto, and during the discussions of American appropriations for the International Monetary Fund and the International Bank for Reconstruction and Development, it urged Congress to consider them not as expenses but as investments in the nation's future prosperity.[18]

The development of trade on a multilateral basis, American foreign aid, and the development of new markets were important goals for the foreign policy of American unions throughout the period of postwar reconstruction. More important factors than just the specter of the Depression were at work. There was a traditional adherence to the idea of expanding American capitalism, which dated back to the turn of the century in the AFL but was still in a formative stage for the CIO. A direct interest in acquiring new markets for American production was closely connected to political strategies and cultural and ideological assumptions. From the beginning of the twentieth century, the craft unions assembled in the AFL under the leadership of Samuel Gompers had seen a way toward civilization and progress in the diffusion of American industry based on free trade, especially in Latin America. Against a strongly nationalist and anti-Socialist background, the AFL supported the growth of foreign trade unions on its own voluntarist and nonpolitical model, whose contract negotiations, by raising wages, would contribute to the formation of new outlets for American exports and reduce competition—based on low labor costs—from foreign goods on the U.S. market. Strengthening the AFL's influence abroad would be in the economic interest of American wage earners and American industry in general. It would also spread liberal democratic values and propagate a way of life that was given the name of consumerism in the postwar period and was regarded as intrinsically progressive. The nationalistic basis and the perceived civilizing mission of this model were much less important for the CIO leaders. An internationalist background and a vision of reform analogous to that of the European social democracies were more prevalent among them than the cult of free enterprise. But the economic logic was not substantially different, even if for men like Philip Murray and Walter Reuther the accent fell more on the social and public benefits of that model of international prosperity than on its advantages for American industry.[19]

The views of these two federations on international economic policy, though they derived from partially different assumptions, tended to converge in the face of postwar prospects in a shared vision of an expansive economic cycle that guaranteed full employment and high income levels for workers both in the United States and abroad, especially in Europe, thus giving rise to hopes for peace, prosperity, and stability.

The AFL and Its Anti-Soviet Policy

Differences in the political orientations of these two groups resulted in radically clashing programs, however. The AFL hoped for the construction of a system of collective security based on the United Nations, but by 1944 it was already distancing itself from Rooseveltian axioms on one fundamental issue: its view of the nature and the international role of the USSR. For the AFL leaders, the Soviet Union was a threatening totalitarian power about which no illusions of collaboration should be cultivated. The federation's program for that year did not mention a postwar unity among the Allies, and it insisted on the importance of individual freedom in a tone which foretold the issues to arise in the anti-Soviet battle: "Freedom of thought and expression must be safeguarded throughout the world. This is the ultimate moral purpose . . . for which we are fighting the Second World War. Tyrannical governments which would crush out freedom of thought in their own lands endanger spiritual freedom everywhere."

On 5 April 1945 George Meany, secretary-treasurer and the AFL's leading light after President William Green, gave a speech whose tone was so harsh, excluding as it did any possibility of cooperation with the USSR, that it provoked censorship of the newspaper reports of the meeting, the United States being still at war.[20] This was not new: the irremediably negative judgment on the USSR and the Communist movements was an integral part of the AFL's ideological and political patrimony. The federation's outlook was dominated by the idea of free bargaining among economic actors in the market. It regarded the independence of union and firm as supreme principles. This independence was violated if the union were bound to a political party, or even merely geared to a program of social change that went beyond the defense of wages in negotiations.

Born of the anti-Socialist polemic of the late nineteenth century, the free trade dogmas of the nonpolitical, bargaining agent union were made more flexible later. During the New Deal, the AFL was able to accept some forms of government intervention and make it possible to have a relationship—although never an easy one—with the Trade Union Congress (TUC) in Great Britain. But the unbreachable wall remained. The AFL's free trade dogmas precluded any relationships not in violent conflict with communism, with which the federation could contemplate nothing but a mortal struggle whose conclusion could be only the triumph of totalitarianism or the emergence of free trade unions in a pluralistic society. In the language of the AFL, "free trade unions" were understood to be free from domination by political parties or governments. But in the 1940s that meant anti-Soviet, pro-West, and anti-Communist. The concept was of primary importance. The existence of free trade unions was for the AFL the fundamental criterion for determining whether a society was democratic or not; it separated its friends from its enemies. It was the primary axis around which to develop every diplomatic and political move. From 1944 on the AFL, by proclaiming that "labor organized in free trade unions . . . will be fundamental for the safeguarding of human rights in the postwar world," gave a foretaste of its chief international commitment, the struggle against communism and Soviet influence in the trade union movement.[21]

Anticommunism was not only the result of the view that a trade union should concentrate on negotiating contracts; it also derived from the historical process by which some of the AFL unions were formed. In the 1920s and 1930s their leaders had fought their way up, sometimes by the expulsion of Communist factions, sometimes after bitter struggles. For some, like Meany, an Irish Catholic, the struggle with the Communists had fortified their view of communism as almost demonically alien from the cluster of strongly American values prevailing in the craft unions. For others, who had immigrated more recently from Europe, the antagonism was supplemented by an aversion to the USSR, giving rise to an overall hostility to Communists. This was the case for David Dubinsky, who grew up in Jewish and Socialist circles in Poland under Russian rule, was exiled to Siberia following a strike, and emigrated to the United States in 1911. In New York Dubinsky had risen rapidly in the International Ladies' Garment Workers' Union (ILGWU), which had many Jewish members and where social democratic backgrounds prevailed. He reached the post of secretary and then president, from 1932 on, after a furious battle

against the Communist faction. In this way the ideal of a nonpolitical, contract
negotiating union was connected to the antiradical assumptions of Americanism
and with the anti-Stalinism of European social democracies: "We have learned from
our efforts that they are never really loyal to their obligations but use the United
Front as a kind of Trojan horse to destroy and to split the organizations of democratic non-Communist labor and to prepare for Communist domination."[22]

Anti-Communist hostility was not limited to the American national scene. In
the 1930s and during the war, the ILGWU had built up a network of contacts with
militant anti-Fascists in various European countries, giving them essential assistance with which to survive in exile. Through these usually Social Democratic
refugees, the ILGWU extended its contacts with resistance groups, especially
through the International Transport Workers Federation (ITWF), which included
among others the European railroad workers. From the moment of the United
States's entry into the war, this network of contacts with exiles and partisans
became one of the main channels of operation for the activities of the Office of
Strategic Services (OSS), the newly formed American intelligence service. Its labor
section was directed by Arthur J. Goldberg, a top-level representative of the CIO.
This led to an extensive network of communication, support, and financial aid to
European trade union leaders, most of whom were Social Democrats and in any
case anti-Stalinist. It hinged on collaboration between American unions, especially
the ILGWU, and officials of the OSS. Thus a commitment to the postwar world
arose among the AFL leaders most in tune with the situation in Europe. Prominent here were Dubinsky and Vice-President Matthew Woll of the AFL, a Catholic who also worked on contacts between the OSS and the resistance. Their goal
was to restore their contacts to leadership positions in European unions and to
prevent those unions from reviving under control of the Communists.[23] These
decisions were made at the AFL annual convention held in the fall of 1944. A
program inspired by Woll and Dubinsky was voted on, based on continuing the
ILGWU's activities after the war. The convention established a Free Trade Union
Committee (FTUC), which the AFL was to finance with a million-dollar fund.
The task of the FTUC was clear: it was to gather information for the AFL and
assist the desired reconstruction of "free" and democratic unions in Europe and
the rest of the world, in opposition to Communist influence. Matthew Woll was
called on to head the committee and Dubinsky was vice-president; both men
belonged to the AFL executive council. The FTUC took over the network of
contacts and the operation of international activities from the ILGWU, but most
significantly, at Dubinsky's behest, Jay Lovestone was nominated secretary-
general of the FTUC.[24]

Lovestone, who had emigrated from Lithuania, had been among the founding members of the Communist party of the United States, becoming secretary-general in 1927. A supporter of Bukharin, he was later expelled from the party and proceeded to organize an opposition. In the 1930s he entered into contact with Dubinsky, supporting his anti-Communist battles in the ILGWU. In 1937 Lovestone participated with his own group in the struggle within the UAW against the leftist faction, providing information and advice with which to defeat the Stalinist group. From 1940 on, having lined up with the Allies against Nazism, he became Dubinsky's adviser in his clandestine contacts with Europe. Violently anti-Stalinist, Lovestone was distinguished among other things for his distinct predilection for the conspiratorial and semiclandestine methods that characterized the activities of the FTUC. He also brought Irving Brown into the committee. Brown, who had worked with Lovestone before, went to Germany in the summer of 1945 to advise the American occupation forces; in 1946 he was sent to Europe as a representative of the FTUC and became the central figure in the AFL's continental operations.[25]

Lovestone's leadership imparted semiconspiratorial operating criteria and a close relationship with the world of the American intelligence services, but more important, it provided a rigorous and obsessive vision of the USSR and the Communist movement as forces firmly committed to world domination, starting with the unions, in the political and organizational vacuum of a war-torn Europe. Lovestone, sharing the desires of the AFL's leaders, foresaw a rupture between the United States and the Soviet Union at the end of the war. He believed that the USSR, having learned from its isolation after World War I, would follow a policy of destabilization in Europe, beginning with the economic and social field. In such a scenario, the unions would have a strategic role, and the USSR would make every effort to control them through Communist parties and a new Soviet-dominated international trade union organization. From these assumptions, Lovestone deduced the crucial importance of American activity in the union field, and he pushed the FTUC to take up its own crusade for the reconstruction of "free" trade unions, the pillars of anti-Soviet stabilization in Europe.[26]

A memorandum prepared at Woll's request in April 1945 set out the FTUC's objectives and the resources needed to act: "The labor movement of the European countries will be divided geographically and ideologically into two main groups, in accordance with the division of Europe itself into two 'spheres of influence.'" There would be no possibility for non-Communist trade unions to survive in the East, but in the Western zone, the struggle would be open: "The Socialist and democratic labor movement will have to endure a very hard struggle for survival. . . . The Communists will enjoy full freedom of propaganda and activity. They will even be represented in the governments and the administration of the individual countries. With the help of the mighty Russian state and a powerful internationally coordinated and streamlined propaganda machine they will strive for the domination of the labor movement in every country." Where the Communists were weak, in the Netherlands, Norway, Luxembourg, the unions would remain "in the hands of democratic elements" and the FTUC would intervene with "a direct contribution" to the treasuries of the union organizations. The cases of Italy and France were different. In those countries, the unitary confederations would be led by both Socialists and Communists: "The only possible way of aiding the reestablishment of a free and democratic labor movement in these countries is to strengthen those elements of the labor unions and the labor parties which are maintaining and defending in their activity the principles of freedom, independence, and democracy." Finally, in the cases of Austria and Germany, the FTUC would work in Western-occupied areas for the rebirth of democratic unions, a task to which it ascribed great importance: "The duty of the AFL will be to support the democratic side as generously as possible." The FTUC was to publish a bulletin in French and German and establish a permanent representative in Europe.[27]

In the first months of 1945 the AFL thus set in motion an efficient mechanism for taking part in European trade union affairs, preparing itself for a fundamental confrontation. The political orientation, the stress, and the organizational means were already those of the Cold War, which the federation's leaders foresaw and hoped for, with a far-sighted point of view and a political will still unusual among American political and social forces. This attitude, which originated in the history of the AFL, was facilitated by the strongly centralized formulation of the federation's foreign policy. International problems remained a topic restricted to a small group of leaders at the national level. In 1945 the autocratic character of a choice of action so at variance with the feeling of the country, and marked by the secrecy inherited from the war, was joined to this centralized tradition. Throughout the postwar period, it was always this small group of leaders—Woll, Dubinsky, and Lovestone, under Meany's supervision—who drafted and applied international policy, limiting itself to submitting some general resolutions for the approval of the conventions and to seeking consent and funding from the AFL executive council, where in any case Meany enjoyed a good deal of influence.[28]

In the FTUC's operations, priority was given to the German situation, with French affairs following. Germany was strategically placed for European power balances and the confrontation with the USSR, and the trade union movement had to start again from scratch. Above all, the AFL saw a powerful tool for its activities in Germany: the Allied military government, especially the American portion of it. The AFL thought it of fundamental importance to have an influence on the choices made by the military government, in order to create the best conditions for the development of trade unions free of Communist influence. It therefore sought to place its own union officials in the military administration. The search for collaboration with government organizations was not limited to Germany, however. On the contrary, it constituted the second instrument, after the FTUC, by which the AFL pursued its twin purposes of increasing its means of intervention and pressuring the American government to join the struggle for "free" trade unionism. The AFL sought to fill the jobs of labor attachés that were then being set up in American embassies with its own men, attempting to become the State Department's privileged consultant on labor matters. The federation could also make its voice felt through the Department of Labor, with which it had traditional ties of collaboration.[29] The AFL's ambition was to stimulate the government through its own programs and to become the primary inspiration for American foreign policy concerning trade union and social issues. This was a logical strategy for the struggle against communism, but in the spring of 1945 it had an immediate urgency because of the isolation enveloping the AFL in the trade union movement worldwide.

The World Federation of Trade Unions

From the summer of 1941, when the German invasion of the USSR created an Allied front with that country, Great Britain, and, shortly afterwards, the United States, a process began of redefining the relationships between trade unions in those nations. The prewar split between the social democratic International Federation of Trade Unions (IFTU) and the Red international led by the Communists was healed in the face of the anti-Fascist power collaborations. The Soviet unions and the British Trade Union Congress in 1941 set up a liaison committee for the duration of the war. This rapprochement represented a commitment to a future international alignment of union forces. However, there was opposition among the TUC unions to participation in this committee. The British unions, in fact, were the guiding force behind the IFTU, and their secretary, Walter Citrine, had no sympathy for the Soviets. But the goals of the anti-Nazi alliance plus strong pressure from the union rank and file made collaboration inevitable, and the TUC finally accepted it. In 1943 the TUC leadership proposed to organize an international conference in London to discuss the prospects for reconstructing the trade union movement after the war—including the Soviets.[30] The invitation was enthusiastically accepted by the Soviets and the CIO, both of which hoped to continue the alliance after the war and extend it to the trade union movement.

The AFL's reaction was quite different. It was working for a revival of the IFTU, with which it had been affiliated since 1937, and for consolidating its privileged relationship with the TUC. During 1944 the situation became increasingly complicated. The CIO saw in the conference the first step toward founding a new unitary international organization, a symbol of Roosevelt's aspiration to cooperation among the Allies and a means of pressuring governments and international organizations to assure guarantees for labor's interests in peace and reconstruction: "International labor unity means a strong union base for all United Nations cooperation now and after the war. . . . United Nations cooperation after the war means world stability, which means world trade, which means jobs and prosperity for workers abroad and for us here at home."[31]

The CIO was also serving its own interests. Up to that point, it had been excluded from any international representation, and its leaders had decided to use the new influence they had gained at home during the war to overcome that minority status. The CIO insisted on being part of the American delegation to the International Labour Organization (ILO), thus breaking the AFL's monopoly. The federation did not fail to press the U.S. government, but it got little response. It finally saw a historic opportunity to defeat the IFTU, from which it had been excluded because of a rule forbidding more than one national representative and thus giving a monopoly to the American delegates from the AFL. For this reason Murray constantly urged the TUC to call the London conference early (it had been postponed for logistical reasons to February 1945) and to distance it from the IFTU. As the delegation was leaving—significantly, it was led by Sidney Hillman, the closest to Roosevelt of the CIO's leaders—the instructions from the CIO executive board were "to make formal representation for the creation of a new world labor organization in which we might be accorded representation."[32]

The rivalry between the two American federations also influenced the AFL, which defended its own status as the sole international representative of American labor. The AFL refused to participate in the London conference but sent a delegate to explain its position to the TUC leaders:

—The IFTU should call a conference of free trade unions.
—Principles followed in calling London Conference would result in disunity and further division. This conference planned to undermine AFL.

—Not more than one national center can be recognized by an international federation—as in constitution of IFTU.

—Russian unions cannot be accepted as free trade unions.

—Protest the destruction of the IFTU by the London Conference.[33]

The AFL unrealistically sought to revive the IFTU, but neither the CIO nor the Soviet unions could be simply left out of the reorganization of the international trade union movement in the anti-Fascist atmosphere of the first months of 1945. No other organization shared the AFL's anti-Soviet intransigence. The TUC did not intend to break away from the AFL and tried to the end to open the London conference with the rebirth of an enlarged IFTU. Its fear, and that of the British government, was to have a new organization form around the dominant axis of the CIO and the Soviets. But the AFL's self-imposed isolation removed a possible counterforce to the CIO-Soviet bloc and left the TUC with no alternative to forming a new organization.[34]

The London conference met in February 1945, overshadowed by the meetings at Yalta—and was dominated by the enthusiasm for unity which the agreement among the Big Three diffused among the Allies. Pressure from the CIO and the Soviets overcame the reluctance of the TUC, and an agreement was reached for the founding congress of a new unitary international organization within a year. The CIO's reaction was triumphal and enthusiastic. The conference had confirmed that unity was possible. Postwar cooperation seemed to be coming alive, and the prestige of the CIO was now being felt on the international scene. Nothing seemed more self-destructive than the isolation of the AFL, which attacked on several fronts.[35] First was the FTUC program, which was the spearhead of AFL foreign policy. The committee, which was trying to convert its contacts with anti-Soviet unionists into a proper international alliance, sought both to eliminate Communist influence and to gather around the AFL the potential protagonists of a worldwide realignment of antitotalitarians in the trade union movement. Secondly, the AFL brought the greatest possible pressure to bear on the American government to deny any official recognition to the new international organization, in particular at the United Nations. In January 1946 the new international was admitted into the United Nations' Economic and Social Council, but later, following American intervention, it was given only consultative status, on a parity with the AFL.[36] Finally, the AFL started a bitter fight with the new organization and its founders. The London conference, according to the AFL, wanted to "sabotage and destroy" the IFTU, attempting to exchange it for a group whose political aspect would prevail over its trade union functions. The presence of the Soviets, irreconcilable with the AFL's principles, would snuff out any hope for the new international's autonomy. "The Soviet trade unions are both formally and actually an organic part of the state machinery, a branch of the Soviet government and the ruling dictatorial Communist Party. . . . The world body of organized labor would lose its freedom to criticize the Soviet Union and the Communist dictatorship. . . . Thus the world labor federation would practically be transformed, in the political field, into a 'yes-organization' of the Soviet government and consequently of world communism."[37]

In addition to its fear of Communist domination, the AFL was driven by its refusal to admit that the CIO, still being habitually denounced as the organization that was dividing American workers, could be publicly legitimated. In a speech at the September 1945 TUC congress, George Meany accused the CIO of having broken the unity of American labor and of being in thrall to the ideological and political orientations of its Communist component. He explained to the British that the AFL would not join any organization with representatives of the CIO and "the pseudo trade unions of Russia."[38] The AFL's polemical campaign, which was destined to intensify, touched the CIO leaders in a sensitive spot since these leaders were not entirely lacking in mistrust of the Soviets and were vulnerable to accusations that they were weak, or unduly influenced by their internal left wing. In the atmosphere of 1945, on the other hand, these accusations did not have quite that much impact. They seemed to indicate nothing more than the AFL's anachronistic isolation. The top ranks of the CIO proudly felt that they were protagonists on an international stage where, on the wave of the anti-Fascist alliance, Europe and the United States seemed to be on the eve of a new period of deep-seated social reforms. The first reports from Europe spoke of hunger and devastation, but also of the people's strong expectation of renewal and a widespread support for leftist organizations.[39] Admiration, curiosity, and respect for an ally's wartime achievements still dominated the popular perception of the USSR. Between the CIO's right and left wings, international activities were a factor for agreement and unity rather than division. An international coalition of workers seemed to be the natural result of the anti-Fascist struggle and the most solid guarantee of a future of peace and progress.[40]

At the end of September 1945 the World Conference of Trade Unions met at Paris and became the founding congress of the World Federation of Trade Unions (WFTU). The new international included the principal world unions except the AFL, the only important exclusion. It reflected the new vitality of labor organizations, whose numbers had doubled between 1939 and the end of the war, from 40 to 80 million. The moving force behind the new federation was the collaboration between the British, Soviet, and American unions, which dominated through their political influence and organizational consistency, and the natural bent for unity symbolized by the French Confédération Générale du Travail (CGT) and the Italian General Confederation of Labor (CGIL). The president was Walter Citrine, who was soon replaced by Arthur Deakin, and the Frenchman L. Saillant was secretary-general. He had three assistants, a Belgian, a Soviet, and an American. The CGIL was represented in the executive board by Giuseppe Di Vittorio. The WFTU's manifesto called for the total destruction of fascism and the democratic reconstruction of Germany and Japan, the extension of Allied cooperation in the framework of the United Nations, the representation of unions at all international meetings on peace treaties and reconstruction, the end of racial and colonial repression, and the adoption of full employment and social security policies.[41] The WFTU's strength was based on a unity that was related more to politics than to trade union affairs. It developed during the anti-Fascist struggle and in the common aspiration to lead reconstruction to full employment and democratization of economic structures. The guiding principle was to achieve a crucial role for the unions, both on the national level, shaping new socioeconomic power balances through the unity of worker organizations in common reconstruction, and on the international level, by representing the social aspirations for peace, cooperation, and progress in opposition to the logic of power, imperial nationalism, and the feared rebirth of fascism.[42]

The United States Government and the Trade Union Issue

Various currents and institutions of American society approached the postwar world with different goals, sometimes in political opposition to each other but with a common, basic inspiration. The very nature of the social compromise reached during the war and the reexamination of the history of the past two decades induced various interests to focus on a key concept, prosperity, on which they all based their hopes that their own projects—at the same time universal and specific, idealistic and supportive of particular interests—could be carried out. The supporters of a free trade approach in the world economy as well as the heirs of New Deal social reformism argued on the basis of a generically Keynesian viewpoint that only an expanding cycle of demand and production could assure those levels of social harmony that would allow for a stable and peaceful international order. The unions logically stressed the role that the workers' representatives should have in this scenario. The CIO trusted that union solidarity throughout the political spectrum would make it possible to restore social equilibrium and international cooperation. The AFL saw the trade union movement as one of the arenas where the coming conflict between the West and communism would be fought and decided. Both federations looked on unions as protagonists of a necessary process for increasing and redistributing income, which by sustaining demand would achieve consensus and consolidate a pluralistic and democratic stability. In warmly supporting these ideas the unions were not alone, nor did they lack interlocutors. At least in principle, the agreement on the importance of pluralistic negotiations among various interests—especially as projected abroad—was widespread throughout the country and the government.

The State Department's Inter-Departmental Committee on Postwar Foreign Economic Policy recommended with respect to labor problems that the United Nations work toward "freeing the world from want" and especially toward reaching "high levels of national income and employment in any country." These ends could be reached as long as international organizations—and especially the ILO—achieved respect everywhere for minimum legal wages and rules of the workplace. These goals were especially important for American industry and unions since they concerned the competitiveness of their products. As for the unions, the committee emphasized how they were "especially important means" to defend the lowest incomes and encouraged "the development of free worker associations."[43]

Similar in tone was the resolution of the ILO congress held in Philadelphia in 1944, where the Americans presented their ideals with warmth and determination. The final statement, personally supported by President Roosevelt, recalled the close interdependence of the economic and social spheres, stating that the poverty of some was a danger to the prosperity of all. To support development in conditions of full employment and increasing income, the efforts of the ILO should stimulate "the effective recognition of the right of collective bargaining, cooperation of management and labor in the continuous improvement of productive efficiency, and collaboration of workers and employers in the preparation and application of social and economic measures."[44]

Within the federal government there was an awareness of the importance which unions and industrial relations would have in determining social power balances and economic conditions in European countries after the war. The federal agencies that would manage the political and administrative aspects of the occupied countries—or were already managing them, in the case of Italy—began their tasks with an assumption that pluralistic negotiation among interests had a positive value and was a leading factor in social stability. The agencies also had the deep, though undefined, conviction that freedom of association for unions could constitute one vehicle for democracy, a means of teaching the desirability of pluralism to societies newly freed from fascism. But in 1944–45, these general ideas were not yet a coherent political design or group of directives to guide precisely the efforts in the union field of the administrators in the occupied zones, most of whom were military. Under the umbrella of some political and social principles—the passive projection, for the most part, of American historical experience—and the absence of any policy on the matter, each agency tended to deal with union issues according to the priorities suggested by its own functions and purposes.

Thus the military government in Italy operated according to regulations that gave priority in union matters to the role of the unions as guarantors of reviving production and keeping order behind the lines, and second place to eliminating fascism. In other agencies geared more specifically to political issues, such as the OSS and the Department of State, the unions were regarded principally as seats of political conflict, particularly as arenas in the confrontation with the more radical left, and thus as political factors rather than economic and social agents. It was symptomatic, for example, that the views on the WFTU—on which the federal government did not draw up a unitary position until 1946—were initially different. Analysts in the Department of Labor, the OSS, and even the Department of State regarded it positively at first, as an organization that would support international cooperation and that did not appear Soviet-dominated. But in the upper reaches of the diplomatic establishment, especially the embassy in Moscow, where the primary focus was on the elements of conflict between the United States and the USSR, it was immediately seen as an "instrument of Soviet foreign policy."[45] In establishing in 1944 a program of labor attachés who were assigned to all the more important embassies, the State Department was clearly aware both of the new importance of trade union issues abroad and of its own lack of preparation and experience with which to deal with them. In the last year of the war, American consideration of the international trade union situation was fragmented and disorganized.

Cultural values derived from the American national experience, and evaluated differently according to differing roles in that experience, influenced a perception of postwar problems that was still extremely vague in comparison with the operational tasks and political and strategic choices that European reconstruction was to impose on the United States government. For this reason, we need to reconsider the importance of the dispute on the origins of American intervention in the international trade union movement that was fully in place from 1947 on. The thesis of Ronald Radosh, that the AFL's anti-Communist activism originated from its subordination to the government's imperial interests, indicating thereby a passive dependence on the Department of State, remains a useful political analysis when it is applied to subsequent developments in a collaboration which reached high levels of integration in the 1950s and 1960s. But it is not relevant for a historical analysis of the first steps in the process. In the last period of the war the AFL was clearer and more decisive on the importance of the union movement as the seat of the struggle against communism, and it pressured the government to more stringent efforts in that direction. Even more evident in that period was the CIO's freedom to make its own policies and operate internationally. On the other hand, the opposing thesis, argued especially by Roy Godson and Philip Taft, which emphasizes the autonomous framework of the AFL's operations and their focus on real trade union issues, is valid only for the purely procedural aspects of the decision-making process within that federation. The AFL certainly operated pursuant to policies of its own governing bodies and not of government offices. But that does not lessen the importance of other factors. The small circle of union officials who drafted the AFL's foreign policy, their close connections with the OSS's intelligence network and with the Department of State, the set of values they had in common—strongly anti-Soviet liberalism, nationalism—and the eminently politico-strategic as opposed to merely trade union character of the AFL's international operations are all elements that show commonality of intentions, methods, and goals, and reciprocal interdependence rather than autonomy. The fact is that from the time of its albeit clearly autonomous origins, the AFL's policy had characteristics that were to lead it quickly to integrate fully with government operations in the international sphere.[46]

Actually, the historical interest in the harbingers of an American international initiative which, with the Marshall Plan, later achieved socioeconomic stabilization and anti-Communist containment does not lie in the dispute about whether the government was behind the initial idea. On the contrary, the most relevant factor was the emergence in American society of multiple tensions that projected onto the international scene power balances that had developed domestically. This social compromise, oriented to industrial production and negotiation, took shape between the New Deal and the war and led the institutional representatives of the social interests to an international activism inspired by the harmonizing and expansive axioms intrinsic to that model. The political economy of prosperity and its implicit social power balances were a product of all the American historical experience of the first years of the 1940s, which burst onto the world stage through the voices, organizations, and ideals—often in conflict with each other—of that society. It gave form to a universal and powerful policy only when the interaction between internal events and federal government initiatives was able to harmonize the separate pressures and resolve the deep conflicts, giving them organic unity and bringing their weight to bear on the reality of postwar Europe.

From the New Deal to Productivity

The characteristics of American international policy, however, were to originate directly from domestic solutions to the great political and economic problems of postwar reconstruction, and these characteristics carried industry-union relations to the forefront. Because of the war, the American trade union movement had reached an unprecedented position of strength. Four years of full employment had swollen the ranks of the principal unions, whose membership had increased overall by nearly 50 percent. With wartime mobilization, the workers' organizations were drawn into a complex tripartite mechanism of government, industry, and labor. Even though they did not have great decision-making power, these organizations derived new solidity from their cooperation with industry and government. But having entrusted themselves to government mediation more than to direct negotiation and industrial conflict, the union organizations, especially the CIO, developed a strong dependence on the government and the benevolence of its policies.[47]

Throughout the war an effective wage freeze had been imposed, while prices were controlled less strictly. Even if real wages had risen through the enormous spread of overtime, the unequal burden sharing gave rise to labor's frustration and discontent. By the last months of the war wildcat strikes were cropping up in various plants. With the end of hostilities and the end of defense contracts, real wages would fall and unemployment would grow. It was easy to predict an outbreak of industrial and social conflict. The problems of reconversion could be summed up in two questions: how to maintain high employment levels during the transition from wartime to peacetime production, and how to modify or remove price and wage controls that governed income variations.

The AFL and CIO greatly feared that the American economy would fall back into the Depression of the 1930s, and they were not the only ones to cultivate these fears. The entire liberal establishment was committed to a vigorous campaign to persuade Congress, through the Full Employment Act, to require of the government a full employment policy. It was feared that business, enormously strengthened by the productive boom, would seek revenge against the unions. The industrialists and a large segment of the press insisted on giving up wartime controls. The Truman administration—although in favor of an agreement between the parties—did not succeed in the first chaotic months of its existence in drawing up clear directives for the transition, either on price controls or on cooperation between industry and the unions.[48]

The AFL's postwar strategy hinged on its request for a quick removal of wage controls and abolition of regulatory agencies, in order to return quickly to full freedom of negotiation. The CIO unions, on the other hand, operated from an entirely different point of view. In the spirit of New Deal reformism, the CIO leaders pushed for an extensive redistribution of economic and political power and an overall expansion of the welfare state. These ambitious goals would evidently need the continuation of governmental controls on the economy as well as the tripartite cooperation carried out during the war. With a perception quite close to that of modern European corporatism, Philip Murray proposed centralized forms of negotiations on economic policy such as to prefigure planned growth. Walter Reuther, looking explicitly to governmental control of the larger firms, considered a supervision of investments governed by long-term social goals.[49]

These points of view had close analogies with those of the main European trade unions, which, in the first stages of reconstruction, were drawing up programs for structural reform based on government controls, the programming of investments, and worker participation in management of industry. The basic priority was a full-employment economy where criteria of collective well-being predominated. On the wave of wartime experience of governmental direction of the economy, these programs had an aura of realism and responded to needs that were widespread in society. The immediate and dramatic necessity of reconstruction made it essential to have a strongly consensual participation of the workers, and this allowed the unions to have significant political influence. The request for structural reforms gave the unions the prospect of achieving "a pivotal position" in the governing mechanisms of the society. It was the similarity of those strategies and ambitions that gave the joint participation in the WFTU both a political rationale and a consistent structural motivation.[50]

As far as the CIO was concerned, these projects of social democratic corporatism needed American government and industry approval, which was conspicuously absent. American industry came out of the war not only strengthened but politically and socially legitimized as the creator of the great boom which had brought prosperity and led to victory in war. Industry's postwar goals were to free itself from the more direct forms of control over its corporate decision making, to limit the authority of the unions, and to reshape the semipublic decision-making sphere, typical of wartime cooperation, in which the two other great powers, government and unions, seemed to strengthen each other. The unions could have a positive role in orderly collective bargaining, but industrial relations should go back to the field of private negotiations. Inside and outside the corporations, in production as in society, management must regain and affirm its exclusive decision-making powers.[51]

The widespread and bitter strikes of the winter of 1945–46 were a trial of strength between these two contrasting views of the future of American society and would involve the government directly in the issue. Its decisions on the fate of the system of wartime controls eventually played a crucial role. In the most indicative of these strikes, the one at General Motors, the United Auto Workers demanded large wage increases with no relaxation of price controls, while management's obstinate resistance took the form of explicit pressure for their abolition and therefore for the dismantling of the whole wartime system of government regulation of the economy.[52]

The resistance of General Motors became the banner of a powerful offensive by industry against union demands for governmental programming and controls. The defense of management prerogatives was elevated to a guiding principle of the industrialists in their negotiations with the unions and the government.[53] When the Truman administration accepted price changes in tune with wage increases, the system of controls began to break up and was quickly set aside. The CIO withdrew from the prospect of a prolonged conflict that would have put it on a collision course with government policy. It concluded its strikes and gave up its demand to retain controls. Industry's victory set new bounds to union power, eliminating from the postwar scene the possibility of strong governmental regulation of the American economy. Although in the framework of a vague Keynesian agreement on public spending in support of growth, the idea of social programming of investments left the political scene.[54]

The defeat of the unions marked a profound change in public opinion and the balance of political power. The difficulties of reconversion were worsened by the steep increase in inflation and were tied to irritation with a new international climate where tension with the USSR was coming strongly to the fore. In the elections of 1946 a deeply felt conservative discontent having antiradical, anti-union, and anti-Soviet overtones took the form of a strong Republican victory. It was a change in the national consensus, which was for the first time explicitly anti–New Deal and post-Roosevelt. The way for decisive changes in labor legislation was open. The new Congress chose to reduce drastically the strength and influence of the unions with the Taft-Hartley Act. The liberals began to redefine their identity in the light of the bitter realities both at home and abroad. For the CIO, a stormy discussion arose about redefining its strategy and its own internal order.[55]

The factional fighting began to take on bitter tones of an ideological conflict, reflecting the spread of a new anti-Soviet mood in the country. Walter Reuther put himself at the head of a coalition in which the Catholic union leaders of the Association of Catholic Trade Unionists were conspicuous and proceeded to attack the left wing of the UAW, accusing it of putting the interests of the Communist party ahead of the union's. After a virulent campaign, Reuther won the presidency of the UAW and began to ease his adversaries out. His vigorous success made him the standard-bearer of a campaign that was getting under way against the left wing of the CIO and marked a decisive change within the federation.[56]

The premises for a corporatist postwar strategy had disappeared, the reaction of industry was threatening, and the hostility of Congress and the antiradicalism of the new political climate appeared still more dangerous. It was essential for the senior CIO leaders to limit their vulnerability to accusations of procommunism and to find a comfortable political orientation close to that of the White House. After the elections of 1946 the liberals began to redefine their creed around criticism of Soviet totalitarianism, substituting anti-Communist prejudice for the anti-Fascist alliance of the united front. Having given up hope of independent political action leading to structural reforms, the leadership of the CIO participated, although with tactical hesitation, in this metamorphosis of the heirs of the New Deal, approaching the Truman administration and cutting its own left wing's room for maneuver.[57]

The Taft-Hartley Act intervened, symbolically and practically, to close an era in industry-union relations. Militant activism was drastically cut off, union negotiations were strictly regulated, the extension of union membership to new areas and sectors was effectively stopped, and new responsibilities were put in the hands of union bureaucracies, starting with guaranteeing the anti-Communist faith of their leaders. The union movement was taken out of social negotiation in the political and public sphere and relegated to private negotiations with management.[58]

The CIO unions, made more cautious by the defeat in 1946, quickly changed their tactics and fell back on wage negotiations and company plans for social benefits. They abandoned any reformist aspirations to control investments, employment, or the construction of a governmental welfare state, and in this their strategies became increasingly different from those of the European unions. From their attempt to achieve the status of representatives of all workers in the public sphere through direct negotiation with the government and political powers, they retreated to the purely market situation and representation of their members before management. In the period of moderately inflationary growth of the American economy after the war, their negotiating tactics were concentrated on the trade-off between efficiency and wages. In exchange for generally increasing wages, the collaboration of the union in productivity growth seemed to offer the key to making workers—or at least union workers—participants in the new consumer prosperity. The new contracts signed from 1948 on assured an ironclad labor truce in exchange for wage increases in line with inflation, productivity bonuses, and pension and health care funds supported by management.[59]

After the war, American industry was virtually free from foreign competition. Its advantage in terms of productivity was such that it did not suffer at all from a policy of wage increases, and this policy had the advantage of guaranteeing harmony and made for a high predictability of economic variables. The inflationary result of a productivity compromise based on relatively high wages could easily be tolerated as long as competition on the domestic and world markets was weak or nonexistent. A new role began for the unions which was heavily restricted by the private sector bounds of negotiating with management, but there were visible economic and organizational benefits, at least in the medium term. As long as the economy continued to grow and the comparative advantage of American industry remained intact, the productivity-wages exchange offered tangible benefits. The relevance of an employment strategy, the programming of investments, and the construction of an efficient welfare state seemed to recede into the far-off and unrepeatable past of the Depression.

The "politics of productivity" that the Marshall Plan would later promote abroad made its name in America as the result of the economic and social conflicts of postwar conversion. In effect, it was the result of the defeat of union efforts at structural reform. The conflict of 1945–47 between conservatives and reformers, and the surrender of the latter, eliminated from the American scene the possibility of a social democratic variety of economic and political development. Together with the lesson of the great wartime performance of the American industrial apparatus and its enormous advantage over all its competitors in the 1940s, this set the character of the economic and political philosophy which the United States was to export to Europe. With the onset of the Cold War, from 1947 on, the United States would elaborate a policy of active reorganization of Europe based on an attempt to overcome political and social tensions, exorcising the conflicts with allegedly "technical" and "non-political" questions of production, efficiency, and negotiation. According to what was proclaimed by the new consensus of the post–New Deal period, the goal was "superseding class conflict with economic growth."[60] For carrying out these policies, whose guiding principle was the promotion of a contractual and private sector model of industrial relations, American foreign policy was to be entrusted to those representatives of unions and industry who, after the decline of the corporatist hypotheses of tripartite collaboration, were beginning to construct systems at home of negotiated division of the benefits of productivity.

In the last phases of World War II, however, there were only the faintest indications of these developments, and the guidelines for U.S. operations were different and much simpler. We must now turn to these guidelines in order to narrate the American involvement in Europe, especially Italy.

CHAPTER

2

The Primacy of Politics: Italy

After the landing in Sicily and the subsequent ascent of the peninsula, the Anglo-American Allies faced a complicated trade union issue in which the fundamental problems of Italy's political, social, and economic reconstruction were all present. Allied operations had to serve immediate military requirements as well as wider-ranging political and strategic interests. Furthermore, they were hampered by significant differences between Great Britain and the United States and an often competitive overlap of civil versus military, diplomatic, and economic administrations, each guided by different priorities and assignments. Basic guidelines and unifying principles were not lacking, but their effect between 1943 and 1946 was scattered in a wide range of interactions with Italy's social realities, in the midst of numerous errors, changes of position, readjustments, uncertainties, and approximations. It is difficult to discuss *a* project or *an* Allied trade union policy—especially *an* American policy—although the American presence was massive and influential and American operations were sometimes a determining factor. It is more appropriate to consider the successive development of partial initiatives, of attempts sometimes energetic and sometimes disordered, but no less incisive, from whose confused succession emerged progressively more coherent and lasting decisions.

The two administrative agencies of the Allied armies, the Allied Military Government (AMG) and the Allied Control Commission (ACC), were charged with supervising Italian administration, to which the AMG restored jurisdiction as the front advanced. The AMG and the ACC arrived in southern Italy armed with a few relatively clear guidelines: to establish a form of indirect control, delegated to the Italian authorities with the exception of areas close to the front lines, and to begin the eradication of fascism. The first guideline, in addition to reasons dictated by military operations, responded to the views of the British, who were more influential in the early stages of the occupation. They looked to a rapid return to normalcy along conservative lines through continuity of the monarchical government's institutions and the traditional governing classes. The second was inspired mostly by the Americans, who were less subject to monarchical and conservative sympathies and who believed in the potentially democratic character of self-determination. But administrative practices that were of purely military origin arose ahead of these principles. They could be summed up in the formula of preventing "unrest and disease," that is, of basing intervention in the economic and social fields on a purely functional dimension limited to guaranteeing order at the rear of the Allied armies. This criterion soon proved inadequate in the face of the administrative breakdown and destruction the war brought to southern Italy. The war lasted longer than the Allies had planned, and the instruments of government initially provided for were soon revealed incapable of dealing with the situation, especially in economic affairs. Indirect control tended to become more direct and strict, but it lacked the resources necessary for other than a purely punitive stabilization.[1]

Only in the summer of 1944 did the State Department begin to consider the outlines of Italy's postwar rehabilitation, based on peaceful international arrangements and characterized by the "creation of democratic institutions" and "an economic reconstruction geared to creating an expanding economy that will offer genuine opportunities to the Italian people for economic betterment." In this way the idea began to be applied to Italy that peace, stability, and prosperity were interdependent. On 26 September 1944 the idea of rehabilitating Italy first took form with the Hyde Park declaration. President Roosevelt, who was also motivated by the necessity of electoral support from the Italian American community, announced the Allied intention to give greater authority to the Italian government and, more importantly, to establish a program of economic aid. This was the first step in a long series of events that was to bring the United States to regard the reconstruction of a democratic, politically stable, and therefore economically sound Italy as a necessary element of the international postwar order. In its decision to commit itself to working against the country's social and economic collapse, Washington's first fears at the emergence of potentially destabilizing factors for Italy and the Mediterranean were involved. These included the entry of the Italian Communist party (PCI) onto the political scene with the agreement to participate in the government ("svolta di Salerno"), the Soviet recognition of the Badoglio government, and on the world level, the advance of the Red Army into central and southern Europe.[2] The American commitment, however, was long to remain bereft of the necessary resources to translate into decisive direct action.

Liberalizing the Trade Unions

The first important decision the Allies made in the trade union field was the dissolution of the Fascist "corporations." This was decreed in Palermo on 3 September 1943 and was subsequently extended to other regions in a series of orders that sanctioned freedom of association for the workers. The liberalization derived logically from the political ideals of the Allied occupation, which looked to the elimination of fascism in Italy. In addition, it was the product and natural result of the trade union traditions of the two Anglo-Saxon countries. Throughout the occupation, liberalization remained a cardinal principle for the Allies and was never revised in spite of the constant changes in the trade union policy of the AMG. In some provinces (under British control), the workers' freedom of association remained a dead letter for months.[3] But this freedom of association did not bring with it the right to bargain or freedom of action. The Fascist labor laws remained in force—especially the prohibition against strikes—and negotiations with management had to be arbitrated by the Allied labor offices set up by the AMG in each province and then in each region. These organizations also served as employment offices and regulated the working conditions of civilians employed by the Allies. The Anglo-Americans thus opened the way for the reorganization of free and representative trade unions, but at the same time they were trying to influence their rebirth with a tight net of restrictions and controls. The AMG wanted most of all to keep the economic situation under control, but its failure to do so hobbled its trade union policy as well. Having arrived in Sicily with the aim of stopping all inflationary pressures, the Allies imposed price and wage freezes. But price controls soon proved to be catastrophically ineffective. Inflation rose at a fast pace, and the Allies had to authorize a wage increase of 70 percent, which was later extended to other liberated areas. In the winter of 1943–44 the Allies were confronted with the clash between a coercive economic policy that could not achieve its desired results and the first results of the liberalization of the trade unions. Before the decrees dissolving the Fascist organizations were in effect, the first nuclei of trade unions sprang up here and there, representing the discontent brought on by the difficult economic conditions, but at the same time capable of constituting an element of mediation and containment of these tensions.[4]

The Allied authorities tended instinctively to establish one union, based on "vertical" industrywide organizations, and therefore leaned toward negotiations on an industry-by-industry basis, without departing from the overwhelmingly economic scope of the negotiations. In a vision inspired by the trade union model, limited by the supervision of the labor offices and generally by the Allied presence, a trade union of this kind, independent of political parties if not totally nonpolitical, could have staved off the tendencies to conflict, trained the workers in orderly bargaining procedures, and guaranteed the Allies a friendly contact. But in the first months of 1944 these desires were unrealistic, and the sporadic attempts to bring them about, such as the meeting held in Matera in February, showed their inconsistency. The rebirth of trade unions proceeded on a different path, marked by the strong presence of politics and influenced by the parties, for which the liberalization decrees had opened the doors.[5]

At the Bari meeting of 29 January the parties represented in the National Liberation Committee decided to call a unity conference. In Naples, Christian Democratic representatives reestablished the Catholic Leagues of the Italian Confederation of Labor on 20 March. Also in the Neapolitan area, the rapid unionization of thousands of workers was marked with the establishment of the General Confederation of Labor (CGL) at the conference of Salerno at the end of February. It was led by Communists who had come from the "scissione di Montesanto," such as Enrico Russo, and Dino Gentili of the Action party. This overlap of frequently conflicting initiatives showed the lack of coherence in the Allied approach to the trade union issue. It brought out the internal differences in this composite administration that often seemed to follow events rather than predetermine them. The Allied officials minutely analyzed each group's activities and programs. But when confronted with the necessity of predicting developments, they surrendered to the impossibility of understanding a situation they habitually described as "in a very fluid state."[6]

As the CGL emerged in Naples as the main trade union group in the south, the priorities of the military government became more elementary. In spite of initial concern about Communist activism, the Allied officials were too uncertain and diffident to give a privileged role to one or another trade union group. The Labour Sub-Commission of the ACC, afflicted with small numbers and lack of trained personnel, was concerned most of all with imposing its authority over numerous controversies that arose from inflation and food shortage. Its offices bore the daily task of dealing with the protests caused by the decision to freeze wages in the face of a steadily worsening economic situation.[7] At the highest levels of the ACC the main concern was to assure social stability. The various decrees dissolving the corporatist unions of the Fascist period, after the labor offices had been established and freedom of association proclaimed, were amalgamated into General Order No. 28 in July. The workers were guaranteed the right to form associations, elect representatives, and negotiate. The labor offices were charged with operating employment exchanges, collecting statistics, and mediating or arbitrating disputes. At the same time, the ACC and the Ministry of Industry drafted a decree to replace the former Fascist regulations with new labor legislation. Noel M. Mac-Farlane, the head of the ACC, explained to Badoglio that he wanted most of all to prevent conflict from spreading. He asked for a "wartime system of labor relationships best calculated to prevent work stoppages and to ensure the greatest degree of industrial peace."[8]

Beyond the immediate requirement for an instrument to regulate labor relations following the departure of the Allied armies, neither the Americans nor the British agreed on or understood the purposes of a law that, however temporary, could govern the reconstruction of the trade union movement in the postwar period. A draft prepared by the Ministry of Industry and the Labour Sub-Commission in the summer of 1944 drew rather sharp criticism from Washington, where it was considered too restrictive. Too much power was concentrated in the labor offices, strikes were rigidly controlled, the unions were subject to minute regulations, and suffocating limitations were imposed on collective bargaining. In short, there was a preponderant role for the government that was unacceptable in the eyes of the American planners, who were advocates of free negotiations among organized interests in a climate of legitimate social pluralism.[9] The draft originated in the encounter between the Italian ministry's tendency to central control and the assumption by the Labour Sub-Commission that the Italian trade union movement needed foreign guidance. One of the originators of the draft, Major Edward P. Scicluna, explained that precautions were needed, given the "sense of irresponsibility" and the "underdeveloped trade union conscience" on the part of the Italian workers at that time.[10] The Department of State instructed that publication of the decree be suspended and the entire matter reconsidered. At nearly the same time Minister Giovanni Gronchi, who approved putting the decree in force, according to Scicluna, decided to postpone any decision until after the liberation of northern Italy, especially following pressure from Secretary Di Vittorio of the recently formed CGIL, who opposed the strict controls provided in the draft.[11] The minister prepared another draft in the first months of 1945, with numerous corrections but without substantial changes in the spirit of the law. This second version was also postponed to the postwar period after CGIL protests. Both the leaders of the CGIL, who had not been consulted in the decree's preparation, and the new head of the Labour Sub-Commission, W. H. Braine, agreed that decisions of such importance should be entrusted to a more representative government, or better yet, to an elected assembly.[12] These postponements marked the collapse of the principal attempt to impose wartime legislation on the rebirth of the unions. General Order No. 28 remained in force, and the labor offices permitted the Allies to influence union activity significantly, especially in contract negotiation. But the process of rebuilding unions, and their organizational and political decisions, was relatively free from drastic restrictions or interventions from abroad, especially in view of the divisions in the Allied organizations.

This entire situation had changed with the founding of the CGIL. It was a very powerful force in the field that could at least partially influence Allied decisions, which up to then had been unilateral. The Allies did not seem to have been aware of the talks in Rome between the Socialist, Christian Democratic, and Communist leaders Bruno Buozzi, Achille Grandi, and Giuseppe Di Vittorio. In the following months, observers became aware of the eminently political character of the agreement reached by Socialists, Communists, and Christian Democrats as the distinctive and innovative element in the CGIL. The CGIL was soon to encompass the entire labor movement, and the Allied organizations seemed inclined to a prompt approval of the new situation. The analysts of the OSS grasped the political consequences of the CGIL's establishment right away, pointing with clear insight to the contradictions inherent in an organization unifying three major parties. This represented the strength of the CGIL in 1944 but after the war became the primary source of its breakup: "If the three 'mass party' representatives succeed in realizing their overall plan, the CGIL will become the single most powerful pressure group in Italy, able to play a decisive role in both the economic and political struggle. . . . On the other hand, the centrifugal forces within the labor movement should not be minimized. The dissidence of particular labor groups is not nearly of such importance as the uneasy character of the three-party alliance."[13]

The coming of the CGIL had a profound effect on the Italian postwar scene. It was a strong, centralized organization that began to spread the influence of the anti-Fascist unity achieved in the north and would soon bring together all the trade union centers spread throughout the country and force the Allies to face their administration's unsolved issues. In the first place, the CGIL carried considerable weight in negotiations, not so much because of the unions it represented—that was still uncertain—but for its political influence. The wage freeze that had been kept in place without too many difficulties was lifted in October when the Bonomi government granted the CGIL's request for an offset to the cost of living, in spite of the ACC's opposition. Thus the anti-inflationary policy was broken and a serious crisis was begun over the methods and terms of Allied control. The contradiction came to light between the principle of indirect control and a practice that tended toward rigid but ineffective controls that, as in this case, could be circumvented and would be subject to a fait accompli by the Italians. Secondly, the unfolding of a stable and unitary trade union situation, based on collaboration between political parties and marked by a strong Communist presence, forced the Allies to redefine their trade union policy. It opened up a discussion of the future that, with the participation of British and American diplomacy and trade unions, went beyond the narrow horizons of the military administration.[14]

The Visit of the Anglo-American Trade Union Delegation

While the Allied administration was trying to keep the development of the trade union situation in check in the spring of 1944, the belief was gaining ground in the British government that the time had come to participate more effectively in the process of rebuilding the Italian unions. The military government and the ACC could guarantee an institutional framework and assure moderation in negotiations, but it was necessary to find other ways to translate the authority and prestige of the British and American democracies into effective political influence. In the formative phase that the trade union movement was undergoing, when it was still open to every option, the Allied interests could be brought to bear more incisively by putting the Italians in contact with their natural counterparts, the American and British trade union leaders. From October 1943 on, the TUC recommended a visit to Italy by a delegation of its members to make contact with and study the possibility of reorganizing the Italian unions. The Foreign Office and the State Department had taken their time, the military commanders had asked for a postponement, and British Minister of Labour Bevin said he was convinced that in the confusion of the moment, a visit could be "premature."[15] But six months later both the Allied government in Italy and the Foreign Office concluded that a visit was appropriate and urgent. On 7 April 1944 the TUC delegation was allowed to depart. Harold Macmillan, the resident British minister in Algiers and most senior British political authority in the Mediterranean, wrote that the TUC visit should take place as soon as possible, "to counteract the spate of Marxist propaganda now flooding Italy."[16] For the Foreign Office, the trade union mission was meant to counter the Communist influence which, after the arrival of PCI head Palmiro Togliatti and the "svolta di Salerno," had become a cause for serious concern regarding the entire domestic Italian political situation.[17]

The TUC leaders extended an invitation to the AFL to join a joint Anglo-American delegation. They did not invite the CIO since this was the preparatory phase of the London conference and the TUC was being careful not to further anger the AFL, with which it was carrying on official relations in the framework of the old IFTU. This was where the first complications arose. The president of the

AFL, William Green, in announcing the nomination of the Italian American Luigi Antonini, an ILGWU vice-president, as the AFL's delegate, stated publicly that Antonini was being sent to Italy to prevent the Communists from taking over the labor movement now being established.[18] There were immediate and heated protests from Italian American groups in the CIO, who requested the State Department to deny a travel permit to Antonini in order to avoid heavy-handed interference in the Italian situation.[19]

Antonini was an especially controversial figure. A prominent member of the Italian American community of New York, he was then preparing to become one of those "prominenti" who were to lead that community in the postwar period in a strong anti-Communist campaign, especially in Italy. Born in 1883 in Vallata Irpinia, Luigi Antonini had emigrated to the United States in 1908, later becoming president of Local 89 of the ILGWU, which consisted mostly of workers of Italian origin. Coming from a reformist Socialist background, Antonini quickly adapted to the negotiating style of the American unions and, in alliance with David Dubinsky in the struggle against the Communists, became an ILGWU vice-president in the 1930s. In December 1941 he had founded the Italian-American Labor Council (IALC) to foster the anti-Fascist movement in the Italian American community, quickly establishing good relations with the State Department and the OSS. The IALC, especially its press officer Vanni Montana, was in close contact during the war with representatives of the autonomous reformist wing of Italian socialism, represented by Giuseppe Modigliani and Giuseppe Faravelli, and more so with the foreign headquarters, organized in Switzerland by Ignazio Silone. Montana claimed that he was the secretary of the Italian Socialist Federation in the United States.[20] At the beginning of the war, Antonini and Montana had collaborated with liberal democratic refugees assembled in the Mazzini Society—Gaetano Salvemini, Max Ascoli, Alberto Tarchiani—to support the emergence of an anti-Fascist leadership in the Italian American community and to attempt to shape Washington's attitude toward Italy's future. But in 1943 the alliance between the Italian Americans and the refugees had broken up. Carlo Sforza's project for the formation of a free Italian government in exile found no support in the State Department.

While the refugees were trying to return to Italy, the formerly pro-Fascist "prominenti" leaders put the finishing touches on their realignment with the Allied cause with electoral support for Roosevelt. The anti-Communist issue became a divisive factor, especially among the trade unionists. Antonini's IALC was among the protagonists of a change in direction. In an attempt to gather the "prominenti" of the community in a strong pressure group based on political support for Roosevelt, Antonini led the IALC to collaboration in the name of anti-Communist moderation with formerly Fascist Italian Americans, among whom the editor Generoso Pope was prominent. The polemic against the unity of the left and his relationship with Pope brought Antonini to the point of rupture with the Italian American union leaders who were less disposed to follow him on his moderate crusade. Augusto Bellanca and George Baldanzi, both of the CIO, left the IALC and established the Free Italian-American Labor Council (FIALC). In a series of accusations, suspicions, and controversies, the Italian American groups split on the issue of aid to Italy without interference versus a vigorous anti-Communist campaign. After the armistice between Italy and the Allies on 8 September, the IALC opened a campaign, supported by the AFL, to collect $250,000 for the reestablishment of "free" trade unions in Italy. The Italian American "prominenti" regained their leadership in the community, consolidated their status in the Democratic party, and became an important pressure group on American policy toward Italy. With the collection and transmission of aid to Italy, and with ever clearer political statements, they played an increasingly important role, culminating in their massive involvement in the Italian electoral campaign of 1948.[21]

Antonini's nomination for the mission to Italy therefore led to some reservations since it was foreseen that his rigid anticommunism would cause bitter controversy. The CIO's protests were followed by a request to authorize George Baldanzi to travel to Italy as its representative. To the fear that Antonini would probably be accused of interference was added the likelihood of incessant squabbling between the two of them. Meanwhile, a formal question arose in the TUC, which had not extended an invitation to the CIO. The State Department's ideas were not very clear. It wanted the CIO to be represented, but it could not force the TUC, much less the AFL, to accept a joint delegation. In addition, the State Department wanted to avoid the risk that the mission would appear as interference in Italian affairs and therefore tried to mitigate these differences before the mission's departure, fearing that the likely disputes between Baldanzi and Antonini would be detrimental to the visit's purposes. After long negotiations a compromise was reached. The delegates from the TUC, the AFL, and the CIO would travel together but would not be part of a joint delegation, and each would represent his own organization alone. Antonini and Baldanzi left for Italy with no other instructions from the State Department—which lacked the Foreign Office's clarity of intention—than to avoid controversy and interference in Italian political affairs.[22]

The nomination of Antonini was also cause for concern in London. A fear arose in the Foreign Office that the delegation would be prejudiced by Antonini's association with former Fascists like Pope, as well as by his well-known anticommunism. If Antonini, whom London considered close to Dino Gentili, were to descend on Italy proclaiming that the Communists as such were to be excluded from trade unions, it would be seen "and not without justice, as an attempt from abroad to destroy the unity of organized labour," with immense profit for the PCI. But these misgivings were not sufficient to reverse matters. There were no fundamental differences on the purpose of the visit: "I do not think we need to pay too much attention to the anti-Communist intentions of Antonini. The whole project for sending a Labour delegation to Italy was conceived as part of our policy to counter Communism."[23]

The TUC raised no objections to Antonini, and London limited itself to recommending to the Americans that Antonini and Baldanzi be persuaded to avoid exaggerated controversies. The TUC named as its delegates W. Lawther and T. O'Brien and at the last minute added the IFTU secretary Walter Schevenels in order to give authority to the delegation. The Foreign Office's reservations—Schevenels was a Belgian and not a British citizen—were overcome due to the conviction that his participation, though less under the control of British diplomacy, would be more effective from the trade union point of view.[24] One crucial doubt remained, however: the attitude of the Soviets. Their participation would compromise the Foreign Office's purposes. The TUC was against the inclusion of the Soviets but would not have opposed a Soviet request to participate. The State Department raised no objections, but the AFL certainly would. The Foreign Office decided to speed up preparations and forestall any Soviet requests: "There is no question so far of Russian representation being included. In fact in supporting the original TUC request we hoped that the visit would encourage Italian Labour to look to British trade union methods rather than to Communism."[25]

The project therefore was in British hands. The delegates were going to Italy to propose a model of trade unionism and—especially in the intent of the Foreign Office—to oppose Communist influence and contest the most explicitly political aspects of the Italian trade union movement. The attitude of the Americans, on the other hand, was much more vague. Antonini combined his bellicose anti-Communist ideas with an ignorance of the Italian situation. Even in the spring of 1944 the IALC hoped unrealistically for reestablishment of the pre-Fascist CGL in a reformist direction and criticized the AMG for not having simply preserved the Fascist confederation, giving the leadership to Socialist representatives and anti-Fascist activists.[26] The IALC also denounced American approval of the formation of anti-Fascist coalition governments as an inappropriate opening to the Communists. Further, it pressured the White House to reintegrate Italy into international trade by opening credits from Washington to Rome and asked for a greater commitment against inflation on the part of the AMG.[27] Even the Italian Americans in the CIO insisted on Italy's rehabilitation, requesting that it be given the status of an ally. They emphasized the urgency of a strong political and economic policy toward Italy, especially in view of Roosevelt's need of the Italian American vote in the coming elections. Concerning the Italian domestic situation, there was explicit satisfaction in the CIO, even among the Catholic elements, at the unity achieved among the anti-Fascist forces, a unity they hoped would be continued after the war.[28] On the eve of the departure for Italy of the union delegations, internal pressures were building up, which were to be aired in the Hyde Park declaration. In the State Department the idea was gaining ground that Italy needed strong economic development most of all, but there was nothing more precise than that. Concerning the purposes of the mission, the officials in Washington limited themselves to asking the AFL and the Foreign Office for clarification, complaining of an "ambiguity" of purpose that was not there. The only instructions they gave were to be diplomatic and prudent, even if in substance there was an implicit agreement on the mission's purpose: to present the British and American trade union movement as a primary representative, if not a model, for the Italians.[29]

All these recommendations proved to be useless. As soon as they arrived in Italy on 27 August 1944, both Antonini and Baldanzi issued statements that were anything but diplomatic. Struck by the misery, lack of food, and low wages, they both criticized the Allied administration, accusing the British of wanting to make a colony of Italy and requesting greater economic commitment from the United States. Baldanzi denounced the failure to purge the Fascists, stating that only an agreement among the workers could defeat fascism and that he looked forward to meeting Togliatti. Antonini, on the other hand, said that the inadequacy of the Allied policy risked leading Italy "into the arms of Soviet totalitarian dictatorship" and announced that he mistrusted the democratic attitude assumed by the PCI. Obviously ignorant of the recent unity of action pact between the Socialists and the Communists, he said he was convinced that only a strong Socialist party could hold communism back, betraying obvious embarrassment at having stepped into a different situation from what he expected. The statements by the two Americans led to strong British protests, and their publication in the United States was censored. It was clear that the State Department exercised no control at all over the two union leaders.[30] Schevenels and the TUC delegates arrived two days later and on 30 August began their mission's activities with a meeting with the CGIL secretaries. All five delegates decided to act together, presenting themselves as a unitary delegation, even though each of them would later draw up a separate final report in the name of his own organization. During the first meeting, Giuseppe Di Vittorio and Dino Grandi explained the CGIL's decisions, insisting that it was a unitary, democratic, and independent federation, while Schevenels and Baldanzi stated that they wanted to gather information, give advice and assistance, if necessary, and support the development "of a free social life and free trade union-ism." It was decided that the delegation would make an extensive trip to the south and hold a joint conference on its return to Rome.[31]

In the south the delegation met with numerous trade union representatives, all of whom by now had become CGIL members. Even the CGL in Naples had joined in August. They discussed the "Anglo-Saxon principles" of trade unionism: absolute independence from political parties; economic and social, but not politi-cal, purposes; and internal democracy. Schevenels emerged as the most authorita-tive and capable member of the delegation, while Antonini, now in his country of origin, was very popular, thanks to his sonorous rhetoric. He stressed two themes in his speeches which caused not a little hostility among the other members of the delegation: he warned of the dangers of communism, and he promised that not only moral support but also financial aid for revival of the unions could come from America.[32] Actually, Antonini was in an embarrassing position. As an AFL dele-gate he had the task of denouncing any collaboration with the Communists, but when he arrived in Rome he found himself faced with cooperation among the anti-Fascist parties, and with ties between his Socialist friends and the PCI. The AFL's plans were revealed to be obviously unrealistic, at least for the moment. In uncertain and defensive tones he wrote to AFL President Green: "The Italian labor movement, as you are aware, is the off-spring of the labor activity of various political parties and it will be some time before the situation can be changed. The Communists have repeatedly made pledges that they intend to fight for democ-racy. . . . Will they keep the promise? This is the question. But the non-Communist elements are willing to try, for the idea of unity is very strong." He wrote to President Dubinsky of the ILGWU, to whom he was close and with whom he shared a social democratic background, that he had been told by all the Socialists that the unity of action pact with the PCI was "only a transitory measure." "I believe the Socialists will be able to assert themselves independently and bid for the leadership of the working class movement. . . . Far from being supine followers of the Communist line, all non-Communist elements are fully aware of the dangers that may come from that side, and lose no time in devising ways and means to strengthen the democratic bloc."[33]

The fundamental choice, to which both the IALC and the AFL were long to adhere, was taking shape: to set their sights on the Socialists and, to a lesser extent, the members of the Action party as a possible alternative to Communist domination of the labor movement. This was a logical and consistent choice, given the AFL's anti-Communist priorities and the ties Antonini and the ILGWU had with the Social Democratic movement. But it bound the ideals and effectiveness of the American federation to the development within Italian socialism of the controversy between proponents of autonomy versus those favoring a united front. It therefore turned the AFL's attention in Italy from the labor movement as such to the more purely political activity of the Socialist party.

The delegation returned to Rome and on 15 and 16 September held a meeting with the leaders of the member unions of the CGIL, together with about a hundred other local and national representatives. The Anglo-American delegation wanted to find a system of guarantees that allowed the CGIL to transform itself into an organization independent of political parties, not subject to their political and ideological controversies, and based mainly on an economic and contractual model. They welcomed the CGIL as an organization that would assure the unity of the labor movement, but at the same time they wanted to exorcise its primarily political nature and origin in the hope of leading it to develop along lines more proper to a trade union.[34] The delegation's views amounted to a recognition of the CGIL, though an unofficial one, at least as far as the Allied administration and the international trade union movement were concerned. The Italian leaders showed themselves quite willing to receive the British and American suggestions. On Di Vittorio's proposal, the conference approved a motion that committed the CGIL to hold democratic elections within three months in all union organizations in order to form national category unions as soon as possible and achieve independence from political parties, rejecting any interference from them. The Anglo-American delegation recognized the CGIL as it originated in the Rome agreement, but it emphasized the urgent need to achieve independence from political parties.

The delegation left Italy with a set of rather cautious judgments. There was no lack of optimism, but there were also serious reservations about how effectively the decisions made in Rome would be carried out. The delegates interpreted them rigidly as formal commitments on the part of the CGIL leaders. The reports from the British and American delegates stressed the seriousness of economic conditions, before which the unity of the trade union movement emerged as a positive factor in the reorganization of the social framework and as a promise for the development of appropriate plans for reconstruction, whose discussion was postponed until the coming CGIL congress. But doubts were growing in the delegation about the nature of this unity, and the delegates' opinions faded into questions about the future. With great lucidity, Schevenels pointed to the crucial development, at least from the Allied point of view, in the evolution of the CGIL: "In the extreme differences, which have existed in the past between the Communist and the Catholic conceptions of trade unionism, the elements are dormant which can produce at the present moment the greatest danger for trade union unity. It is therefore essential that the greatest care must be exercised in avoiding even the appearance of political supremacy of one current upon the other. There is the field in which the international trade union leaders can immediately assist the Italian comrades in the most effective way."[35]

The views of those considering the political more than the trade union aspects of the matter were far less trusting. The State Department observer agreed with Schevenels's diagnosis but was skeptical about the possibility that the CGIL's commitments could prevent political interference. In the Foreign Office it was noted with disappointment that the anti-Communist impact of the visit was substantially lacking: "The Delegation was here trying to warn the Italians against allowing the Communists to run their unions. The retort of the Italians on the other hand was extremely clever, and really left the foreigners with no come-back."[36]

Of quite a different nature was the reaction of Major Scicluna, who had been assigned a few weeks previously to follow the visit of a Soviet trade union delegation, which arrived in Italy on 23 September. His reports, after the popular enthusiasm brought on by the joint meetings between the Soviets and the CGIL leaders, accused Di Vittorio of having transformed the visit into a great Communist propaganda operation. Scicluna contended that Di Vittorio was violating the agreements reached in mid-September with the Anglo-Americans and that they were facing the rapid advance of a plan for the totalitarian suppression of democracy. He therefore put forward a drastic plan of action. Legislation should be launched with strong controls over the unions. The anti-Fascist alliance in the CGIL should be broken, and the greatest possible support given to non-Communist factions. More generally, Scicluna suggested the support of an immediate and right-leaning solution of the crisis in the Socialist party, the establishment of a front of the moderate forces, and finally, "forcing the revolutionary issue before the withdrawal from Italy of the Anglo-American troops." His paper was not followed up. The Foreign Office deemed it extremist and unworthy of attention, and in the ACC his ideas fell on deaf ears. Nonetheless it bore witness to the obsessive fear with which some Allied officials regarded the increasing influence of the PCI, both inside and outside the CGIL.[37]

The view of the CIO delegate, on the other hand, was completely different. George Baldanzi denounced the American policy, "or rather lack of policy," that imposed intolerable sacrifices on the workers, with wages lower than what they had been when the Allies arrived. The Allied government was responsible for the failure to purge the Fascists and for perpetuating antique ideas in contrast to the unitary will of the people for deep social change: "All in all, we are faced with a new era and it will be necessary for us to decide whether Italy is to be given an opportunity to reconstruct itself on democratic lines, or whether it will be sub- jected and reduced to the status of a colony. . . . The tendency of the people of Italy to look towards Russia is not because the people are communistic, but rather because the ruling classes of Europe have been autocratic and have refused to improve life for the majority of the people. This hemisphere is very definitely moving towards new concepts of government—no power on earth will stop it." The emotional account by Baldanzi summed up the hopes and illusions of the left and many of the liberals in America. It reflected that firm desire to participate in history that animated all of the CIO at the end of the war. Within that federation Baldanzi was lined up with the right; he was anything but soft on Communists. His concluding recommendations were clear. The Allies must give power and responsibility to the Italians, send supplies and credit to stimulate the revival of production, guarantee free elections, and not put obstacles in the path of purging the Fascists. As for the CGIL, Baldanzi praised its unity, requested that it be given the greatest possible freedom to negotiate, and recommended that the CIO give it "its full support."[38] In this way an official relationship between the CGIL and the CIO began that was to find its natural framework in joint participation in the World Federation of Trade Unions, where the Italian union was admitted at the insistence of the CIO, which overcame objections from the British.[39]

The report that Luigi Antonini sent to the IALC, the ILGWU, and the AFL emphasized the mistakes of the Allied administration and recommended giving more responsibility to the Italians. In the economic field he sought better food supplies, effective price controls, employment growth, and a wage increase. But here the similarities with Baldanzi's paper stopped. Antonini dissented from the joint conclusions of the delegation, noting that the transformation of the CGIL "into a genuine and independent federation of workers' unions, not dominated by any political party" was still far off in time and far from certain. At the moment, "some guidance by the parties" was "inevitable," but preparations should be made in advance in view of the inevitable clash between opposing perceptions. Antonini distanced himself from the inclination of the Christian Democrats toward a compulsory union founded on public law. Then he took up the problem of the

Communists: "Fundamentally, the Communists are the same the world over. Their conversion to democracy is of recent vintage and should be strongly doubted." Anti-Fascist collaboration was necessary, but it would be only transitory. "The really democratic forces" should be reinforced and watched over to prevent the Communists "from dominating the workers' organizations." Antonini therefore looked to a battle for domination in the Italian labor movement and believed that America, which had great political responsibilities, should contribute to its outcome: "Almost instinctively, there is a widespread desire in Italy for a new social order modelled on the American way of life. . . . Nothing would be worse than a short-sighted policy on our part in dealing with the Italian people. That would push them to adopt ideologies foreign to its traditions and character and detrimental to the interests of Italy and democracy worldwide. Such conduct on our part would be disastrous not only for Italy but for all of Europe as well."[40]

Antonini's report was approved by the AFL convention of November 1944 and formed one of the bases for the federation's interventionist policies in international affairs, as exemplified by the creation of the FTUC. But how does one implement aid to the democratic forces in Italy? In the course of his visit, Antonini had met many figures in the political and trade union worlds, most of whom were Socialist, and to the Socialist and Action parties, with which he hoped for close collaboration, he had extended $11,000 collected by IALC "for free trade unionism." A few months later, at the request of Lizzadri, Grandi, and Di Vittorio, the IALC sent $5,000 to the CGIL as well, "provided that the federation be guided strictly by what was decided at the Rome meeting."[41] But this was not an enthusiastic contribution, and it was not repeated. Antonini was receiving contradictory reports from Italy. His correspondent, Serafino Romualdi, wrote that the September commitments were being respected and that the Communist domination of the CGIL reflected their effective representation, while Vanni Montana, also in Rome, referred to a Communist-dominated Nenni and compared Di Vittorio to a Frankenstein who, with IALC money, was on his way to subjecting all the CGIL to its will.[42]

On 10 February 1945, in a dispute with the American Communists, Antonini accused Togliatti of receiving money from the USSR. A controversy arose in which none of Antonini's Italian friends came publicly to his defense. On the other hand, friendly but firm requests came privately from Italy not to complicate the situation and to trust in the choices made by the Italian Socialists. Nenni wrote, "But your dispute with Togliatti is a mistake. . . . Believe me, dear Antonini. It is not right for you to bring your polemic into Italy. We need unity." The conflict was between Antonini's fear that the Italian democratic left would be damaged by cooperation with the Communists and the intolerance of the Socialists for the paternalistic recommendations of intransigent anticommunism that accompanied the IALC financial aid from across the ocean.[43] This small storm was calmed a few weeks later thanks to the mediation of Romualdi, surely the most acute of the Italian American observers, who recommended that Antonini not bring into Italy the anti-Communist controversy that was raging in the American trade union movement: "The situation in Italy is quite different than the one in the New York trade union movement. The Socialists must give absolute first place to the Italian working class. In their honest opinion, this requires collaboration with the Communist party. . . . They cannot shape their tactics to the requirements of the Italian-American colony of New York and its trade union movement."[44]

In a peacemaking letter to Nenni, Antonini wrote that the incident was closed and that he recognized the distinction between the Italian and American situations. He announced that the IALC would continue its financial contributions to the Socialist party, earmarking them for the trade union office. With the liberation of northern Italy the CGIL's organizational framework was set in place, and Antonini hoped that energetic action by the Socialist and Action parties—the IALC was still sending support and financial assistance to the latter as well—would finally restore internal equilibrium in the federation, giving rise in the workers' movement and the entire country to a progressive and democratic bloc that would form an alternative to the Communists.[45]

The Allied Administration and the CGIL

The meeting with representatives of the British and American unions, and the one immediately following with the Soviets, brought the Italian labor movement back into contact with the international movement after its post-Fascist revival. The CGIL took its place before the Allied powers as the legitimate workers' representative and an essential protagonist in Italian society as it moved from fascism to democracy. Multiple and widely varying relations began with the American trade union movement which were to undergo important changes in the postwar period. The CGIL's advent brought about important changes for the Allied administration.

The new British labor attaché, W. H. Braine, arrived in Rome at the end of September. An official of the Ministry of Labour, he had been warmly supported for the assignment by Ernest Bevin.[46] His arrival coincided with a public crisis in the Labour Sub-Commission—and more generally in the relationship between the ACC and the Italian government. Plans for new labor legislation were blocked, and wage controls were eliminated by the CGIL's agreement with the government. Braine clearly understood the implications of the crisis. The ACC had to change its methods, he wrote, and give up any claim to exercising detailed control. The spirit of the draft labor law and the rigid regulation of wages from above were incompatible with the long-term purposes of the Allied presence. What was needed was a redefinition of the relations between the ACC and the Italian authorities and a beginning of negotiations between labor and management: "Development on British trade union lines seems likely to hold out the best hope of future Italian political and social stability." Braine felt that the achievement of stability needed not so much a system of controls as an extension of greater responsibility to Italian institutions and representative organizations, especially the CGIL. His suggestions were favorably but cautiously received at the Foreign Office since they brought up the delicate issues of the timing and methodology of Allied operations. But Braine's views were supported by events. The "new deal" stipulated in the Hyde Park declaration implied a mitigation of Allied control. The CGIL was entering the scene as an important Italian reality, and the prospect of the liberation of the industrialized north required more long-range decisions in the labor-management field. At the beginning of 1945 the chairmanship of the Labour Sub-Commission was assigned to Braine.[47]

The CGIL congress opened in Naples on 28 January 1945. Braine participated, with other Allied authorities, in a spirit of friendly cooperation. In his first report he praised the congress as "a landmark in the development of democracy in Italy." The Allied observers praised the highly representative character of the CGIL and the political and public relations success of the congress: "The Italian Labour organization is probably the most powerful national force in the country today, with objectives on a corresponding scale." The presence of a Communist majority and of a resolute minority of Christian Democrats produced an atmosphere of tolerance and reasonableness in the name of unity instead of the divisions some had feared. This brought about the most important result: "The moderate tone of the convention and the moderation exhibited in the reforms advocated by both left and right."[48] Braine pointed out the opportunity offered to the Allies by this role of bringing people together, which appeared as one of the few moderating factors in the country's social fabric: "It is to the interests of all to foster a publicly recognized influence which can be of importance in restraining violent elements in the labor field."[49]

The Labour Sub-Commission issued instructions to its local commands for facilitating the CGIL's consolidation, overcoming the reluctance of many AMG officials. To be avoided in these local situations was a revival of the union "on unorthodox lines" and its falling prey to "subversive elements." Since the CGIL was proceeding in a moderate and responsible fashion, Braine recommended giving "as much encouragement and stimulation as possible" to rebuilding the unions in liberated territories. CGIL officials were to be guaranteed all possible movement and communication so that they could guide "the development of the unions on a proper basis."[50] Braine also attempted to reduce tensions between the Italian labor offices and the CGIL, which opposed their controls, especially in hiring activities. The Italian government would decide on their future; in the transition period, Braine assured them, they would operate in collaboration with the CGIL.[51]

With the coming of Braine, the Allied bureaucracy started moving in the direction indicated by the Anglo-American delegation. Braine, like Schevenels, understood that the trade union unity stipulated by the pact of Rome and made official in Naples joined several currents of opinion and steered the CGIL on a course to political and economic decisions whose consequences could only be social moderation. In a way not unlike that of other European countries, the arrangement called for in the name of anti-Fascist unity and the need for wide social representation induced the CGIL to assume responsibility for reviving productivity, maintaining discipline in the workplace, and containing tensions over demands and trade disputes.[52] In the vacuum left by the dissolution of the Fascist organizations, all the political parties—in pursuit of their differing ends—understood the temporary mutual necessity of extending their roots in the country and preventing a socially disruptive conflict. It was especially important to mend the social fabric and reestablish relationships between the masses and the institutions. The CGIL was under heavy and multifaceted pressure to attenuate and conciliate tensions. It originated not only in the obvious need to start up economic recovery, but from the very nature of the equilibrium that had been provisionally arrived at by the political party system that was coming into being.[53] This conferred on the CGIL a set of values where political and ideological elements prevailed, as well as the aspiration to be the reception point for political demands that went far beyond union issues.[54] Such aspirations inspired no enthusiasm among the Allied union leaders and officials, who looked at Italy through a perspective of trade unionism. But they were obliged, however unwillingly, to bow to the historical realities of the Italian trade union movement. They believed that an evolution of the CGIL to a mere bargaining role would be possible only in the very long run. The habit of collective bargaining would have to be developed, and the CGIL's center of gravity would have to move toward the industrial unions. Above all, any diminution of the CGIL's political character could not be imagined, unless as a result of the compromises that the cohabitation of the various currents made inevitable. "But with all its faults the present immature organization is recognized as an improvement upon the Fascist system and it is hoped that encouragement to take open responsibility in the labor field will diminish or, alternatively, expose political maneuvering."[55]

In any event, these were future concerns. With the approaching liberation of the industrial north, the political compromise on which the CGIL was based appeared increasingly important, with the strong "moderating centralization" that derived from it.[56] The compromise offered the Allies the opportunity of dealing with labor unrest and economic tensions not only with their political and military presence, which remained the basic controlling factor, but also through collaboration with an organized and representative point of contact that was free of extremism. In anticipation of the liberation of the north, Braine drew up an agreement with Grandi and Lizzadri. The CGIL and the Allies would collaborate through the labor offices. Allied officials would refer to the chambers of labor and would arrange for distribution of the CGIL's newspaper *Il lavoro*, provided there were no political propaganda articles in it. Concerning wage negotiations, Braine limited himself to hoping that the AMG would be promptly informed of every development. Braine instructed all the Allied commands to encourage bargaining between the parties, to act like a "good employer" with its own civilian employees, and to avoid "any appearance of the intervention of military power to suppress strikes." The focal point of this policy remained the labor offices, which were to be established immediately in every province and region. They were to mediate between parties to labor conflicts, guarantee an orderly bargaining process, and facilitate establishment of management and labor organizations.[57]

In the spring of 1945, while Braine was setting up collaboration with the CGIL, the labor attaché arrived at the American embassy. John C. Adams was among the first officials sent to Europe with the task of establishing contacts and transmitting analyses on trade union problems, especially their political ramifications, which the State Department anticipated would be of crucial importance in the postwar reconstruction of Europe.[58] He concentrated on the issue of the Catholic presence in the CGIL, on the occasion of a meeting organized by the Christian Associations of Italian Workers (ACLI) in Rome from 8 to 10 March, which concluded with an audience at the Vatican. Pope Pius XII pronounced words of explicit recognition for workers' rights and of appreciation for the CGIL. Myron Taylor, President Roosevelt's special representative at the Holy See, referred to a conversation with Monsignor Tardini, "the principal adviser" to the pope for foreign affairs. According to Tardini's authoritative interpretation, the speech was mainly an appeal to the Catholics to carry out "within the 'unitary federation' a series of operations that would be very useful to the affirmation of doctrine, to the safeguard of justice, liberty, and moderation against revolutionary and splintering tendencies." Taylor recorded how the pope had warned the federation to stay strictly out of politics and respect religious liberty. He concluded that the Vatican appeared "to be throwing the influence of the spiritual power of the Catholic Church into the Italian trade union movement. . . . Apparently the Holy See is not losing any time in placing itself in a favorable position by showing a sympathetic attitude towards the CGIL in which the Communist element is playing such a prominent part."[59] The accent therefore fell not so much on the recognition of the CGIL as on a commitment by the Catholics not to allow any changes in the tenuous compromise between the forces of the left and the Christian Democrats, which was based on the confederation's totally nonpolitical character. Adams commented on the meaning of the pope's speech with a brutal summation: "The Catholics are, therefore, free to retire from the CGIL whenever it becomes too Communist."[60]

The American attitude toward ACLI and the trade union activities of the Catholics combined attention and mistrust in a blend whose final result was one of extreme caution. A marked alienation from their union values (especially ideas inspired by corporatist doctrine, as well as the notion of compulsory unionism) proceeded side by side with Allied interest in the restraint the Catholics exercised on Communist influence in the CGIL. Romualdi, though quite close to the Socialist right, explained to Antonini that the opposition by the Christian Democrats in the CGIL was the most watchful and effective.[61] On the other hand, the Catholics' solidarity, autonomy, and good organization, which became increasingly obvious as the ACLI consolidated, was also a potential threat to the unity of the confederation. There was a clear and calm awareness of this: "The ACLI is significant, however, less for what it proposes to do at present than for what it may decide to do in the future. Without seriously altering its present structure, the ACLI can become a full-fledged labor union. All that would be required is a word from the Pope and the willingness of the members. The Pope's speech left the door open for such a word in the future."[62]

For the moment, the American embassy, like the Allied administration, was concentrating chiefly on the influence that the unified reality of the CGIL could bring to bear on a social and political situation in rapid evolution. On the eve of the liberation, these factors of moderation and responsibility, which Braine had indicated among the more prominent characteristics of the unified CGIL, were the elements that lay closest to the heart of the American diplomats. To make it

possible for the confederation, management, the Allies, and the Italian government to cooperate in stabilizing the country, the peaceful and unitary coexistence
of the currents within the CGIL was a primary requirement. Adams gave unstint-
ing praise to the reciprocal tolerance shown by the Christian Democratic and
Communist union leaders. Their capacity "to continue this collaboration and at
the same time to pursue a policy of active leadership in Italian affairs will be a vital
factor in determining the future of Italy. Failure on the part of these labor leaders
would play into the hands of the extremists on either the right or the left. Their
success would mark a victory for tolerance, democracy and mutual understanding."[63]

The Liberation

A few days after the liberation, Braine left for a rapid turn through the northern
cities. In Bologna, Milan, Turin, and Genoa he ran into an unexpected situation.
The industrial plants were in good condition and working order. Activist optimism was to be seen everywhere. There were many serious problems, but the
social fabric did not seem as torn apart as it was in the south. The first decrees of the
Committee of National Liberation in Northern Italy (CLNAI) and its rudimen-
tary but effective administrative framework unequivocally demonstrated the existence of a new government. It was thin but widespread, and the Allies had to
reckon with it. "The most important step," Braine wrote, "is perhaps to dispel the
false optimism which pervades Italian circles." Expectations for a prompt recovery
of production were soon to be frustrated by the lack of raw materials, especially
coal. The solutions envisaged by the Committee of National Liberation (CLN) in
the economic and social field were subordinated to decisions by the government in
Rome and by the Allies. It was useless, even inadvisable, for the Allies to take on
administrative functions directly, but "there must be formulation of policy and
direction from above . . . the Committee of National Liberation is not itself able to
provide this, although it has assumed a position of authority which rivals or even
challenges AMG control." Braine requested immediate decisions on three important issues. He asked for suspension of the CLNAI decrees blocking all dismissals,
paying a "liberation bonus" to the workers, and establishing worker-management
councils (CDG) in industrial plants. The Allies and the Italian government must
prevent the "arbitrary replacement" of business leaders with commissioners appointed by the workers or by the CLN. The Italian government must promptly
prepare regulations, under the guidance of the ACC, to govern bargaining over

wages and layoffs. The firms needed to be freed from the burden of excess workers, and the resulting unemployment must be alleviated by extraordinary public works and assistance projects, which could be arranged by the Allies but would be implemented by the Italian administration. Unemployment seemed to be the most serious problem, but in the long run, Braine concluded, "that is, however, Italy's own problem."[64]

The problem that was pressing the Allies more strongly, and which they handled more urgently, was the power struggle that came to light with the liberation. In the final rush to establish a new administration and a new source of authority in the larger industrial centers, the CLN had arrived before the Allies. The AMG did not have a power vacuum to deal with, but rather a network of powers, which may have been uncertain but were recognized and active. The resistance, useful though it was from a military point of view, had always inspired mistrust among the Allies, since it was a free political and social movement that was hard to control. It was coming out at this moment as a source of independent power and as such had to be changed. It was urgent to eliminate the uncertainties and plurality of these powers, reestablishing the uniqueness of the constituted authority, represented by the government of Rome and, in a provisional way, by the Allied administration. Thus a beginning was made to disarm the resistance and bring the CLN to order. The first goal was to safeguard property rights and the Allies' control of industrial plants where workers' mobilization and CLN decrees seemed potentially capable of making significant inroads. The AMG took control of purging the Fascists from industry and prevented radical changes in the business sector from being formalized.[65]

The attitude of the Allies—especially that of the Americans, whose position of greater power and responsibility was then coming to the fore—to the social and political problems brought on by the liberation was dictated by new strategic concerns that had arisen with the conclusion of the war in Europe. After the end of military operations, American interests were concentrated on the already difficult confrontation with the USSR over reconstruction, on defining the peace, and on the postwar international order. In the State Department there was growing concern at the role the Communist parties in France and Italy might play in the global rivalry between the United States and the USSR. It anticipated an attitude on their part of hostile challenge to the United States and expected that "Communist-inspired labor disputes" would exacerbate social and political tensions. Outlining a posture that was to become an axiom of the American viewpoint, the State Department advised intransigence before internal subversion of Western nations, in terms of the need to appear resolute toward Moscow.[66] The prevalence of a hard line during the first months of Truman's presidency was in conformity with the need for an overall redefinition of American initiatives toward the Soviets. The temptation was emerging to bring America's superior economic and strategic power to bear in negotiations with the USSR. The failure of the Potsdam conference in July 1945 stiffened the division of Germany and Europe into separate spheres of influence in which the leading power had freedom of action.[67]

The tie between the new anti-Soviet tone of American policy and the Italian situation was described by Admiral Ellery Stone, head of the ACC, in a document that circulated widely among Allied offices and was dubbed "excellent" by the State Department. Admiral Stone wrote that Italy, divided by intense political conflict, economically prostrate with little chance of recovery because of lack of raw materials, and prey to unemployment that was likely to increase unchecked, was at a crossroads:

> If present conditions long continue, Communism will triumph—possibly by force. Communistic growth cannot be blocked by restrictive or repressive measures. Since the conditions which engender it are both material and moral, the only hope of restraining it in Italy is to ameliorate these conditions—to assist Italy economically, and to lift her morale by admitting her to a position of respectability in the family of nations. . . . The great majority of Italians desire to see a democratic Italy. . . . But unless they receive help and guidance from the democracies, particularly the United States and the United Kingdom, they will inevitably turn to the USSR and join the group of "police" states, united by Communism, which is extending westward from Russia. It is in the material interests of the United States and Great Britain to prevent this.

"An expression of positive policy" was accordingly necessary from the Allies, one that would help the country to build itself "as a healthy nation politically and economically," actively participating with the Western powers and able to act as a "bastion of democracy in southern Europe." Efficient armed forces and police needed to be reestablished. The Allies would have to maintain a military presence on Italian territory, and the future peace treaty must not be a punitive one. The United States, above all, should help reconstruction with ample supplies of coal and raw materials, by granting credits, and by dispatching a mission to help Italy "in correcting the basic defects of her former economy." Finally, Stone dedicated special attention to "the education of the minds of the Italians towards a democratic way of life." "Not enough has been done in this direction. . . . We cannot expect, nor should we try, to impose Anglo-American methods on a Latin country: but in the field of national and local government, of justice and police methods, of agriculture and labor, of electoral systems and social welfare, the Allies still have much to teach and the Italians much to learn. If the Italians are to become partners with the Allies they must be prepared to assimilate their national characteristics with the principles of democracy and take advice from the two democratic powers who are willing to help them materially."[68]

Stone was not the only one to underline the importance of Italy's economic and political rehabilitation for American strategic interests. The Italian embassy in Washington, headed by Alberto Tarchiani, tied its request to the American government for economic aid with the urgent necessity of "opposing Soviet efforts to give a position of influence to a unified bloc of the left in Italy."[69] These suggestions found fertile ground at the State Department, where Stone's fears were widely shared and where—as in London—the thinking tended to a moderate solution of the Italian crisis. There was a clear propensity to greater American activism in search of a collaborative relationship with moderate and reformist Italian political forces that could oppose the feared influence of the Communist left, but there were difficulties. It was still difficult to find the appropriate Italian contacts; Stone himself emphasized the absence of a clear political leadership in the country. Moreover, the Americans suffered from a lack of functioning programs, due to the confusion produced by the end of military operations in Europe—though not in the Pacific—and the simultaneous transition from the Roosevelt to the Truman administrations.[70] This problem was particularly serious in the most important area, economic aid. The Foreign Economic Administration (FEA) was about to be dissolved, and the most reformist circles in the federal government, the New Dealers who inherited Roosevelt's social progressivism, placed their hopes in a United Nations Relief and Rehabilitation Administration (UNRRA) aid program. However, this was not due to begin until 1946, with very limited resources. The most important State Department official in the economic area, William L. Clayton, was drafting a plan for reconstruction geared to freeing commercial exchanges, but he lacked the resources necessary to push the Italian economy—with appropriate credits, by means of which to bring pressure to bear on the government in Rome—toward a reconstruction based on free trade policies.[71]

At the highest levels of the American political apparatus the conviction was gathering strength that the influence of leftist forces, and the serious socioeconomic conditions that presumably provided their attraction, had disquieting strategic implications for American interests. From this derived a greater sensitivity to the outcome of the social conflict and its political aspects. Stone's paper principally marked an awareness that the Italian crisis should be handled from several sides. Most evident was the importance of seeking economic solutions and a start of democratic transformations and greater efficiency in the institutions that governed the society. The diagnosis was incisive and to the point, but the cure would have required financial and organizational resources that the United States was not then in a position to extend. As for the aspirations to modernization, implementing them was to be entrusted mostly to the reformist groups among the Italian political forces. However, neither the mode of the social conflict nor that of the political confrontation then in progress led in that direction. On the other hand, Italy's limits and historical conditions restricted the boundaries of American and Allied operations in the months after the liberation.

On his return from the inspection tour in the north, Braine had tried to divide the complex of questions that the liberation of 25 April posed for the Allies into single problems, and as many hypotheses for action and perhaps solution, but they were by no means reducible to trade union problems alone. All the tensions and deep undercurrents that had grown up in the struggle against fascism were present in the industrial world and were feeding on each other: the yearning for political regeneration and the need for reconstruction; the desire to overcome the bitter sacrifices and the class-based aspirations of the often armed workers to overthrow the management hierarchies; the ideological suggestions for restructuring the social order and the collective ambitions for a new balance of power. The convergence of resistance military power on the factories, the mobilization of the workers, and the desire for a purge of the Fascists gave life to an anarchic plurality of industrial powers.[72]

The Allied administration, alternating authoritative measures with others geared to attenuating friction, set out immediately to defuse these tensions according to a twofold order of priority. The Allies took drastic steps to prevent the worker and partisan mobilization in the enthusiasm following the liberation from leading to durable power structures, from imposing radical changes in property ownership and hierarchy in industry, and from setting up an uncontrolled anti-Fascist purge inspired by class-based criteria. The resistance armed forces must not develop into formal authority; the control of many firms by the workers must not lead to the dismissal of the managers and owners; the momentary power imbalance between workers and management could not be transformed into a permanent alteration of the social hierarchy. Making use of its political authority, the AMG proceeded to disarm the partisans, nullifying the appointment of factory commissioners by the CLN if they were not ratified by the Allied authorities and taking under its own control the removal of Fascists from industry.[73]

The AMG's attention was drawn in particular to the worker-management councils, whose legitimacy was contested, in accord with the views of the industrialists and the moderate political forces, and which, it was feared, could evolve into instruments for socializing industry.[74] The intention was to restore all power and responsibility for the operation of industrial plants to the hands of management, leaving a purely consultative role for the worker-management councils. An agreement reached on 23 February 1946, which restored Vittorio Valletta to the control of FIAT and spelled out the worker-management councils' functions, sanctioning the end of attempts to make them effective instruments of control, was greeted with satisfaction as "a definite step toward recovery."[75] It was Admiral Stone again who described most clearly the Allies' intentions and their accord with those of the industrial leaders:

> Professor Valletta, Managing Director of FIAT, called on me last week to say that he had concluded arrangements with the C.L.N. labor representatives, and with the Ministry of Labor, which he felt would satisfactorily resolve the difficulties which had arisen in his company due to the taking over of management functions by C.L.N. labor committees. When he conferred with me last year, I suggested that he not try to eliminate labor committees as such but that he should limit their functions to the subjects generally covered by labor-management committees such as were common in the United States and, as I believed, in Great Britain. This, he assured me, he had now accomplished and he was very pleased at the outcome.[76]

Parallel with these initiatives to return to normalcy, the Allied administration tried to establish the bases for a system of industrial relations founded on tripartite cooperation between government, industry, and unions. The AMG proposed to establish regional committees composed of representatives of all three sectors which would become headquarters for negotiation and mediation of industrial conflicts. They were to serve as temporary consultants to the labor offices, which were to make the final decisions on all agreements reached by the parties involved. On two more urgent questions, wage adjustment and layoffs, the AMG tried to impose precise, though temporary, limitations on the conflicting demands coming from labor and management. An order of 25 May allowed the negotiation of wage adjustments but subjected their implementation to AMG approval. Its concern was to curb inflationary pressures and mitigate the pressing claims of the workers. A second order forbade all layoffs until 30 September, reflecting an agreement reached in Milan by the chamber of labor and the industrialists' association to encourage the gradual transfer of workers to sectors such as construction, which were expanding.[77]

But the measures taken by the Allies in these fields did not have very positive effects; in many ways they were an attempt to keep up with events rather than to effectively control them beforehand. First the AMG had to agree to the payment of the "liberation bonus," even though it thought it harmful. To resist pressure from the workers in the first weeks of May might have led to excessively strong tensions after the government in Rome refused to make a common front with the Allies' anti-inflationary intransigence.[78] Analogously, the government's acceptance at the end of June of the Milan agreement to introduce cost of living compensation into the north forestalled a possible Allied veto.[79] On the question of unemployment, the Allied administration, although it deemed increasing productivity and lowering of industrial costs to be fundamental, had to accept the logic of a temporary freeze of layoffs, without which public order, already in a precarious state, would probably have gotten out of control. In principle the Allies shared management's desire to unfreeze layoffs so that the financial burdens could be lightened and, more important, so that order and discipline as well as full management control could return to the workplace. This layoffs freeze was looked on as a transitory means to allow public works to get under way and to lower the number of excess workers without adding to the unemployed. But as the end of the freeze approached, no positive signals came from the government. No plans were being prepared, and the pressures from the left and from the unions made an indefinite continuation of the freeze likely.[80]

Braine deplored the government's incapacity to take the situation in hand. It seemed to surrender to the mutually exclusive positions of the parties and the absence of an effective spirit of collaboration under the leadership of the public authorities.[81] This feeling of disappointment was summed up well by the British ambassador, who said of the "consultation and cooperation" structures which Braine suggested to the government and the parties: "It remains to be seen whether the Italian authorities will continue to operate this machinery when Allied Military Government is withdrawn. There is unfortunately much evidence of mutual distrust which may prevent full cooperation between the respective interests when the initiative and stimulus of Allied authorities are no longer available."[82]

The progressive demobilization of the ACC in anticipation of the restitution of northern Italy, with the exception of Venezia Giulia, to the control of the Italian government on 31 December 1945 transformed the officials of the Labour Sub-Commission from protagonists to witnesses of events in the trade union field. The AMG's measures that summer, thanks to the cooperation of the CGIL, had checked the tensions coming from the factories. The chaotic and impetuous mobilization of the first weeks after the liberation had been partially channeled by the AMG's decrees into more controllable forms that were of less concern to the

Allies, when the first CGIL organizations had begun to translate the workers' claims into negotiations inspired by notable moderation. The intense political burden of those first days, represented for the Allies by labor's control of many firms and by the widespread presence of the Communists, had been mitigated, leaving more room for mediation by the chambers of labor. Fears were calmed and reports from industrial centers expressed satisfaction at the return to some kind of order, although with many reservations, emphasizing the containment achieved by the CGIL. The moderation shown by the confederation was the most reassuring factor in a situation which then was anything but stabilized. A sudden outbreak of agitation—the "political" strikes that so worried the Anglo-Americans— was still a possibility that kept the future uncertain.[83] In the face of the seriousness of these tensions, the economic difficulties, the political uncertainty, and the lack of the government's capacity to lead the recovery in an authoritative manner, the only reliable factor now was the CGIL's moderation.

The Allied administration was beginning to close out its operations and the picture was both bright and obscure. AMG power had been able to keep the working-class drive for political power in check, to rein in the most radical impulses of victorious antifascism, and to place the structure of industrial power under control, thus saving the prerogatives of the entrepreneurs. Sufficient bounds had been placed on labor mobilization to channel it into less damaging courses, laying a basis for institutionalizing and regulating the bargaining process. But here the results were much more meager. On the economic level, the American proposals for growth foundered on lack of resources and of contacts among Italian management circles who agreed with these ideas. Similarly, a model for industrial relations based on collective bargaining and collaboration was unsuccessful in breaching the complex of political and social conflicts that was present throughout the labor field. The Allied presence had delineated the boundaries within which the dialogue between classes could occur. But the attempts to defuse the social conflict, to reduce it to its technical aspects with self-regulating bargaining methods, were stopped by the absence of any initiatives from the Italian government.[84] The center of attention turned, therefore, to possible developments in the CGIL and its precarious internal equilibrium.

The Confederation and the Political Parties

The British attitude toward the CGIL was similar to that formulated by Braine at the beginning of 1945. To encourage a moderate role on the part of the confederation, the method was to encourage a gradual watering down of its political nature. Following the victory of the Labour party in the July elections, the British embassy saw "a great opportunity for assuming the leadership" of the "moderate component" of Italian trade unionism.[85] However, this was a somewhat vague possibility. When a delegation from the TUC arrived in Italy in December 1945 there was a dialogue of the deaf. On the Italian side, requests for assistance alternated with rather harsh speeches, especially from Di Vittorio, against industrialists and landowners, the Liberal party, and the political right. (The government of Ferruccio Parri had just fallen.) The British responded with offers of unspecified support. They did not hide their resentment at Italy's Fascist past and, with paternalistic insistence, "emphasized on all occasions the necessity of avoiding party politics in trade union organization."[86]

In American circles, the analysis of the CGIL was more attuned to the novelty of a tumultuous mass movement's entry on the scene in the industrial cities. The ambivalent relationship between the CGIL and labor agitation dominated Adams's reports and those of his collaborators. In a summary of events in Milan over the summer, an American official on the Labour Sub-Commission, Joseph Di Fede, recorded how the workers in the first weeks after the liberation tended to impose their demands on industry "by show of force." Large demonstrations or strikes of a political nature—"totally unnecessary and absolutely futile"—brought out the popularity of the leftist parties as well as the capacity of the chambers of labor and the CGIL to control events. Their leaders, especially the Communists, knew how to use the threat of agitation in successful negotiations with management, showing themselves very adept at playing a double role of leaders of the movement as well as its efficient moderating force: "Thus while the movement is stronger than any political party it is often subservient to the parties." The peripheral structures of the CGIL were warmly appreciated as "strong stabilizing powers in the labor field." In a very short time "they have asserted their power and prestige over all workers throughout Italy." For the Allied administration, the union leaders had been "of great assistance in maintaining calm and public order," but, however useful the CGIL's moderating influence was, the situation was not encouraging. The pressure from the workers, loosely connected to leftist forces and very influential in the CGIL, was destined to last. Poverty, lack of food and shelter, low wages, and unemployment were cause for concern. "All these are symptoms of the complete collapse of Italy. Labor unrest is due to several factors. . . . All in all we may say that labor unrest has been well contained so far. This, however, should not lead responsible authorities into a false sense of security. The underlying situation is explosive and steps must be taken to remove the detonating apparatus."[87]

The solutions that were hoped for referred to the beginning of a cycle of prosperity, the basis for which was very weak at the end of 1945. The picture painted by Di Fede cast new light on the importance and fragility of the equilibrium among the factions in the CGIL. Although there was strong pressure from below, originating in the social crisis and politicized as it was, the CGIL could mitigate some of its manifestations. At the same time it was directly affected and conditioned by it, becoming one field of the political battle then taking place in Italy.[88] Swollen by the multifaceted political demands of the workers, the CGIL's activities tended to take on a centralized character and a more markedly political aspect as the overall representative of the working classes.[89] Adams noted the assertion of these characteristics with concern because they made the CGIL even more unlike a trade union: "Its present activity is primarily of a political nature. . . . At present this organization is in an amorphous state: it is formally a labor union and functionally a political party, while its structure, if indeed it has any, is of neither."[90]

As a result, there was more concern for those forces which would have been able to achieve not only moderation, but some hope of greater CGIL attention to more purely trade union tasks, since they were not bound to a class concept of trade unionism. Some officials of the Labour Sub-Commission were critical of the decision to collaborate with the CGIL, since it had reportedly helped the Communists to attain a dominant position in the chambers of labor.[91] But a drastic change in its position on the CGIL met with more fear than agreement. At the end of September, when Achille Grandi published a letter to Di Vittorio and Lizzadri recommending greater tolerance on the part of the leftist factions, the view spread through the Allied administration that the Christian Democrats were about to leave the CGIL. Scicluna, not hostile in principle to a breakup, stressed the risk that the departure of the Christian Democrats could drive the Socialist workers into the arms of the Communists.[92] Braine was concerned about the reinforcement of the leftist factions in the CGIL and sympathized with the Christian Democrats' impatience, since the tolerance of the Catholics and the passivity of the Socialists were giving too much influence to the Communists. Concerning the Christian Democrats, Braine wrote, "They must either recover their lost ground and assume some more public share of the leadership of the working-class masses; or they will split away from the CGIL and resuscitate the 'white' unions of the pre-Fascist regime." But the head of the Labour Sub-Commission maintained that the political battle should be waged within the CGIL, whose unity was one of the few elements of stability, all the more valuable as political and social tension turned bitter: "It would be regrettable if the Christian-Democrats broke away from the trade union movement which would not only be weakened as an organization but would dissipate its energies in recrimination and counter-propaganda. . . . The dangers attending a secession of the Christian-Democrats from the trade union field have been pointed out to their leaders who are giving serious consideration to all the issues."[93]

Fears of a split soon abated, but the problem remained. An organization like the CGIL, based on a coalition of political parties, politicized and guided by majority Marxist elements, was the exact opposite of what the Allies desired. Nonetheless, the alternatives seemed even more risky. The CGIL when unified was the only filter of, and sometimes the only barrier to, the uncontrolled spread of social agitation in a transition phase in which every aspect of life in Italy, from the institutional framework to the political balance, from the dynamics of economic activity to Italy's place on the international scene, even to the very sense of the nation's identity, was undefined and uncertain. For the moment there was no substitute for the moderation and centralization of bargaining produced by the unitary compromise on which the CGIL lived. At the end of 1945 the first signs of recovery in output and the industrial agreements—which linked wages to inflation, allowed the resumption of piecework, and sanctioned the unfreezing of layoffs, at least in principle—marked the beginning of a return to the normal social order and to factory productivity, all in a framework of strong centralized control over industrial relations.[94] The importance of a CGIL anchored to the moderate strategy imposed on it by the disparate elements existing in its midst was still given high priority by the American observers with respect to the necessity of weakening the Communists. This latter goal had by then been raised to the primary purpose in the American scheme of things. Long analyses from the embassy in Rome tried to explain the reasons for this contradiction. Certainly the union was "controlled by the Communist party," Adams wrote, but this was not through "an acceptance of Communist principles." The Communists had better leaders and better resources, and they enjoyed the confidence of the masses thanks to their "personal integrity" and their "unequivocal anti-Fascist records." Their strength lay more than anywhere else in the connection they had been able to develop with popular aspirations: "The Communist Party is a true mass party whose principal aim is the improvement of the material conditions of the worker." If the workers' favors were to be granted to a nondemocratic force, the explanation would lie in an entire historical and existential experience. "Twenty years of Fascism cannot be forgotten overnight, and there are many Italians who feel unsure of democracy and who seek the type of order and discipline for which the Communist Party stands."[95]

What possible alternatives were there? Concerning other political forces, Adams stressed how cultural affinities and similar political choices offered scope for a dialogue with America: "The Socialist and Action party labor leaders tend to look at things and want to act in an American, democratic way, and the Christian Democrats almost to a man try to ingratiate themselves with the United States and seek her protection."[96] But the Action party was small, and sympathy for communism prevailed among the Socialists. "The only non-Marxist group within the CGIL which is given serious consideration as having a potential mass following is the Catholic group. . . . Many people . . . rely on this group as a nucleus for the creation of a democratic, non-Communist labor movement in Italy." Adams was extremely critical of the Christian faction, however. Its religious inspiration tied it too closely to the church; its operations appeared to be surrounded by an "aura of the parish house" that was completely inappropriate for defending the workers. Its dependence on the Christian Democratic party gave it a cast of mind "so at variance with the sentiments of large sections of the working classes that it can never succeed in gaining their support." The Catholic union leaders, of whom only Giulio Pastore had sufficient ability and energy, according to Adams, were subject to too many nonunion ties, and they were not representative enough to be able to lead successfully the reestablishment of the confederation. But they had a valuable "moderating influence" on the CGIL and therefore played an important role from the point of view of the Americans, to whom stability and anticommunism were very important: "While the Christian Democrat labor movement is too small and weak and too impermeated with basic fallacies to form even the nucleus of a strong independent labor movement . . . nevertheless it is sufficiently powerful to affect the policy of a united labor movement of which it is a part, and those who look on this more modest role as its true function can be reasonably optimistic of its continued success."[97] As long as the relative strength of the factions did not change, and the CGIL's moderation worked in favor of economic recovery and social stabilization, the view prevailing in the American embassy did not depart from Adams's realistic approach.

Changes in the American political atmosphere at the end of the war had immediate effect on the activities of the Italian American union leaders of the ILGWU. The diplomatic clashes between the United States and the USSR strengthened the anti-Communist propensities of the AFL. The end of the anti-Fascist struggle eliminated the weak obstacles to Antonini's encouragement of a break between Socialists and Communists after his visit to Italy. He wrote to Pietro Nenni on 11 September 1945:

When the two of us discussed the Italian situation and the position of the Socialist party, I agreed that the unity of action pact could not be dispensed with. . . . Now, after the outcome of the elections in England with the Labour Party's formation of a government and the position taken by the French Socialist party, it is impossible to understand why the Italian Socialist party, instead of taking advantage of and inspiration from those examples, still persists in sailing towards the rocks of fusion that will undoubtedly bring it to shipwreck. This would be seriously detrimental to Italy because if Italy wants to earn respect, esteem and above all aid from America and the Western democracies it is necessary that there be a democratic Italy that distances itself from any kind of dictatorial systems.[98]

Antonini's new position reflected the opening in the Socialist movement of a split, destined to widen, between the two poles of international influence, which Nenni hoped could be reference points for Socialist activities: Soviet socialism and the reformism of the British Labour party. The totally Western orientation of the victorious Labour party indicated the unreality of Nenni's dream of staying above the international split and accelerated the conflict within the Italian Socialist movement.[99] The IALC decided to "take a different route" and no longer sent aid to the union office of the Socialist party, but to the autonomists and Action party members in whom Antonini had greater confidence.[100] After a meeting with Leo Valiani in New York, Antonini announced that the IALC funds would be distributed to three committees: a joint committee for northern Italy (composed of Giuseppe Faravelli, Antonio Greppi, and Leo Valiani) and two for the rest of Italy, one composed of Socialists (Giuseppe Modigliani, Ignazio Silone, Emilio Canevari, Matteo Matteotti, and Vasco Cesari), and the other made up of Action party members (Alberto Cianca, Emilio Lussu, and Bruno Pierleoni). The purpose of this was to reinforce the antifusionist position in light of the Socialist congress and to favor the anti-Communist forces in the CGIL, in the expectation of overturning the confederation's majority: "Our aid to the periphery and lower reaches of the CGIL are not meant to divide it to its detriment. It is intended to make it possible for *our people*, the sincere and true democrats, to have available the means to stand on guard to keep the Italian labor movement effectively free and democratic."[101]

Neither the IALC nor its Italian contacts were thinking of breaking up the CGIL. If anything, there was the hope that if Nenni were defeated, an autonomous and anti-Communist Socialist party would have been able to reshape the status of the Communists in the confederation. The political struggle in the CGIL was still regarded with great caution, because of the difficulties inherent in the Italian situation as well as the uncertainties in the international field, which set clear limits to the AFL's operations. The anti-Communist battle in the international trade union movement had hardly begun. It was to require not only organizational efforts but profound changes in the political balance in European countries before it could achieve significant results. As long as the center of the political trade union movement was occupied by organizations that derived from the anti-Fascist alliance—coalition governments, unitary confederations, and a world federation that included the Soviets and the American CIO—the AFL's policy of breaking up the CGIL was limited to almost clandestine opposition, to assembling its forces, and to patching together unstable alliances among the Social Democratic and Liberal Democratic groups. Undoubtedly the AFL was beginning to benefit from the growing attraction and influence exerted by America in the eyes of many non-Communist European political forces. But that federation was not yet in a position to put itself forward effectively as a point of reference. As long as the international trade union movement was dominated by the WFTU, the attraction exerted by American power did not precipitate the conflict that the AFL expected and prepared for. The aid sent by the IALC was meant to bring on the best conditions for a clash with the Communists, but that, however, was still far off.[102]

Political Alliances

At the beginning of 1946 the Allied administration left Italy completely under the jurisdiction of the government in Rome and Italian institutions, with the exception of the territory of Trieste and Venezia Giulia. Even though the peace treaty that defined the nation's international status was still to come, relations with London and Washington returned to normal, at least from the institutional point of view. In relations with the victorious powers, and increasingly with the United States, the ordinary channels of bilateral relations—diplomacy, economic contacts, and private exchanges between similar social and political organizations—became the protagonists once again. Regarding trade union issues, the change was quite significant; the people involved remained, but their roles changed. Both Adams and Braine, as labor attachés at their respective embassies, took on the duties of observers or, at most, of liaisons between the Italian unions and the American or British ones. Relieved of their political and administrative responsibilities, they became witnesses to events in the Italian trade union movement. A more active role was eventually to depend on their governments' decisions to intervene in Italian trade union issues, but for the moment such a choice was not being considered. Between 1946 and 1947, even though preparations were under way in the United States for a strong diplomatic role on the international trade union stage, the embassy in Rome in general, and Adams in particular, remained passive though very attentive spectators of the course of Italian trade union affairs. In the months that saw events of decisive importance for Italy's political structure and its relations with the United States—the referendum on the monarchy, elections to the constituent assembly, drafting the peace treaty, the Socialist split, De Gasperi's trip to America, and, finally, the breakup of the coalition governments—the CGIL was the subject of constant and thorough investigation, but not yet the object of active political initiatives.

One organization operating in a progressively more incisive fashion was the AFL, through the IALC. As a pressure group in American political debate, the Italian American trade union movement gathered around Antonini intervened repeatedly in favor "of a just and speedy peace with Italy." With mass demonstrations and propagandistic initiatives, including Antonini's presence in Paris during the peace conference to bring pressure to bear on the American delegation, the IALC incessantly argued the necessity of tying the political and economic rebirth of Italy to the influence of the United States: "Our country, as the strongest and most influential power, has as its first responsibility to exercise international leadership. . . . Let America redouble and invigorate its efforts to assure a speedy and just peace settlement with the new Italy. Only America's complete fulfillment of its pledge to the Italian people who fought on our side, only the unyielding opposition by the United States to Russian aggrandizement against Italy, will enable her talented and hard-working people to serve as a pillar of world peace and progress."[103]

The efforts of the IALC to consolidate a moderate anti-Communist left were meant to contribute on the internal level to the complete rehabilitation of Italy as a Mediterranean power and an anti-Soviet force. There were even requests that Italy keep its colonial possessions. As the Socialist crisis became more heated, Antonini's ties with autonomist groups, especially with Giuseppe Faravelli, became more intense. With the Socialist congress in Florence in April 1946, Antonini nourished for the last time the hope that party's wounds could be healed without splits or movements toward the PCI, in a full reaffirmation of Socialist autonomy. During the precongress maneuvering, Antonini recommended to Faravelli that he not intensify the clash between the factions. He let Nenni and Rodolfo Morandi know that he would wait for the outcome of the congress before deciding to whom he would send the IALC aid. Antonini wanted an agreement among the centrist and *Critica sociale* factions that would safeguard the party's independence and make it "the linchpin of a Social Democratic bloc in the future Italian Republic."[104] To Saragat he sent "the wish that everything be done to avoid a split," which would have weakened the democratic forces and caused a crisis in relations between Italy and the United States—the pivot, from the Italian American viewpoint, around which the future should be designed. "A success at the Socialist Party Congress, from both a 'unitary' and 'democratic' point of view would contribute a great deal to reinforcing the confidence of America or at least its influential worker-progressive sector, in the sense of the responsibility and maturity of Italian democratic forces of which the Socialists can if they desire be the fulcrum."[105]

The unitary compromise arrived at in Florence was greeted with satisfaction by Antonini, who immediately agreed with the party's new secretary, Ivan Matteo Lombardo, who was in New York at the time of his election, to contribute $25,000 to the party for the coming electoral campaign. This was not a permanent step by the IALC. The *Critica sociale* group and its liberal Socialist viewpoint remained Antonini's preferred reference point. But the Italian American trade unionist was aware of the importance of the time frame before the elections and the referendum of 2 June, which required a united party. He was especially aware that the stages of the anti-Communist struggle, inside and outside the party, would be influenced by international developments.[106] But Antonini's pro-unity viewpoint was short-lived. On the day after the elections, the reasons for the conflict on the left regained primacy. Faravelli, requesting the urgent dispatch of IALC funds for the *Critica sociale*, made clear in no uncertain terms his own desire for a breakup: "When the struggle is described in the terminology of the fusionist faction there can be no alternative to a rupture. The problem is to bring about the break in the shape of the Communist fifth column's exit from the party." Antonini answered by confirming his confidence in Faravelli and his faction.[107] It was the union situation especially that caused concern in the IALC. One of Antonini's associates, after a trip to Italy, emphasized the necessity of furnishing every assistance to Saragat and Faravelli. He referred dramatically to conditions within the CGIL: "The unity action pact with the Communists, as Nenni has shaped it, has been greatly to the advantage of the Christian Democrats and the Communist party, who are contesting supremacy over and control of the CGIL. . . . The situation in the union is worrisome from every point of view. . . . Seven chambers of labor are controlled by the Socialists as opposed to eighty-four by the Communists. A feeling of tremendous hatred for the Communists prevails among the Italians. And since the Socialists in the confederation are represented by fusionists or 'fellow travellers' (like Lizzadri) the workers, no longer able to take comfort from the Socialists, are turning towards the Christian Democrats."[108]

The alarmism of the Italian American union leaders was exaggerated, but it had

a factual basis in the growth of tension within the CGIL. Even a calmer observer
such as Adams, who was critical of Antonini's involvement in the Italian Socialist
Party of Proletarian Unity (PSIUP), fearing that it might contribute to a breakup
in both the party and the union, noted during the spring the increasing concern of
the Christian Democrats and the appearance of obvious hostilities among the
factions, which led him to foresee the approach of a "showdown which cannot be
indefinitely averted."[109] The imbalance due originally to the numerical predominance of the Communists and the left was now tending to develop into political
differences. The industrial agreements of December 1945 and May 1946, which
brought back piecework, indexing wages to inflation, and virtually lifting the ban
on layoffs, had made possible a truce on the labor front and the beginning of a
recovery in production, sanctioning managerial control of industry with the FIAT
plant agreement on the worker-management councils. The containment of wage
changes and the advent of unemployment stirred up social tensions that were
increasingly difficult to check.[110] Worker participation in reconstruction, marked
by a drive toward greater productivity and by the CGIL's moderate demands, was
not significantly reciprocated. From the fall of the Parri government to the failure
of the currency conversion and the partial liberalization of foreign trade, economic
policy decisions were articulating the abandonment of a view based on government controls and structural reforms, thus weakening any desire for programming
and giving reconstruction a distinctly private-enterprise cast. The subjection of the
left to free trade formulas and its abandonment of any strong pressure for economic reforms—in order to give priority to institutional reforms such as the
republic and the new constitution—forced the CGIL into an ambiguous, unstable
position.[111]

   With the victory of the republic, and in the presence of growing inflation that
gave rise to frequent labor demonstrations, the split in the CGIL became explicit.
The Christian Democratic component wanted to give more influence to the
electoral result that had given their party a relative majority. The forces on the left,
when the goal of a republic was achieved, no longer believed in the firm policy of
moderation in wage increases that was beginning to eat away at the prestige of the
confederation.[112] In the CGIL's directive of mid-July, the confrontation on wage
policy clearly showed the irreconcilable distance that separated the two strategies
of politics and trade unionism. Di Vittorio emphasized the risks of defense of the
status quo ("if our confederation breaks up there will be no moral authority in our
country that can take matters in hand"). The CGIL could not accept lifting the ban
on layoffs or the decline in real wages. Investment and public works were needed
to give jobs to the unemployed; the government was requested to institute real

price controls, but the confederation had to concentrate its efforts on achieving wage increases. Diametrically opposed was the solution put forward by Grandi: the greatest danger for democracy was inflation, from which the workers should defend themselves by wage indexing, not with wage increases which, in turn, would drive up prices. Recovery should be encouraged, and therefore lifting the ban on layoffs should be accepted. The government should safeguard the workers until economic recovery was complete by getting public works under way and reining in prices. On the problem of intolerance among the various CGIL components, a compromise was achieved with the establishment of a commission of investigation. But on the course of action to follow, the directive was divided over two motions reflecting the differences between majority and minority.[113] This was not only the end of internal unanimity, but the opening of a phase in which the value of unity in the trade union movement was to be reconsidered continually by every member in the light of the compromises and sacrifices it required. "The question of union-government relations was a background to this disagreement on trade union policy and was its ill-concealed detonator. . . . A little more than a year after the liberation, the idea was losing ground that the mere presence of the traditionally worker-oriented parties in government could in itself furnish guarantees to the workers on sharing the successes of the recovery of productivity."[114]

All parties in the government had asked the CGIL for a substantial subordination of objectives to those of Treasury Minister Corbino, a liberal, and those of De Gasperi. The confederation was to accept a wage freeze and the unfreezing of layoffs.[115] The inflationary surge that was to accelerate in the second half of 1946 began to shatter the precarious ties between the parties of the anti-Fascist coalition, causing the failure of the labor peace that followed the liberation. One of the first effects of this was to bring to light the absence of any coherent program on the part of the leftist forces, which were culturally and politically subjected to the free trade principles of Corbino and of the industrialists.[116]

Adams rapidly grasped the potential consequences of the split that had opened up in the CGIL. The wave of local strikes found little justification in economic conditions, the labor attaché wrote, since wage increases were canceled by inflation. The high prices caused by insufficient production should be met with "more production and therefore more work." For this reason the workers were losing sympathy in public opinion and the CGIL's prestige was falling. To the extent that they were not planned from above, these agitations probably derived from a "more aggressive policy" of the Communists, following a partial electoral disappointment and a fear that the first signs of recovery could "adversely affect the progress of their cause." According to Adams, the divisions in the July directive originated from the Communist decision to push for new wage increases. This had put the Socialists in a difficult position and made the Christian Democratic minority the only focal point for opposition to Di Vittorio. The stand taken by the Christian Democrats, together with a notable increase of ACLI groups in various industrial centers, marked the growth of Catholic influence in the labor movement and opposed the Communist domination of the CGIL ever more conspicuously. Once again there was talk of a possible split, but not in the immediate future: "Although in many ways, the Catholics would like to split, they do not see what practical gain they could achieve by these tactics." Furthermore, according to Adams, the Catholics still did not constitute a genuine union alternative because of their subjection to the church and the Christian Democratic party. Their partial success "is primarily a reflection of and a reaction to Communism." Adams, however, pointed to two very important questions for the future. In the first place, the nature of the CGIL was changing. As long as the CGIL had represented "more or less accurately the aspirations and viewpoint of the working people as a whole," albeit more in a political way than as a trade union, "the CGIL could perform a useful function."

Because of Communist domination and internal differences, however, the CGIL was now losing "any autonomous function" and appeared increasingly like "a political adjunct of the Communist party." Above all, the confederation was showing itself to be deeply influenced by the psychological, economic, and political conditions of the country: "If general conditions become more stable . . . the CGIL will have a better opportunity to effect gradually those changes and improvements which will make it an adequately functioning union. If instead the situation should become increasingly chaotic, the present organization would be wholly inadequate. Italian labor organizations are for the most part too sick and weak themselves to give much impetus or aid to Italian recovery; rather they must themselves look to an improvement in the general situation as a condition of their own recovery."[117]

The idea that the CGIL was turning into a political tool in the hands of the Communists, whose dominance was checked only by a minority too small to become an effective alternative, was to set off alarm bells in the State Department, where concern at the expansion of Communist influence had by now taken root and become constant. Furthermore, Adams's analysis foresaw a new relationship between the confederation and economic recovery. The CGIL no longer appeared as a positive element on the Italian scene. On the contrary, its desired transformation into a union whose main purpose was to assist in collective bargaining now appeared subordinated to a period of stability and development. For the first time, in the picture of the CGIL conveyed to Washington, negative aspects began to get the upper hand over the positive light in which the labor attaché had viewed it up to then, however imperfectly.

Between the end of the summer and the fall, the succession of economic and political difficulties and the intensification of the political conflict added further shades of gray to Washington's analysis of the Italian crisis. In the first months of 1946 the Truman administration's view of the international situation, as well as the political climate in America, had veered toward a resolute and intransigent confrontation with the USSR. From the speech in Fulton, Missouri, where Churchill denounced the "iron curtain" that was dividing Europe, to the Iranian crisis in which the United States showed that it wanted to block any further expansion of Soviet influence, to the decision to proceed to the reorganization of a divided Germany announced by Secretary of State Byrnes in September, Washington's attitude was based on two assumptions: first, that it was confronting Soviet plans for global expansion, and second, that only inflexible firmness could safeguard American interests. Henry Wallace's September 1946 departure from the government, where he had been secretary of commerce, marked the defeat of Roosevelt's previous policy of collaboration with the USSR.[118]

U.S. policy toward Italy derived logically from this scenario and adapted itself progressively to the priorities defined in Washington. At the beginning of 1946 a program of UNRRA aid was set up that was led by prevalently Keynesian and New Deal–oriented officials, who intended to establish democratic forms of planning that would favor the increase of production for the internal market through governmental controls and fiscal policy. A greater availability of consumer goods was deemed necessary to combat inflation and the widespread poverty that was considered the primary cause of social instability and the attraction of communism. But New Deal reformism, already weakened by the growth of conservative viewpoints in Washington, clashed in Italy with the resistance of Corbino and the industrialists. The hostility of the Italian treasury minister to the Keynesian formulas, the abandonment of price controls, the partial liberalization of foreign trade, and the priority given to exports made UNRRA's programs useless. At the end of the summer, the mission had been reduced to impotence. In the face of inflation, even the economic offices of the State Department were having difficulties. The opening of the Italian economy to international markets was impossible without a drastic stabilization of the lira. One of the New Deal officials of UNRRA even came to the unhappy conclusion that welfare costs and employment levels would have to be cut to bring the situation under control ("save the lira at the expense of the people").[119] But could such a policy be adopted by a coalition government that included the leftists and the PCI? The break with the left seemed to be necessary for the success of economic stabilization. In September the "new course" of the PCI, which obtained the resignation of Corbino, was interpreted by the State Department as an indication of the party's desire to prevent the recovery of Europe. This strengthened the view that ending the crisis would require solution of the political problems by the weakening of the left.[120]

The intensification of the political crisis became more tangible in the fall. Tensions and strife, for the most part submerged but sometimes visible, were multiplying both in the society and in the political sphere, involving the CGIL as well. The confederation agreed on 27 October with the employers' association CONFINDUSTRIA on a "wage truce," fulfilling the government's request and continuing its efforts to contain wage increases that were at the base of postwar recovery.[121] But the effectiveness of the confederation's mediation and its role as a "political guarantor" of collaboration were rapidly diminishing.[122] In an atmosphere of increasing tension—the protests of the former partisans were being added to the strikes, while on the opposite side of the political spectrum there was the virulent "Uomo Qualunque" ("Man in the Street") campaign against all democratic parties—the inability of the political parties to live together struck the confederation with greater immediacy.[123] The Christian Democratic party increasingly argued against the exploitation of the CGIL by the left and the succession of conflicts in industry. In September it established a committee to reach agreement on labor matters and to coordinate ACLI activities and those of the Christian current in the CGIL with those of the party. The ACLI, at a congress at the end of September, restated its choice of unity in the confederation but showed increasing skepticism about the idea's validity. They strengthened their independent organization and stepped up their polemics with the left. Ideas and proposals for a new Christian trade union were by now circulating explicitly in Catholic circles.[124] The PCI entered this arena in November, when Togliatti, perhaps in anticipation of a coming political crisis, asked for the "democratization" of the CGIL, that is, the abandonment of equal representation in favor of a proportional division among factions. In the bitter reactions from the Christian Democrats, the possibility of a split was publicly aired.[125]

Antonini, then on a trip to Italy, did not lose the chance to become involved in the controversy. He stated in a radio broadcast: "The workers want free and independent unions. This is a condemnation of those who wanted to box in the trade union movement for political and totalitarian purposes."[126] Lizzadri rebutted by accusing Antonini of having given ILGWU aid not to the confederation but to its splinter groups from 1946 on, isolating himself from the labor movement without succeeding in breaking up the CGIL. Antonini then replied that the

CGIL had become a "totalitarian political monstrosity," subservient to the Soviets like the WFTU, and that only the free unions from America offered solid economic victories to the workers.[127]

The deepening international split and the intensification of the crisis in Italy were irreparably widening the division of the Socialists—who also had problems in the confederation following the polarization between the Communist and Christian Democratic parties—precipitating the crisis in their party.[128] Antonini announced to the administrative secretary of the PSIUP that the IALC no longer intended to "finance the social-communist idyll in any way."[129] Shortly thereafter, assuring Faravelli of the IALC commitment to the *Critica sociale* group in view of the coming PSIUP congress, Antonini abandoned caution and any further procrastination: "We have always been careful to give no pretext to Di Vittorio and his Lizzadri to accuse us of promoting disunity in Italy. But, these scruples apart, I think that now is the time to help all those who are working to have a free and democratic labor movement in Italy."[130]

Antonini was convinced that this was the moment to join battle, first in the party and then in the labor confederation, just as his Italian counterparts wanted. Faravelli wrote that he had reached an agreement with Saragat in connection with the congress. After having mentioned the possibility of winning it over—as if merely pro forma—he announced that it had been decided, in case of defeat, to "leave in a body to found the true Italian Socialist party." The tactics to be followed therefore would be to "reject any compromise whatsoever" and, on the contrary, to "energetically accentuate the points of disagreement with the fusionists" in order to prevent any further postponement of the break.[131] Antonini was fully aware of this exceptional moment ("in which facts count more than words") and urgently sent funds raised by the ILGWU and the AFL.[132] On 14 December the IALC sent an official message to the Italian Socialists, in rhetorical but unequivocal tones: "You and perhaps you alone can save Italy from the danger of totalitarianism. . . . America wants a free, independent, democratic, and prosperous Italy and is prepared to give it concrete aid in order to reach these objectives. . . . To you, Socialist comrades of Italy, goes our hope that in the decisive turning point where history has given you an appointment for the new year, your intention to free yourselves definitively from every suffocating totalitarian tentacle will be fulfilled and that you will be able to be yourselves, Socialists and only Socialists."[133]

Antonini's conviction that the moment had come to break with the Communists and to split up the PSIUP derived not only from the Italian situation and the state of that party, but also from the debate in American political and trade union circles. The November elections for Congress, with widespread Republican victories, had marked a decisive political change in the conservative direction. Antonini interpreted the Republican victories as "a solemn rebuke to Truman's shaky policy, pro-Communism and 'appeasement' in the style of Wallace with the Russia of Stalin and Molotov."[134] The AFL believed that this was the moment for a direct attack on the WFTU and on every variety of anti-Fascist coalition in the countries of Europe. It organized its own operations there and established a close network of relationships with the Social Democratic forces. It also prepared to open a permanent office in Europe and distribute the journal of the FTUC in several languages.[135] The IALC approved an action program for 1947 based on "the urgent need of rendering all-out moral and material assistance to the militantly anti-totalitarian and genuinely pro-democratic groups inside the Italian Socialist Party and the Italian trade union movement."[136] The State Department, which had attentively followed the preparations for the Socialist congress, was not involved in carrying out the split of that party that occurred at Palazzo Barberini. But it greeted the split with great satisfaction, hoping that it would open the way to a reformist coalition between Catholics and Social Democrats to isolate the Communist left and take votes from it.[137] When the split occurred, the Social Democrats' preferential relationship with the IALC led them to an alliance with the AFL. That American federation throughout 1947 considered the consolidation of the Italian Socialist Workers' party (PSLI) and the reinforcement of its activities in the union field to be the fundamental goals of its policy to Italy. Immediately after the break, Antonini wrote to Saragat: "What had to happen has happened." The IALC "will help you with all its forces and to the limit of what is humanly possible."[138] A month later, at Antonini's suggestion, President David Dubinsky officially committed the ILGWU to support the PSLI and give it financial aid.[139]

At the same time as the breakup of the Socialist party, another and much more important bond was being forged between the United States and Italy, that between the Truman administration and Prime Minister Alcide De Gasperi, then on a visit to Washington. The Christian Democratic leader's trip was the starting point of a long, steady convergence between his political program and the American decisions for a Western stabilization of Italy. It represented the beginning of a complex partnership, both diplomatic and expressly political, that matured over the following two years. The closer relations between De Gasperi and the American foreign policy establishment had fairly remote roots in the dialogue carried on during the war between Roosevelt's personal envoy, Myron Taylor, and the Vatican. A communality of interest had emerged, centered on the struggle against communism, between Christian Democratic moderate elements and Washington's aspirations for the postwar reconstruction of Europe and Italy.[140] Then, with De

Gasperi as head of government, and with the active involvement of Italy's Ambassador Tarchiani in Washington, the contacts with the United States had often taken on aspects of collaboration toward partially common goals. The desire to anchor Italy's international status to a primary relationship with the United States and to limit the role of the leftist forces within Italy constituted the principal areas where the two countries were already drawing closer together in the first half of 1946.[141] De Gasperi's efforts to find international conditions which would favor his own domestic position and America's interest in a solid, moderate partner led both parties to mutual dependence and a marriage of interests.[142]

The feeling from that summer on that a crisis was imminent accelerated the process. The left's opposition to Corbino's economic policies, the return of inflation, the spread of social disorder, and the immobility of the coalition government in the light of the international divisions all convinced the two parties of the urgent need for both economic and political action.[143] In September De Gasperi confided to the American embassy that he foresaw and hoped for an accounting with the Communists, which could only take place, however, after ratification of the peace treaty. The results of the local elections in November, in which the Christian Democratic party lost from both the right and the left, increased a feeling of alarm in the State Department. To help De Gasperi and to aid Italy, at first with credits and economic aid, appeared in Washington to be urgent priorities.[144] Looking to a decisive confrontation, De Gasperi meant to guarantee himself maximum support and concrete promises of aid for Italy from overseas.[145] This convergence of views lay behind De Gasperi's trip, which was desired both in Rome and Washington— in parallel and separate ways, but directed to similar ends. The economic results of the trip were minimal, given the scant willingness of the new Congress to take on any more financial commitments. However, they were symbolically effective as a promise for future American commitments to support Italian reconstruction, as soon as Italy set out on a politically reassuring path, and when the Truman administration succeeded in overcoming internal resistance to using vast resources for its own international policy.[146]

While the Italian crisis made it possible to foresee a definitive clarification of the lines that reconstruction was to follow, many bonds of political collaboration and plans for alliances between forces of differing nature but with strong common interests—such as between the AFL and the PSLI—were being consolidated between Italy and the United States. The CGIL, at the beginning of 1947, was not yet torn by the polarization in party politics then taking place, even though it suffered its paralyzing effects. Its capacity to initiate action was drying up. Not even the international situation—where the albeit combative isolation of the AFL stood in opposition to the unified existence of the WFTU—was likely to force on the CGIL political conflicts deep enough to threaten its unity. But in the eyes of the more attentive, or more interested, American observers, both the bipolar hostility and the incipient radicalism of Italian political confrontation were causing the CGIL's image to take on radically new colorations and contours. For Antonini and the AFL, the period of mutual toleration and compromise among the groups in the anti-Fascist coalition was long past. For Labor Attaché Adams, who was less inclined to take up arms against communism, the CGIL was nevertheless no longer in a position to play its mediating role, so useful in reconstruction, for which the Allies had initially welcomed it with interest and confidence. From what the CGIL did, or rather from its quarrelsome lack of action, there no longer emerged those results of realigning the labor arena and deradicalizing the conflicts that in 1945 had seemed so reassuring and indispensable. In the rigorously defined framework of Allied power just after the liberation, the CGIL's emphasis on labor's responsibilities to the nation had prevented the start of a conflict over the power structure in industry or the lines of economic policy. The confederation had acted as a filter and a barrier, leaving to the currents within the government and the political sectors of the country as a whole the debate on reconstruction, thus keeping it out of range of the most disruptive social tensions. Collaboration with the CGIL had given the Allies a valuable contribution toward governing the society as a whole, but it had not advanced at all the more ambitious objective of depoliticizing the federation and making it more of a trade union. The necessary premises, conditions, and desire for this change, so wanted in both London and Washington, were lacking in Italy.[147]

On the contrary, the progressive deterioration of the governing political alliance was significantly reducing the CGIL's remaining capacity to mediate and to achieve a truce in the labor arena. This made it impossible for the confederation to contribute to any reforms. The progress of a reconstruction whose costs weighed heavily on wages and employment lessened the scope for bargaining and reconciling the various factions in the CGIL. The AFL, tying its intervention in Europe and Italy to the Social Democratic hypothesis of a break to the left, began to blow on the fires of internal conflict in the CGIL. American foreign policy was now lining up decisively in the battle on Italy's economic and political reconstruction. The decision to fight the left and to establish a privileged relationship with De Gasperi's leadership made obsolete any positive evaluation of the CGIL as a factor for stability and unity. In the analysis of the CGIL made by the State Department, praise of its unity vanished and the hegemony of the PCI came to the fore, along with its inclination to support worker protests, and the role of internal minorities.

Toward the latter, the official American attitude was still one of passive benevolence. It oscillated between frustration at the weakness of lay leftist groups and a contained admiration for the combativeness of the Christian Democrats, offset by the degree to which their different social and industrial background set them apart from Americans. But if the reduction of Communist influence in the confederation depended on the progress of economic stabilization and political clarification, then the establishment of an axis of collaboration between the Truman administration and De Gasperi, which had began with his trip to Washington, laid the basis for overcoming that passivity. When the United States, with its programs of economic assistance, became a participant in reconstruction and the political conflict on the form it would take, the internal power balances in the CGIL would soon become a subject of decisive interest for American foreign policy.

Part Two
THE WORLD SPLITS IN TWO, 1947–1951

CHAPTER

The Truman Doctrine and the Marshall Plan:

Toward Anti-Communist Stabilization

"It must be the policy of the United States to support free peoples who are resisting attempted subjugation by armed minorities or by outside pressures." The principle announced by President Truman on 12 March 1947 in a message asking Congress for $400 million in aid to Greece and Turkey signaled the starting point of the Cold War and the criterion for a new global activism on the part of the United States. Based on the assumption that the world by then had split into "two differing ways of life," Truman's new international doctrine went beyond the momentary situation in Greece and Turkey and committed the United States to a generalized effort at containment of the influence of the USSR and the Communist movements.[1] The appeal came at a time when the foreign ministers' conference in Moscow had been unsuccessful in reaching agreement on the fate of Germany. There was a strong conviction among American leaders that it was up to the United States to take the lead in a Western front against the expansionist threat perceived in Soviet attitudes. When word had come from London a few weeks previously that the British government would no longer be able to bear the financial burden of supporting the two Mediterranean governments—especially Greece, which was involved in a civil war—it went without saying for the Truman administration that the United States would replace Great Britain in its stabilizing role as dominant power in the Mediterranean area. For the United States the moment had come to assume publicly the responsibility for and the leadership of a settlement of postwar Europe that would safeguard free market economies and guarantee political stability. It appeared as a historic choice from which there was no possibility of appeal. "We must either take or surrender leadership."[2]

The Truman Doctrine translated the anti-Soviet axioms of the American leaders into concrete political action, set containment programs under way, and projected the American initiative to that assumption of direct international responsibilities that later took the form of Marshall Plan aid and the establishment of the North Atlantic Treaty Organization (NATO). Within the administration there was a substantial unity of views. The real problem was to find the agreement necessary for an American international commitment, both in public opinion and in a Congress that was as sensitive to anti-Communist issues as it was hesitant to undertake new foreign obligations, especially financial ones. The government therefore set out on a campaign of deliberate dramatization, raising the Greek problem to a crisis of the first order where the security of the United States and the Western world was at stake. Basing their approach on the widespread conviction that the appeasement of totalitarian powers inevitably led to catastrophe—a view unassailable by then in the thinking of the average American, after Munich and Pearl Harbor—administration strategists, and Under Secretary of State Dean Acheson, in particular, offered to American and international public opinion the first version of the domino theory:

> In the past eighteen months . . . Soviet pressures on the Straits, on Iran, and on northern Greece had brought the Balkans to the point where a highly possible Soviet breakthrough might open three continents to Soviet penetration. Like apples in a barrel infected by a rotten one, the corruption of Greece would affect Iran and all to the east. It would also carry infection to Africa through Asia Minor and Egypt, and to Europe through Italy and France, already threatened by the strongest domestic Communist parties in Western Europe. The Soviet Union was playing one of the greatest gambles in history at minimal cost. It did not need to win all the possibilities. Even one or two offered immense gains. We and we alone were in a position to break up the play.[3]

To convince the country, the administration so magnified the danger inherent in the European situation as to confer on the Truman Doctrine the tone of a global anti-Communist crusade, which was to characterize international and domestic affairs in succeeding years.[4] In the face of the ultimatum conveyed by such an appeal, not only Congress, which quickly approved the aid request, but all social and institutional forces were inevitably called to join in. For the trade unions, the government's entry into a program of anti-Communist containment in Europe changed all the reference points of their international activities. Most important, the commitment to economic stability in countries threatened by Communist forces led the federal government to insert the issues of social equilibrium, and therefore the concerns of union policies, into the gamut of American foreign policy priorities.

The American Mission in Greece

At first, the Truman Doctrine gave rise to various reservations among liberals. The heirs of Roosevelt's vision, though strongly anti-Communist, could not fail to greet with suspicion an initiative that tied American policy to the support of reactionary governments, bypassed the United Nations by lessening its role, and pointed to commitments that were too extensive for the United States. And the fact that it was accompanied by domestic policies that were anything but liberal, such as the Loyalty Program, fed their mistrust.[5] The reactions of the trade union leaders were diverse. The AFL immediately declared its unconditional agreement. The direct entry of the government into the struggle against the Soviet and Communist threat was the realization of the policy the federation had been asking for since 1944. This resulted, if anything, in a more extensive interpretation of the American commitment—the FTUC was asking for the immediate revitalization of the German and European economies as an anti-Soviet bulwark—and ensured that the union organizations would be directly involved in formulating progressive social policies in countries under American guidance. The IALC sent enthusiastic congratulations to the president, requesting that the policy set forth by Truman be "also applied to democratic Italy which is the very frontier of the civilization to which we belong." The ILGWU as a whole, under Dubinsky's leadership, was the first union to adhere unreservedly to the principles of the new doctrine.[6]

The CIO, on the other hand, was the main victim of the initial transitory reservations of the liberals. Truman's initiative did not run counter to the ideological inclinations of those on the right, but it gave rise to some distrust concerning its practical implications. President Murray, especially prudent about domestic political balances of power, took no position on the matter until the summer, when the announcement of the Marshall Plan and, above all, Truman's veto of the Taft-Hartley Act brought the union leaders closer to the White House. Over several months, the CIO newspaper mentioned the matter only in an article by James Carey, who decried the lack of union representatives in the mission to Athens. Carefully avoiding the problems raised by the Truman Doctrine, the article brought out the unease in the CIO, almost as if Carey had wanted to conceal the reservations he did not dare to voice as open criticisms. "What the workers of the United States would like to know is whether they are expected in the case of Greece and Turkey to shore up reaction. . . . Do the American people have more than two choices on the matter: communism on the one hand and the divine rights of a reactionary government on the other?"[7]

The CIO leaders, more than the American people, were faced with this dramatic alternative. Not yet fully convinced that negotiating with the USSR was impossible, Murray and his associates feared that the commitments taken on with the Truman Doctrine would lead the United States to line up with the most conservative political currents in Greece or other countries. The danger was all the greater due to the simultaneous shift to the right of the domestic political axis, especially on labor-management issues. Defeated by the resistance of the industrialists in the strikes of 1946, deprived of the corporatist influence it had hoped at the end of the war to obtain over the government apparatus, the CIO interpreted the antiunion Taft-Hartley Act as the symbol of an energetic return of reaction to the center of the American political scene: "The first real step toward the development of fascism in the USA."[8] Although in agreement with the anticommunism that then dominated the country's attitude on international affairs—or, more important, lacking effective alternatives—the leaders of the federation wanted to avoid having to support, in a subordinate role having no influence, foreign policy initiatives that were under the influence of a purely business view of labor relations, free trade economic doctrines, and an antiradical hysteria. If it was necessary to go abroad to forestall Moscow's designs, this should be done in the democratic spirit of the New Deal, with its models of organized social pluralism and an expanding mass-consumption economy.

On 18 March Dean Acheson met the union leaders and painted a dramatic picture of Greece: the country was on the verge of economic collapse; the armed forces were insufficient to keep order; and the public administration was incapable of governing. If American aid had not come, the Communists would have taken control of the country and their influence would be extended throughout the Mediterranean area. The representatives of the AFL "expressed unqualified approval." Among the CIO's men, Clinton Golden said he was impressed by Acheson's presentation and convinced of the necessity of aiding Greece; James Carey said that "a chance at democracy" should be offered to the Greeks. Albeit without any formal commitments, the CIO representatives declared themselves in favor of aid and emphasized the importance of aiding the reconstruction of a "free Greek trade union movement."[9] Having accepted the anti-Soviet priority, the principle in the name of which it was vital to prevent Communist subversion, the acid test for these union leaders was the degree to which the social and economic proposal brought by the missions to Greece and elsewhere was democratic. Taking this position could lead only to the direct involvement of the unions. Only the presence of the American unions would be sufficient assurance of giving a democratic cast to the missions' activities, encouraging the development of trade unions and free collective bargaining. Any real change for the advancement of a social model marked by pluralist bargaining among organized interests—by industrial democracy, as the CIO understood it—came down to a joint leadership of the mission by diplomats or technical personnel and representatives of the unions, who would advise the Greek government and unions on social affairs.

What the AFL had long advocated—the use of its members as consultants by American administrations abroad—now became, in the face of the uncertainties brought out by the Truman Doctrine, the touchstone for the anti-Communist leaders of the CIO. It was something to hold on to in the face of the dilemmas of a political stand that was becoming rapidly obsolete with the outbreak of the Cold War. As soon as the State Department addressed these problems, the CIO's reservations about the Truman Doctrine vanished and its leading members associated themselves with the containment policy without any further fears. A prestigious CIO representative, Clinton Golden, was called as consultant on labor affairs to the mission in Athens. While the State Department was drawing up the project for aid to Europe which Secretary Marshall was to make public in June, Acheson returned to his discussions with the CIO leaders. Perceiving the concerns of the union leaders, he did not limit himself to airing the Communist danger or the domino theory: "Mr. Acheson explained the significance of this doctrine in relation to the collapsing economic systems in Europe." Carey replied that this "put a new light on" the importance of Truman's policy.[10] These openings by the State Department were more than enough. Murray stated that the CIO completely supported the mission and its democratic purposes.[11]

The choice of Golden was no accident. He was a fervent anti-Communist and the most prepared to support the Truman Doctrine. A man who enjoyed Murray's confidence, Golden had represented the CIO during the war in various government agencies, and he was the leading exponent of a philosophy of cooperation with management in the name of orderly, productivist, and nonconflictual industrial relations.[12] The program he brought to Athens reflected his confidence in efficiency, in the possibility of offering technical solutions to problems that were mainly political. While the mission pursued a rigidly deflationist economic policy, both for balancing the budget and out of a general skepticism about the possibility of expanding a poor economy such as that of Greece, the labor division headed by

Golden drew up programs typical of an industrial economy in expansion, with two fundamental objectives: "to aid promoting sound, peaceful, and constructive labor-management relations," and to develop "a sound wage and salary structure designed to promote industrial efficiency and equitable wage-price relationships." But the atmosphere of civil war and the increasing weakness of the liberal and centrist forces—which the American mistrusted increasingly, preferring to support the right for a military victory over the Communists—did not offer space for social reform projects founded on collective bargaining and collaboration among the parties.[13]

Golden's position, already made difficult by the financial austerity that imposed a rigid wage freeze, became untenable after only four months, when the Greek government voted in a law in December that punished strikes with the death penalty. Isolated even in the American mission, which had pressed for a drastic law even though it thought the death penalty inappropriate and counterproductive, Golden thought of resigning and requested the CIO and the AFL to protest vigorously at the State Department. This subsequently led, following the intervention of Secretary of State Marshall himself, to an official American request to revoke that law.[14] Golden stayed at his post, but the basic problem remained unsolved. The priority given to the anti-Communist struggle and the need for rapid stabilization brought the United States to support restrictive economic and political solutions, especially at a time of military conflict, which cut off any possibility of developing the reformist programs of the CIO leader. Golden was aware of this: "We talk about 'recovery' in a way at least here in Greece, that conveys the idea that we are trying to recreate an old order that no one particularly wants. We are not talking about the possibility of making Greece anything but what she has always been—a poor country where most of the people grub a precarious living from the barren hillsides and narrow valleys."

But in the now frigid atmosphere of the conflict between the United States and the USSR—the Cominform had been established and the Marshall Plan was getting under way in Europe—that analysis did not give rise to any serious second thoughts. The urgency of the struggle against the Communists was not being discussed; on the contrary, that viewpoint was reinforced by the experience in Greece. As for the best way to carry it out, the imminent launching of plans to aid not backward countries like Greece, but industrialized nations of Western Europe, promised greater success for union-inspired reformism. The conclusions Golden reached—he left Athens in 1948 to join the administration of the Marshall Plan as head of the labor division—were that the American union organizations must get involved with American missions abroad with more commitment and effectiveness, in order to have more influence over them. The policies of the Truman Doctrine were not under discussion. On the contrary, the American commitment abroad to containment and social stability was being strengthened. It was up to the government—and pressure from the unions—to see that the commitment was fulfilled under progressive, enlightened, and socially creative auspices.[15] If, as Golden conjectured, the mission to Greece was serving as a pilot operation for the administration of American aid, the unsolved problems brought out by the conflict between the labor division's perceptions and those of the mission as a whole—not to mention the Greek government—clearly indicated the problems the CIO was to face with the Marshall Plan. But in Golden's view these problems could be dealt with only in a situation of international and social peace. First the Communist threat had to be stopped; then it would be possible to consider social reforms.[16]

The mission to Greece, however, was not the main result of the Truman Doctrine, even if it constituted the first official commitment of the CIO at the side of the government. Much more important was the reexamination of international balances of power among trade unions worldwide, and the change in policy undertaken by the State Department following the choice of containment. The fundamental postulate of the Truman Doctrine, the American assumption of direct responsibility for stabilizing countries "threatened" by communism, inevitably enhanced the importance of the political coalition of the workers and their organizations and the consensus these organizations could provide to governments. The instructions sent to the embassy in Rome during the May 1947 government crisis contained clear indications of the importance the State Department was ascribing to the issue of political representation of the working classes and the economic causes of their discontent:

> It is evident any non-Communist government formed following De Gasperi's resignation must achieve early, visible improvement economic conditions.

> Communists intend charge new Italian Government as undemocratic, without representation working classes, while attempting portray US as supporting reactionary Italian elements. . . . You might explain to PSLI leaders, US view that Italian situation requires loyal cooperation all truly democratic elements in national interest. With Christian Democracy leaders, you might point out need, which applies to all European governments today, for support of democratic left and of fullest possible representation working classes.[17]

In the conflict with the Communists, the workers and unions throughout Europe became one of the more important arenas in the struggle for popular consent and for the adversary's political isolation. In the State Department's scheme of things, if the unions were to become important political factors for solving Europe's strategic equation, some attention would have to be given to the WFTU, and first of all to the CIO's delicate position in that organization.

The Attack on the WFTU

The Department of State had never been particularly friendly to the WFTU, nor had it been openly hostile, even if there was a strong concern at the way Moscow was using this international trade union movement. These fears increased during the winter of 1946–47 and were crystallized in a long report that began to circulate at the beginning of 1947. The document, citing Lenin, emphasized the enormous importance traditionally attributed by the Communists to union organizations. "Communists regard trade unions fundamentally as political weapons and therefore seek to gain control of them whenever possible. . . . Once they achieve a dominating position in a union the Communists use it for mobilizing public opinion and for exerting direct political pressure in favor of the interests of the Soviet Union." The ideas and the language were close to those of the AFL, especially the initial, firm conclusion: "The Russians have achieved considerable success in utilizing the WFTU as an instrument of Soviet foreign policy."

Soviet influence was limited only by the caution with which the Communists up to then had avoided positions unacceptable to the British, or to the Americans of the CIO. Any breakup would have made the organization weak and too vulnerable to the accusation of serving Soviet interests, thereby lessening its effectiveness. "The Russians, therefore, do not desire an open break." In spite of this prudence, the Soviets—especially thanks to the secretary-general, the Frenchman Louis Saillant, whom even the CIO considered excessively pro-Communist—had succeeded several times in getting the WFTU to act in consonance with Soviet interests and in open contrast with American or British policy. The document cited the WFTU's statements against Franco's Spain, the Greek government, and the Western colonial powers, and concluded that the WFTU served to induce union leaders in every country to believe that the USSR represented "a friend and an ally" of the workers. It was therefore a means of pushing the worldwide trade union movement to support "the foreign policies of the Soviet Union" and to oppose those of the Western powers. It also served "to prevent cooperation either on a national basis or an international basis of labor unions which are opposed to Communism." The criticism was deep and total. The negative view of what the

WFTU was doing took up the condemnation that the leaders of the AFL had already expressed. The last paragraph referred to the views of the CIO and the AFL without explicitly taking a position on either of them. The tone and language, however, indicated a preference for the unyielding criticism of the AFL over the arguments of the CIO and the TUC. The latter two organizations believed that the Western unions should stay in the world federation to prevent the Soviets from bending it completely to their own political and national purposes. The State Department had not yet made a decision on whether or not anything should be done to divide the WFTU, but this was still a tactical choice, which would depend on developments in the CIO's political crisis and on decisions made by the British. From this point on, in the picture painted by American diplomacy, the WFTU took on the negative and sinister aspect of an instrument in the hands of the Soviets for striking at and destabilizing Western governments. In the clash between the two superpowers, especially in the conflict around the stabilization of Europe, the WFTU was an obstacle to American interests, if not their enemy. This was the political message that arrived at all the embassies on 23 June, a few weeks after the announcement of the Marshall Plan, when the document was circulated with a letter from Acheson that stressed the "substantial importance" of the views of the unions to American foreign policy. The embassies were instructed to study the best ways of conveying that policy to the unions in every country and obtaining their support for it.[18]

It was equally crucial for the Truman administration to undo the complex network of internal and international interests that bound the CIO to the WFTU. The CIO leaders themselves, well aware of the contradiction—which could easily intensify—between their cooperation with the Soviets in the WFTU and the choice of containment that their country had made by then, felt the need of discussing their positions, especially their uncertainties, with the Department of State. On 19 May 1947, just before they left for a meeting of the WFTU executive board, James Carey and Michael Ross met with Acheson to discuss the State Department's views on the world federation. The meeting was seen there as an opportunity to make known the department's critical view of the WFTU and ascertain whether the CIO wanted to continue "to drift along" or whether it intended to take a more determined position in the WFTU, insisting on the replacement of the secretary and assuming greater executive responsibilities, for example. The State Department wanted to convey "the desirability of stronger CIO influence in the WFTU to counter Soviet influence and to make the WFTU more responsive to the interests of trade union movements in the Western countries."[19] Given such negative views of the WFTU, the State Department officials probably did not believe that was possible. Nevertheless, Acheson told the union leaders that the department was "disturbed" by the WFTU's activities and that "perhaps some improvement in the present WFTU situation might take place if the CIO and the British and the other Western labor movements take a firmer and more active part in the WFTU as proponents of genuine trade union problems." The answers evaded the question, showing more than anything else the unionists' hesitation in the face of Acheson's certainties. Carey defended some of the WFTU's actions but said that the CIO was also concerned by the totally pro-Soviet management of the world federation. The fact was, Carey maintained, that "the CIO has never gone fully into the WFTU. Its attitude has been, since the beginning, to wait and see what develops," without assuming any direct responsibilities. Now it had to decide whether to be fully in the federation, as Carey preferred, or to get out. But neither he nor Ross offered any indication that the CIO had plans to reinforce its presence in the WFTU and firmly take positions on the main political issues.[20]

The group of CIO leaders was in obvious difficulty before the changes occurring on the international scene, especially the American attitude. Concentrating almost entirely on domestic affairs, since the Taft-Hartley Act seemed to threaten the very bases of the union's role in American society, Murray and his collaborators had seen the political grounds for their past adherence to the WFTU disappear in the course of a few months. This had been the linchpin of the CIO's international activities. In the atmosphere of the anti-Communist crusade which was taking over the United States, the criticisms of the AFL and the Department of State began to make themselves felt on a group of leaders that was ideologically prone to oppose communism but still politically unprepared to make anti-Sovietism the main theme of a new international policy. Nor did the situation within the CIO make drastic and rapid decisions easy. Adapting himself to the country's antiradical atmosphere, Murray was beginning to move against the left wing. He was driven chiefly by Walter Reuther, who was steadily eliminating from the UAW all those who were close to the Communists. The first sign of obvious hostility to the left was the replacement of the editor of the *CIO News*, Len DeCaux, one of the most influential leftists at the national center, with Alan Swim, who immediately came out in a polemic way as "politically democrat, ideologically right-wing."[21]

But the conflict had hardly begun, and some caution was needed before rushing into important political choices. And so the CIO, although forced into the powerful stream of anti-Communist containment, was still tied—though with little conviction—to the groupings created in the immediate postwar period, and it participated without enthusiasm or ideas in the WFTU's activities. Only a further worsening in diplomatic and strategic relations between the United States and the USSR could change the situation enough to make it impossible for the CIO to stay in the WFTU. The unified structure of the world trade union movement was divided by contrasting interests, but it was not yet at the breaking point, even though the forces driving in that direction, at least from the American side, were by then quite strong. The Department of State was also aware that more time would be needed. Commenting on a WFTU meeting in Prague, the American ambassador wrote to Washington, barely a month after the meeting between Acheson, Carey, and Ross, that the WFTU's future depended on the relations among the three great powers. The Soviets had showed themselves conciliatory, and the British, like the CIO, were reluctant to take steps that could threaten the organization. Things were held up pending the next foreign ministers' meetings, which would make clear whether the break in the international community was irreversible. The CIO, wrote the ambassador, "was torn between its allegiance to the traditional principles of trade union movements and the realization that it was in danger of being used for the purposes of Soviet foreign policy." The recommendation sent to Washington was not to press the CIO to break with the WFTU, which would have been unrealistic at that time, but to have faith in the anticommunism of its leaders, allowing the crisis to mature. In the meantime, the CIO would be assisted in moving astutely on the international scene, to "enable it to pursue more effectively its own interests, and when the chips are down, the interests of the United States."[22]

The attitude of Carey and Murray toward the WFTU was already changing and was far from the enthusiasm of two years previously. In the CIO's public statements the tone for the first time was defensive, as if to apologize for belonging to an organization where the Soviets were also present. Its newspaper compared the WFTU to the United Nations, "a forum" where it was logical that radically differing positions would coexist. The CIO's steady adherence to "the American democratic principles" was emphasized, and there began to be talk of a commitment to aid workers in European nations to oppose "the forced evolution of those European unions into political institutions."[23] For the first time, the CIO was voicing the AFL's traditional view (but much less forcefully), according to which it was the task of the American unions to help European organizations not to be dominated by the interests of political parties. The equation of "free" with anti-Communist trade unions thus entered the political and propagandistic baggage of the New Deal leaders of the CIO.

For the AFL, these developments set in motion by the Truman Doctrine came as repayment for years of intransigent anti-Communist efforts. The basis of its international strategy emerged as the nucleus of the U.S. government's official policy. The federation's activities abroad came out of isolation, and some much more promising prospects began to open up. Between 1946 and the spring of 1947 the AFL had already begun on its own to prepare its policy of attacking the WFTU. With the rise of bipolar tension, the anti-Communist plans it been announcing since 1944 were finding ample scope for operative as well as symbolic application. In the middle of 1946 the FTUC was reconsidering the European situation and was ready to seize the opportunity. The rapid erosion of the anti-Fascist fronts was causing "a psychological and moral rift" between Socialists and Communists, and this made it possible to suppose that the moment had arrived "for the ideological and psychological emancipation of Labor from Bolshevism." The AFL's international activities could finally emerge from isolation and find fertile ground. Overcoming its own theoretical and ideological prejudices, the AFL was to recognize and accept the eminently political nature of European trade unionism. The lowest common denominator represented by an alliance against the danger of Communist domination would have offered common ground for working with the Social Democratic and Catholic trade union movements. It was then possible "to establish a harmonious cooperation between the AFL as the American form of Democratic Labor and the Socialist parties (and the Socialist led trade unions) as the historically given form of Democratic Labor in the Old World." In this context, the task of the AFL was to come forth as the great opponent of the WFTU, offering itself as the linchpin of a new international trade union group united by the opposition to communism. Before the prospect of a frontal clash between the Western democracies and the Soviet bloc, the group would develop into "the nucleus of a new International Federation of Unions freed from totalitarian control."[24]

Important operational decisions came out of this formulation. Irving Brown was appointed permanent AFL representative in Europe, and in November 1946 he opened an office in Brussels to coordinate contacts with European union leaders. The FTUC began to publish a "free" trade union bulletin in four languages. Even the AFL's structure was reorganized, with the establishment of a permanent department for international relations. The economic and political reconstruction of Germany would be at the center of the conflict on Europe's future, and the AFL sent men and resources to collaborate with the American military government in the reestablishment of a solidly anti-Communist trade union movement that was to stand out as an anti-Soviet bulwark in "the industrial heart of Europe." Joseph Keenan, the official of the International Brotherhood of Electrical Workers who served as labor assistant to General Lucius Clay, summed up the goals and ambitions of the FTUC program: "We can defeat Communism in Germany instead of the United States."[25]

The first target of this activism was obviously the WFTU, which was accused of being "a worldwide fifth column organization" by means of which the USSR was trying to subjugate workers to its influence and so carry its "program for world domination." The propaganda against the international labor organization became incessant and concentrated in particular on the CIO, whose participation in the WFTU was explicitly condemned as a betrayal of the American national interest.[26] But the assault on the WFTU was not limited to words. It extended to the search for allies with whom to collaborate in weakening the organization. In the summer of 1946 the AFL, with the support of the State Department, began to work toward the establishment of an Interamerican Labor Confederation (CIT) for coordinating and reinforcing anti-Communist trade unionism in Latin America.[27] A second and more important front against the WFTU was located in the International Trade Secretariats (ITS), which coordinated the international trade union federations of various crafts. The AFL had excellent relations, in particular, with J. H. Oldenbroeck, the Dutch secretary of the powerful ITWF. A fervent anti-Communist, Oldenbroeck had a good deal of influence in the ITS, and this could be useful for the AFL's crusade. The ITS, reluctant to be absorbed by the WFTU both because of hostility toward the Soviets and because of a jealous attachment to its own autonomy, was busy with inconclusive negotiations at the top levels of the WFTU to define the terms of their relationship. On the world scene, the ITS and the AFL were the only union organizations external to the WFTU. Their independence constituted the weak link in the WFTU's attempt to achieve worldwide unity. Oldenbroeck and the AFL perceived that the ITS in general, and the ITWF in particular, could constitute the potential nucleus for coordinating anti-Communist trade unionism on an international scale. Therefore the AFL committed its own unions, and the Latin American federations that it directly influenced, to assume a high profile in their respective ITS so as to bring the greatest possible pressure to bear against any plan to agree with the WFTU.[28]

When the Truman Doctrine intervened to produce a strong direct commitment by the United States against Communist influence, the AFL was well prepared to step up its offensive against unified trade unionism on an international scale. The convergence of its axioms with those of the Department of State laid the foundations for a powerful American drive in the union field. The government agencies involved in international affairs rapidly and almost naturally developed close collaboration with the international activities of the American unions. The State Department's consultations with those responsible for international affairs of the

AFL and the CIO became frequent and regular. The Office for International Affairs at the Labor Department was strengthened, and within it a Trade Union Advisory Committee on International Affairs was established, composed of the main leaders of international activities in the two federations. The committee became the most important permanent center of political arrangements between government and unions in foreign issues.[29] From 1947 on, moreover, the foreign operations of the AFL, and to a lesser extent those of the CIO, were meshed with those of the main embassies, with a high level of coordination and integration, based on their common anti-Communist position in the struggle for the reconstruction of the European trade union movement. Contrasting "free" and Communist trade unions became a concept and operational guide that was common to the representatives of the FTUC and the American diplomatic establishment. Coordinating meetings of the labor attachés at the American embassies in Europe were held in the presence of Irving Brown and other American union representatives, while the selection of new labor attachés was passed on by George Meany, Matthew Woll, and Jay Lovestone.[30] The leaders of the AFL soon succeeded in obtaining a near monopoly on the appointment of union men to be sent to diplomatic missions abroad. The junction of the political purposes of American diplomacy and of the AFL after 1947, and the specific nature of the union problem—which demanded a certain experience, mentality, and terminology all its own—made the connection between Foreign Service personnel and union officials so close that it was sometimes difficult to tell whether the labor attaché was working for the Department of State or the FTUC, or in some cases the CIO. In most cases he had a double loyalty, representing both his own union and the government.[31]

The integration of the foreign operations of American unions and the administration developed on another plane after 1947. This was the area of clandestine operations and the concealed financing of anti-Communist European forces, activities that were carried out in common by Lovestone's FTUC and by the government's intelligence services. This kind of cooperation was not unknown. It was rooted in operations of various union members for the Office of Strategic Services in the Second World War. The connections established then presumably remained open in the immediate postwar period, even if they do not seem to have been used for important operations throughout all of 1946. The onset of the containment policy changed the situation decisively. One of the principal institutional changes brought on by the coming Cold War was the establishment of a permanent intelligence organization by the American government, the Central Intelligence Agency (CIA), which was founded in July 1947. Its origins were accompanied by a long discussion on whether psychological warfare operations should be carried out. In the spring of 1947, faced with the perception that the Soviets were seriously blocking American operations in Europe with the many organizations of the international Communist movement, the Truman administration judged the possibility of starting clandestine operations to be a necessity. The fear that Moscow would operate on all levels, beginning with the clandestine ones, and the global necessities of containment pushed the government to equip itself in a great hurry. The debate was concluded at the end of 1947 when the National Security Council officially entrusted the CIA with the responsibility for conducting "covert psychological warfare operations."[32]

The AFL, with its stress on the Communist danger in Europe, was one of the earliest and strongest forces advocating clandestine operations, in a way preceding the CIA in secret financing of the anti-Communist trade union movement. In the last months of 1947 Brown financed with huge sums the split of the French group Force Ouvrière from the Confédération Générale du Travail. The CIA inserted itself into the operation, probably assuming part of the financial burden, and in this way initiated its own clandestine operations.[33] Only a few months later, again in collaboration with the AFL, the CIA's first large-scale psychological warfare operation began, to finance anti-Communist propaganda for the Italian elections of 18 April 1948. This first experience of the CIA coincided with a clear formalization of assistance programs to anti-Communist forces in the American security organizations. They provided explicitly for collaboration with the unions. As part of a "world-wide offensive against Soviet directed world Communism," on 30 March 1948 the National Security Council issued its directive to "encourage and assist private United States citizens and organizations in fostering non-Communist trade union movements in those countries where they could contribute to our national security."[34]

The way was thus officially opened for collaboration between the CIA and the FTUC to send funds (originating partly in the union, but mostly of government origin) to the AFL's European contacts. The details and the course of these operations obviously were secret, undocumented, and thus impossible to reconstruct. However, several sources within the CIA itself have subsequently testified to this close collaboration. The operations in support of the Italian and French non-Communist unions, one of the FTUC's main activities, were financed in large measure by the CIA.[35] The cooperation was not limited to financing operations useful to the common policy of support for anti-Communist forces. In the course of the 1950s, especially with relation to countries outside Europe, the ties between Lovestone and the intelligence services became stronger, to the point of reaching

joint collaboration.[36] Even the CIO, although unfamiliar with clandestine operations and less tied than the FTUC to a line of pure support for anticommunism,
was sometimes involved in providing financing from the CIA to European trade
union leaders.[37]

There is not a sufficient documentary basis for a considered historical judgment
on the effectiveness of these operations, or more generally on the ties between the
FTUC and various government agencies. But it is certain that they were an
integral part of the Cold War fought on the union field and that they had their
practical effect on events. On the other hand, the theory that collaboration with
the CIA constituted a change in the FTUC's policy or blind obedience to the
government is to be rejected. Such relationships rarely exist, and in this case it is
abundantly clear that there was a convergence of interests and complementary
political goals. It certainly was rare for a trade union organization to commit itself
to such operations, but the reasons for its behavior lie in the history of the group of
AFL leaders and in its interpretation of the Cold War, not in the pay records of the
CIA (although if they were opened they could shed useful light on the whole
matter).[38] In analyzing the events subsequent to 1947, it is well to keep in mind the
existence of this underground and partially invisible level of action, especially on
the part of the AFL, in close collaboration with the CIA and other government
organizations. Its importance, however, should not be exaggerated: the clandestine operations probably only implemented well known political positions that
had been widely and publicly documented, without substantially changing the role
and the fundamental directions of the various protagonists of that period of the
Cold War.

The Marshall Plan

On 5 June 1947, in an address at Harvard University, Secretary of State George
Marshall announced the United States government's intention to furnish economic aid to European countries necessary to deal with the crisis in which the
continent's postwar reconstruction seemed to be foundering. Three months after
the Truman Doctrine, the American government in this manner publicized its
political commitment to the reconstruction of a solid economic base that would
support a stable order leading to self-sufficiency in European societies, thereby
implicitly recognizing the insufficiency of the measures taken up to that point. The
announcement came at the end of a heated debate in the spring, which had seen the
responsible officials in the State Department all agreeing that the European situa-

tion was at the edge of a profound and dramatic crisis and that only American intervention could head off collapse. Various factors contributed to the perception that a crisis in Europe was imminent: production shortages and social dislocations, lack of confidence and financial resources, and unsolved problems and exasperating conflicts. Men like Clayton and Marshall returned from Europe convinced that the United States must inevitably intervene in an organized manner and on a large scale to prevent a history-making collapse and to solve the cluster of problems left unresolved by the conclusion of the Second World War.

> Further deterioration might be disastrous to Europe. It might well bring such hardship, such bewilderment, such desperate struggle for control over inadequate resources as to lead to widespread repudiation of the principles on which modern European civilization has been founded. . . .
>
> United States interests in the broadest sense could not fail to be profoundly affected by such a trend of events.
>
> In the first place, the United States people have a very real economic interest in Europe. This stems from Europe's role in the past as a market and as a major source of supply for a variety of products and services.
>
> But beyond this, the traditional concept of U.S. security has been predicated on the sort of Europe now in jeopardy.[39]

This dark, nearly apocalyptic vision united widely varying elements of judgment and vested interest. Research on the factors that led the American leaders to promote the Marshall Plan has given rise to an extensive historical debate, especially following the revisionist criticisms of the first, nearly hagiographical interpretations of American aid as humanitarian and idealistic assistance to European democracy. The revisionist historians, on the other hand, accented the economic interest of this developing American imperial power in safeguarding the possibilities of multilateral trade for the opening of markets and the furtherance of its exports so as to stave off the danger of a depression at home. Seen in this light, the anti-Communist bent of the Marshall Plan was secondary, the result more than anything else of the Truman administration's need to dramatize the Soviet threat in order to spread an emergency psychosis throughout the country to assure agreement for an expansive international economic policy.[40] However, another interpretation of the Marshall Plan's origins emphasized the need to solve the economic and political problems of the Western occupation zones in Germany in a manner compatible with France's strategic and productive requirements, which could be guaranteed only in the context of a more general European recovery.[41]

Other analyses have given up the claim to specify a single cause for the plan, turning their attention to the complex interaction of geopolitical, economic, commercial, and strategic objectives that were bound up with the formulation of a plan where the will to start an expansive cycle of the international economy was fused with the strategy of anti-Soviet containment and the anti-Communist stabilization of Western Europe. Based on a set of political assumptions that entrusted the maintenance and defense of United States security to the spread of prosperity on an international scale, the Marshall Plan sought to respond at the same time to other needs: to assure the economies of Europe the necessary financing to import from the dollar area; to stabilize their currencies and increase international trade, thereby staving off the danger—in the multilateral U.S. perception—of bilateralism and government economic planning; to favor the economic consolidation of those countries, particularly France and Italy, where the political strength of the Communists appeared dangerous, thus reinforcing a Western sphere where the Soviet influence was reduced to a minimum; and to start the economic recovery of the Western sectors of Germany—in contrast with the Soviet demands for reparations—in full coordination with the reconstruction of other European countries. These ends were perfectly compatible with pressures from the American productive apparatus for an expansion of exports and the multiplication of foreign trade, but the primary purpose was undoubtedly the grand design of reinforcing the West economically and politically and isolating the USSR. Containment, stabilization, multilateralism, and the ideology of prosperity came together in a single political and economic initiative to which the State Department planners entrusted the hope of finding an overall solution to the problems of the postwar settlement of Europe.[42]

The many-faceted nature of the Marshall Plan corresponded to the global nature of the crisis in Europe that the Truman administration believed it was facing. In 1947 one could not really speak of an economic crisis in the strict sense of the word, except for the specific but relevant crisis in the availability of international payment means due to the lack of dollars, which made it difficult to supply raw materials, foodstuffs, and investment goods from the American market. The most recent research has shown that industrial output was well on the way to recovery, even though inequalities and food shortages, which fed social discontent, persisted. The real problem and the true crisis consisted of the increasing trade deficits resulting from the high level of imports of investment goods from the dollar area, due to this same recovery of industrial production. In most European countries—especially Great Britain and France, and with the notable exception of Italy—economic policies were markedly expansive because of the political and social requirements that developed between the Depression and the war, which gave priority to seeking full employment, opening significant channels of social spending, and—especially in the case of France—to a decisive modernization of the industrial apparatus. These were historical conditions reflecting the strength of the Social Democratic parties, which American strategic requirements, based on the need to support democratic governments against the Soviets, could not ignore. The growing international payments crisis was faced in the light of these national priorities in the European economic policies. Without them it would have been very difficult to imagine a growth of consensus and hence an effective political and social stabilization. The coincidence, in great part, of these expansive goals with New Deal prosperity dogma was to be useful for the liberals who were to apply the Marshall Plan. When the plan was being put together, it was the whole policy of containment—the basic strategic goal of both the Truman administration and a large part of Congress—that had to confront directly those political and social rigidities common to most European countries. A break or a crisis here would have thrown the key countries into an instability that would have permanently damaged the reasons and purposes of containment: "These strategic necessities meant that what the government of the United States actually paid for with Marshall Aid was not to increase the rate of recovery in European economics and to prevent Europeans in dislocated and deteriorating economies from starving, but to sustain ambitious, new, expansionary economic and social policies in Western European countries which were mostly already in full boom conditions."[43]

In this context, the solution of the international payments problem was directed not only at reaching convertibility and multilateralism, but also, and with much greater urgency, to consolidating the economic bases of anti-Soviet containment. The intrinsic purposes of the Marshall Plan were joined on two levels that were woven together and interdependent. On the economic level, it meant supporting, stimulating, and assuring the growth and ultimately the prosperity that, according to American historical experience, could develop social consensus, transform protest and discontent into pluralistic negotiation among interests, isolate revolutionary ideas, and therefore remove the reasons for the Communist proposals: "American effort in aid to Europe should be directed not to the combatting of communism as such but to the restoration of the economic health and vigor of European society. It should aim, in other words to combat not communism, but the economic maladjustment which makes European society vulnerable to exploitation by any and all totalitarian movements and which Russian communism is now exploiting."[44]

Seen in a political light, the plan's basic goal was to promote—and occasionally to attempt to impose—a supernational approach to the continent's economic problems, with an objective of achieving integration among European countries. Here again, American historical experience of a large unified market was joined to the strategic requirement of setting up a robust, economically strong, and politically solid bloc to face Soviet control of Eastern Europe and the destabilization maneuvers in Western countries: "American leaders . . . turned to integration as a method of solving the German problem, restoring Europe, halting Communist advances, and promoting multilateralism. They came to believe, moreover, that subsuming restricted national markets within a larger, interdependent economic order could point the way to a revival of European productivity and to a new era of permanent peace and abundance on the continent."[45]

The emphasis placed on the supranational approach to European recovery at the time the plan was launched constituted one of the main reasons for its anti-Soviet political impact. The USSR in fact walked out of the Paris conference where the European governments were discussing the allotment of American aid and forced its satellites to do the same, because coordination on a continental scale of the use of this aid would have threatened its jealous defense of Eastern Europe as its hermetically sealed sphere of influence—and presumably would have reproduced a model of exchanges between an industrialized West and an agrarian East that would be unacceptable for economic reasons as well. In this way, the Marshall Plan, even before it was launched, achieved its first political and psychological success, which had been deliberately pursued by the State Department. It placed on the USSR the responsibility for dividing Europe into two separate, noncommunicating areas, putting an isolated Moscow in the difficult position of one who refused and then boycotted an offer of extremely necessary aid.[46]

This first result was not only a propaganda success, but also the cause of deep and decisive changes in both public opinion and the main political groupings in the West, starting with the American ones. In the ten months from Marshall's announcement to the beginning of the plan's implementation—that is, well before its economic and social effects were felt—the political impact of the new American initiative was such as to alter decisively the character of the international conflict, to gather an extensive and solid consensus around the Truman administration, to set important processes of realignment in motion in Western Europe, and to put the Communist parties and their allies on the defensive.

In America, the complex character of the plan and its presentation as a global approach to European problems made possible the creation of extensive political and social support for it. The conservative forces, beginning with the Republican leadership in Congress, were gradually brought to support the Marshall Plan and to participate actively in its formulation because of its strategic value as the key to the entire anti-Soviet containment policy. Truman used the anticommunism theme skillfully, especially in the fall of 1947, when, after the latest failure of the foreign ministers' conference, the establishment of the Cominform, and the onset of strikes against the Marshall Plan in France and Italy, the atmosphere of open international conflict foretold the approach of a dramatic emergency. In the name of anticommunism the president then sought and obtained urgent aid ad interim for France, Italy, and Austria. A few months later, at the end of March 1948, Congress voted the European Recovery Program (ERP) in a crisis atmosphere, approaching prewar intensity, brought on by the coup in Czechoslovakia, the coming electoral confrontation in Italy on 18 April, and the rumors of a possible armed encounter coming from Germany.[47] On the other hand, the liberals of the New Deal tradition could easily support the proposal for aid—and reconcile themselves fully with the administration's foreign policy, which the Truman Doctrine had made appear too unilaterally concentrated on the anti-Communist struggle—because of the social and humanitarian factors and the promise of international economic prosperity that the Marshall Plan emphasized. The fusion of the anti-Communist impulse with the aspiration to reconstruct an international economy geared to growth forged a solid bipartisan consensus in Congress, and a wider convergence of social forces and opinion in the country. It was this nearly all-inclusive nature of the plan, as well as direct economic interests, that caused the principal interest groups to focus on it, beginning with the farmers' and industrialists' associations, whose representatives, together with those of the main unions, participated in the many committees to study the ways of applying the plan, its economic impact at home and abroad, and the criteria for managing it.[48]

The political effects of the ERP were even greater in Europe. The international division that it confirmed—between a Soviet-controlled Eastern zone and a Western one under American influence—was reproduced, not in territorial but in political terms, within the leftist forces in each Western nation. Inserting the Cold War divisions directly into the field of economic policy, in the debate on the ends and methods of reconstruction, the plan brought out and sharpened the contrast in viewpoints, already rather strong, between the Communist forces versus the Social Democratic and British Labour ones, something that corresponded to the State Department's political desires. "The trend in Europe is clearly toward the Left. I feel that we should try to keep it a non-Communist Left and should support Social-Democratic governments."[49]

While the Communist left rejected the Marshall Plan and mobilized against carrying it out, the Social Democratic forces, often participating responsibly in governments, greeted it with enthusiasm, to the point of sometimes taking it over as their own. American aid brought with it a point of view and a promise of growth that allowed the possibility of mitigating social conflict through a negotiated and pluralist division of the future benefits of greater productivity. This aid served to loosen those balance of payments constraints which, by generating deflationary pressure, could have strangled economic policies geared to full employment and increased social spending. The Marshall Plan did broaden and facilitate the way to those expansive economic policies to which the Social Democratic left was devoted and bound.[50] On the wave of a proposal characterized by the inseparable pairing of economic growth and anticommunism, there thus arose an extended array of political and social forces that coalesced on both sides of the Atlantic in an almost physical representation of that "consensual American hegemony" that distinguished the entire postwar period in the industrialized West.[51]

In the trade union movement, the political effects of the ERP were deep, decisive, and lasting in the United States, Europe, and on the international scene. Both the economic strategy and the political ends that dictated the launching of this program required for their complete success the achievement of a general agreement and active participation by workers' organizations, the American ones above all, not only for the support they could give to the steps leading to its enactment, but so that the Marshall Plan could appear to the Europeans as a social and democratic initiative. It also needed the support of those European workers' organizations whose attitudes were to be largely decisive for the success or failure of the task of building a social consensus for expansive capitalism that was the most ambitious long-term objective of the ERP. The unions were the principal means of organizing this consensus among the working classes for the productive efforts to which the European economies were called and whose results, in terms of employment and salaries, were to appear only at a later time. It was therefore essential to integrate the workers' organizations into the management of the plan, in each country and on the international level. The unions, moreover, represented the main area of direct conflict with the Communist opposition to the aid program. "For so long as the objective conditions for widespread mass discontent enable the Communists to assume leadership of the mass movements dedicated to improving or eliminating these conditions, so long will they be able to exploit for their own purposes the widespread non-communist sentiment for trade union liberties."[52]

"The struggle for hearts and minds," as the American leaders had just begun to call the psychological and social front of the Cold War, was fought first among the workers, and the political allegiance of the unions was the main stake. The Marshall Plan was meant to offer the Europeans not only financial aid, but also a model of an economy and a society in which the way to improving the conditions of life was indicated not by a Communist appeal to the class struggle, but by an American picture of democratic capitalism and relative opulence: "We are not capitalistic in the sense most Europeans understand capitalism. . . . Capitalistic government in most European countries today is thought to be a government which protects the interests of the rich and powerful and which does little for the people. . . . If the United States is to win permanent friends for capitalism as opposed to Communism, then we should do everything possible to make the capitalistic system more attractive to the people. . . . We cannot permanently head off Communism, or some other type of revolutionary government, unless we convince the peoples of the world that the interests of the people can be protected under a capitalistic system."[53]

The AFL on the Offensive

The leaders of the AFL were the first to realize the political and trade union implications of the Marshall Plan, especially after the Soviet withdrawal from the Paris conference and the subsequent prompt establishment of the Cominform made clear the central role that the program for European reconstruction would assume in the clashes of the Cold War. The crusade for "free" trade unionism found in the Marshall Plan an economic program and a wide political perspective around which it could launch its own anti-Communist campaign with much more strength and authority. It was not just the propaganda advantage that could be had from accusing the Communist opposition of sabotaging economic recovery. The Marshall Plan was much more: for the first time, the appeal to "free" trade unionism lost its purely ideological connotation to assume the powerful guise of a wide-ranging socioeconomic proposal, supported by a political plan of the United States government and a good part of those in Europe. For the AFL the plan became the linchpin of a renewed and confident international political project. While the FTUC journal began its incessant campaign of propaganda for the Marshall Plan, the AFL's representative in Europe began an ambitious attempt to bring the unions in countries adhering to the ERP into contact with each other: "Irving Brown informs me that he has been endeavoring arrange for calling conference of labor leaders of sixteen countries represented Paris to discuss Marshall Plan and guarantee that its execution will benefit workers. . . . Brown's object is to counteract Communist propaganda of US imperialistic, capitalistic designs."[54]

Aside from counterpropaganda, the AFL saw in the Marshall Plan a potential gathering point for a new international union grouping in which it might be the nucleus and driving force. After the establishment of the Cominform and the departure of the Communist parties from the coalition governments in France and Italy, the economic reconstruction projects became the principal field of battle in the frontal clash in which the international lineups were faithfully reflected, with all their rigidities, on the national scene. In the fall of 1947 the onset of strikes—in Italy and even more in France—against the Marshall Plan and the economic decisions of the governments was interpreted as a direct challenge to the American initiative, a threat to sabotage the ERP, and above all as a choice of head-on conflict on the part of Moscow.[55] As the AFL perceived the situation, the strikes had a strategic importance and the unions involved had an almost political-military role inasmuch as they were the instruments of Soviet operations to destabilize Western Europe. France was the key country for European recovery and political stabilization, and for this reason the Communist-led strikes in the mines and railroads became, from that point of view, acts "as close to a military, or a politico-military operation as you can get anywhere in the world short of armed warfare or short of a declaration of war."[56]

The increase in tension to the point of direct conflict—to uncompromising opposition not only between economic programs, but between political strategies that reflected Europe's bipolar divisions—led in December 1947 to a split in the French trade union movement. The clash on the Marshall Plan and relations with the government exploded into open conflict before the intransigent Communist opposition and its strikes, and a minority of the Force Ouvrière left the CGT. This was the first radical change in the unitary alliances that originated at the end of the war, the first sign of how much the Cold War was shaking the structure of unionism, after having begun to reshape affairs in political and governmental circles, imposing the establishment of new groupings and new alliances. For the AFL's strategy of breaking with the Communists, this was a victory of the first order, since the conditions that had previously relegated it to international isolation were now crumbling. This was a clear confirmation from France that the strategy of anti-Communist discrimination was right, because it was beginning to function and achieve results. It indicated especially that the Marshall Plan was the focus for the trade union movement's reconsideration of its strategies and alliances, a wedge destined to split the international unity created around the WFTU.[57]

The top-level leaders of the AFL threw themselves into the fray with the self-confidence of those who feel they are confronted with a historic occasion. The federation's annual convention proclaimed its complete support for the Marshall

Plan, and on 19 December 1947 Green, Meany, and Woll presented Truman with a program which, in perfect agreement with his administration's international operations, sounded like a call to arms for the Cold War: "Mankind is now confronted by a race between starvation and security, civilization and chaos, democracy and totalitarian dictatorship, peace and war. In this contest, the American people can play only one role. We *dare not* remain neutral. . . . America *must* assume the decisive role in helping the world to help itself." The Marshall Plan must be approved without delay to give the Europeans an "enhanced economic security"; the aid was to stimulate "higher levels of production and consumption at home and abroad," to "promote higher living standards and purchasing power and firm social security." Even in its political aspects, the Marshall Plan, according to the AFL, should turn more than anything else to the world of labor: "Full and free collective bargaining must be assured. . . . We must not support reactionary forces of the right or the so-called left (Communist). The strengthening of bona fide trade unions—free from all government, employer and political domination—is of paramount value in this respect." The AFL thus entered the discussion around the character the plan would assume, indicating that its main value was in the possibility that it could overcome Communist influence among the workers, reinforce the "free" trade union movement, and bring it into the structure where economic policy decisions are made. The workers' representatives should therefore participate in the preparation and management of the aid, to stimulate an "enthusiastic and energetic cooperation by the working people in carrying out the ERP." The AFL offered its own men and its organizational experience as a trade union guarantee for the Marshall Plan.[58]

From that moment the AFL was one of the most actively engaged forces in the campaign to approve the ERP, distinguishing itself for the insistence with which it stressed how the Marshall Plan should offer European workers an alternative to communism, based on "free" unions and therefore managed at first by American union leaders.[59] The leadership of the AFL was ready to seize the great opportunity the ERP represented for its international policies. The direct confrontation taking place in Europe, exemplified by what was going on in France, caused the AFL to see "the complete bankruptcy of the illusions of those democratic trade unionists who thought that they could "domesticate" the Soviet totalitarians . . . by cooperating with them within the framework of the WFTU."[60]

The European Social Democratic or Christian Democratic trade union movement, the greater part of which favored the Marshall Plan, was clashing with the Communist opposition and was led inevitably to take sides, even at the cost of serious ruptures, with their governments and in favor of the American proposal.

Staying in the WFTU was to be difficult, if not impossible. The secretariat of the WFTU had already criticized the "capitalist" imprint of the American aid. It had come out several times in favor of the strikes promoted by the CGT, and in reply to a request by the CIO for an open discussion of the Marshall Plan, it had postponed the issue because of its embarrassment at facing a subject that would have brought out deep internal divisions.[61] At this point the AFL set in motion a detailed plan to precipitate the crisis of the WFTU, forcefully joining the controversy on the Marshall Plan. The federation decided to furnish a maximum of aid to representatives of "free" unions in countries where Communists dominated the labor movement and where the opposition to the Marshall Plan would be the strongest. In France and Italy, the battle was decisive. The political fate of the ERP was to a large extent bound up with the policies—and the futures—of the French CGT and the Italian CGIL. And the AFL strengthened its presence in the ITS federations, trusting in their capacity to gather forces hostile to the WFTU. Brown principally was charged to work with the greatest commitment to convene a conference of unions from the sixteen countries adhering to the ERP. The purposes were ambitious but very clear: to "rally European labor around an economic program with democratic objectives" and to "break the WFTU as an instrument of Soviet foreign policy."[62]

With this gathering of unions favorable to the ERP the hope arose—for once realistically founded—of laying the foundations for a new international organization to set against the WFTU. But the British TUC, however much it favored the Marshall Plan, and however resolutely hostile it was to the Communists, was hesitating at a step which would have threatened the line it had followed up to then by opening a split in the WFTU and putting it in opposition to the TUC. Without the cooperation, or at least the full support of the TUC, no one in Europe could even think of calling the conference with any hope of success. The AFL decided to work around the obstacle, sending Brown to a series of confidential meetings with Ernest Bevin, the British foreign minister and prestigious leader of the Labour party union movement, to persuade him to bring decisive pressure to bear on the TUC. The lucid Bevin was quick to understand what was at stake in the international controversy over the Marshall Plan and was successful in overcoming the uncertainty of the union leaders.[63] When told that the TUC was prepared to attend the conference and had even decided to open a discussion on it in the WFTU, Brown pronounced himself "delighted." "Brown interprets this . . . as move on part of British indicating general stiffening towards Communist movement, international and internal, since it will probably result in breakup of WFTU as now constituted owing to withdrawal of Americans, British and other trade unions."[64]

There were still two months to go before the approval of the ERP; the operating characteristics of the plan were anything but defined, and the relation it was to have with the unions was even vaguer. But its political impact was already so strong as to make people see, in the not too distant future, a break in the trade union movement of worldwide importance.

The Crisis in the CIO

The effects of the ERP on the international trade union movement were especially profound, particularly on the CIO's internal crisis. From the fall of 1947, the federation began to cast off all the ambiguities in its political identity and its international position. At the beginning of the conflict, which was to lead to the elimination of its left wing and to its becoming more homogeneous, based on the centrist and anti-Communist policies of President Truman, Murray guided a steady but rapid realignment of the federation's foreign policy, placing it squarely within the Western grouping that plunged into the most dramatic conflicts of the Cold War in 1948.

Like other liberals, but to a greater degree, the leaders of the CIO were soon attracted by the prominent place that the idea of economic prosperity had been given by the Marshall Plan in United States foreign policy, recalling as it did the Rooseveltian notion of an America idealistically committed to democracy and the well-being of peoples. In Marshall's message, Murray and Reuther found a propensity to international collaboration finally joined to the ambition of the New Deal period for social progress founded on economic growth, in contrast to the unilateral intransigence of the Truman Doctrine. It was the cultural background and the humanitarian and expansive cast of the Marshall Plan—before the political proposal—that attracted the union leaders, as they joined the international initiative promoted by the State Department. The Truman administration knew how to play on these affinities skillfully, transforming them into participation, involvement, and support. Some of the most prominent trade unionists (Green and Dubinsky, Murray and Carey) were called on to represent their organizations in several consulting committees that were organized as the Marshall Plan was being set up.[65]

On the political level, the Soviet rejection of American aid and the establishment of the Cominform gave the coup de grace to any remaining faint hopes on the part of the CIO leaders in the possibility of international cooperation founded on the shattered anti-Fascist coalition. The irresistible adversarial polarization in the international community changed all the points of reference that had been guiding the CIO's foreign policy. The federation's representative at the WFTU, Elmer Cope—a fervent anti-Communist—deplored the CIO's absence from the daily struggle in which the AFL was engaged in Germany and throughout Europe for the "free" trade unions, and he hoped for a wider and more committed participation: "It is really a challenging situation. If the big four powers fail to make an agreement on Germany at the forthcoming meetings in London, no doubt there will be a definite split between the East and the West. This will have its repercussions within the unions."[66] The strikes in France and Italy and the alarming messages from Golden on the Communist guerrilla warfare in Greece convinced the leaders that collaboration with Moscow was impossible; the terms of trade union cooperation in the WFTU were therefore reviewed.[67] The naive and propagandistic pretense that the WFTU could be an international forum like the United Nations disappeared quickly when the unions, with the spread of the Cold War to the field of political economy and decisions for reconstruction, were now directly involved in the great conflict between East and West.

It was the domestic situation more than anything else, with its urgent political factors, that pushed the CIO toward a reversal of policy. In the government, Congress, the mass media, and public opinion, the anti-Communist and antiradical mania was spiraling steadily upward, fed continuously by the eagerness of everyone involved to seem more energetic and absolute in the observance of an anticommunism that was becoming enshrined as an incontestable national dogma. This crusading spirit entered the CIO as well. The offensive of the right registered its most important success in the UAW. Walter Reuther, turning on the pro-Communist left the pressures of the Cold War that pervaded the nation, got rid of all internal opposition over the course of 1947 and achieved absolute control of the union. Using wisely measured doses of characteristic union arguments and repressive instruments (such as the oath of nonadherence to Communist organizations required by the Taft-Hartley Act), Reuther brought one of the three principal unions in the CIO into the anti-Communist camp, decisively changing the balance of power in the federation and emerging as the most energetic and authoritative leader against the left.[68] The Truman administration, for its part, stepped up pressure on the union—the only large institution where the left was still widely represented—for an anti-Communist switch, which was necessary for the White House both for the presidential elections in the fall of 1948 and for its foreign policy. Truman courted the principal figures in the CIO to obtain electoral support, while the Department of State repeatedly encouraged an anti-Soviet realignment by the unions, beginning with the American ones, around the ERP. The role of the CIO, especially because of its ambiguous presence in the WFTU, was crucial. Secretary of State George Marshall, in an unheard of and surprising move, appeared in October at the annual CIO convention, asking it to support the Marshall Plan unreservedly.[69]

At the CIO convention, foreign policy problems were in the forefront. Marshall wisely limited himself to the economic and humanitarian advantages of his plan, but Reuther attacked the CIO's left very heavily, proposing a resolution of explicit support for the purposes of the program to reconstruct Europe. The left weakly resorted to an anachronistic distinction between aid for peace, which in the Rooseveltian spirit could be approved without difficulty, and aid for political ends, which should be rejected. Able mediation on the part of Murray, who was still reluctant to precipitate an internal crisis, especially on a foreign policy question, was successful in getting a motion approved that spoke of aid against misery and for peace "without political or economic strings." The final resolution, still cloaked in Rooseveltian language of cooperation for international peace, was approved by all factions, and support of the aid policy thus became a binding commitment for CIO members. The Marshall Plan was not mentioned explicitly, but since carrying out the resolution would be the task of the central leadership, this was a purely verbal distinction that was to disappear as soon as the convention closed its doors. This was a very severe defeat for the left, even though it was concealed in an ambiguous formulation that made it possible to preserve the federation's superficial unity. The compromise developed at the end of the war between the left and the right had been broken. Cold war politics came directly into the internal debate, and, given the increasingly rightward balance of political forces, especially at the top, this signified the beginning of the final clash. Mediation efforts could no longer hide either the weakness of the left or the determination of the right, which was now free to move in coordination with the government's foreign policy.[70]

On the delicate question of the WFTU, the convention merely renewed its decision to stay in. But here too the official formulas barely concealed a changed point of view on the part of the group of leaders. Barely a month before, James Carey had presented to the executive board of the WFTU a formal request for a discussion of the Marshall Plan. The board stalled, suggesting a postponement of this thorny issue to the next congress. Carey's activities, however, received a good deal of attention in the European press, and the CIO seemed for the moment to be satisfied with this first result: "There are few people in France at least who do not know that there is one union in the WFTU that supports American aid to Europe."[71] But to submit to the WFTU the most controversial question, the one on which East and West were opposing each other in an extremely sharp conflict in

France, and more generally throughout Europe, represented a historic turning point both for the CIO and for the internal affairs of the WFTU. The expansion of the Cold War was now penetrating openly into the headquarters of international trade union unity, threatening to break up its already precarious cohabitation. Carey's initiative, together with a simultaneous AFL proposal for a conference of unions in favor of the ERP, handed the international trade union movement an issue so divisive that it put all the existing organizations into a state of crisis. The anti-Communist right that governed the CIO's foreign policy was now marching by the side of the American government in an anti-Soviet direction.

The fragile compromise Murray had imposed on the convention lasted only a few weeks. The division of the liberals on the anti-Soviet issue was made final when Henry Wallace, the former secretary of commerce, came out as a presidential candidate on a platform of open criticism of Truman's international policy. Recalling Roosevelt's themes of collaboration with the Soviets in international forums, Wallace's third-party candidacy gathered the most radical heirs of the New Deal and all the pro-Communist left. This was an extreme version of the popular front that was more a coherent witness to a minority viewpoint in Cold War America than a realistic plan for a political regrouping. Based primarily on foreign affairs, especially against the division of Europe brought on by the Marshall Plan, Wallace's campaign steadily lost relevance with the spread of the most fervent anticommunism following the coup in Czechoslovakia and then the Berlin blockade. But his candidacy caused a serious political problem at first, since it appeared to preclude any chances Truman and the Democrats might have had, therefore favoring a conservative triumph of the Republicans. This at least was the fear of the CIO leaders; the electoral dilemma struck the union as an opportunity to resolve a long internal conflict. Both because of the international situation and, even more, because of the fear of a yet harder antiunion offensive by the Republican right, the relationship with the federal government had become essential for the CIO. Only a Democratic administration seemed able to guarantee that the Taft-Hartley Act was not just the first step in an attack on the most well established union rights. To the CIO leaders, Wallace's candidacy at the head of a third party seemed to threaten the existence of conditions regarded "as absolutely critical for the survival and prosperity of their unions."[72] Murray convinced himself that Wallace should be isolated and defeated. The CIO left would have to bend before this priority or accept a frontal clash at the worst place and the worst time. Murray, as Reuther had done before him, was able to make the conflict appear to pit the union's interests against those of an external political minority. In the middle of January 1948 a motion to condemn the attempt to form a third party split the CIO executive board, where the two currents were facing one another openly. The motion was approved 33 to 11.[73] The right had given up any further delay and opened the final confrontation; the division was explicit and irremediable. Wallace's candidacy, around which the leftist front gathered for a last desperate battle, had become a touchstone for the CIO, "a test of loyalty" from which none of the factions was to hold back.[74] With the vote of the executive board, the CIO set out to regiment its internal left and participate fully in the anti-Communist front that supported Truman's activities. At that same meeting it was decided to support the ERP explicitly. Its approval by Congress was declared the "top legislative priority" for the CIO in 1948.[75]

Congressional debate on the ERP in the first three months of 1948 reflected the same irreparable divisions within the federation. The opinions presented in Congress by the CIO member unions led by the left attacked the Marshall Plan as an extension to Europe of the Truman Doctrine's political goals. Taking advantage of the need of aid for reconstruction, the State Department was really trying through the ERP to "reimpose the pre–World War II economic relations of the European countries," keeping the agrarian areas backward and favoring the recovery of German heavy industry. The real objective of the Marshall Plan was to impose "the American kind of economic system in Western Europe," and to entrust to the United States a degree of control over economic policy so extensive as to transform America into "the economic dictator to the Marshall Plan countries." The economic maneuver called for in the plan served the interests of the most reactionary monopolistic groups in America and divided Europe by boycotting all nations, starting with the USSR, that did not bend to the domination of the United States.[76]

An opposing interpretation came from the CIO leadership. Philip Murray indicated three objectives for the plan: "1) To take care of destitute people; 2) to aid those people in reestablishing their own economies; 3) to permit participating countries to solve their internal problems without political interference." The accent was on the necessity that the aid not be accompanied by political conditions or financial terms such as to impose monetary austerity measures on participating countries to repay the debt. Europe had to return to self-sufficiency in the common interest of peace and prosperity, in the face of which the mere financial interests of the United States would have to take second place. Attentive to its country's problems, the CIO requested that the Marshall Plan be supported by the expansion of the American economy and, if necessary, by measures to control inflation. Finally, it requested extensive participation of unions, "who can win the confidence of the people of Europe" in the administration of this aid.[77] The official position of the CIO sought to avoid, or at least to suppress, the potential political effects of the ERP—its anti-Communist function and the consequent formation of two opposing blocs—preferring to emphasize its open and humanitarian character.

Once more the person with no hesitations was Walter Reuther, whose clear vision united the economic with the political in clarifying the ERP's objectives, which the UAW president unreservedly supported: "We believe that adequate aid is an economic and political must if democracy is to have a fighting chance in the rest of the world. . . . If we fail, free men and free institutions in the world will not be able to survive." The tone was the more dramatic one used by the government to make clear the anti-Communist emergency. It bore witness to the extent to which Reuther was fully immersed in the spirit of the Cold War. But his political proposal went beyond the boundaries of anti-Sovietism to describe a way toward prosperous, organized, and socially responsible capitalism, which followed the path of the clearest and most optimistic New Deal traditions, on the international scene no less than on the domestic one:

> The American economy, as we see it, because of its tremendous productive capacity, is freedom's greatest asset in the world today. . . . Production won the war. We were the arsenal of democracy. Production will win the peace. . . . The thing that bothers us is that too many people in America in high places in industry are fearful of abundance. They are afraid of America's capacity to produce. . . . We have to gear America's future, and the future of the world, to the economics of abundance. We get in trouble in the world when we divide up scarcity. You get in trouble between nations, you get in trouble between citizens within nations. . . . That is what the Kremlin is counting on. The Kremlin is counting upon serious economic dislocation in America. I think they know that they cannot beat us. They are counting on our beating ourselves. They hope to take over by default on our part. . . . I think the people of the whole world are watching us. And they are asking the question: is it possible for people so to arrange their economic life and their political relationships so that they can achieve economic security and material well being without spiritual enslavement? That is really the nub of the whole thing. . . . We in America have the practical challenge, and we have all the things required to solve it, of showing that democracy can give people economic security without spiritual enslavement.

The domestic and international objectives, in Reuther's words, were inseparable. America had to overcome any restrictionist temptations and set out on the road to a bold expansion of output, based on social consensus and seriously regulated in order to avoid the threat of inflation, something that required controls no less effective than those adopted in wartime. Industry and unions both had the task of cooperating, not only in the productive effort, but also in its international projection. Reuther asked for an important position for the workers' organizations in the management of the ERP: "Psychologically, that would do more than anything else to begin the break-down of the propaganda of the Cominform and give the working people and the great mass of people in Europe greater confidence and belief in the basic motives behind this program."[78]

The law approving the ERP, appropriating funds for its execution, and establishing an organization to carry it out—the Economic Cooperation Administration (ECA)—was voted by the U.S. Congress, with an overwhelming majority, on 31 March 1948. The Marshall Plan was launched with the consensus of the two American labor federations and with their active participation in its economic and political purposes, in which the union leaders, although from partially differing viewpoints, saw the expression of many of their own specific political objectives. For the AFL, the Marshall Plan was mainly the basic way of carrying out its own international campaign for the break in the world trade union movement along anti-Communist lines, the kernel of a policy for realigning the international union movement that was to find the best conditions for its success in the ERP. For the CIO leaders, the ERP—after having precipitated the political battle against its own leftist faction—became the privileged area of integration into the government's foreign policy, one of the crucial factors in its rapprochement with the White House and, furthermore, the political and ideological project on which to launch the prospects of a productivist collaboration with industry. The Marshall Plan, with its fusion of the ideal of prosperity with the policy of anticommunism, took on many themes that were proper to the American trade union movement. Its implementation offered to the workers' organizations a means of further integration into the government's policy and into the Western community that the Cold War was creating. The American commitment to stabilizing Western Europe required, because of its complexity, the confluence of political plans and socially diverse experiences and ideological assumptions. The ERP laid the foundations for that "interlocking relationship"[79] between unions and government which, in foreign policy, became a constant on the American scene for the entire postwar period.

CHAPTER

4

The Breakup of the International
Trade Union Movement

Between the end of 1947 and the beginning of 1948, while Congress debated the ERP, and while anti-Communist change was taking place in the CIO, the Department of State followed the daily developments in the conflict that had begun in the international trade union movement. The efforts under way in the AFL, in consultation with Benelux and British unions, to call a conference of unions in countries adhering to the ERP promised more than just a widely organized consensus for implementing the Marshall Plan in Europe. The main result of this AFL move was to precipitate the crisis in the WFTU, bring the East-West conflict to the surface in the trade union movement, and definitively break the unity of that international federation. The Department of State looked on this with expectation and interest, concentrating its attention on the TUC and the CIO, whose attitudes would be crucial since they were the most important and authoritative organizations which supported the Marshall Plan and also belonged to the WFTU. When it appeared that both these unions had decided to demand a vote from the WFTU executive board, or an explicit statement on the ERP that would have no chance of being approved, a prediction was circulating in the State Department that represented a hope more than anything else: "Having made their position on M [Marshall] plan clear and having failed elicit WFTU endorsement, TUC and CIO will then feel morally free to convene or participate in international trade union conference of M plan countries outside the WFTU. Conference will in effect produce a rival trade union body because it will include AF of L and French Force Ouvrière; it will be boycotted by CGT and Italian trade union movement."[1]

The Trade Union Conference for the ERP

The matter was not so simple and linear. The ideas of the TUC and the even more uncertain ones of the CIO did not fully coincide with the AFL's plans and Washington's desires. The TUC leaders did not intend to be driven into hasty actions, both for reasons of their international prestige and in order to avoid being blamed for a split they wanted to lay at the door of the Soviets. They therefore advocated the prompt convening of a trade union conference on the ERP under their direct supervision, to leave the role of the Americans obscured and to saddle the WFTU leaders with the decision of how or if to react to the formation of a new trade union reference point around the Marshall Plan: "TUC leaders regard ultimate split in WFTU as almost inevitable, but wish to move in such a way that onus for split can clearly be put on Communists. CIO views similar."[2]

The leaders of the CIO were even more hesitant in the face of the rapid succession of events which made it progressively impossible to reconcile their decision in favor of the Marshall Plan with their adherence to the WFTU. James Carey met with the leaders of the Soviet trade unions to seek a compromise, perhaps thinking that the WFTU could discuss the ERP, assume an officially neutral position, and in some way continue its unified course. But the meeting did little more than record disagreements. At its end the Soviets published a statement that was strongly critical not only of the Marshall Plan, but especially of the conference then being prepared among the unions that adhered to the ERP. In spite of the failure, Carey, who was acting on instructions from Murray not to precipitate a break with the WFTU, said he was still confident of possibilities for discussion within the WFTU, and in private he stated that he was against immediate decisions, preferring to await the Soviet reaction to the conference on the ERP. This attitude was criticized in the Department of State. On the future membership of the CIO in the WFTU, Carey showed himself uncertain, tying it to the outcome of the discussion in the world federation. This caution derived from the lack of decisiveness in the CIO national leadership, which obviously was hesitating in the face of a break in international unity.[3]

Urged on by the AFL and the Belgian and Dutch unions, the TUC leaders called the labor unions' conference on the ERP for 9–10 March 1948. The AFL was taken by surprise and, since it did not want to submit to a unilateral move of the TUC, threatened not to send its representatives. But it was promptly dissuaded by pressure from the State Department, which certainly did not want an initiative so important for the ERP and for a possible split in the WFTU to be compromised.[4]

Also, the leaders of the AFL and their closest European allies set too much store in the formation of a group of unions in favor of the ERP to hold up the project for reasons of pure prestige. Oldenbroeck, who was leading the ITS toward rupture of negotiations with the WFTU, implored the AFL to take part in the London conference and pointed clearly to the most urgent goal for all the forces hostile to the WFTU: "An international trade union conference is necessary to explain the Plan and to arouse that wave of enthusiasm which is not only needed to make the Plan a success, but also and above all to engender a popular campaign against those who are trying to sabotage the Marshall Plan."[5]

The ERP was about to enter into its operative phase at the moment when the political conflict throughout Europe became more bitter and implacable. The delegates to the conference, including those from the AFL, gathered in London on 9 March 1948, at a time when an electoral campaign was starting in Italy and when the impressions of the Communist coup in Czechoslovakia were still strong. The coup appeared to confirm the grimmest forecasts on Soviet intentions, spreading alarm throughout the West and making definitive the break between the Communists—now isolated more than ever—and the European Social Democratic left.[6] The conference, in which representatives of twenty-eight organizations participated—significantly including the delegates from the minority of the CGIL (Pastore, Canini, and Enrico Parri), those from the Force Ouvrière, and the German unions from the Western occupation zones—assumed a symbolic significance. It clearly represented the split in the left and in the European trade unions and gave signs, whatever may have been the intentions of the participants, of "the germ of another world labor federation."[7] The final communiqué proclaimed support for the ERP from all the participating unions, which recognized the indispensability of American aid and declared themselves satisfied with the absence of unacceptable conditions or attempts at interference. The trade unions had the task of supporting each government's policies for applying the plan and of cooperating with its administrative organizations, contributing "to the establishment of the social, economic and political conditions which are essential to safeguard the principles of free citizenship and democratic institutions, and which alone can assure improvement in the life and labour of the people."[8]

The meeting was only preliminary—the ERP had not yet been voted on by Congress—and it postponed all detailed discussion of economic reconstruction problems to a second conference to be convened in a few months. A permanent committee was formed, however—the ERP Trade Union Advisory Committee (ERP-TUAC)—and charged with preparing the next meeting and establishing contact with the Organization for European Economic Cooperation (OEEC) in order to define the terms of union participation in the administration of the aid. The permanent committee was the most important result of the conference. In addition to the representatives of the American, British, Scandinavian, and Austrian unions were Giulio Pastore for the CGIL minority, Hans Boekler for Germany, and Leon Jouhaux from Force Ouvrière. The AFL's plan to gather all the representatives of "free" trade unions was beginning to take form. The ERP-TUAC was the first international coordinating body for European and American unions outside the WFTU. Equally new was the joint—and especially harmonious—presence of the CIO and the AFL in an international assembly. This showed how important, and potentially dominant, American influence had become in the international trade union movement. The AFL delegates left the conference on a note of decisive optimism: "Everyone was impressed by the unity of purpose. . . . There is great potentiality in this first step towards the reconstitution of a real free international trade union movement."[9]

The political importance of the London conference did not escape the Department of State, whose interest in trade union issues was becoming especially intense in connection with the launching of the Marshall Plan. A meeting was arranged between Secretary Marshall and Presidents Green of the AFL and Murray of the CIO to coordinate the activities the American unions would be able to undertake "in connection to E.R.P. and in our effort to repel further Communist aggression." Both Green and Murray offered the assistance of their organizations and requested close ties to the ERP administration. The department's interest was especially concentrated on France and Italy, and its pressure was directed first at the CIO: "As evidenced by the success of the trades union meeting recently held in London, . . . most European labor movements are actively supporting ERP. . . . An active program by AFL and CIO in support of European labor would be most effective in the situation outlined above. It is evident that Communist power derives primarily from their influence in the trades union movement; the only effective American force to combat this influence is American labor. . . . The full support of American labor should be thrown to anti-Communist labor elements in France and Italy."[10]

These were the two countries where opposition to the ERP would probably be the most intense and where the success of the plan would therefore be more significant. Furthermore, the rapidly approaching Italian elections concentrated all energies on a challenge held to be strategically relevant for the success of anti-Soviet containment. The State Department was convinced that a split in the CGIL, similar to what had occurred a few months before in France, was not only desirable but inevitable and urgent. To this end all the energies of the American unions were mobilized. The CIO, still uncertain whether these splits were appropriate, either in the WFTU or the CGIL, was brusquely challenged by a proposal for dialogue brought forward for the CGIL by Di Vittorio, who, in connection with the London conference, had made one last attempt with Carey to try to maintain the connection between the two hostile camps into which the international trade union movement was irretrievably divided over the issue of the Marshall Plan.[11] The State Department's concerns derived chiefly from the lack of commitment on the part of the CIO and the TUC to quick action leading to a split in the WFTU. Carey openly opposed any split and Murray was not yet ready for immediate decisions, while an eventual split would need long preparation.[12] On the other hand, the department thought it indispensable to present an attitude so intransigent that it would exclude any possibility of an accommodation at the next WFTU meeting. The minorities in the CGIL were waiting, among other things, for the CIO and the TUC to break away from the WFTU before leaving the CGIL.[13]

Irving Brown shared the State Department's fears, not only of the CIO's hesitation, but of the TUC's reluctance to take decisive action against the WFTU. After a meeting of the ERP-TUAC, whose leadership had been entrusted to Vincent Tewson, secretary-general of the TUC, Brown told the American embassy in London that he was "bitterly disappointed." "Although initiative and vigorous action were necessary to associate European Trade Unions with ERP, and to capitalize on Communist defeat in Italy and growing dissatisfaction in Italian and French Trade Unions with Communist leadership, no initiative or imagination was shown by Tewson. . . . Brown said AFL leaders will be exasperated by lack of speed and vigor and will soon indicate their displeasure."[14]

The resentment of the AFL toward the TUC reflected not only the traditional rivalry for the leadership of the trade union movement in the West, which was present, or the difference in style and organizational methods in the two organizations, although that too was important. At the basis was a disagreement on the lines of action to follow. Neither the TUC nor the Foreign Office thought it appropriate for the Westerners to bring about the split in the unitary organizations, differing here with the AFL and the Department of State. Rather, the minorities in the CGIL would have to expand and perhaps seize control of the organization instead of bringing about a minority secession. As for the WFTU, the TUC intended to break away and walk out only after preparations to isolate the Communists and to lead the greatest possible number of unions into a new international. But the Americans, concentrating on the effectiveness of the Marshall Plan, wanted an immediate break, which would symbolize a new, clamorous defeat for Moscow. For the

British, the ERP-TUAC should not act as if it were the new international. It was only a first, cautious, and implicit step in that direction. The AFL, after all, was not a member of the WFTU, and the TUC did not want to be dragged out of the world federation just because of American pressure.[15] For the Department of State, the priority was unequivocal: "Basic dept. policy is to do everything possible to strengthen non-Communist labor elements. It is essential to success of ERP that non-Communists regain and hold control of European labor organizations."[16] Neither the caution of the TUC nor the uncertainties of the CIO could satisfy the AFL or the department, which expected a prompt anti-Communist realignment to result from a break in the WFTU, beginning with the minority in the CGIL.[17]

At the executive meeting of the WFTU in Rome from 5 to 10 May 1948, Carey sought and obtained a compromise. After a discussion on the brink of breaking off, in which Carey threatened to walk out, an agreement was reached according to which Saillant's leadership would be subject to various controls and the federation's propaganda would avoid attacks on policies supported by one of the member country federations, as was the case with the Marshall Plan. The CIO withdrew its request for an official debate on the ERP.[18] This result was publicized by the CIO as the triumph of its choice to stay in the WFTU and struggle against Soviet claims to dominate the body; the changes decided in Rome had even revitalized the WFTU. But the AFL launched a furious attack against the CIO. According to Woll, it should have left the WFTU to "prove its respectability" to the American people and "free" trade unionism.[19] For the ambassador in Rome, James Dunn, the agreement was a personal victory for Carey and an affirmation of the CIO: "Communists including Di Vittorio told us that Carey's evident sincerity in seeking to prevent WFTU split made deep impression and that CIO influence within WFTU has notably increased as result. From Communist standpoint, however, severe scolding of Saillant and . . . restrictions on his administration . . . represent satisfactory price for preservation of facade of 'unity of world labor.' " The compromise, however, was considered fragile and incapable of restoring effective unity to the WFTU. Its effectiveness and durability would depend only "upon threat of constant readiness of CIO to withdraw from WFTU." The ambassador's disappointment was clear: "Split of WFTU especially over ERP issue would have stimulated split of Italian CGIL, strengthened Force Ouvrière and further justified their split from French CGT in December 1947. Split would have weakened Communist and strengthened Socialist labor forces in ERP countries where Communists are already embarrassed by their enforced role of opposing American aid."[20] Another message sent from Rome to Washington summed up the views of the American embassy: "The reluctance of the American CIO and the British TUC publicly to recognize that the WFTU has ceased to be a genuine organ of world labor will inevitably discourage the non-Communist labor organizations throughout western and southern Europe in the struggle, against Communism, for the loyalty of the European working class."[21]

Actually, the patching up of the WFTU executive board was very feeble and could not heal the overall disagreement between the two sides over the Marshall Plan. In the summer of 1948, with the Berlin blockade, international tension reached its high point. The implacable hostility between the two geopolitical camps was reproduced without mitigation in the world trade union movement. In the unions in the Berlin territory, the "Western" forces, under increasing pressure from Henry Rutz and other AFL figures, completed a split that ended the previous unitary experience.[22] In Italy the breakup of the CGIL was already under way. Starting with the defeat of the leftist forces at the polls, it needed only an appropriate occasion, which came unexpectedly in July with the tensions that broke out after the attempt on Togliatti's life. With the start of ERP operations in Europe, American pressures intensified for the trade union realignment to be made final. On 29 and 30 July the second trade union conference of the ERP met in London. The senior official in the ECA in Europe, Averell Harriman, inaugurated the meeting, together with Clinton Golden and Bert Jewell of the AFL, who had just taken positions at ECA headquarters in Washington as consultants on union affairs. "Of all groups, the international labor movement can do most for the European Recovery Program. . . . We want your help. We need your help."[23]

The AFL delegation arrived at the conference in a rather skeptical mood, fearing that the TUC wanted to dampen the American spirit of initiative. In a preliminary meeting with the CIO delegates an agreement was reached to act jointly, even against any TUC reluctance, to take concrete measures "to advance international trade union cooperation for the ERP." The American delegates criticized the "hesitation" of the Europeans at jumping into a vigorous propaganda campaign for the ERP and succeeded in placing in the final resolution two amendments to which they attributed the greatest importance. The first advocated the lowering of all trade barriers to arrive at a gradual unification of Europe, which would allow for a more rapid recovery and constitute a defense "from menacing pressures from the outside." The American insistence on an integrated continental approach to the development of the ERP took the form, on the more immediate level of trade union interest, of the decision to entrust the ERP-TUAC to "give guidance to the national centers in the mobilization and coordination of their activities." The committee would have thus taken on not only the appearance but substantial functions of a new international. The second amendment concerned the type of economic recovery that the Marshall Plan was to favor, and it explicitly recalled the ideal of prosperity; while the British talked of a "balanced economy," the AFL and the CIO indicated as one purpose an "economy of abundance." The difference in emphasis took on political importance for the Americans, since a promise of prosperity could be the key theme to mobilize the unions and those in favor of the ERP. The only American request to be defeated was the one to launch an immediate publicity campaign to magnify the conference and solemnize it as a historic event. This in fact would have marked the existence of a new international, and the TUC did not want to hear of it. The American delegations left much more satisfied than when they had arrived. Throughout the conference they had exercised an undoubted leadership. There was not a new international organization yet, but its existence was closer each time the ERP-TUAC met. Furthermore, the CIO, driven by its obstinate conviction that the ERP could democratize European society, had for the first time shown itself prepared not to follow the authority of the TUC and was freed from special precautions to safeguard its relations with the WFTU. Irving Brown commented that this was the "first step in the formation of a new [international] labor organization."[24]

The American delegates felt that their influence was increasing and that the "free" trade union grouping around the ERP was now taking form. But to bring the realignment to its logical conclusion and definitively weaken the WFTU, a continental leadership would be necessary that would lead the European trade union movement to break from the Communists, and only the British TUC could play this role. Lovestone returned to America with the following recommendations for the AFL: "We must carefully and patiently develop ways and means of bringing to bear sufficient friendly pressure on the TUC to have it assume such leadership. It may require a more frontal and sharp collision for the TUC with the Communists on the continent and also a sharp change in their relations with trade unions dominated by Communists. We have to work out our tactics carefully with all due allowance for British sensitivities."[25]

The prudence of the TUC was also of concern to the leaders of the ECA and the Department of State, where officials lamented British reluctance—more on the part of the government than the unions—to accept the American viewpoint centered on integration in one great continental market to increase productivity. The TUC was specifically criticized because it was blocking the formation of a committee to consult on union matters at ECA headquarters in Paris.[26] But it was chiefly the question of the WFTU that concerned the Americans.

The Breakup of the WFTU

The initiative for a split in the world federation was obviously up to the British, but for the moment, they had no intention of assuming the responsibility. As the American diplomats complained: "Privately they condemn WFTU and hint they mean withdraw at appropriate moment, but publicly they defend WFTU. . . . We now doubt whether initiative to withdraw will come from TUC, whose leaders seem incapable of taking decisive action." Attention was then directed to the CIO, where there were rumors that Murray, pressed by Reuther, was making up his mind to withdraw from the WFTU. The Department of State was informed that the AFL was preparing "long term plans regarding new non-Communist union organization."[27] Irving Brown ascribed the TUC's caution to its "extreme nationalism," but he believed that the Berlin blockade was leading to greater anti-Communist vigor even on the part of the British. More important, he thought the Foreign Office could push the TUC to decide on a break. The AFL was beginning to bring public pressure to bear on the TUC—and the CIO—with a press campaign for the formation of a new international organization.[28] The situation was building up from day to day. In preparation for another executive meeting of the WFTU, the executive board of the TUC gave carte blanche to its secretary to decide on the TUC's affiliation with the world federation. Tewson confided to the American embassy in London that "TUC was prepared for a showdown and break. . . . But CIO had indicated unwillingness to break at this time." The Department of State intervened at that point, through Clinton Golden, "to stir the CIO to break off relations with the WFTU." The embassy in London reported that "a split in WFTU may occur at any time."[29] The CIO's leaders were divided. Carey and Frank Rosenblum, delegates to the WFTU meeting, opposed an immediate break, while Reuther and Emil Rieve were in favor. Murray, by now leaning to departure from the WFTU, replied to the State Department that the delegation sent to Paris by the CIO executive board had instructions not to break with the WFTU, but to coordinate with the TUC the procedures for an early joint departure. The CIO executive board would then make a definitive decision.[30]

The decisive event occurred in September, when the International Federation of Transport Workers, led by Oldenbroeck, decided in conjunction with other ITS federations to reject any collaboration whatever with the WFTU, breaking off any negotiations. The maneuver begun two years previously by the AFL and Oldenbroeck was thus completed, and the WFTU was completely isolated from the other important international rallying point for trade unions. The isolation of the

Communist unions was complete. The withdrawal of the ITS was, according to the leaders of the AFL, "the most crushing defeat the WFTU has received."[31] This was an opportunity for the TUC to walk out of the WFTU under the best of conditions. In the formal sense, the breaking off of negotiations between the ITS and the WFTU gave the British a reason for accusing the WFTU of absolute ineffectiveness, since the TUC's WFTU membership was originally conditioned on an agreement with the ITS. The WFTU's moment of greatest political weakness could be exploited. On 27 October the executive board of the TUC decided, with significant concurrence, to start an internal campaign to repress Communists and to seek the suspension for a year or more of all WFTU activities because of the federation's incapacity to settle its internal disagreements and operate in a unified fashion. In this way, an attempt was being made to lay at the door of the Soviets the official responsibility for a break that by then was inevitable.[32]

Meanwhile, the conversion of the CIO to the values of the Cold War and its adherence to containment policy were nearly complete. The CIO was a full participant in the changes undertaken by the American liberals, who were setting aside the progressivist thrust of the New Deal and coming to define themselves as a vital center that opposed totalitarianism on two fronts and was based on a philosophy of economic growth. But it was losing its role as a critical voice and a goad from the left in order to adapt itself nearly completely to the nationalist and antiradical consensus that dominated the United States.[33] After its rejection of the third party represented by Wallace's candidacy, the CIO completed its realignment with the administration in September, when the federation came out explicitly for Truman's reelection. The unexpected success of the president, who was reelected in the first days of November, opened the way to full collaboration between the CIO and the government at home and abroad. In 1949 the national crusade against the Communists achieved its most conspicuous political success when the CIO launched a purge in the grand style, culminating at the end of the year in the expulsion of leftist-led unions, among them the crucial electrical workers' union. In this brusque and definitive way the experience of more than ten years of association between liberal or social democratic unionism and Marxist-inspired unionism was broken off.[34]

The CIO convention of 1948, immediately after the TUC's decision to ask for suspension of the WFTU, voted for a foreign policy motion with harsh anti-Soviet tones that was fully in agreement with the American government's plans. Unconditional support for the ERP was accompanied by a commitment to help the European unions that accepted the Marshall Plan. The usual ritual motion of support for the WFTU was made on this occasion solely by the delegates from the left, and it was soundly defeated. The final resolution stated that the executive board was authorized, in consultation with the TUC, "to take whatever action in relation to the WFTU and the international labor movement as will best accomplish CIO policies and objectives."[35] It was a blank check for CIO leaders, clearly indicating that the break with the WFTU was now only a matter of when and how.

At the same time, the AFL was pressing the FTUC to increase its contacts with "free" trade unions and to bring delegations to the United States "so that they may see for themselves how American democracy functions, how our free trade unions work." Irving Brown, in a talk to State Department officials, explained how the struggle against the Communists for union leadership, now in its crucial phase, constituted the decisive front for victory in the Cold War throughout Europe, especially in France and Italy. This was because the Communist parties were sacrificing their popularity in a losing effort to block the Marshall Plan with the mobilization of trade unions.[36]

The delegates from the TUC and the CIO met in London in mid-January, the day before the WFTU executive meeting. The British now were very firm. They would demand the suspension of the WFTU for a year, without accepting any compromise. James Carey, however, was still uncertain. He had received no binding instructions from the CIO, and the final decision was up to him. He was personally opposed to withdrawal from the WFTU, on the basis of his conviction "that the Communists can be most effectively fought from within the WFTU." But having seen the TUC's determination, which made it certain that a break would occur, Carey decided at the last moment to "take the lead, ahead of TUC" in precipitating the break.[37] The WFTU meeting in Paris on 17 January 1949 therefore became the scene of this rupture. When its executive board rejected the British proposal, the representatives of the CIO, the TUC, and the Dutch union left the session. The unity of the international trade union movement, which had developed at the end of the Second World War on the basis of the anti-Fascist alliance, was definitively shattered. In its place, two hostile groups faced each other, exactly mirroring the polarization of the Cold War. The CIO rejected the accusation that it fomented the break: "When the Communists sought to pervert this organization to serve their ends, they irrevocably split this body in two. The WFTU became inactive and ceased to exist. There is nothing left for us to split."[38]

The propaganda machine of each front hurled virulent accusations that the other was responsible for the break, ascribing the blame to "Soviet totalitarianism" or to "an imperialist Wall Street plot," according to the rigid reciprocal logic of bipolarity. In the historical field, the causes of the break in the international trade union movement—in addition to the obvious finding that it was just about inevitable because of the Cold War's global division—were sought mainly in the Marshall Plan.[39] By fusing the strategic purposes of containment with the task of Western Europe's economic reconstruction, the ERP brought the divisive effect of the conflict between the United States and the USSR directly into the field of economic policies and into the center of gravity of trade union strategies. When Moscow's hostile reaction to the Marshall Plan, with the establishment of the Cominform, confirmed the fundamental role played by the economic reconstruction of Europe in the global confrontation of the Cold War, the unions in Western Europe—and before them the CIO—were faced with a stark choice. On one side was a proposal of productive expansion that could support economic policies geared to full employment and the formation of a welfare state; on the other was a refusal of the American proposal based on anticapitalistic principles or the choice of the pro-Soviet camp. The political differences that were present previously in the structure of every union and within the WFTU took on gigantic proportions. They became rigid, along the lines of opposing choices that had become violently incompatible because of their all-embracing nature, whether economic, political, ideological, or strategic. Where the anti-ERP left was in the minority it was reshaped and purged, while in areas where it had majority positions—in the CGIL, CGT, and the WFTU—the unitary association was split and the forces favoring the Marshall Plan broke away.

The American decision to challenge its Soviet antagonist in the first place on the field of economic stabilization, productivity growth, and expansion of the social consensus behind the promise of capitalistic prosperity acted as a catalyst for political and social conflicts that were already entrenched in European society. This precipitated the internal conflicts in the trade union movement with a force which the AFL's crusade for a "free" trade union movement by itself could not even approach. The activities of the American unions, crucial for the transformation of that political force into a concrete realignment of the European trade union movement, had great importance not only for the AFL's untiring pressure for a break, but principally for the role of the CIO. Its political transformation, strongly stimulated by the Marshall Plan, constituted perhaps the main element, and certainly the most surprising one, of the adherence of a majority of American society behind the Truman administration's foreign policy, which allowed the containment strategy to be presented as a proposal that was also a social and economic one. The CIO's anti-Communist realignment was not only of importance in the breakup of the WFTU; in a deeper sense, it was the first decisive victory of the Marshall Plan in winning over institutions in the trade union movement to the anti-Soviet prosperity strategy, which first had to gain the allegiance of the principal forces in the American union movement in order to have any effect in Western Europe.

"Western" Trade Unionism

The rupture of the WFTU was only the last act in a now complete polarization of the union movement into two camps: the Western group around the ERP and the pro-Soviet one based on the WFTU. It therefore seemed a foregone conclusion that the forces favoring the Marshall Plan would immediately unite in a new international federation. The leaders of the AFL had long been looking on the ERP-TUAC as the embryo of this new federation. At its next meeting, barely a week after the break, on 22 January 1949, the question was at the center of the discussions, even though the representatives of the TUC and the CIO were actively denying that the committee was an alternative to the WFTU. It was clear that the ERP and the experienced group of unions around it represented the common ideological and political base for a new international federation. Furthermore, both the iron-clad anti-Communist political logic of American activities, interpreted in an extreme fashion by the AFL, and the urgent need of an international affiliation for forces such as the Free Italian General Confederation of Labor (LCGIL), which had left unitary organizations, required prompt official recognition of the new Western alliance of trade unions.

A coordinating committee was therefore established, in greatest secrecy, on the sidelines of the ERP-TUAC meeting, to study the steps that would lead to a new federation. In addition to representatives from the TUC, the CIO, and the AFL, Pastore of the LCGIL, Jouhaux of Force Ouvrière and Kupers of the Dutch union also participated. The first problem was to request all the national federations that were not committed to Communist positions to leave the WFTU. This step would require diplomatic caution because some, such as the Swiss and the Scandinavians, were not firmly in the Western camp, and all those outside Europe were not necessarily involved in the dispute on the ERP, nor had they been brought into the polarization between East and West. A more serious problem, however, was the reciprocal mistrust deriving from the competition among the three large Western powers in the trade union movement: the AFL, the CIO, and the TUC. The ERP-TUAC meeting brought this conflict into the open again. It was necessary to nominate a permanent secretary who would direct the committee's activities in conjunction with the OEEC and the ECA. The British proposed the Belgian

Walter Schevenels, secretary of the former IFTU and then deputy secretary of the WFTU, from which he had just resigned. The AFL, however, was opposed, since it mistrusted Schevenels because of an aversion against anyone who had worked with the Communists in the WFTU, and also for fear that the TUC was imposing a man of its own as the possible secretary of the future international. The battle over Schevenels's candidacy was bitter and disproportionate, showing how the problems relative to the establishment of a new international federation were dominated by the rivalry between the TUC and the AFL.[40]

It was a rivalry deriving partly from the different choices these federations had made in the immediate postwar period. The AFL feared that the CIO and the TUC would make up a common bloc which would assume the leadership of any new international trade union federation. Furthermore, it had not fully accepted the idea that it had to associate with its CIO rivals in an international setting. The TUC was naturally reluctant to accept American preeminence and was trying to retain its own unopposed primacy in the European trade union movement. The path to the new international federation seemed fraught with difficulties, even though there were no profound political differences. The AFL's executive council, though emphasizing "the burning urgency . . . of an all-inclusive international federation of genuinely free trade unions," was on its guard against hasty preparations that might be vulnerable to a sudden attack from its large rivals. The AFL responded to the danger of a TUC-CIO axis with an appeal to all those minority groups—such as the Force Ouvrière, the LCGIL, or the Asian and Latin American unions—with which it had close and privileged relations.[41]

In official American circles it was believed that the union leaders should cease to indulge in "the luxury of dispute and bickering" as soon as possible. The ECA believed that the WFTU should not be given time enough to recover from the blow it had been given: "ECA, as a government agency, of course, cannot become involved in the controversy. However, we have a vital interest in the maximum implementation of ERP and the strengthening of the democratic forces. . . . There is no question that delay in the formation of a new trade union international is harmful to European recovery and to the cause of democracy. Prompt and quick action is needed." The high degree of union involvement in the foreign policy of the American government made it necessary to keep the fundamental objectives in mind.[42] Since it was not a case of "genuine differences of interest," but only "prestige and personality issues," the State Department informed the American unionists in no uncertain terms about where its own priorities lay: "We would welcome creation of an international in which AFL, CIO and railway labor organizations would participate. It would give support to U.S. policy aims, helping strengthen democratic trade unions and helping to counter Communist-WFTU drives in colonial and semi-colonial areas."[43]

At the end of March a TUC delegation traveled to the United States for consultations with the AFL and CIO, but they had difficulty in reaching an agreement. The rivalry between the two American federations was very strong. The AFL did not concede to the CIO the right to participate in a future international with the same level of representation. Most of all, each proposed procedures that would give itself the greater influence, if not complete control over a future international. The CIO wanted a limited group (the CIO, the TUC, and the AFL) to convene a constituent conference, selecting those to be invited. The AFL, on the other hand, advocated a large provisional committee made up of all the organizations in Europe and the Americas and insisted that the new international be established free of all "domination and manipulation by political parties and political ideologies," a formula that alluded to the dangers of Social Democratic dominance in Europe. The State Department urged the CIO to be accommodating, and at the moment when difficulties were greatest, Carey even suggested an intervention from the White House to settle the differences between the American union leaders.[44]

Even though this was not done, official pressure had its effect, and the two federations finally reached an agreement. The delegations from the AFL and the CIO would be on equal footing in the executive organizations of the future international, but in the plenary assemblies, their numbers would be proportional to their members (7.5 million for the AFL and 6 million for the CIO). The two federations also committed themselves to prior bilateral consultations in order to present a single American position, when possible, at the international congress. At the same time, the TUC called a preparatory meeting in Geneva for the end of June. The Department of State greeted with great satisfaction the news that the way to the formation of the new international was finally open: "Its chief activities are likely to be essentially political, since its firmest characteristic will be its anticommunism, and its chief members will be supporters of their governments, especially in foreign policy. . . . An anti-Communist international will be a sort of projection of the foreign policy interests of the governments of its members, most notably the United States and the United Kingdom." The embassies were to assist the establishment of the new international in every way, although avoiding "unwise interventions," and were to make great efforts to broadcast the positions of the American unions.[45]

On 25 and 26 June 1949 the preparatory conference meeting in Geneva called for the founding congress of the new international to convene before the end of the year and nominated a permanent committee for its preparation. The atmosphere of the meeting was inspired by the necessity of consolidating the non-Communist trade union movement to struggle totally against the WFTU and its claims for control of the workers' movement by the Communist parties. The concept, dear to the AFL, of "free" and nonpolitical trade unions tended to emerge as the central reference point for the new organization. For the first time, the CIO representatives publicly embraced the idea that a union movement guided by a political project or tied to a political party could not be considered "free." The two American delegations acted with total unity of purpose. The new international, according to the AFL and the CIO, should be aggressive and militant, solidly organized both at the center and in the regions, and provided with important financial resources to launch massive campaigns against the WFTU and to assist in the formation of "free" unions in all the countries outside of Europe. In opposition to the TUC, which looked on the new international in a politically analogous way but did not share the grandiose activism of the Americans—both because of British problems with colonial issues and for fear of American financial predominance—the AFL and the CIO proposed very elastic membership criteria so that they could assemble a large number of unions in the countries of Asia, the Middle East, and Latin America. Furthermore, they were fighting for the admission of the Christian unions, mainly to strengthen the new anti-Communist organizations like the Italian LCGIL. Against this admission were the Belgian FTGB and the NVV in the Netherlands, which because of internal rivalries demanded the exclusion of organizations with ties to religious denominations. Finally, the Americans advocated close cooperation with the ITS, again in connection with the struggle against the WFTU, and the AFL advanced the candidacy of J. H. Oldenbroeck, its closest ally and the most prestigious leader of the ITS, as secretary of the new international. A spirit of unity prevailed at Geneva, and the conference proceeded without delay to the establishment of the new international. The disagreements were postponed to the constituent congress.[46]

The final phase in the creation of the new international was marked by growing hegemony on the part of the American union organizations. This was the result not only of their numerical and financial preponderance, but also of the international political situation, especially the series of events that gave life to the new Western trade union coalition, whose formation over the previous two years around the proposal of the Marshall Plan had defined its political and conceptual horizons according to two rigid coordinates. On one hand was adherence to a program of European reconstruction that pointed out to the unions the path to negotiating the benefits of expanding capitalism, which carried political and ideo-logical values as well as economic and trade union ones. On the other hand, the political, class conflict model of trade unionism under Communist influence, organized in the WFTU, stood out as an antagonistic and negative countervalue. In the face of this situation, the competition lost its purely trade union character to assume the total commitment of an ideological confrontation. The progressive international polarization had molded a good half of the common identity of the developing Western trade union movement around the philosophy of the Marshall Plan. The other half was provided by the antagonist, by the very existence of the WFTU, and by its solidarity with the Soviet camp. In proposing their own union model and their own political orientation, the American unions extended to the labor world the guiding role that the United States had in the formation of the Western bloc.

The Department of State was lucidly aware of this: "The formation of the new organization is important to us because, by working through it, American labor can support our objectives in helping to change the attitude of politically-minded foreign trade unionists who are suspicious of 'capitalist' governments, especially the U.S." For Washington it was no longer just a case of assuring the agreement of the European union movement for the ERP, but much more universally, to develop a united front in the Cold War, especially in the areas outside Europe that were being increasingly affected by the bipolar division. For this reason, the establishment of the new international was accompanied by detailed support operations on the part of the American government. The State Department, in connection with the Geneva conference, initiated an impressive propaganda cam-paign for the new international, issuing instructions that the trade union issue be given "a high priority" for at least six months. United Nations recognition would be immediately requested for the new organization. The American unions would be given assistance "to expand their efforts . . . especially in Asia, Africa and colonial areas." They would be given new positions in the embassies, and their international activities would be followed through close consultation.[47] The ECA was active too, with a publicity campaign for "free" trade unionism and against the WFTU: "The workers of the free nations have chosen liberty; WFTU: a symbol masking a Communist organization."[48] In this framework of closest collaboration, the AFL and the CIO reached an agreement to present joint candidates, according to criteria of sharing rather than competition, for the positions of labor attaché in the American embassies. The CIO, during the annual convention that dramatically concluded its internal Cold War with the expulsion of the unions led by leftists, also completed its realignment on foreign policy issues, approving the establishment of NATO and triumphantly greeting Dean Acheson, the new secretary of state.[49]

The International Confederation of Free Trade Unions

The International Confederation of Free Trade Unions (ICFTU) was established at the end of the year, after a long constituent congress which met in London from 28 November to 9 December 1949. Participating were fifty-eight union organizations representing fifty-three nations for a total of approximately 48 million members. All the main union federations of the non-Communist world joined, with the important exceptions of the Italian CGIL and the French CGT, which remained in the WFTU. The American union leaders went to London with the firmest resolve to put political considerations explicitly at the center of both the congress and the ICFTU's activities. Thus the CIO announced the establishment of the new organization: "A large portion of the world's ideological warfare is being waged on trade union fronts. The new group will speak for freedom and democracy—and against totalitarianism."[50]

The idea of the struggle against totalitarianism—to exalt parliamentary democracy and individual liberties, but even more, to defend against attempts at "infiltration and subjugation of labor organizations by totalitarian or other anti-labor forces"—was reflected in the preamble to the constitution, together with social justice, as a principle that inspired the ICFTU.[51] The congress in London represented the international triumph of American trade unionism. The CIO and AFL delegations made a powerful bloc with the representatives of the new European anti-Communist unions, which had been founded with their support, and those of many non-European organizations with which they had close ties. Many delegates from Latin America, for example, had come to London at the expense of the AFL. "The net result of the conference," Dubinsky wrote, "is that we carried practically every point." Almost all the controversies with the TUC and other European organizations were settled in favor of the Americans. The right of the Christian unions to join was approved, and ample representation was given in the management structure to unions from minor countries, especially the non-European ones. Giulio Pastore was placed on the executive board, primarily because the AFL wanted him there, to represent the LCGIL's anti-Communist struggle. The Americans were also able to have the president, Belgian Paul Finet, and Secretary-General Oldenbroeck ("the best man we could have") assisted by a permanent committee where the European representatives of the AFL and the CIO were to control the ICFTU's daily activities. Finally, the British suffered the most telling symbolic defeat when they had to accept the placement of the new international's headquarters in Brussels instead of London. "As a whole, the Conference recognized the leadership of the Americans," Dubinsky concluded.[52]

The constitution of the ICFTU, in addition to its strong antitotalitarian tones, took up another theme—the right to self-government, development, and national independence of the underdeveloped countries—to which the Americans ascribed great value because it was at the same time anti-Soviet, anticolonial, and therefore anti-British. The commitment to self-government and economic development in fact called the Europeans' colonial responsibilities into question, presented American trade unionism as the best ally of the non-European countries, and was a foretaste of an international aggressively bent on assisting the growth of "free" trade unions in underdeveloped areas. The decision to establish close cooperation with the ITS, and especially to assign regional missions to the ICFTU for the continents outside Europe, enforced the American perception of the international as a "fighting unit" on a global scale from the organizational point of view.[53] The affirmation of this idea of the ICFTU as a dynamic and aggressive anti-Communist organization seemed to mark the decline of the British TUC's guiding role and the passage to the Americans of leadership of international non-Communist trade unionism. This reflected the relationship between the two countries and the new postwar balance of forces. The American union leaders were proudly aware of this. Jay Lovestone wrote from London: "The British crowd is dull, slow, and colourless. They are living in the nineteenth century but they do not run the world any more. This is hard on them." In a more meditative and less disdainful reflection, Dubinsky wrote a few months later: "The new International represents a fundamental departure from the pattern of all its predecessors. European trade-union aims and actions, though very important, are not its main wellspring. The present and potential strength of the new organization stems in large measure from the strength of labor in the western hemisphere and from rising trade-union movements of Asia and Africa."[54]

From the vantage point of union strategies and organizational models, the establishment of the ICFTU showed the new influence of the voluntarist and collective bargaining views in the American matrix, even if in this field the program documents all reflected more a compromise with European tradition than an explicit American dominance. The ICFTU constitution did not mention aspirations to transform society, nor the value of capitalist freedom of enterprise. It did not indicate strategies based on government planning and nationalizations, nor did it exalt the free market and private property. The omission of the most controversial ideas marked the compromise achieved, the ideological nonbelligerence between the prevalent Social Democratic viewpoints of the European unions and the liberal capitalist outlook of the American ones. The American leaders, however, made no mystery of their conviction that their union model was going to be spread on the international scene. In Paris, immediately after the congress, Walter Reuther stated: "One of the real weaknesses of the European unions is that they are continually fighting against ideological windmills. In our struggle against Wall Street reaction, we have learned something about fighting capitalism in a practical sense. Our program is as progressive, if not more so, than any European one; it is simply not based on ideological issues but on humanitarian ones." And a leader of the steel workers union of the CIO, David McDonald, stated unequivocally what the American expectations were: "I don't want the confederation to be a branch of the world socialist movement. I'm proud of the kind of free democratic capitalist union movement we have here."[55] After all, the compromise of silence and omission in the ICFTU constitution rewarded the American viewpoint. No national federation was bound in its activities by the principles of the ICFTU charter. But that document left out the political dimension and limited itself to indicate the economic and bargaining route to take to improve the workers' living conditions. This reflected the basic principle in the American trade union model: the possibility of raising incomes and consumption by means of collective bargaining. Indicating full employment and the improvement of working conditions and standard of living as economic objectives, the ICFTU charter—following a typical formula of the American voluntarist tradition, introduced as an amendment by the AFL—defined unions as "free bargaining instruments" whose authority derived from their own members.[56]

The ICFTU thus came into being under the banner of the antitotalitarian battle in defense of political and economic democracy. It united organizations with Social Democratic, Christian, and liberal and capitalistic inspiration in the anti-Communist cause. At least as a lowest common denominator it pointed the way for collective bargaining in an expansive economy. The ICFTU increased the power of the American trade union movement on the international scene and projected its image, especially in the industrialized world, but not only there, as a concrete and victorious example of an organization to represent the workers in a capitalist economy. American unions, especially the AFL, presented themselves openly as models for the cultural and practical regeneration of unions in the Western world. The ICFTU was to be an effective instrument in the Cold War if, and to what extent, it succeeded in propagating a pluralist and pragmatic formula for the settlement of social conflict, multiplying in the world the experience of "free" American trade unions. Dubinsky defined the ICFTU as "the new weapon" of labor in the world:

> The ICFTU does not rule out competitive enterprise. Neither does it rule out public or government ownership, but in both public and private enterprise, the ICFTU insists that the workers shall enjoy certain basic rights and have an adequate voice in the economic life of their country. . . . An increasing number of people in the European labor movement have begun to doubt that state control is the panacea for social ills. As this doubt grows, there is a growing confidence in the usefulness of independent trade unionism. . . . Foreign trade unionists . . . have come to realize that, though American labor has a different and less radical-sounding philosophy than their own, the labor movement in the United States has in practice been very successful in defending and expanding the workers' interests. . . . American trade unionism provides the practical way of building a democratic labor movement free from denominational limitations. . . . More and more the forces of free labor throughout the world are facing the complex problems of our difficult era in an undogmatic way; more and more they are freeing themselves from rubber-stamp phrases and absolutist philosophies, to seek practical, realistic solutions for present-day problems.[57]

The results of the London conference were greeted with great satisfaction in American government circles as well. The State Department emphasized the importance of a political program that committed the ICFTU to move "generally along U.S. policy lines."[58] The ICFTU's dynamic and aggressive nature, its organizational structure that was open and freed from European Social Democratic domination, and the affirmation of a guiding role for the American unions, which finally were united, gave reason to hope that the ICFTU would become an important protagonist in the ideological and social struggle that made one of the main fronts of the Cold War. The most immediate interest related to Europe. The ECA showed that the programs of the new international, fully in tune with the fundamental message of the Marshall Plan, were directed to achieving security and economic well-being for the workers in addition to their political freedom. The ERP was strongly supported in all the speeches at the congress and in the final resolutions, even though there were frequent repetitions of the request that the American aid be more specifically directed at improving the workers' living conditions. A new, important ally was indicated in the ICFTU: "ECA would make a mistake if it tries to take a hand in the conduct of ICFTU affairs. But it would be a still greater mistake to ignore the organization entirely. In fact, we should establish the fullest possible liaison, should use such opportunities as developments within the organization permit for the dissemination of propaganda supporting ECA and American policies."[59] The American government gave the greatest possible diplomatic and propaganda support to the ICFTU, and it was immediately given official recognition both by the United Nations and by the ILO, thanks to pressure from Western nations.[60]

In the first two years of its existence, the ICFTU performed mostly as an instrument of the Cold War, as both the American government and the American unions had wanted. The international conflict reached greater intensity with the outbreak of the war in Korea, the Soviet nuclear tests, and the accelerated rearmament in the West. The bipolar conflict spread geographically, affecting new areas outside Europe and assuming universal importance, especially in the eyes of the main protagonists. In these conditions, anticommunism and the vigor brought by the Americans had their maximum effect on the ICFTU, characterizing its activities almost totally. In Europe, in addition to coming to the aid of "free" unions, as in Greece, or in attempting to support their reunification, as in Italy, the ICFTU took the first steps to make itself a part of the major international initiatives for stabilizing the western part of the continent. An organization was established for liaison with the ECA and the OEEC, coinciding in good part with the ERP-TUAC, to provide union participation in carrying out the Marshall Plan. A subcommittee was formed for participation in negotiations for the Schuman coal and steel plan, which the international supported. American pressure in that direction was constant, because the CIO, and even more the AFL, wanted the ICFTU to exercise the maximum influence for the economic and political unification of Europe. The American unions, furthermore, were ceaselessly driving the international to anti-Communist propaganda activities directed not only against the WFTU, but at Soviet policy in general. The American requests were directed to activating the ICFTU in areas outside Europe, primarily in Asia, with the aim of making the international an instrument for organizing unions in a pro-Western manner in those underdeveloped countries that had greater importance in the eyes of the United States now that the Cold War had reached them. In 1950 and 1951 the ICFTU established regional offices for Asia and Latin America—the latter largely independent and governed wholly by American union leaders, especially from the AFL—and also organized the first study missions in Africa and the Middle East.[61]

The influence of the American view of the ICFTU as a militant instrument in the anti-Communist battle on a global scale was at its height in the years when the bipolar conflict was most intense, but it began to decline just as rapidly. At the second congress of the ICFTU, held in Milan from 4 to 12 July 1951, the conflicts with the main European figures started up again, breaking the feeling of un-challenged unity created during the initial enthusiastic crusading spirit, and mark-ing the decline of absolute American domination. The main European unions, beginning with the TUC, looked on the international more as the locus of coordination and discussion of union affairs than as a combat group. This led to a certain passivity and intolerance for the activist pressures that were coming from the United States. The AFL, on the other hand, could scarcely tolerate the lack of dynamism that the Brussels headquarters demonstrated, especially in the field of propaganda and publicity. Many AFL proposals got bogged down there. The American federation did not stop at these continuous pressures but expanded its own independent activities through the FTUC in Europe, Asia, and Latin Amer-ica, thus giving rise to mistrust and protests in many other national federations. These tensions came out in Milan. The American delegations arrived with a draft resolution against Soviet totalitarianism that was modified by the Europeans with additional references to Fascist totalitarianism. Moreover, the replacement of President Paul Finet by the secretary of the TUC, Vincent Tewson, was considered by the AFL to be a breakup of the internal balances achieved two years previously in London. Against the background of the first criticism from the unions of the economic results of the Marshall Plan, whose implementation did not yet produce the expected benefits for the workers, American insistence on the absolute priority of the political and ideological dimension of the Cold War was beginning to encounter resistance and competition from other priorities. The AFL, with an important address against totalitarianism by George Meany in Milan, urged an extreme unilateral anti-Soviet activation of the ICFTU. The CIO showed itself less intransigent and more attentive to Europe's problems and to more properly union issues. In the face of an increase in the more peaceful and less ideological points made by the Europeans, the diminished unity between the two American federa-tions already presaged a fall in the ephemeral American dominance. From the time of the Milan congress on, while the AFL was emphasizing the independent character of its international activities and harboring a resentful and suspicious attitude to the ICFTU, the influence of the principal European unions rose to balance, but not overturn, that of the American ones.

Born on the wave of the antithetic separation of the East and West brought on by the Cold War between 1947 and 1949, the ICFTU had its origins in the anti-Communist conflict and in the urgency of an Atlantic alignment for stabilization and economic growth in Western Europe. These factors led to the initial domi-nance of an American political, cultural, and trade union model. But as economic issues began to arise, as European forces slowly gathered again, and as the stark perceptions of the Cold War began to ease, the original characteristics of the ICFTU were mitigated and the preeminence of the American organizations and their models gave way to a more articulated variety of viewpoints. The ICFTU continued to act in many situations as an instrument of the West in the Cold War, but it no longer constituted, in its entirety, the pure and unilateral international projection of anti-Communist aggressiveness with which the AFL leaders had baptized it at the bitterest time of the bipolar confrontation.[62] The relative decline of American union influence was marching in tandem with the decline in the attractiveness of the American models of industrial relations and social organization, as European reconstruction found its own way to develop, leading to the great boom of the 1950s and 1960s.

CHAPTER

Divisions and Realignments:

The Italian Case

The Truman Doctrine, announced in March 1947, only two months after De Gasperi's visit to Washington, substantially changed the American attitude toward postwar stabilization in Europe. From the varied and unresolved mixture of attempts to promote social cohesion, a revival of productivity and political solidarity among the nations of Europe, and their adhesion to a system of multilateral exchanges, there now emerged a vision of order guided by one clear priority: the consolidation of democratic regimes, in an area of undisputed American influence, into a position of anti-Soviet containment. "The stated goals of American policy remained constant: stability through democracy, free trade and peace. However, United States tactics radically altered the meaning of these concepts. Democratic state building gave way to an anti-Communist crusade throughout the American sphere of influence."[1]

With the definition of containment as the strategic priority, Italy's position rapidly took on a new importance. From a beaten and unstable nation whose democratic reintegration into Europe was to be encouraged, the country rose in Washington's plans to become one of the main fronts for success in the global conflict with Soviet communism. Italian affairs were seen in a new light, dominated by the outcome of the political conflict that opposed the moderate forces to those of the left. In the weeks after Truman's announcement, the discussions between the American embassy in Rome and the Italian Foreign Ministry brought out an explicit analogy with the situation in Greece. This allowed the Italians to solicit a similar American commitment in the form of a substantial loan for the country's economic stabilization. The dispatches from Ambassador James Dunn emphasized the spread of social disorder, in direct relation both to economic deterioration and to intensification of conflict in the governing three-party coalition. They called the State Department's attention to the many difficulties the PCI would have if faced with a significant American commitment of aid to Italy.[2] From the spring of 1947 on, American policy took the form of clear and vigorous action to lessen the influence of the Communists in Italian society, and the CGIL became one of the principal targets of these efforts.

Reformism and Anticommunism

In Washington, the process of revising international economic policy—later to result in the proposed Marshall Plan—was an attempt to combine efforts to revitalize Europe's economy and international exchanges with the urgent need of social stability as defined by the containment strategy. The government's analysts were working to define objectives and economic instruments for alleviating the reasons for social discontent, primarily low wages and unemployment, which were believed to contribute to the power of the Communist parties. The political interests of moderate and conservative anticommunism were thus linked to aspirations from the New Deal period for widespread social prosperity, gathering a large bipartisan consensus behind Truman's foreign policy. The Italian situation was seen as an extreme example of the viability of Communist proposals because of poverty and backwardness. On 4 April 1947 a study by experts in various departments concluded that Italy's industrial production must be expanded and concentrated on the domestic market, supplying a large quantity of goods at low prices so as to convert the poor into consumers and backwardness into development of a modern economy of mass production and consumption. The spread of even a moderate consumerist prosperity would realign the social bases of adherence to the PCI, making possible a lasting democratic stabilization. The United States would have to greatly increase appropriations for aid and credits to allow Italy to shift the priority of its economic programs away from exporting and toward the domestic market, to adopt effective anti-inflationary measures, and to take steps to stabilize prices and wages.[3]

The Department of State accepted the priority given to long-term stabilization, asking the embassy in Rome for an evaluation of its possible impact and at the same time conveying its urgent desire to strengthen the moderate pro-Americans and consolidate the authority of the government at a moment when the economic and social crisis threatened to come to a head.[4] The ambassador's reply, however, concentrated on the short term—ten days afterward, De Gasperi was to open the crisis in his third government—and on the intensity of the contrast between the mass parties. For Dunn the crisis was basically a psychological one: "Population generally and particularly more responsible banking and industrial leaders have lost confidence entirely in the Government. . . . A flight from the lira is beginning: rise in spiral inflation is unchecked. The pity is that there exists all over Italy a real will to work and there could easily be a general confidence in the future if it were not for the political agitation of the Communists and I doubt if there can be any real effective measures taken to improve the situation as long as the Communists participate in the Government. . . . I do not believe it is too late for a government to be formed without their participation." Dunn was therefore wedded to the reasoning of De Gasperi on the confidence of the "fourth party"—industry and finance—and pointed to the problem which was to be at the center of the coming government crisis, the presence of the Communists in the executive branch. The granting of American aid was to depend on its resolution, accompanied by un-equivocal moves that would make clear how the American aid depended on weakening the Communists, or, as Dunn told De Gasperi, on the Italians' capacity "to put their house in order."[5] In difficult times, the measures for restoring the government's authority and opening the way to an American aid commitment needed to be based, according to Dunn, on "draconian" steps which, striking at the social interests represented by the left, could not be accepted by the Commu-nists. These included the abrogation of laws that "intimidate and paralyze strategic economic groups," a wage freeze, lifting the ban on layoffs, control over strikes, controls over exchange and credit, reductions in government spending, and a return to order and respect for law. The ambassador's position reflected the views of CONFINDUSTRIA, the Italian employers' federation, and the free traders. They favored abrupt measures centered on lifting the freeze on layoffs and the abolition of political prices, accompanied by the departure of the Communists from the government.[6]

In the face of the May crisis, economic stability and political normalization, with the exclusion of the left from the national leadership, became for the Americans a single indispensable step. The course of the government crisis, which De Gasperi opened on 12 May, saw the convergence of American desires with the Christian Democratic leader's decisions, to the extent of an informal agreement that was solidly based on common interests, according to which Washington was to furnish the maximum of aid to a government from which the Communists had been excluded. On 31 May 1947 the birth of De Gasperi's fourth government was greeted with an unusual message of congratulations from Secretary of State

George Marshall. The government was composed entirely of Christian Democrats—the Socialists and Communists being excluded—and free trade technicians
led by Luigi Einaudi, who was given responsibility for economic policy. Marshall's
message marked the American commitment to support the stability program on
which De Gasperi had set out.[7] A few days later, the address at Harvard with
which Marshall announced the aid plan for Europe soon bolstered confidence in
the possible success of the political and economic shift undertaken with the May
government crisis.[8]

For the State Department, the departure of the Communists from the government represented not only a welcome clarification, but also a significant political
success. With De Gasperi firmly in power and the left in opposition, the best
conditions existed for the Western stabilization of Italy, supported by American
aid, to get under way. The crucial point, however, remained that of social cohesion, in particular the consensus of the popular masses and the workers. Washington showed its disappointment that the PSLI was not in the new government
and indicated to De Gasperi the need to obtain the support of the moderate left
and to acquire the widest possible representation of the working classes. Dunn
emphasized the urgency—more political than economic—of an expansive program that increased consumption: "If a democratic government of present type is
to succeed, its fundamental task must be to shift from present phase of an emergency hand-to-mouth economy to one providing maximum employment and
production and their corollary of improved standards of living necessary for
eliminating social unrest. For democratic leadership in Italy to survive it must
accomplish this position towards a more permanent basic economic reconstruction which offers Italian people concrete hope for a betterment in standards of
living in a foreseeable future. . . . Should the present effort to govern Italy without
the Communists fail, the future of democracy in Italy may be most seriously
endangered."[9]

Now that the political clarification had taken place, the decline in the confidence
of the "fourth party" had been halted, and De Gasperi's Christian Democratic
party had assumed full control of the executive branch and obliged the forces of the
left to follow the government's activities from outside, it was time to begin work
on the reformist modernization of the Italian economy, so as to bring the workers
into an ascending cycle of prosperous and consumer-oriented productivism
which, according to what was learned from the American experience in the New
Deal and the war, would dry up social extremism and propagate a democratic
consensus. The American design, even though it had its own linear logic, was
nevertheless fraught with deep contradictions as it faced Italian political and

economic realities. Measures to reestablish financial equilibrium, stabilize the currency, and rein in inflation flew directly in the face of others to bolster production, internal consumption, and especially employment. From the political viewpoint, the incipient polarization between a Christian Democratic group in the government and a Marxist-leftist one in opposition relegated ambitions for reform to the category of unrealistic abstractions. The deflation on which Einaudi embarked stabilized prices and the Italian lira, but it kept down production and employment levels. The freeze on layoffs was chipped away and progressively eroded. The reorganization of industry was directed to penetrating foreign markets, taking advantage of the competitiveness brought on by low wages, while the domestic market and consumption for the people were stifled. An alliance of intent arose between industry and governmental bodies whose goal was to restrict the political and bargaining power of the workers. Its main political result was to make useless any attempt at social reform.[10] In American policies, the gulf between the imperatives of anticommunism and projects for modernization steadily evolved into a strident contrast that was to emerge with the implementation of the Marshall Plan. From the deflationary shift of 1947, and for several years after that, the contradiction between anti-Communist political stabilization and the possibilities of socioeconomic modernization remained an unresolved problem for American policy in Italy. The American planners looked on it initially only as a matter of timing, placing their hopes in a brief, sharp anti-inflation plan followed by a vigorous productive expansion supported by the first ERP funds.[11]

The American attitude toward the CGIL obviously encountered the difficulties inherent in this contradiction. In the brief interval from January to May 1947 when three parties—Christian Democratic (DC), Socialist (PSI), and Communist (PCI)—governed Italy, while internal conflicts in the CGIL were becoming more intense and explicit during preparations for the second congress, the views of the embassy began to decline decisively into pessimism. The labor attaché, John C. Adams, referred to a weakened, confused, and disorganized confederation that was shot through with strong centrifugal forces. The clash between Communists and Christian Democrats had no source of mediation within the union, bringing to light its lack of autonomy and strategic independence and therefore its vulnerability to splits in the political world. "The basic failure of the CGIL is that it has not become a labor organization. It functions almost exclusively in the political sphere rather than the labor sphere. . . . The CGIL has done more to safeguard labor's political rights and gain new ones than to improve labor's economic position. . . . If the work of the CGIL had dealt primarily with labor problems, it would not have been so difficult to create a strong unified movement. . . . It has been the emphasis on political action that has caused the rift in the CGIL, because in this field Communists and Catholics cannot go hand in hand."[12]

The centralized structure of the CGIL and its eminently political origin, based on the unity of the anti-Fascist parties at the time of the pact of Rome, determined its division and its substantial impotence from the moment in which the political break between the DC and the leftist forces was imminent.[13] For the American observers, the basic political factors, which were to decide the outcome of the clash in the confederation and therefore its future orientation, took on greater importance. These factors were the solidity and extension of the Communist dominance—which seemed to be expanding without apparent obstacles in the period prior to the congress—and the potential strength of the internal opposition. After the Social Democratic break of January, the AFL, through the Italian American union leaders of the IALC, came massively to the aid of the PSLI. Giuseppe Faravelli, announcing the establishment of an office for union affairs in the party, under the direction of Ludovico D'Aragona, requested a maximum of support from Antonini for the struggle that the PSLI was preparing to undertake against the "Communists" "to rescue the unions from subservience to them." He also requested direct contact with the European representative of the AFL, Irving Brown.[14] The IALC sent its contribution, but the PSLI wanted much more substantial political and financial aid. The party secretary turned directly to President William Green of the AFL and to David Dubinsky of the ILGWU, asking for a long-term loan of $150,000. The leadership of the AFL, which was putting together its campaign for the "free" unions throughout Europe, guaranteed its assent. Dubinsky invited Giuseppe Saragat and Matteo Matteotti to the ILGWU's annual convention in June, where an interest-free loan was agreed on with terms so generous as to make it effectively a free gift.[15]

The AFL chose to entrust the success of its anti-Communist crusade to the Social Democrats because in Europe they were the alternative to Communist unions, and also because of the traditional ties that the American federation had in Italy with Antonini and the ILGWU. But in the embassy in Rome no one was cultivating any illusions about the real capacity of the PSLI to have any effect on the struggle within the CGIL. The Communists, Adams wrote, not only had the best-trained cadres and a better organization, but they enjoyed great popularity among the workers because they seemed to be the only ones capable of offering an effective defense of their interests and the prospect of improving their future social conditions. Other trade union organizations lacked that capacity to convince and offer hope. The Social Democratic union leaders were few and weak; the Socialists were nearly incapable of acting independently. Both groups had a "truly pathetic" attitude, because they did not have the will to oppose Communist domination in a concrete way. The labor attaché's impetuous judgment was softened a little with respect to the Christian faction. According to Adams, it would have difficulties in becoming "a dominant force" in the Italian trade union movement, both because of its strongly religious character and because of its ties to the DC. But it constituted "the only group which can combat the Communists," even though it was numerically inferior to the Socialists. It was considered "actually more secure," in view of its compactness and ideological determination.[16]

The embassy's lack of confidence reached its culmination in June, when the second congress of the CGIL convened in Florence immediately after the formation of the new De Gasperi–Einaudi government. The voting gave the Communists a wide majority (57.82 percent) and control of the federation's executive bodies. The Socialists obtained 22.61 percent of the vote, the Catholic faction 13.4 percent, and the Social Democratic and Republican minorities about 4 percent. These results confirmed the Communist domination the Americans now considered to be part of the nature of the CGIL. What disturbed the American observers most of all was the course of the political conflict that took place on the floor. The recent break in the government's coalition had naturally been reflected in the union. The leftist majority showed itself relatively accommodating because of its obvious interest in safeguarding the unity of the trade union movement, and because it hoped in this way to support the reestablishment of political collaboration.[17] The Catholic faction was anxious to stem the Communist predominance and to defend the stability of the government from possible attacks in the union field. It had openly struggled against the political use of strikes and the right of the CGIL to assume political positions, requesting the abolition of Article 9 of its bylaws. The conflict ended with a compromise formula on which the Christian Democrats abstained, which mitigated, but did not eliminate, the possibility of political action by the CGIL.[18]

The American embassy judged the congress "disheartening from political viewpoint." Communist domination was ascribed mostly to the ineptitude of the opposition, beginning with the Social Democrats. The political battle against the leftist majority was waged without determination. The Christian Democrats, in spite of their belligerent intentions, had then "backed down ignominiously," accepting the compromise, and they were definitively beaten. Unity was restored and thus "the way was paved for the Communists to achieve their immediate aims."[19] The bitterness of these comments originated in the disappointment of excessively great expectations. The recent solution of the government crisis, with the iron will that De Gasperi demonstrated and the decisive defeat of the left, probably led to hopes that a vertical crisis would open up in the CGIL. The opinions of Dunn and Adams were hasty and mistaken, but they revealed the hopes and views of the embassy, especially concerning the anti-Communist minorities in the CGIL. The congress of Florence, with the opening of an inner conflict on relations between the CGIL and the government, and between union activity and the political scene, was the first step in a deep crisis of the CGIL, which began to feel the explosive effects of the political division between the moderate forces and the parties of the left.[20]

The internal conflict came out in the open three months later, at the beginning of fall. The withdrawal of the Soviets from the Paris conference on the Marshall Plan, and the subsequent establishment of the Cominform, induced the PCI to break the social truce, well or ill kept as it had been, and descend into the arena as an opposition force. In Italy, as in France, a bitter struggle was beginning between the government and the left, which the deflationary austerity made especially dramatic on the social and economic level. The agreement on internal commissions between CGIL and CONFINDUSTRIA on 7 August put an end to the freeze on layoffs and, with the anti-inflationary measures, opened a period of intensive reorganization of industrial plants. Unemployment was beginning to threaten even the most protected areas of the workers' organization. Torn between increasing political conflict and a very difficult economic situation, the union saw confidence in its social base crack and the internal debate between the factions fester.[21] The atmosphere of the Cold War, the international clash over the Marshall Plan, and the open conflict between leftist forces and the DC colored social agitation and strikes with obvious political overtones. The precarious internal unity of the confederation was subject to increasingly strong tensions, and it began to break up. Every kind of compromise formula was immediately overcome by the virulent political polarization taking place in Italy.[22] In September the DC took a position against the agitations the CGIL was planning because they were directed against government operations and therefore for political purposes. In the course of the fall all the Catholic forces, from the Vatican to the DC to the union faction, entered the field of battle explicitly and vigorously against the attempts by the left at social mobilization.[23] The news of AFL financing for the Social Democratic minority touched off violent controversy. The Communist vice-secretary, Renato Bitossi, accused the American union leaders and their Italian contacts of working to break up the unity of the workers' movement.[24]

The atmosphere of violent conflict was regarded with alarm by the State Department, which interpreted it as the result of an offensive coordinated by Moscow to bring on a crisis in Western Europe and obstruct the Marshall Plan. It believed that

Communist mobilization could even be a prelude to an insurrection against the government, whose defense therefore began to take on an absolute priority. The bonds of collaboration that tied the Department of State to De Gasperi, the Vatican, and the Catholic world became even closer.[25] For the Americans the reinforcement of a nonsectarian and modernizing political force was still the most desirable alternative. This force would contend with the Communists for representation of the workers and set out on the reformation of Italian politics. The expansion of De Gasperi's government to include representatives of the PSLI and the Italian Republican party (PRI) in the first days of December was seen as a salutary enlargement to the left of the anti-Communist front.[26] It was similarly hoped that the minority currents in the CGIL would be able to expand, perhaps through a coalition, to contest the PCI domination and promote a "regeneration" of the Italian trade union movement away from politics and toward collective bargaining. In more immediate terms, there were hopes of blocking the CGIL's capacity to mobilize, which threatened the stability of the government and the coming implementation of the ERP.[27]

The AFL, calling all the forces of "free" trade unionism to gather around the Marshall Plan, was considering an increase of its support to the minorities in the CGIL, which it realized were quite weak. In addition to its privileged relationship with the Social Democrats, it began to make contact with the Catholic current, led by Pastore.[28] Both David Dubinsky and Irving Brown were very disappointed in the PSLI. After they had invested money and hope, they observed neither effective progress nor any better prospects for the future. They were most disturbed by the internal quarreling of Saragat's party, which threatened its political and operational effectiveness as an opposition force within the CGIL. Brown, now established in Europe and closer to the theater of action, especially wanted to find more trustworthy contacts and possibly to remove Antonini, whose bias in favor of the Italian Social Democrats was deemed excessive and counterproductive.[29] With the onset of the Cold War, the AFL saw many opportunities opening up for its anti-Communist operations, and it demanded that its money be used to produce immediate political gain. The DC, which led the anti-Communist battle with tenacity, probably began to appear as the most trustworthy force to combat the Communists in the CGIL. The Christian faction strongly denounced political agitation, and Pastore, speaking at the DC congress in November, explained that the unity of the trade unions was possible on the condition that it not turn into political dictation to the minorities.[30]

Time seemed to be running out, and the political conflict took on the air of a direct, frontal clash. The political preferences, the cultural affinities, and the long-run decisions were subjected with increasing rapidity to the imperatives of the moment and the now absolute priority of the decisive battle against the Communists. At the State Department's request, the labor attaché prepared a report on the strength of the Communists in the union, which excluded the possibility of a significant reversal of the power balances in the short term. The ACLI was available as an alternative organization of the Catholic trade union movement, but its influence on the workers was still extremely limited. The one alternative to Communist domination would be a vigorous growth of the Socialists, and especially of their independence from the PCI.[31] But at the moment when a leftist front was formed with the 1948 elections in view, such a hypothesis was a long way from reality. The battle against the Communists, as the Americans saw it, had to be won soon, and there were neither the conditions nor the time to draft long-range programs for taking the Socialist party away from its unitary relationship with the PCI.[32] The stabilization of Italy was entrusted in the long run to programs of rehabilitation and economic modernization. But the importance of the strategic imperative of containment led the United States to a frontal clash with the Communists and their allies. The American National Security Council (NSC) issued its first directive, significantly dedicated to the Italian situation, indicating that America's primary interest was to "give full support to the present Italian government," with a series of diplomatic, military, and economic measures. In view of the election, it ordered a powerful anti-Communist propaganda campaign, which, among other things, would inaugurate the first clandestine operations of the CIA, with financing for Italian government parties.[33] The State Department was well aware of the Italian social problem and did not conceal the weakness of a reform entrusted to the Social Democrats: "The situation is all the more serious because no party except the 'Blocco del Popolo' has become associated in the minds of the people with the basic reforms urgently required for the peasants, the workers, and the humble white collar class so numerous in this country. Up to the present the Communists have been successful in rendering completely ineffective the dissident Socialists who should represent the main hope for the Italian worker." In the face of the specter of a Communist electoral victory there were only two forces that could be counted on, the Christian Democratic party, "a reassuring bulwark," and American intervention, which in large measure supported the economic credibility of De Gasperi's government. The United States, according to Ambassador Dunn, should furnish every possible aid to the government and intervene with the greatest authority and clarity to make it obvious to the voters that the way to American aid was open only if the leftists were defeated, that the Cold War constituted an absolute and impassible watershed.[34]

The CGIL, the ERP, and the Elections of 18 April 1948

In the most intense months of the Italian electoral campaign, the vital United States interest in a victory for the anti-Communist forces took the form of an extensive and heavy-handed intervention. The De Gasperi government was given the maximum diplomatic and political support. The campaign of the government's parties was sustained with every means. The American diplomatic apparatus and media were mobilized in an unceasing pro-Western propaganda campaign. The Italian American community and various union organizations were active in a thousand ways to convince the Italian electorate to deny its votes to the forces of the left. Between March and April, Italy became the principal field in the battle that set the United States against the USSR at the height of the Cold War; it had to be won at any cost.[35] The dramatization of the Italian election, which also served to facilitate passage of the ERP bill in Congress, reached its extreme after the Communist coup d'état in Czechoslovakia, from which American propaganda drew the main lesson by analogy: the danger of totalitarianism and the incompatibility of a Soviet government and democracy. The second basic argument was economic aid. Only the United States would be able to assure the survival of the Italian economy. The ERP, which became law on 31 March, would make Italian democracy prosper, but the basic requirement was that aid would be forthcoming only to a democratic government that was solidly in the Western camp, to an Italy where the power of the Communists was reduced to a minimum.[36]

The ERP, in its twin guise of an economic program and an implicit but obvious political prospect, played a decisive role in the Italian political events of 1948. In particular, it involved itself in the CGIL crisis with widespread influence. As a program for economic reconstruction, the Marshall Plan put the PCI in a seriously embarrassing position and made even more difficulties for the CGIL. The importance of aid for the expansion of the Italian economy and its popularity in public opinion made it very risky, if not counterproductive, to oppose a plan whose political effects weakened the position of the leftist forces and solidified the moderate front guided by De Gasperi. Out of respect for the position taken by the Soviets, the PCI followed the party line of opposition, which the Cominform had adopted, but, at least at first, it avoided the Cominform's virulent tones and presented its own criticism in nonultimatum form. This prudence evaporated during the electoral campaign, when the question of American aid became a central issue in Christian Democratic campaigning and the Truman administration stated explicitly that there would be no aid for Italy if it were governed by leftist forces. Then the PCI came out in the open and embraced the intransigent arguments of the Soviets, who saw in the ERP a plan to subject European countries to American monopolies, snuffing out their independence and limiting development of production.[37]

The CGIL, where the embarrassment of the PCI was added to the uncertainties of the Socialists and was in contrast to the explicit agreement of the minorities to the Marshall Plan, was even more out of the fray. In January it declared its neutrality on the ERP, while its Catholic faction came out in favor of it. Only on the eve of the elections did it denounce the potential negative effects of the plan for Italian industry, which according to the confederation would be suffocated by competition from American goods and forced into further dismantling.[38] In the meantime, however, the CGIL had been deeply torn apart, driven not so much by the American economic proposals as by their political implications for Italian affairs and, above all, by the realignment of the international trade union movement around the ERP. While the proposed Marshall Plan was getting tangled up over the delicate question of relations with the government and was splitting the confederation's unity vertically—as had occurred a few months previously in France—the AFL's proposal for a trade union conference on the ERP, and the crisis in the WFTU that had begun by then, had direct effects on the conflict among the various CGIL factions, forcing them to make decisions inevitably in opposition to one another. The pro-Western realignment of the European trade union movement was the goal pursued by the AFL and the government when they opened the campaign for the adherence of the unions to the Marshall Plan. The Italian CGIL was one of the main subjects of the operation.[39] Barely a month before the union conference on the ERP, neither the AFL nor the State Department thought an early breakup of the CGIL was possible: "Brown foresees possible Italian CGIL split thru church influence but agrees realization more difficult than in France." Growing opposition on the part of the Christian current and the existence of the ACLI now pointed to the Christian Democrats as the main points of contact for the American plans for realigning the Italian trade union movement. But any break under these auspices still had the specifically Italian character of a Catholic project linked more closely to the Vatican's attitude than to the WFTU crisis and the operations of the American unions.[40]

Events then succeeded one another with great rapidity. The disputes of the fall of 1947 led to a final attempt to find a modus vivendi in the CGIL based on freedom to dissent, together with a prohibition against opposing measures decided on by a majority vote of the executive bodies. But in the preelection atmosphere, the agreement on the modus vivendi—voted for on 24 February with the abstention of the Christian Democrats—rather than safeguarding CGIL unity, seemed to point to its comatose state.[41] The debate on economic policy, on which measures to propose against the recession, revealed the open gulf between the left and the minority currents that were supporting the government's decisions. The CGIL executive council finally faced the question of the union conference on the ERP, scheduled for 9 March in London, and here the break took place. Even though the Socialists proposed to participate as observers, the Communists were decisively opposed, both because the conference was taking the form of an attack on the WFTU and because the ERP by now was De Gasperi's war-horse. The CGIL executive council declined the invitation. At this point Pastore announced, together with the Republicans and Social Democrats, that the minorities were going to send their representatives to London. The crisis had begun. The embassy in Rome noted that the Communists were more concerned with placing responsibility for the break on their adversaries than they were with the break itself, which was already in progress. From the Christian Democratic side, even a formal break would be welcomed. "Thus it would appear that CGIL unity is presently hanging by very slender threads indeed, with neither of the major groups vitally interested in its maintenance."[42]

In London, coordination was developing among unions in favor of the Marshall Plan through the ERP-TUAC, which was to lead to an international grouping in opposition to the WFTU, precipitating a year-long crisis. The Italian representatives in London—Pastore, Giovanni Canini for the Social Democrats, and Enrico Parri for the Republicans—obtained important international recognition and entered officially into contact with the American unions, becoming an active part of the project to realign the trade union movement on a European scale. Pastore and Parri met with James Carey, who was still opposed to a break in the WFTU and advised them not to bring about an immediate break in the CGIL. But they were officially recognized by the CIO as its interlocutors in Italy, while that American federation issued harsh criticisms against the CGIL for not adhering to the ERP, even though theoretically the CGIL was a fellow WFTU member.[43] The Social Democrat Giuseppe Faravelli ascribed to the finally united minorities the mission to "liberate the CGIL from the unbearable despotism to which it is now subjected."[44]

The leaders of the CGIL tried to repair the damage at the last moment, seeking an agreement with the CIO, which seemed the most open and available among the organizations in the new pro-ERP grouping. Di Vittorio asked for a meeting with Carey to head off an open crisis in the WFTU, to preserve the connection with the American trade union movement, taking advantage here of the CGIL's neutral policy to the Marshall Plan, and to prevent the Italian left from appearing isolated in its unpopular opposition to American aid. But the CGIL leaders were too late, having probably underestimated the speed with which the CIO was aligning with American foreign policy, especially the Marshall Plan. The Department of State advised Carey not to trust Di Vittorio, whose purpose was to "make political advantage for Italian Communist party in coming Italian elections"; to repeat the American viewpoint in no uncertain terms, denying to Di Vittorio the "slightest encouragement"; and to inform the press after the meeting that "Italy's best interest, if she desires American aid, is to support ERP."[45] Carey met Di Vittorio and Fernando Santi in London on 12 March, but it was a dialogue of the deaf. In addition to protesting the break in the unity of the international trade union movement produced by the London conference, Di Vittorio proposed an agreement between the CGIL and the CIO in which the CGIL would accept only those parts of the Marshall Plan it deemed favorable to the Italian economy. Primarily, the CIO was to promise that American aid would come even to a government other than De Gasperi's. Carey rebutted that the ERP would have to be accepted in all its aspects "good and bad," that the CGIL would have to collaborate with the Italian government and unite with the ERP-TUAC, and finally that the CIO did not sign agreements which might imply that only a Communist government would continue to receive American aid. Carey's ambiguity on just that last politically delicate point—Carey also told Di Vittorio that the CIO could accept the idea of aid being extended to any kind of government—caused the meeting to end on an indefinite note. This left the way open for differing interpretations, even though the discussion as a whole certainly brought out deep disagreement.[46]

The CGIL spread the news that an agreement had been reached, stating that the CIO would push to give aid to any Italian government. The Marshall Plan was not to be rejected but criticized, because it did not assure sufficient resources and pushed the Italian economy into the substantially closed dollar area. The CIO did not issue a communiqué, contending that no agreement of any kind had been reached. At this point the State Department intervened brusquely, asking the CIO to deny any agreement with Di Vittorio and to publicly support a recent official statement by Marshall according to which aid to Italy would be suspended in the case of a victory of the left at the polls. The CIO denied the interpretations published by the CGIL, accusing the Italians of having falsified the outcome of the meeting.[47] There was no longer any room for the CGIL's ambiguous neutrality. Its international views were restricted to those of the pro-Soviet bloc in the WFTU, and, more important, its unity was now openly threatened.

The success of the London conference, where union representatives from all the countries participating in the ERP were united in their support of the American aid program, had a profound effect on Washington. The Department of State believed that the time had come to coordinate operations with the American unions, to consolidate the non-Communist international trade union lineup, to promote the split in the WFTU, and to drastically reduce the influence of the Communists in the European unions. The leaders of the AFL and the CIO were requested to commit themselves totally—politically and financially—to bolster "free" trade unions and lead them to a definite choice for the pro-Western camp. If the influence of the Communists in Western countries depended in large measure on their ability to achieve domination of the unions, the polarization that opened up around the Marshall Plan at the London conference offered the opportunity to decisively alter the power of the Communist parties in Europe and at the same time to obtain the maximum social and political consensus to implementing the ERP. In the strategy of anti-Soviet containment, these were two vital objectives, on which depended the possibility of stabilizing Western Europe and, therefore, the outcome of the confrontation with the USSR for domination of the continent. The most urgent front was in France and in Italy, where Communist strength was significant and where the CGT and the CGIL seemed to constitute the most serious threat to the success of the ERP. The efforts of the American government and trade unions were to be concentrated on these two countries. "The anti-Communist minority of CGIL is actively supporting ERP, and is seriously considering whether to force the issue and break away from the Communist group so as to make their position clear to the Italian workers. . . . Only American labor can combat Communist influence in the European trade movement. . . . The full support of American labor should be thrown to anti-Communist labor elements in France and Italy."[48]

The AFL promised maximum collaboration, while the CIO leaders, still uncertain on the timing of a break in the WFTU and therefore reluctant to precipitate a break in Italy, nevertheless promised to work for the success of the ERP and to establish relationships with the minorities in the Italian unions immediately after the elections. The Department of State then announced to the American embassy in Rome that it was time to begin working for a break in the CGIL: "Dept. feels that split away of CGIL minority and formation non-Communist trade union center will inevitably occur as in France since Communists will almost certainly call strikes designed cripple Italian economy and ERP if they lose election. We indicated to Murray and Carey they can help materially if disposed to encourage CGIL minority breakaway and give moral support and financial aid. . . . Will you evaluate possibility and timing of CGIL split?"[49]

The reply by the embassy was succinct: "Formal split in CGIL along lines of present majority-minority division is inevitable." But everyone had to wait for the elections, after which the minority factions intended "to force showdown with majority on issue of ERP." It was also necessary to await the meeting of the WFTU executive board, scheduled for the end of April in Rome, where it was expected that the pro-Communist majority would probably break with the CIO and the British TUC. The embassy, in the meantime, was to organize a meeting between the leaders of the minorities in the CGIL and the American union leaders, whose visit was expected as soon as the postelection situation was clarified.[50] Meanwhile, initial consideration was being given to the nature of a future union organization in opposition to the CGIL. The attention of the embassy fell first on the ACLI, "the organization [the Catholics] would promote as their own national labor union in opposition to CGIL." But the ACLI was a Vatican organization and was tied to the more conservative sectors of the Catholic world. Its undoubtedly solid organization could from one moment to the next become a new union federation. But serious doubts remained on its capacity to garner agreement, become a modern and efficient union, and compete successfully with the CGIL.[51]

The defeat of the popular front and the Christian Democratic victory in the 18 April elections represented a geopolitical success of supreme importance for the Truman administration. But at the same time, the triumph of De Gasperi, the fall of the Socialists, and the scant success of the Social Democrats restricted the options for American policy to a privileged, but nearly exclusive, relationship with the DC. The 1948 elections became a referendum against communism and brought on the success of the moderate forces. But it also compromised the potential for the development, if there really had been any, of a reformist and modernizing policy, which was the only one Washington thought could lead to lasting stability in Italy.[52] As for the CGIL, the electoral outcome constituted the turning point. The whole range of anti-Communist forces began immediately to mobilize to shatter Communist hegemony in the trade union movement. The CIO declared itself enthusiastic that Italy had taken a first, decisive step toward its transformation into "a functioning democracy." The AFL leaders, rejoicing with the CGIL minorities, explicitly indicated what the next step should be: "AFL confident that free Italian labor will move quickly to eliminate Communist control of trade unions and thereby safeguard victory of democracy on political field."[53]

There was no unanimity among either the Italians or their foreign allies,, however, about how to achieve a substantial change in the balance of political forces in Italian unions. The British labor attaché, W. H. Braine, the pro–Labour party leaders of the TUC, and the Foreign Office, for example, deemed inadvisable a break that would have left the Communists in complete control of the CGIL.

They advised instead that the minorities reinforce themselves to win control over the confederation. The Italian minister of labor, Amintore Fanfani, brought forward the same argument, trusting in an early victory of the minorities.[54] Antonini also opposed a break, believing that the electoral success should be used by the anti-Communist forces to attract the Socialists and expand their following in the CGIL.[55] In the days immediately after the election, Irving Brown met in Rome with the minority leaders and strongly advocated a break. The Christian Democrats Pastore and Roberto Cuzzaniti said they would favor the establishment of a new separate organization if and when the CIO and the TUC would break with the WFTU. Alberto Simonini, responsible for union affairs in the PSLI, believed like Braine that it was more appropriate for the minorities to strengthen themselves in order to win at the next congress, while Canini, the Social Democratic vice-secretary of the CGIL, would have preferred the immediate convening of an extraordinary congress with subsequent withdrawal from the CGIL.[56] Brown thought the idea of achieving a majority in the CGIL was nothing more than a fantasy, and he left the meeting with scant confidence in his Social Democratic counterparts: "If the Sarragat [*sic*] boys will follow up on the trade union work, they can really finish the CP. However, I find this the weakest part of the Italian picture. The Catholics are doing a better job than any other group in the CGIL. But because of their fear of the Catholics, the Sarragat crowd are not doing too well on trade union matter."[57]

One who fully shared Brown's position, as well as his sympathy for the Christian Democrats and his ill-concealed contempt for the Social Democrats' uncertainties, was the new labor attaché at the American embassy, Colonel Thomas Lane, who had arrived in Rome at the beginning of the electoral campaign.[58] The executive meeting of the WFTU, with the compromise that momentarily preserved the federation's unity, did not resolve, but rather further complicated, the confusion arising from differing opinions on how to proceed against the Communist majority in the CGIL. The embassy deplored the failure to achieve a break in the WFTU, which lessened the possibilities of a break in the CGIL and made things even more difficult for the minorities.[59] To the embassy's request for instructions, the Department of State responded in politically clear terms that were still indefinite from an operational point of view: "Basic Dept. policy is to do everything possible strengthen non-Communist labor elements. It is essential to success of ERP that non-Communists regain and hold control European labor organizations." On the timing and modalities of a break, Washington preferred not to make any pronouncements yet, as it waited for the intentions of its Italian contacts to become clearer. But the State Department did not seriously consider the hypothesis of a prolonged struggle for control within the CGIL. On the contrary, it advanced the idea that Catholics and Social Democrats should coalesce in one unified, non-political trade union organization. In short, a break was regarded as a foregone conclusion in Washington, though at an undetermined time. For the moment, the embassy would gather more information and avoid "any impression of US government intervention."[60] The CGIL leaders, only partially guessing what was going on in the wings, accused the AFL of conspiring against the unity of the Italian federation. The CIO informed the Department of State that it believed a break was necessary at one time or another, but that it regarded it then as premature and, in any event, as a decision for the Italians to make. The same idea was expressed by senior officials of the Foreign Office in London, who stated that, for the Western governments, it was a matter mostly of being prepared to furnish the maximum support to the non-Communist factions as soon as they had carried out the break. On 20 May, Washington told the embassy in Rome that the "ultimate decision whether to split and timing is of course up to the Italians."[61]

In the meantime, "the Italians" had not been sitting idly by. During the electoral campaign, the entire gamut of Catholic organizations was mobilized against communism in a manner unprecedented for its expanse and intensity. The triumph of 18 April was experienced as a historic turning point, and it set the Catholic world on a final offensive against the PCI, especially its hegemony over the CGIL. The world of trade unionism was the field of the second great anti-Communist battle. The unity of intent of the Catholic organizations stopped here, however. Neither the tactics to be followed nor the ultimate goals of the new union program—a sectarian trade union, or a nonpolitical organization that united all the non-Communist factions—were agreed on by the different Catholic organizations: the Christian Democratic party, the ACLI, the union faction, the civic committees of Luigi Gedda, and even the church itself. The ACLI, strong in its independent union organization and supported by the Vatican, was strongly in favor of a break and the establishment of a new union. The ACLI's national council decided at the beginning of May, in a resolution that was not made public, to commit the organization to the preparations necessary for a breakup of the CGIL. It was estimated that the operation would require a few months to be achieved, but the way was indicated.[62] Pastore and the DC, who in some ways were in competition with the ACLI for control of Catholic trade union policy, proposed at that time, with the union leaders of the PSLI and the PRI, an "alliance for trade union unity and independence." This was publicly announced on 11 June and reflected the formation that had grown up around the Marshall Plan. While even the pope seemed to be in favor of a break, Pastore and the alliance, whose very existence showed how deep the split in the CGIL was, leaned toward a decisive battle within the confederation, which would have probably brought on the breakup of the CGIL. The formation of the alliance responded to the need to be prepared for that eventuality but did not yet constitute a definitive and operating plan for a split.[63] On the other hand, the collaboration between Christian Democratic, Social Democratic, and Republican union leaders, which had been relatively easy as long as it concerned opposition to the Communists, ran into difficulties as soon as it raised its sights to the future. The Social Democrats feared the dominance of the Catholics within every form of future union association, and they mistrusted the restrictive economic policies of the DC, to which they would have preferred to oppose more advanced ideas for social reform, in line with the expansive promise of the ERP.[64] These difficulties were only at their beginning at this point, but they were soon to grow into problems of the first order, constituting obstacles not only to reciprocal collaboration, but to the hopes of the Americans as well.

In May and June the final phase of a traumatic accounting in the unitary labor federation began. Its imminent breakup was a prospect that figured in everyone's actions and comments, but there was still no operative plan for dismantling the federation. The American embassy, well informed about the projects being discussed in the Catholic world and the disagreements concerning them, naturally looked with special favor at the formation of the alliance and informed Washington on 25 June that "for the present split CGIL is academic question."[65] After the first enthusiasm over the electoral victory had subsided, and with the prospect for a breakup of the WFTU further away in time, the expectation of a CGIL breakup was also relegated to a later date. This was not reassuring for the Department of State where, in addition to the desire to deal powerful blows to the Communists, a certain impatience was beginning to gain ground over the lack of vigor by the De Gasperi government in the face of the most serious economic and social problems. It was hoped that a new union organization, influenced by the ERP's idea of expanding output, and committed to collective bargaining with industry and government, would be able to call up and stimulate this vigor. The diplomats were not the only ones to have these concerns. One of the most important stands was taken by the CIO, with a document sent to Truman from the federation's committee of Italian American union leaders and officially authorized by the national leadership. It was a long appeal that American operations in Italy should favor a policy of social reform on the model of the British Labour party, without which there could be no hope of defeating communism in the long run. Agrarian reform was indispensable; the unions should be reinforced and given a public role; the reconstruction of the cities should consider plans for popular housing; the main financial and industrial institutions should be put under public control:

> The Italian people, like the people of all Europe, envision an economic order in which production is carried on for the benefit of all people, not the profit of a few. . . . The old order is done for. If we seek to rebuild in the old patterns, we will fail. . . . Mr. President, if the new Italian government and the Western democracies are to retain the advantage the election has given them, political events in Italy must move forward promptly into economic democracy, must result in democratic social ownership and control of the central elements of the Italian economy by the Italian people. Nothing less than such a basic transformation of the Italian social order can stem the otherwise inevitable advance of totalitarian Communism in Italy. Not all the economic aid in the world can.[66]

The suggestions of the CIO had little to do with official American policy toward Italy. But they did reflect, even though in a rather unusual Socialist tone, the growing disappointment at the conservatism of the moderate Italian forces by wide sectors of American liberalism. The CIO program did touch on one issue, that of ways to achieve social, and therefore political, stabilization in Italy, to which the State Department was sensitive. Furthermore, the CIO was among the forces that supported the ERP and the whole European policy of the United States, and its opinion needed to be considered in some way. When information on this was sent to Rome, it was pointed out that the CIO document represented "the left-hand view of an American prescription for Italy." But that did not eliminate agreement with more widespread points of view. "In general, American opinion seems to be pleased with the vitality of free enterprise in Italy, but disturbed that Italian capitalism may not be sufficiently 'enlightened' for this industrial era of ours." Walter Dowling, the State Department official in charge of Italian affairs, agreed it was urgent to have a strong reformist initiative, and once again it was the New Deal that emerged, as it did in the CIO document, as a model for action: "What is needed is a dramatical and perhaps even theatrical program such as that with which Franklin D. Roosevelt so ably captured the imagination of the people in 1933."[67]

The impatience with the De Gasperi government came from a fear that discontent, if not desperation, brought on by continuing difficulties and wide economic inequalities, worked to the advantage of the Communists, who had been defeated but not routed. For this reason, the center of the struggle in Italy became the union field; control of the CGIL seemed to the American analysts to be the principal reason for the strength of the PCI, and the most serious threat to the stabilization program undertaken by the ERP.[68]

The Catholic Withdrawal from the CGIL

The withdrawal of the Catholics from the CGIL was precipitated by three factors: the attempt on the life of Palmiro Togliatti, head of the PCI, on 14 July 1948; the immediate reaction by the workers; and the subsequent proclamation of a general strike by the CGIL. De Gasperi accused the confederation of planning an insurrection; the Christian faction denounced the majority for having "violated the pact for trade union unity," and indicated the "necessity of an independent and democratic union . . . truly free from any and every influence of political parties." The break which the Christian Democrats were preparing—although beset by their own internal contradictions—had been in the air for months. This split became an unforeseen and profound gulf in the face of the direct confrontation between the leftist forces and the government in the days of popular mobilization.[69] The union leaders in the PSLI and the PRI who had assented to the general strike did not follow the Christian Democrats. The alliance, in its first decisive test, was already shattered. The American embassy was taken by surprise, not only by the events but by the Christian Democratic reaction. It showed its disappointment at the unilateral measure taken by the Catholics that buried the unity among the minorities in the CGIL: "Embassy believes since PSLI and PRI are not going along with CDs there is good chance split will not take place and situation will be allowed to blow over. We hope that this will be the case since independent CD organization, we think, would, at its present stage of development, have practically no chance of competing successfully with CGIL on national labor scene. Simply does not control large enough sector of laboring group."[70]

In the heat of the moment, the first reaction was still dominated by lack of confidence in the prospects of a Catholic union, which would have compromised the American plans for a nonpolitical and unified organization of all the anti-Communists. The two proposals for a new union which had taken shape up to that point—the Catholic one, especially ACLI's, and the one desired by the Americans that was inspired by the ERP and partially embodied by the alliance—were unexpectedly in competition, if not in opposition. On 22 July the national council of the ACLI met with the leaders of the Christian faction and decided to found a new union, but only after the majority of the CGIL drove the Christian Democrats out of the confederation. This occurred on 26 July, when the CGIL executive council declared the Christian Democratic federation leaders "dismissed." The split was now a fact, and the majority had no further interest in attempting to avoid it. The controversy of those days consisted mainly of attempts by each adversary to blame the other for the break.[71]

Meanwhile, David Dubinsky and Luigi Antonini had arrived in Rome on 16 July for a visit scheduled long before. As soon as they received word of the crisis, the two most senior leaders of the FTUC, Jay Lovestone and Irving Brown, also came to Rome and met immediately with alliance representatives. On 25 July, before Dubinsky, Lovestone, and Brown left for the ERP-TUAC conference in London, they discussed the prospects for the break and outlined a project for a union newspaper. Pastore explained that the Christian Democrats were proceeding with plans for a new union. The Republicans and Social Democrats, on the other hand, were anything but convinced that a break was appropriate. They would remain in the CGIL, but they wanted to produce the newspaper with the Catholic unionists all the same. Faravelli told the Americans in confidence that the Social Democrats did not intend to "substitute Communist domination with Christian Democratic domination." The AFL leaders, who more than anyone had urged a unified withdrawal of all pro-ERP components from the CGIL, began to bring great pressure to bear for an agreement between the Catholic and lay forces. Brown said that the AFL would not give aid to any one group in particular, but only to all the anti-Communist forces, once they were outside the CGIL. Now that the crisis had begun, the AFL wanted to support the maximum possible withdrawal from the CGIL. Lovestone said he was ready to finance every representative of the PSI under Pietro Nenni who was disposed to support the Marshall Plan and participate in the ERP-TUAC conference. Pastore, Canini, and Parri also left for London for further consultations with the American union leaders.[72] In successive weeks, the embassy reported Christian Democratic plans for a new confederation that would be nonpolitical and capable of attracting other non-Communist groups in the CGIL. But it was skeptical of the claim that a new union could be established that would be effectively independent of the Christian Democratic party. Labor Attaché Lane went to Washington to consult with the leadership of the AFL, which was drafting its plans for a new non-Communist international.[73] Antonini, who stayed in Italy, continued his consultations with the Social Democrats. At the PSLI's conference on union affairs, which met in Milan from 22 to 24 August, he advocated an immediate withdrawal from the CGIL, but the Social Democrats had a different view. The conference decided to stay in the CGIL and to struggle—at least until the next congress—for greater democratization in the organization. The embassy defined the PSLI's hopes as "completely unrealistic" and ascribed them to the desire to keep a dialogue open with the autonomist components of the PSI, then in crisis within the party but not yet prepared to withdraw from it.[74]

The crisis in the CGIL was open, but it was not going in the direction the American State Department and the American unions had hoped for. A new union was taking shape, at the behest of the strongest and most determined among the groups favoring the ERP, but its debt to the Catholics was heavy and there was a risk that it would turn out to be only a branch of the Christian Democratic party, with little influence on the flux of social affairs in the country. At that point the State Department, closely coordinating with the AFL through Lane, decided to take resolute action. On 1 September Marshall sent a telegram—"Ambassador's eyes only"—to Ambassador Dunn: "Dept. studying possibilities of U.S. aid to new non-Communist Ital. labor organization, provided organization receives united support of principal non-Communist labor groups, i.e. moderate Socialists and Republicans as well as Christian Democrats, as non-partisan, non-clerical labor federation." Financing was to be transmitted to Italy through the American unions, which would contribute in such a way as not to expose the American government to accusations of interference. But that was not all; the Americans also wanted to give the new union scope for its operations and a positive bargaining function. "Dept. on Lane's advice also considering encouraging Ital. industry through Embassy and ECA to sign wage contract with new labor organization along lines of granting skilled workers 4–8% increase, both as incentive to Ital. labor and as essential promotion point for new organization."[75]

Ambassador Dunn replied that it was very difficult to purchase with contributions the withdrawal of the nonsectarian groups from the CGIL, but the new union Pastore was working on could by no means be allowed to fail. Lane explained to the AFL leaders that in the anti-Communist union movement, Pastore was certainly "the ablest and most effective leader." He should have the maximum support because only he could unify all the non-Communist union forces and resist Catholic pressure for a religiously oriented union.[76] The AFL leadership decided to descend into the arena at Pastore's side. The FTUC committed itself to finance the planned union newspaper. Dubinsky, at Lane's suggestion, stopped payment on a check to Saragat and decided to reduce the ILGWU contributions to the PSLI, at least until the Social Democrats changed their mind about staying in the CGIL. Lane insisted at the Vatican that the idea of a religiously oriented trade union should be abandoned.[77] The most urgent problem for Washington was to fend off the danger that the new union which the Christian faction and the ACLI were hastening to establish should begin life with the image—already present in press coverage—of a Catholic organization: "Any indication Vatican leadership new labor organization would seriously jeopardize chances anticipated split from CGIL of PSLI, PRI and some PSI elements, also long range prospects unity these groups with DC in single anti-Communist labor confederation needed successfully combat Communist dominated Ital. labor."[78]

These fears were soon alleviated, at least from the formal point of view. The factional clash in Catholic organizations was being resolved according to the desires of the State Department. The ACLI met in an extraordinary congress on 15 September and approved Pastore's project, deciding to establish soon a new independent trade union confederation that would be nonsectarian and free of political overtones. The ACLI deliberations were to lead to the founding of the LCGIL, and thereafter to the Italian Confederation of Workers' Unions (CISL), and put an end to the organizational and doctrinal tradition of Christian trade unionism in Italy.[79] The embassy noted with satisfaction that the ACLI resolution for a nonpolitical union had no reference to the church, to the Christian Democratic party, or to Catholic trade union doctrine, and it often mentioned the necessity of obtaining the support of other non-Communist forces. The main task of the American officials now became that of encouraging a rapprochement between the Christian Democratic union leaders and the Social Democratic and Republican ones who had stayed in the CGIL. The primary ground for cooperation was logically the support of the Marshall Plan and negotiations and propaganda relative to applying the ERP to Italy.[80] In Washington, the State Department was insisting that the AFL and the CIO finance an early visit to the United States by Pastore and representatives of the PSLI and the PRI.[81] As soon as the ACLI congress concluded, Pastore met with Ambassador Dunn to discuss the new confederation that was being established. The Christian Democratic majority, Pastore contended, had to be contained, and the formation of factions along political party lines was to be avoided in order to facilitate the future gathering of the nonsectarian groups. Concerning the financial problem, which weighed on him the most, Pastore presented a detailed explanation of his expenses. For its first nine months, the new union would need about 900 million lire, after which it would have achieved self-sufficiency through dues income. Pastore found firm agreement with his program at the embassy in Rome. Dunn summed up the problem for the secretary of state: "In our opinion Pastore group, in absence of any concrete action on part of PSLI and PRI, offers best means to combat Communist labor control, especially as it leaves door open to adherents of other non-Communist labor forces. We, therefore, hope Department will explore all possible means of obtaining financial assistance for this group."[82]

The primary objectives remained to weaken the Communists, to reduce the degree to which they represented different social classes, and to limit their capacity to mobilize. This pursuit seemed so urgent as to impose only partially thought out decisions that were even contradictory in some ways with the ultimate goals of American policy toward Italy. The need to facilitate the implementation of the ERP, taking the greatest possible advantage of the left's isolation after 18 April, gave first priority to the prompt setting up of a union as a vehicle of consensus for the aid plan. Since the CGIL was feared as the most serious threat to the success of the ERP, the formation of a new alternative organization in opposition to it had an immediate influence over American operations. Washington's program for modernizing Italian society and its institutions, beginning with the unions, took the form in Rome of contingent decisions that pursued the ups and downs of Italian politics much more than it determined them, tying the success of American policy to those among the moderate forces who were able to take the offensive against the Communists in the union field. It was Antonini, the American most in agreement with the nonsectarian anti-Communist groups, who succinctly summed up the American lack of understanding for PSLI and PRI decisions not to join the Christian Democratic withdrawal and to remain in the CGIL: "Frankly, I think you have missed the boat. If you had set your scruples aside and taken your courage in hand, even though a minority, you could have seized the controls of the union movement as it was getting off the ground. . . . I do not understand your reservations about collaboration with the DC. With whom should you collaborate?"[83]

The ironbound confrontation of the Cold War was entering and influencing fields of choice that were apparently more restricted and minimal. While the long crisis of the WFTU was sliding toward its traumatic conclusion, the reasons for the break and the opposition to the Communists became the main, if not the only, standard for American sympathy and support. For groups and institutions like the leaders of the AFL or the Department of State, which looked mostly, if not totally, to the political goal of curtailing Soviet and Communist party influence, an alliance was initiated when action had to be taken with those who not only wanted the break but brought it about. The CIO later judged the Catholic withdrawal as premature, inopportune, and excessively political, but in the judgment of the moment it was enthusiastically greeted as one of the many indications, together with the crisis of the WFTU, that the struggle against the Communists was beginning to reap success.[84]

In the field of Italian history, the influence of the United States on the breakup of the unitary CGIL—aside from the obvious observation that the split originated from the tensions of the Cold War—has from time to time been exaggerated or minimized.[85] The breakup of the CGIL is part of much more than the history of the relations between Italy and the United States, and it is in relation to events in Italy that it should be evaluated, especially if one looks beyond the split to the global confrontation that pitted industrial interests and government power against the class conflict trade unionism of the CGIL and the forces of the left.[86] The American interest, however, was so constant and active as to constitute a significant factor. Given the importance of the close interaction of international polarization with domestic social and political divisions, the American influence on trade union affairs can be evaluated with sufficient precision. In the first place, the promotion of the Marshall Plan broke every barrier between the polarizing events of the Cold War and the political confrontation within the unions, in Italy as in other West European countries. All the unions and political organizations were directly invested, with no mediation, in the responsibility for a choice for or against the Marshall Plan, which at the same time included socioeconomic, political, and strategic themes. It was therefore impossible to distinguish economic policy views from geopolitical location, or specifically trade union choices from international loyalties. The call to line up politically with the United States or with the USSR fell unavoidably on every union organization, bringing about a clear dichotomy—as proposed by American policy—between pro-Western and pro-Soviet forces. In the first place, the Marshall Plan offered the prospect of economic growth and a bargaining role—to negotiate the benefits of productivity—that from the union viewpoint had an undoubted and important attractive force. In the second place, the campaign for "free" trade unions launched against the WFTU by the AFL, and from 1947 on by the State Department, also strengthened the anti-Communist side in the convulsive process of postwar union affairs. In the Marshall Plan it found a solid rallying point and a political and economic prospect that joined antitotalitarianism with an institutional and negotiating model for reinforcing the union. The formation of a union grouping in support of the ERP prefigured the establishment of a new international, in this way offering a reference point for the minorities in the CGIL, unifying their political action, and giving an official character to the AFL's activities in their support.

The descent of the American government into the arena against the WFTU elevated the membership of trade unions in international federations to a primary ideological and geopolitical issue in every European country. All of American society, from government to industry and the large unions, was proposed as a model of prosperity in democracy. The anti-Communist forces in the CGIL thus found not only material support, but also alliances, international legitimation, promises of expansion, and suggestions for a new scope and union identity. From the London conference on, Pastore, Canini, and Parri, leaders of the minorities, became within the CGIL the representatives of the alliance of Western unions and governments, the bearers of a wider political plan that was incomparably stronger than their respective union factions. The impulse to and the possibility of opposing the CGIL to the point of rupture, in the name of a global alternative, were greatly invigorated. Finally, from the winter of 1947–48 on, the CGIL became one of the prime targets of American operations. The Department of State, the AFL, and, to a lesser extent, the CIO gave the greatest encouragement and assistance to a break in the Communist hegemony of the unitary federation. That this would be accomplished through a split was the obvious wish of both the AFL and the American government. It was equally clear, however, that carrying out this aim depended on choices and decisions by Italian parties and union leaders who were largely independent, rather than influenced by American pressure. The effective breakup of the CGIL in July 1948 was brought on by those among the United States allies who had their own political and union agenda, greater independence and autonomy, as well as their own strength. On the contrary, those like the PSLI, who were culturally closer and materially more tied to American influence, especially trade union circles, remained nevertheless in the CGIL—though for only a short while—even when strong indications to the contrary were coming from Washington. American policy interacted with the Italian political and trade union battle in ways that were often effective but sometimes without influence. If America's strategic, ideological, and political and economic weight on the global scene was very great, its capacity for direct control of Italian events and decisions was rather reduced.

A Single, Large Anti-Communist Union

The Catholic withdrawal from the CGIL and the resulting formation of the Free Italian General Confederation of Labor on 16 October 1948 drastically changed the situation. The American embassy, in addition to committed support for Pastore, the secretary of the new confederation, was obliged to update its tactics and redraft an action program for its relations with the new union movement, in order to reconcile the basic aims of American policy toward the conflicts, complications, and tendencies to political struggle in Italy. The process of forming the new union was under way, but the Social Democrats and the Republicans took no part in it, nor was there any sign that their disagreement with the Christian Democrats was abating. The secretary of the PSLI, Alberto Simonini, said of the LCGIL that it "smells from afar of the sacristy." Faravelli argued with Antonini that the LCGIL was "neither free or independent," for which reason "it was not worthwhile to leave the Communists high and dry in order to become Pastore's sacristans and bell-ringers." Only by staying in the CGIL could they attempt to bring the Socialists together again and "take the masses away from the Communists and rebuild an entirely free political (socialist) and trade union movement."[87] The leaders of the new confederation said they were confident that the lay minorities in CGIL would sooner or later come into their organization, and Pastore was careful to avoid any action that would confirm the widespread perception of a LCGIL subjected to the church and the government.[88]

In the embassy, the ideological reasons for the disagreement did not enjoy much consideration. The fact that the Social Democrats and the Republicans stayed in the CGIL was ascribed to their "opportunistic desire to ride the fastest moving and largest band wagon." As soon as the LCGIL was consolidated enough to constitute a genuine alternative to the CGIL, they would withdraw and join the "free" confederation. The embassy based its operational plan on this premise: "The ultimate objective is the creation of a national non-Communist, non-political, non-sectarian labor organization in Italy. The immediate objective is convincing the Moderate Socialists and the Republicans that they should withdraw from the CGIL and join in such a movement or union." The way was shown by the political formations gathering around the ERP. As a new international was taking shape in Paris around the ERP-TUAC, in Italy it was necessary to bring together the LCGIL leaders and those of the nonsectarian minorities of the CGIL in a similar consultative committee for the ERP, which would collaborate with the government and the ERP mission in Rome and, above all, would serve to attract the trade unionists in the PSLI and PRI away from the CGIL. With the "moral and material support" of the Italian government and the American unions, the committee was to publish an anti-Communist newspaper for the workers. The funds, however, were to be transmitted to Pastore alone, at least as long as the non-sectarians stayed in the CGIL. This was a stratagem that "will quickly impress on them the desirability of making the break."[89]

The program was the same as the AFL's, which requested the unification of all the non-Communist forces and prepared for an official visit by Pastore, Canini, and Parri to the United States.[90] Both the American leaders and Pastore aimed first of all for favorable public recognition. Contacts with British and American trade unions and their common base in the ERP would bring the LCGIL leaders closer to the idea of collective bargaining. The idea of a struggle against totalitarianism and the more specific trade union goal of pluralistic negotiation within an expansive economic cycle—in a framework of productivist collaboration between government, industry, and unions—seemed to offer a role model to the newly established confederation. Barely a month after the LCGIL was founded, Pastore stated that he looked to the example of the AFL, the CIO, and the TUC, "where militant Catholics, Protestants, and Socialists work together for the defense of workers' interests outside of any political influence. This form of trade unionism, independent of every party and every government, is our highest aspiration."[91] While the crisis in the WFTU was coming to a head and observers were already looking to the next anti-Communist trade union international, both the AFL and the CIO sent official messages of solidarity and promises of assistance to Pastore.[92]

On 22 December 1948 the ERP's consulting committee on union affairs began meeting. Its members included Lane and ECA officials as well as Pastore, Canini, and Parri. Its operations consisted mostly of promoting "free" trade unions and the ERP among the workers. At the beginning of 1949, Lane reported to Washington that the LCGIL was a consolidated, continuously developing organization, with nearly a million members and led by a national board "of high quality." It had not yet been able to attract the Social Democrats or the Republicans to its ranks, but there was reason to hope that would come about in the not too distant future.[93]

The breakup of the WFTU in January 1949 opened the way for the formation of a "free," anti-Communist international trade union federation on the outlines of the union group established around the ERP. For the AFL the formation of a united non-Communist union in Italy was an important symbolic step in that direction. If "free" trade unionism was able to prevail over the CGIL and CGT in Italy and France, the battle against the Soviets on a world scale had begun with better chances of success. A strong "free" Italian confederation, furthermore, would constitute a useful ally for the AFL within the new international. Pastore was among the most convinced advocates of forming this new confederation at once. It would support the legitimation of the LCGIL and probably facilitate the withdrawal from the CGIL and the realignment of the nonsectarian minorities.[94] Both the unions and the United States government intended to move rapidly to consolidate the pro-Western group that came together in the course of 1948. The reunification of the non-Communist forces in Italy represented one of the essential elements of such a design. In Rome, Lane began to see some possibility of success. Simonini said he was convinced that the Social Democrats should in any case withdraw from the CGIL and unite at a later date with the LCGIL, but in the transition period they were to establish a third confederation. Financial resources were lacking, however, and according to the embassy, so was the necessary courage to withdraw from the CGIL.[95] Lane, the ECA mission, and the leaders of the AFL thought the moment had come to pressure the Social Democrats. Direct collaboration on the ERP committee provided a basis for an agreement between the lay factions remaining in the CGIL and the LCGIL. It was a question of carefully calibrating pressure and encouragement to persuade the PSLI and PRI leaders to cease further delay. The ECA thought that a visit to the United States by Pastore, Canini, and A. Claudio Rocchi, a Republican, as representatives of the ERP's consulting committee on union affairs, would provide the ideal atmosphere and stimulus to induce them to agreement and joint action. Pressure from American trade unionists, promises of aid, direct contact with American reality, as well as constant attention from government officials, would break down the last reservations on the part of the Italians.[96]

The trip, which began on 10 March and ended on 12 April, brought the three union leaders, with Lane always in tow, to numerous industries and union headquarters, with a tight schedule of meetings culminating in a short call on President Truman. The three were especially impressed by the combination of political freedom and material well-being in America, by the technical and bargaining capabilities of the unions, and by the efficiency of a system of industrial relations based on collaboration for productivity. They came back with a message and a model to propagate. "The United States is undoubtedly at the forefront of social progress and the standard of living of American workers is the highest in the world, morally and materially."[97] More important, they returned with a secret, detailed agreement to move quickly toward unification. On 12 April Secretary of State Acheson informed the embassy in Rome: "During visit US and Canada Pastore, Canini, Rocchi reached preliminary agreement form united free labor federation. . . . In talks with Antonini and Baldanzi before leaving US April 9 they obtained tentative approval this plan. . . . Plan calls for PSLI and Republicans leave CGIL by end June, merge with LCGIL by November, using intervening months for local reorganization and other preparations. Department pleased with plan but regrets schedule slow."[98] Lane had stimulated and presumably mediated an agreement which amounted to the financial support promised by the AFL to carry the operation out rapidly. In succeeding weeks, the FTUC began to send the first payments.[99]

At first the plan drafted in the United States seemed to go smoothly. In Italy, PRI trade union officials, after a referendum among their members, left the CGIL in May. The Social Democrats, although continuously divided by internal disagreements, left the CGIL following the violent incidents with Communist workers and the police which occurred on 17 May at the chamber of labor of Molinella, where the PSLI had the majority. On 4 June, Republicans and Social Democrats established the Italian Labor Federation (FIL). Antonini promised maximum support, "now that the die is cast." The embassy, noting that the new federation was soon to merge with the LCGIL, reported to Washington: "FIL is highly desirable new comer on Italian scene and should be given every possible encouragement."[100] Brown arrived in Rome at the end of June and took up with Lane the implementation of the plan worked out in America for the prompt unification of the LCGIL and the FIL. In the meantime, the independent union leaders in the PSI, Italo Viglianesi, Renato Bulleri, and Enzo Dalla Chiesa, had left the party and the CGIL and began talks on joining the FIL. Canini and Parri, secretaries of the new federation, preferred to avoid this, both for the sake of their own influence and from the fear that it would postpone the planned fusion with the LCGIL, if not cause it to fail. Brown also promised to help the autonomists when they had reached an agreement with the FIL and embraced the idea of joining Pastore promptly.[101]

But serious complications began to arise over the summer. The FIL leaders were complaining about the continuous pressure from Brown and Lane to speed up the merger; the promised aid was slow in coming; and both the FTUC and the ECA, in a chaotic succession of conditions and petty extortions, seemed bent on pushing a still weak and disorganized FIL into the arms of Pastore, whose organization was already consolidated and much more numerous. The disagreements became rancorous and mistrustful: "They want to prevent us from getting under way, they want to choke off our movement to prevent us from dealing as equals. . . . Do they think we're some poor clowns that jump to the bosses' daily whims?"[102] At the end of July Brown was able to convince Canini and Parri to establish a committee with Pastore to set up the merger. The AFL and the Department of State wanted solid assurances that it would be complete in early fall before the founding congress of the new international, to which Washington attributed great political importance.[103] In Rome, Lane took into his own hands the embassy and the ECA mission contacts with the Italian trade unionists. Together with Brown and the FTUC leaders, with whom he shared both the anti-Communist bent and a hasty, very undiplomatic way of operating, Lane intervened none too subtly in the negotiations between the Italian union leaders. With a bias toward Pastore, whose firmness and vigor they appreciated most of all, Brown and Lane would tolerate no delays in the unification process arising from reservations in Socialist and Social Democratic circles. They thought these reservations were founded on a myopic perception of the trade union movement and were based on the interests of the parties. If their goal was a united, formally nonpolitical union federation, a weapon above all in the battle against communism, then the concerns of the PSLI for the Socialist area, or the mistrust of the laymen for the preponderance of the Christian Democrats, seemed to them to be mere obstacles on the chosen path, barriers to be knocked down without much hesitation or fine language.[104]

The agreement reached in America among Pastore, Canini, and Rocchi found the most opposition among the autonomist Socialists and the FIL itself. Some wanted more time to strengthen themselves and negotiate with Pastore on a basis of equality; others contended that only a nonsectarian and Socialist union federation could induce a significant number of members to leave the CGIL. With the exceptions of Canini and Rocchi, the small array of union forces the Americans would have liked to reunite with the LCGIL all thought that the schedule dictated by the financiers from overseas was too tight. This resistance was supported in America by Vanni Montana, Antonini's right hand in the IALC. Montana was closely tied to the Italian Social Democrats and severely criticized Brown's activities, especially the decision to give Pastore and the LCGIL a privileged position. The leaders of the AFL, however, had no intention of setting their program aside. Irving Brown saw the possibility of success in the anti-Communist struggle only in unification: "Those who oppose trade union organization or unification because of political or religious reasons are going to find themselves eventually without any mass following." Lovestone suspected that the resistance derived from competing plans, not to join LCGIL, but to oppose it: "Unless, of course, our friends have the notion that they can go into competition with a third federation. If they have such notions, they are dead wrong. The AFL is not interested in organizing and supporting a mass of competing organizations in Italy or anywhere else." Vanni Montana was brusquely reined in—"Cut out your 'behind-the-scenes' operations and intrigues against the AFL policy in Italy"—but the problems were anything but solved.[105] On 8 September 1949 in Rome, the leaders of the LCGIL, the FIL, and the autonomist Socialist group met in greatest secrecy with Brown and Lane. The FTUC threatened to cut off aid if reunification were not decided upon by November. The FIL and the LCGIL agreed to hold their respective congresses by that date, with a motion for merger that the two federations were to formally vote on. But the autonomist Socialists rejected the agreement because they were opposed to merger with the LCGIL. A few days later they published an appeal for the establishment of an independent trade union organization.[106]

The disagreements, which had been kept under wraps up to this point, suddenly burst into the public eye. On Montana's suggestion, the American Socialist leader Norman Thomas complained to the State Department about American operations geared to "force prematurely an artificial unity," since they actually brought about the opposite result, "a new split among anti-totalitarian unionists," thus strengthening the Communists. The Social Democratic organ *l'Umanità*, for which Montana was a correspondent, published the news conspicuously, precipitating a scandal and setting off a storm of controversy in Italy as well.[107] Out in the open and shot through with an array of accusations, the operation conceived by Brown and Lane was compromised. The postponement of unification was inevitable. The Department of State, seriously embarrassed by Lane's role, which involved the United States government directly, advised more prudence and secrecy at the embassy in Rome. The AFL was advised to cease its pressure until calm was restored. For the State Department, the reason for the scandal and the failure of unification was to be found in the attempt—which British Labour party members supported—to promote Socialist unification between the PSLI and the autonomist Socialists. The Italian Social Democrats believed that this operation had priority over the drafting of union alliances. In spite of all this, the State Department repeated that "with or without socialist political unification, early Italian non-Communist trade union unity is desirable."[108]

Luigi Antonini, embarrassed before the AFL leaders, distanced himself from Montana's operations and complained that the funds sent to Italy, nearly $200,000, had not achieved the desired results. Montana was peremptorily ordered not to involve himself further in FTUC operations in Italy. Norman Thomas made up with the AFL, stating that he had never wanted to criticize its foreign activities. On the American side at least, the incident was nearly closed and the controversy simmered down.[109] Lovestone, who was furious at the Italian and American Socialists, to whom he attributed responsibility for the failure, stated that the FTUC would let the Italians fend for themselves from then on. The Italian American Augusto Bellanca of the CIO, who had thought it a mistake to break off from the CGIL, advised the Department of State to avoid pressure and interference, give up the idea of unification, and support joint action among the various non-Communist Italian trade union organizations. In a careful retrospective analysis, the State Department blamed the failure on underestimating the importance of political traditions and party groupings in Italian unions and, to a lesser extent, to the fact that the agreements were limited to the leadership of the organizations concerned, without sufficient preparation to make it possible to carry them out.[110]

But in Italy the problem persisted. At the end of October, the embassy in Rome made a substantially positive assessment of the trade union situation, without departing from the line it had been following up to then: "During last year important strides have been made by non-Communist Italian Labor groups toward development of independent anti-Communist Trade Unionism. Such Unionism in long run should make important contributions to political and social stability by breaking Communist stranglehold on Italian Labor movement, providing workers with energetic non-Communist champions and improving workers often grievous economic lot. Achievement these objectives would probably be facilitated by unification all non-Communist Labor organizations, particularly, FIL and LCGIL." This could not be achieved immediately, but it remained a goal for the not too distant future. What was important was for the LCGIL to expand. To the embassy the federation showed no sign of being dependent on the DC. But the weak and uncertain FIL received little consideration.[111]

Paradoxically, the temporary failure of the attempt at unification served only to further reinforce the convictions, prejudices, and traditional preferences of both the embassy and the AFL. Pastore and the LCGIL were earning more confidence on the part of the Americans for their clarity of intentions, organizational strength, and affinity of views on political and trade union matters. The FIL was weak, and the autonomist Socialist forces seemed even weaker. In any event, the small amount of confidence that Lane and Brown previously had in them had completely disappeared by this time. The future of the anti-Communist trade union movement in Italy was, more than ever, entrusted to the LCGIL. In the first days of November it held its first national congress, which officially marked the new organization's appearance on the Italian trade union scene. Pastore's idea for an anti-Communist trade union movement, geared to integration in Europe and the West, closely coordinated with the ERP, and attentive to making labor's claims compatible with the national interests set by the government, was triumphantly affirmed. The embassy commented enthusiastically; Brown, for the AFL, greeted the congress with warm praise.[112] The ICFTU came into being only a month later, on 9 December, ratifying American leadership in the Western trade union movement. For the Department of State, the new international would move "along U.S. policy lines." In American official and trade union circles an extraordinary optimism was spreading for a situation that represented "an event of historic importance, in many respects the most significant development in the struggle for a free world," according to the *New York Times*. Pastore obtained significant recognition when, with AFL and CIO support, he was elected to the ICFTU executive council. On his return to Italy, the secretary of the LCGIL had greater influence, strengthened as he was by the solidity of his relations with the American allies. To officials of the embassy in Rome, "he was proud to be able to say that the LCGIL was the only labor union in Europe which followed completely the American concept of trade unionism."[113]

The founding of the ICFTU began again the unification of Italian non-Communist trade unionism, although on a more restricted basis. In the first days of December, the autonomist Socialists established the new Unitary Socialist party (PSU) under the leadership of Giuseppe Romita. In addition, a group of trade unionists led by Italo Viglianesi opted definitively for an independent confederation, given the failure of negotiations with the FIL. That organization's leaders, even at the cost of clashes with their political parties, especially the PRI, decided to merge with the LCGIL. Together with Pastore, they agreed with the AFL leaders in London on a new calendar for the merger of the two organizations, finally gaining the confidence and the aid of the American trade unionists. On 15 December a joint committee, the FIL-LCGIL, decided to call the congresses of the two federations, obtain the approval of a unification plan, and proceed to merger within two months.[114] The American embassy also supported the plan with satisfaction. Though there was no lack of internal opposition, the FIL congress of 5–6 February 1950 approved the unification proposal, as did the general council of the LCGIL ten days later.[115] This merger gave rise on 1 May 1950 to the CISL. The autonomist trade unionists, together with dissidents from the FIL, established the Italian Workers' Union (UIL) in March. The Italian trade union movement was taking the shape it was to hold for the entire postwar period.[116]

The CISL was greeted by a wide range of American opinion as the anti-Communist, independent, and nonpolitical union federation for which they had been working since 1948. The AFL, the IALC, and the Department of State had complete confidence in Pastore's leadership and looked on the CISL as "the final consolidation of free trade unions in Italy." They were especially reassured by the political and economic program of the new confederation. Lane referred with satisfaction to the collective bargaining viewpoint with which the CISL looked on industrial relations, rejecting the class struggle in the name of social pluralism and productivist cooperation among the parties. He also described how Pastore's vision favoring European integration and a continental market with free exchanges was close to the basic lines of American foreign policy, especially the ERP. George Meany met in Rome with Pastore, Canini, and Parri, promising them maximum assistance from the AFL, while Brown and Lane made an extensive trip to CISL locals, receiving an impression of a vigorous, determined organization progressing rapidly. The CIO too, although it had had a marginal and uninfluential role in American activities in favor of unification, greeted the advent of the CISL with praise of its unitary character and productivist spirit.[117] In the middle of 1950 the long, tortuous activities of the State Department and the AFL seemed to have achieved their goals: the CGIL's monopoly in union affairs had been broken;

"free" trade unionism was solidly organized and integrated into the Western camp as represented by the ICFTU; and the ERP had a trustworthy contact in the social sphere most crucial for its success, that of labor.

But problematic and somber aspects were not lacking. In the first place, there were two non-Communist, pro-Western trade union federations rather than a single unified organization, less subject to political domination, that was under American auspices. The UIL, although of less influence than the other two confederations, did exist and sought a collaborative relationship with the ECA and the American unions, referring internationally to the ICFTU. But these affinities were not enough, in the early 1950s, to overcome the residue of hostility and suspicion, of mistrust more than any real political differences, that had been inherited from the twisted process of splits and reunifications that characterized the period from 1948 to 1950. The AFL for years followed a policy of privileged relations with the CISL and of extreme coolness to the UIL. For two years the American federation opposed the UIL's admission into the ICFTU in a vain effort to force it to merge with Pastore's CISL. Even at the end of 1951 when, in spite of strenuous opposition from the CISL and the AFL, the ICFTU finally voted the affiliation of the UIL, the American federation did not cease its pressures for merger with the CISL. In the State Department the idea was often brought up, in the first years of the 1950s, of extending the same recognition and assured support that was given to the CISL. But in the Rome embassy Lane continued to operate in close coordination with the AFL leaders and repeatedly blocked these attempts, contending that only Pastore should be supported since a reinforcement of the UIL would bring on political and religious polarization in the non-Communist trade union movement. Lane's hostility to the UIL came both from his deep mistrust of its leaders and from his hope that American ostracism would finally force it to unite in a subordinate position with the CISL. On the other hand, the CIO, which was less involved in establishing the CISL, soon came to the defense of the UIL, first within the ICFTU. It established a collaborative relationship that had its roots in the Social Democratic sympathies of some CIO leaders and their desire to promote a more progressive and militant non-Communist trade union in Italy than the CISL, which the CIO felt was too subordinated to the government's economic interests.[118] And so the competitive divisions of the non-Communist trade union movement were reflected in the American movement, with neither the Department of State nor the AFL succeeding in their unrealistic attempts to transcend the traditions and political bases of the Italian trade union movement to achieve a unified and nonpolitical organization of all the forces of labor that rejected collaboration with the Communists.

In the second place, even though the "free" trade union movement was now an organized reality, the signs of the improvement that it should have brought about in industrial relations and on the social scene were not apparent. There were no indications of effective scope for that reinforcement in the economic and bargaining areas to which many of the American hopes for victory in the anti-Communist struggle had been entrusted. Pastore himself expressed disappointment at the rigidity with which the economic policies of Italian treasury minister Giuseppe Pella pursued the balancing of the budget. Pella conceded no margin for reabsorbing unemployment, or for delays in beginning agrarian reform. The government and CONFINDUSTRIA appeared to prefer a frontal clash from a position of strength, with strikes promoted by the CGIL, over a negotiated settlement of matters through the LCGIL and then the CISL. The incidents at Modena of 9 January 1950, when police fired on workers, demonstrated tragically that in the face of violent social conflict and the intransigence of industry, the government was unable or unwilling to begin a serious policy of social conciliation. The American desire to see an agency of reform and bargaining develop in the working classes found no fulfillment in the realities of social conflict in Italy.[119] Both the AFL and the American government had cultivated hopes of miraculously achieving a complete reversal of the Italian situation, first in the plans to split the CGIL, and then in the construction of a "free" trade union federation. The exaggerated, and sometimes terrorized, fears at the possible subversive success of the CGIL, united as it was under Communist hegemony, alternated with the conviction that a "free" trade union federation would bring about peaceful social relations free from ideological and political tensions and would thereby exorcise the specter of class conflict and communism.[120] But the first steps of this non-Communist trade union movement that had been so stubbornly desired and attended to were taken in an atmosphere of frustrating disappointment of the American expectations.

The European Recovery Program:

Toward a New Model of

Society and Trade Unions

With ERP aid a new phase was inaugurated in 1948 of more intensive and extended American commitment for the economic and political stabilization of Western Europe. In the direction defined by the containment strategy, the Foreign Assistance Act—passed by Congress on 31 March 1948—established the principles, goals, and operative criteria for the aid program announced ten months earlier by Secretary of State George Marshall. The ERP originated under the banner of an explicit connection between political and economic ends: "The Congress finds that the existing situation in Europe endangers the establishment of a lasting peace, the general welfare and national interests of the United States, and the attainment of the objectives of the United Nations. The restoration or maintenance in European countries of principles of individual liberty, free institutions, and genuine independence rests largely upon the establishment of sound economic conditions, stable international economic relationships, and the achievement by the countries of Europe of a healthy economy independent of extraordinary outside assistance." The economic purposes consisted of the attainment of conditions that would allow consolidation of vital and self-sufficient economies in participating countries within the four years the plan was to be applied, stabilization of currencies and balance of payments, a sharp increase in production and foreign trade, and development of international economic cooperation.[1]

Because of fears of inflationary pressure, the emphasis in the first phase fell on the necessity of normalizing the financial situation, balancing budgets, and stabilizing prices and wages. But overall the operating philosophy of the ERP was decidedly an expansive one, and it looked to the formation of an integrated continent with increased productive and trading capacities. The main effect of ERP aid was to allow higher levels of imports and investments in the participating countries. "At no time was it an objective of E.C.A. policy to produce deflationary policies in Europe. . . . Marshall aid remained throughout a device to permit expansion in Western Europe."[2] The ERP's intrinsic characteristics led to a rise in production levels and productivity and expansion of trade in Europe. A concern to avoid permanent support to European economies had led Congress to set a limit of four years to the aid program and, furthermore, to decrease ERP appropriations steadily, so that each participating country had a strong incentive to achieve independence from American aid by 1952. In this way, both the ECA and the European governments were encouraged to direct aid into new investment so as to increase productive and exporting capacity before the termination of the ERP.[3]

The character and purposes of the ERP were also influenced, however, by other considerations that were not solely economic. The ERP originated in an orderly convergence of different needs: strategic consolidation of the Western sphere, extension of multilateralism and overcoming economic nationalism, integration of Germany in a free-market international area; and lasting social and political stability in participating countries. For this reason it was not directed exclusively at eco-nomic recovery; it also contained more ambitious American goals for a global redefinition of the Western European political and economic order. Through the Marshall Plan the government and social forces of the United States projected into Europe their vision of a unified, productive, and prosperous continental society that, because of pluralist negotiation among social interests, was free from atavistic class conflicts. They did this by calling up the model which American historical experience, especially that of the previous fifteen years, seemed to indicate as a winning combination: "American leaders tried to forge an organic economic order in Europe. The new order would be balanced between a paternalistic statism and the old capitalism, would be tied together by market forces and institutional coordi-nators, and would be founded on economic interdependence and supranational-ism, American mass-production techniques, and American labor-management programs for a productive abundance in which all could share. A similar order had supposedly cleared a path to social harmony and affluence in the United States. And once in operation, or so the Americans believed, it would also lead to a new era of peace and plenty on the Continent."[4]

It was no coincidence that the similarity with the Second World War was frequently brought up during the months of intense debate on the purposes and means of aid to Europe, not only through the frequent comparison of the Soviet antagonist with Nazi totalitarianism, but also through the constant reference to productive growth and the integration of social interest and government achieved in America during the Second World War. What the United States had done between the New Deal and the war was what was now proposed for Western Europe and was what the New Deal liberals and the industrial and union leaders hoped for. These groups in the early 1940s had been protagonists of corporatist negotiation in a growing economy, and in the spring of 1948 they were eager to manage the exportation of that socioeconomic recipe into the Europe of the Cold War.[5] The American experience suggested a system of deradicalization and of recasting the industrial conflict based on voluntary collaboration in productivity growth and on the distribution of its benefits by means of free bargaining among the social parties. Motivated by the need of moving union representation away from Communist influence and of bringing forward social consensus as an aid to stabilization, the ERP stressed both a political realignment and a theoretical and strategic review of the European trade union movement, with a goal of recasting the old continent's industrial relations system along the lines of productivity. The ERP's operating agency, the ECA, itself represented many social interests, in this way investing not only financial resources but conceptual and organizational ideas of American society. The collaboration of the AFL and the CIO with the ECA expanded the boundaries of the campaign for a "free" trade union movement beyond the narrow ideological frontiers of anticommunism to include economic issues and concerns of collective bargaining more characteristic of a trade union, in the attempt to educate European trade unions in the expansive philosophy and negotiatory propensity of the American ones. The operations of the American government and the unions—merged in the ECA's pluralistic composition—met, not without conflict, in the effort to link the economic stabilization of Western Europe with the regeneration of its union policies and industrial relations. The campaign for productivity that the ERP undertook throughout Europe, but with special vigor in countries like France and Italy where social and political stability looked more fragile, was a substantial attempt to export American techniques and solutions under the banner of social modernization. But its success was only partial and, especially in the union field, it ended up a semifailure, as shown in the extreme but not entirely anomalous case of Italy. This failure shows how, in the interaction between Europe and America and in the priorities set by the various governments, the goals of an American-style modernization were subordinated, at least in this brief period, to the imperatives of political stability, to the continuation of national traditions and strategies, and to an economic growth that in the early 1950s could not yet deliver mass-consumption prosperity.

The ECA and the Unions

Congress established the ECA as a temporary and independent agency, separated from the federal government's permanent bureaucracy, guided by management criteria, and closely tied to economic and technical principles in its implementation of the ERP. The emphasis was on both public and private interests, since the agency was based on the use of the human resources and knowledge held by the industrial, financial, social, and technical sectors of American society. Also, its foreign operations were to develop international private channels of commercial and technological exchanges and organizational and educational collaboration. ECA headquarters in Washington, the Paris office of the special representative in Europe, and the various missions in each country were to recruit personnel with specific skills and make use of qualified consultants from the private sector. Congress itself gave the clearest example of this direction when it nominated Paul Hoffman as director of the agency. He had been a successful manager in the automobile industry, with long experience collaborating with the government. Like James Zellerbach, head of the mission in Italy, and many others, Hoffman represented the industrial circles that were most open to a genuinely pluralistic view of collaboration between interest groups, and which had experimented with the most advanced labor relations schemes. Assisting Hoffman and Averell Harriman, the special representative in Europe, was a large staff coming from business, banking, the professions, and research institutes. They were placed both in the functional sections into which the ECA was divided (industry, finance, technical assistance, etc.) and in central management positions. The ECA, moreover, operated on advice supplied by consulting committees that included representatives of the main social interests. Chief among these was the Public Advisory Board, which cooperated with the agency's headquarters and where George Meany of the AFL and James Carey of the CIO represented the unions. Thus the operating guidelines and the structure of the ECA reflected the mechanisms of corporatist integration that had long been practiced in American society.[6]

In this framework the collaboration between the ECA and the American union organizations took on a special value. The complete success of the ERP required explicit and vigorous support from the labor movements in the participating European countries. For promotion of anti-Communist social consensus and economic stabilization of Western Europe, not to mention the goal of redefining the continent's political economy in a productivist direction, it was indispensable to have the active participation of the unions in ERP. With the ERP conference on union affairs and the establishment of ERP-TUAC, the first decisive step had been taken to bring the European unions closer to the Marshall Plan. The most efficient instrument for obtaining union consent to the ERP was found logically in the American unions. If AFL and CIO support had been important in assisting the ERP through Congress and for its popularity in public opinion, their involvement became crucial when the ECA was founded. Only the participation of American trade unionists could assure in some way that the ERP would not work to the disadvantage of labor, countering Soviet propaganda about an "imperialist Wall Street plot" and aiding the "free" unions where the clash on the plan was tearing the union movement apart. There was thus an impelling political need to associate the American unions with the ECA and with the whole plan to aid Western Europe.[7]

The leaders of the AFL and CIO insistently requested to be represented in the administration of a plan on which they had based a good part of their international operations. The CIO had even based some of its strategic decisions for its political stance and its internal power balances on this involvement. The AFL's anti-Communist campaign in the international union movement was finally beginning to make itself felt due to the realignment of the European trade union movement that the ERP had stimulated. For the CIO leaders, the rapprochement with the Truman administration was the determining factor in its now public clash with its own left wing. Furthermore, both federations saw in the ERP an instrument to reinforce their presence abroad, to increase assistance to "free" trade unions, and to bolster their ambitions to take the leadership of the international trade union movement. Finally, the AFL and, even more, the CIO both saw in their direct, and possibly influential, participation in the administration of the ERP the possibility of moving it toward views more favorable to the economic interests of the European workers. The union leaders thought the ERP should be directed toward increasing wages, giving incentives to union bargaining, expanding not only investment but also consumption and social spending, and pursuing stabilization through prosperous and dynamic growth. They believed that these goals and aspirations should be those of the ERP, which they interpreted in the light of their own confidence in the potential of "industrial democracy." If the ECA appeared as a microcosm of bargaining pluralism as it had developed in American society, it seemed indispensable, in the eyes of the most convinced union interpreters of that model, to have their negotiating role in its projection abroad as well.[8]

The convergence of these needs led to the recruitment of many trade unionists in the ECA. The collaboration between unions and government in foreign policy, which had been initiated in the Department of Labor and in frequent talks at the State Department, was expanded, in an extended and formalized version, in the administration of the Marshall Plan. Paul Hoffman called Bert Jewell of the AFL and Clinton Golden of the CIO to Washington as advisers on union affairs. Golden, because of his experience in the American mission in Greece and his technical and practical activities over an extended period promoting collaborative and productivist labor relations, was undoubtedly the more important. In the European office in Paris, a labor division was established under the direction of Boris Shishkin of the AFL, while responsibility for publicity directed at labor was entrusted to Harry Martin, president of the journalists' union and representative of the CIO. Several other trade unionists were sent to American missions as consultants on union affairs, information attachés, or for liaison with local workers' associations.[9] The primary task of the union offices of the ECA was political and propagandistic: to explain the value of the Marshall Plan to the European workers and unions, to promote knowledge of the methods of American trade unionism, and to counter propaganda that was hostile to the ERP. It was a matter of organizing publicity campaigns on the freedom and comfort of the American way of life. These activities, from the end of 1948, had been particularly conspicuous because of a special fund appropriated by Congress. The labor division and the two American federations were assigned management of visits by European trade unionists to the United States to study productive ideas, systems of industrial mediation and collaboration, and the techniques of collective bargaining and union organizing in America.[10]

Even though concerned principally with the ERP's immediate political impact on the anti-Communist realignment of the European trade union movement, both the AFL and the CIO and part of the ECA bureaucracy soon began to take an interest in the profound effects the plan could have on the economic and social order in participating countries. Believing that unions that were strong at the bargaining table and close to the mechanisms of government would be the main basis for democratic stability, the leaders of the AFL and CIO looked on the ERP as a powerful instrument to spread their own conception of "industrial democracy" in Europe. The European representatives of the two federations were consulted by the Department of Labor about the policy to follow in German reconstruction. They recommended reinforcement of the unions and extension of collective bargaining to initiate a close collaboration on social affairs directed to growth and democratization of the economy, from business firms to the highest economic policy decision-making levels. A systematic collaboration between industry, unions, and government would exert democratic control over German reconstruction: "This is the only approach that offers a hope of preventing either the old employing class or a new state-managerial class alliance from shaping Germany into a new totalitarian force."[11]

At the second trade union conference on ERP, the American delegates solicited the full participation of the unions in formulating and managing the recovery policies that the ERP would stimulate, both on the national and the continental level, through close consultation between the ECA, the OEEC, and the ERP-TUAC. Only the active participation of the unions in implementing the ERP could direct its operations to the development of that "economy of abundance" which the American trade unionists thought should be the ultimate aim of the program. The unions would have to accept temporary sacrifices, but the implementation of the ERP should lead, by means of multinational integration, to the reconstruction of Europe's economy "in conformity with the wishes and aspirations of the people," that is, by assuring the workers "a fuller and more abundant life."[12] At ECA headquarters, Clinton Golden studied ways of having the ERP bring about a greater integration of the workers and convert increased economic efficiency into an increase in their wages. With a characteristic reflection of American experience, he indicated that the basic direction would be an improvement of productivity and cooperation between labor and management. The opportunity which the ERP offered to the unions was that of an efficient modernization of industrial relations. In the summer of 1948, the British government and Paul Hoffman began the first important initiative in this field, founding the Anglo-American Council on Productivity, an organization where representatives of industry and unions in the two countries would compare the systems of production used by English and American firms, in order to distribute the most efficient technical and organizational devices in Great Britain. The committee, whose founding was chiefly an exercise in public relations in favor of labor-management collaboration, hoped to stimulate the export of American mass production systems, find and solve obstacles to productive organization, and educate unions and management in a productivist philosophy as the ECA intended. Its operations, which extended to 1952, consisted mainly of bringing groups of British economic entrepreneurs and trade unionists to visit American industry and publishing studies and reports on systems for standardizing industrial procedures.[13] At the beginning of 1949, on the wave of this initiative, the ECA established its largest program to raise productive efficiency in all the European countries, the technical assistance program, coordinated by a division of that name within the agency. The program responded to the ambitious goal, fixed in OEEC planning, of raising productivity in participating countries, in four years, by 15 percent over prewar levels of 1938. The program, also dedicated to bringing economic entrepreneurs, technicians, and trade unionists to America to learn the most efficient industrial systems, was based on two premises: to diffuse more productive technologies and organizational systems and to promote better relations between labor and management through collective bargaining.[14]

The philosophy of productivity, intended not only as economic growth but, through that means, as a solution to social conflict and thereby an instrument for political stabilization, was one of the main planks in the entire ERP platform. All the social and institutional forces gathered around the Marshall Plan identified with it. But from the first steps taken by the technical assistance program it was obvious that serious problems would arise for the unions. Technical renewal and the intensification of production would have very serious effects for the workers, especially in countries with high unemployment levels such as Italy and Germany. If the unions were not completely integrated into the program, it would be reduced to mere assistance to businesses to increase the pace of work and the degree of management's control over the workers, clearing the way to a weakening of the union's bargaining position. As the productivity campaign began, the European and American unions tied to the ECA faced a challenge—of which they were partially aware—whose outcome was to depend on the influence they would be able to bring to bear, within the ECA and in negotiations with their respective governments and industrial counterparts, on the policies and methodology by which the ERP was to be implemented.[15]

The ECA and Productivity: Between Stability and Modernization

In the middle of 1949, after a year devoted to putting the organization on its feet, defining projects, and publicizing their worth, the ECA began to formulate its labor policy in relation to the basic aims of the Marshall Plan. It was no longer sufficient to secure the support of the "free" unions and publicize their image in contrast to Communist totalitarianism. The necessary programs had to be drafted for modernizing industrial relations and trade union policies, as an integral part of the restructuring of the continent's economic fabric to which the ECA aspired. A theoretical and practical commitment was necessary to activate "the objectives of ECA in the development of multilateral trade, economic unity in Europe, and the elimination of restrictive practices which have been the pattern of world trade since the war."[16]

The concept of "restrictive practices" did not refer solely to foreign trade. In the ECA's vocabulary the term took on increasingly extensive value and meaning. It came to include all those characteristics of European economies that American policy set out to overcome and reform, through the ERP, in the light of the American model. These characteristics ranged from oligopolistic practices limiting competition to regional and national market fragmentation, from systems of bilateral exchanges to the complex of behavior on the part of industry and labor that checked the spread of low-cost mass production and consumption. In the ECA's scheme of things, "restrictive practices" meant not only political or techni-cal decisions, but the sum total of traditional economic behavior and social attitudes that seemed to hamper growth and delay the spread of prosperity, which was given a key role in achieving stability in the West. The ECA therefore focused on ways of overcoming such obstacles to expansion, and the solutions were found in two principal goals. The first of these was the integration of Western Europe into one large market that would encourage large economies of scale and higher productivity levels, as a first step in the continent's political and economic unifica-tion. The second was to raise productivity levels to assure uninterrupted growth and a constant increase in incomes in all sectors of the society.[17]

The ECA's activities in the trade union field were geared to these primary ends. The labor division was to contribute to "bringing into being a new economic structure." The idea of productivity was thought of as a way of changing histor-ically rooted customs and altering individual and collective attitudes. The first discussions in the Anglo-American Council on Productivity brought out the differing, nearly opposing, casts of mind in the attitudes toward work of an American versus a British—and in general a European—worker. The American looked first to increasing his income; the Englishman, to guaranteeing his security. The American worker was mobile; the British worker was tied to a static idea of society. "The British worker has been immobile. He thinks of himself as a member of the working class. If we talk of increasing productivity, we have to talk about some kind of incentive which will encourage workers to gamble in part, and take a chance with security for the sake of better wages and working conditions." The productivity campaign could not be restricted to technological innovation. It sought to promote a new approach to industrial relations based on collaboration among the parties and to replace the traditional class conflict with an agreement to increase growth. For the unions, this would imply constant attention and pressure so that "the gains from increased productivity in participating countries are broadly shared. If monopolistic practices maintain high prices, low wages and limited production, increased productivity will be of small benefit. Productivity must not become a speed-up device." The labor division worked in three areas. It arranged study trips to American industry; it solicited the greatest possible collaboration between governments, industry, and unions in formulating productivist plans; and it studied projects for retraining workers and for their emigration, to reduce tensions in labor markets where there were wide areas of unemployment— the Italian case being the worst.[18]

In this way the productivity campaign began with ambitious but potentially contradictory, if not incompatible, goals: to stimulate technological investments and organizational innovations, but at the same time to prevent this from degenerating into an increase in work load and a reduction of employment, and to reinforce industry economically and at the same time to induce it to lower prices and to dialogue on an equal footing with unions. There was also hope of replacing adversarial relationships with orderly collective bargaining inspired by the subordination of vested interests to the common ones of stability and growth: "The real advantages of increased production can only be realized if workers and consumers as well as the owners receive their fair share in the benefits resulting from increased productivity." The point of equilibrium was seen in the long run in the possibility of social harmony deriving from a socially balanced distribution of the benefits of growth. If a high degree of opposition originated from scarcity, mass consumption would allow for peaceful negotiations free of ideological overtones. In the short run, confidence was placed in the ECA's capacity to convince governments, businesses, and unions of the advantages of the American productivist model and therefore of the necessity of collaboration.[19]

The labor division and the labor information division were given the task of assuring that the workers and the "free" unions were integrated in the plan, putting them in contact with American unions, furnishing them with propaganda and study materials, and seeing to their association in the ERP management institutions in each country. But the most serious problem was to persuade business and conservative politicians to cooperate with non-Communist unions and to meet the most basic claims of the workers half-way. The union offices in the ECA looked with concern at the economic conditions of the wage earners. The moderation showed up to then by non-Communist leaders began to ebb, especially in France and Italy. Wage demands seemed so essential and so justified that they could no longer be ignored or postponed. The "free" unions "can no longer afford to leave the initiative to the Communists; indeed they must recapture it." Officials in the labor division, in natural solidarity with their European trade union colleagues, suggested that the other side, and the political authorities, should take responsibility for the situation. "Strikes should be reduced to a minimum if employers and governments approach the problem judiciously and realistically. . . . Employers and the governments should recognize that it is a better policy to make reasonable concessions before a strike is called than to make those concessions after a strike has occurred."[20]

But neither in France nor Italy—or even in Germany or Belgium—was the moment right for wage concessions and encouragement to unions, since this was the high point of anti-Communist tension. The same union leaders who had guided the realignment around the ERP were beginning to criticize privately the plan's results. Aid was helping recovery and with it the consolidation of the governments in the face of a weak and sidetracked Communist opposition. The great fear of Western society's collapse had been overcome, but the workers were not getting substantial benefits from economic improvement. Industry and governments were benefiting from expanded production and investment, from the consolidation of public finances and trade, but wages were not increasing and unemployment was still extensive. Even the AFL, which was much more sensitive to the ERP's political priorities, urged a change of course that would obtain for the workers "a just share of the benefits of the economic progress achieved under ERP. Only a reduction in unemployment and an improvement in living standards can guarantee a healthy social peace."[21]

The trade unionists in the ERP-TUAC complained of feeling used since they had obtained agreement for the ERP and given it essential political support but had not received the expected benefits. The plans for investment, the import programs, and the financial policy choices had been decided upon without any real consultation with the unions, which did not have any viable means of turning the situation around. The entire strategy of a non-Communist trade union movement was based on participation in the ERP, and the need for stability ruled out the use of strong adversarial pressure. The basic decision for freeing up trade and integrating European economies was shared in principle by all the members of the ERP-TUAC, but fears for its impact on employment and wages were very strong, especially in view of the unionists' scant influence on decision-making processes at the national and OEEC levels. Reactions varied; some, like the TUC in the United Kingdom, were solidly integrated into the political mechanism of their countries and had confidence in their capacity to negotiate on a national scale. At the opposite end, organizations such as the French Force Ouvrière and the CISL, which were still weak, asked the ECA to pressure their respective governments for greater social equity and close collaboration with the unions. The AFL and CIO representatives repeatedly called on their European counterparts to develop common programs to submit to the OEEC in order to take concrete steps toward integration and to organize nationwide social programs with their own governments to deal with unemployment. But this was something most union confederations had no power to negotiate or impose. The feeling emerging in the ERP-TUAC and the ECA labor offices at the end of 1949 and the beginning of 1950 was one of powerlessness and pessimism.[22]

Within the ECA the largely positive evaluation of two years of operations was accompanied by a will to begin restructuring the European economy before ERP aid terminated. "The Marshall Plan in its first two years has been a dramatic success. Hope has replaced despair in western Europe; new stability and virility have been given democratic institutions; the Communists have suffered one defeat after another. . . . In the second half of the Marshall Plan, we are urging the Europeans to make a substantial start toward correcting their deep-seated economic errors. . . . The context in which we are working today is no longer so much an immediate European emergency; it is a grave and long-term problem of world economic adjustment as a basis for peace and prosperity."[23]

The political priority now became that of reshaping Europe's entire economic framework. American techniques would intervene and correct the "errors" of the "Old World's" economy. The productivity campaign was to launch a comprehensive effort to increase the efficiency of Europe's entire productive structure with the rationalizing stimulation of greater competition. "Objective is to increase volume of man-hour output at lower unit cost, permitting lower unit prices as well as equitable wages, salaries and profits. Important that benefits from increased productivity be thus shared among consumer, labor and industry. . . . Competition is most effective mechanism to assure passing on of benefits of increased productivity to whole economy in form of lower prices." While the missions were to study plans for technological and organizational modernization, consulting as appropriate with businesses and government organizations, the American trade unionists had the task of rebutting the "prevailing conception among European workers that Marshall Plan helps employers but not labor." Permanent productivity centers composed of technicians, public officials, and representatives of industry and labor were set up in each country to direct this huge task of economic and social modernization. The basic political guideline was to assure "maximum participation of labor and management." Collaboration among the three parties was indispensable. Without this, it would be impossible to hold the resulting social tensions in check: "Improved productive efficiency will increase employment in long run, but immediate impact likely to release many workers from existing jobs." The unions, which would bear most of the brunt of these tensions, were requested to reexamine their theoretical and practical baggage in the light of improvements to come and to visit America, on trips arranged by the technical assistance division, to learn the new field of industrial relations.[24] The ECA labor offices, reflecting the concerns of European trade unionists, emphasized the risks of the campaign, fearing in the first place that consumer prices would not fall as rapidly as production costs. They sounded the alarm on the weakness of the social balance of forces: "In our care not to interfere with the governments of the participating countries, we have permitted to develop over the past year a feeling among European workers that the Marshall Plan is being oriented against them and toward the vested interests. . . . We face a grave danger of losing completely the support of European labor *at the worker level*, which is where it counts, even though continuing to hold *lip-service* at the leadership level."[25]

The pluralistic makeup of the ECA was such that the internal discussion proceeded along parallel, noncommunicating lines. While officials in the industry division saw to the application of new forms of technology and to technical retraining in industry, those of the labor division concentrated on the social problems of the campaign. The productivity program was intended to be "directly geared to the maintenance of full employment" and to bring about "an increase in the standard of living." To achieve these goals—which were rather improbable given the high unemployment levels in Italy and Germany—it was recommended that the unions participate fully in the campaign and that industry assume some responsibility for its social aspects. There was no common thread to the discussion, or rather, it was defined a priori by the political and economic imperative of growth. The contradictions of the campaign, and especially its scarce compatibility with the unions' interests, would be countered with a propagandistic effort at persuasion: "Workers must be made to understand that this is not a speed-up program but a program whereby more goods can be produced with less effort." The European unions of the ERP-TUAC, for their part, arrived at a "resolution on European economic reconstruction" that supported the ERP's objective of European integration and an increase in productivity but specified that economic growth must be accompanied by full employment and a more equitable income distribution.[26]

In May 1950 the ECA's discussion of trade union issues reached its apex with two important conferences. The first was in Washington between ECA management and a large group of AFL and CIO leaders. The second, in Paris, gathered the entire personnel of the labor division. The most important point of departure was that the conflict between East and West was being fought first among Europe's workers. "If we fail to win the minds and hearts of Europeans . . . we will have lost this fight." In France, Italy, and, to a lesser extent, Germany—that is, where the political implications of productivity were more urgent—the battle had not yet been won. The absence of a dynamic economic and social plan opened a void in which extremism could thrive, and the governments had not been able to eliminate the workers' adherence to communism. The American planners reacted, characteristically, without questioning the basis of their concept for stabilizing Western Europe. Quite the contrary, they replied to the challenge by reemphasizing the importance of completing those original ERP plans which had not been fully realized in the first two years. It was therefore a matter of forcing the Europeans to accept and apply the solutions dictated by the most recent American experience.

> There is a program, however, that can fill the vacuum and provide the vision around which the free forces of Europe can rally. It is European unification. . . . The ECA program is, briefly, the creation of a single, dynamic, expanding economy in Western Europe, within a larger North Atlantic framework, which could be able to provide rising living standards for all Western Europeans. . . . History has proven that a divided, compartmentalized Europe cannot survive in the modern world. Europe has never caught up with the industrial revolution. . . . Under such conditions, efficient, low-cost mass production and mass consumption cannot exist. . . . A gross disparity between low wages and high profits persists. The strength of the economy is therefore sapped not only by low, inefficient production, but also by the most inequitable distribution of income.

Only expansion, only a bigger pie, could ward off social antagonism about its division. Only integration could lead to prosperity. A program to restructure the European economic order was therefore imperative, but both management and the "free" trade unions were opposed, or at least undecided and hesitant. This resistance, however, could be defeated: "The democratic forces of Western Europe must seek not to prevent such change, but rather to cushion the shocks and facilitate readjustment." If management did not take leadership of the modernization process, the task would fall to "free" unions, which would learn from their American counterparts to fight for greater productivity and introduce greater flexibility and mobility among the workers. "The European worker must come to believe in European unification and increased productivity not only 'in principle,' but concretely as it applies to his daily life, his standard of living, his security. He must be shown the real immediate and long-term benefits to be derived from joining a non-Communist union."

A special program was proposed for France and Italy, where "the noncommunist unions—though they are free—are not yet strong, stable and dynamic." The ECA was to finance an extraordinary effort to strengthen the "free" unions and educate and train their members. Long periods at American industry and unions, and a massive commitment by members of the AFL and CIO as ECA consultants at the CISL and the Force Ouvrière, were to provide those European federations with the theoretical and technical know-how to become effective bargaining unions well integrated into the community and capable of stimulating productivist modernization. Receiving instruction from their American counterparts, the Italian and French trade unionists would learn what "the role of trade unions in a dynamic industrial society" consisted of. The leaders of the AFL and the CIO, insisting on the need for the ERP to contribute concretely to raising wages in Europe, declared themselves in favor and guaranteed a commitment unreservedly.[27] The labor division analyzed the reasons for the weakness of the non-Communist unions. In France and Italy there were no wage increases to correspond to rises in production and national income. A high rate of unemployment persisted in Germany and even more so in Italy. In both France and in Italy the bargaining role of the non-Communist unions was not encouraged, either by the governments or much less by the industrialists. In countries with strong commitment to reform, such as Great Britain and the Scandinavian countries, the Communists were very weak, but where the governments participating in the ERP did not effectively resolve social problems, the workers blamed the Marshall Plan. The non-Communist unions were often held back by their recognition of the imperatives of stability. "European unions—rightly or wrongly—contend that frequently they cannot ask for wage increases because A) it adds to inflation and B) that it would not be in the interest of the economy." The answer of union officials in the ECA, expressed in timid but clear and unequivocal language, was that the agency must begin to force governments to correct their economic and trade union policies, even to the point of tying aid to a decisive social commitment.[28] The idea of placing such conditions on the governments was obviously not formalized and remained only a temptation on the part of the officials from the trade unions. But the labor division asked for a revision of the whole ERP program in favor of labor and wages. It was proposed that the ECA officially include full employment among the Marshall Plan's primary objectives, that the program of each country's mission be reexamined in light of the priority given to "full employment and rising real income," and that each participating government be required to make an immediate commitment toward its most pressing social issues.[29]

Within the ECA, the labor division began to come forward as a pro-union pressure group requesting a readjustment of ERP priorities, or at least a change of emphasis, using for leverage the crucial importance of workers' consensus for the success of the anti-Communist stabilization effort. The outbreak of the war in Korea in June 1950 further accentuated this tendency since it dramatized the urgency of ensuring the solidarity of Western societies. The progressive militarization of the confrontation between the United States and the USSR in 1949 and 1950 had led the United States to draft a rearmament policy, which took shape after the explosion of the Soviet nuclear device and was then rapidly and vigorously applied during the Korean conflict; it was directed both to military superiority and to accelerated growth throughout the West under the stimulus of military expenditures. Economic and defense goals were seen to be closely tied as components of a single process of reinforcing the anti-Soviet camp. For weaker countries such as Italy, American policy even regarded both NATO's presence and military production more as factors leading to political stabilization and economic strengthening than as elements of purely military value.[30] Between Paris and Washington, the trade union officials in ECA repeatedly insisted on a sense of agreement, indispensable for "mustering the strength essential to successful resistance against Communist aggression." "The working people, whose will to resist determines the ultimate outcome of any warfare, must through actual experience come to know that democratic institutions are well worth fighting for and must be defended. . . . Economic aid of the US must raise real wages in the participating countries, so that the workers will have tangible evidence of America's concern for their well-being."[31]

The pressures within the ECA were joined by those from the American unions. In July a delegation from the UAW visiting Great Britain was invited by the ECA to extend its trip to France, Italy, Germany, and Austria, since a meeting with the American trade unionists would be "a good morale booster to the non-Communist unions." At the end of their European tour, however, the head of the delegation, UAW vice-president John Livingston, stated to the *New York Times*, to the great disappointment of the ECA, that observations in the field and many discussions with European trade unionists had convinced him that the ERP had been a "miserable failure" for the workers, who had derived no benefit from it.[32] In CIO headquarters, criticism of the Marshall Plan's results was by now explicit and concentrated especially on the state of affairs in France and Italy. The Communist parties were keeping their hegemony over the workers, and the "free" unions were very weak, it was noted, because the industrialists were pursuing a policy of holding wages down and limiting consumption levels among the workers. The governments, in spite of American aid, were not taking steps against unemployment, nor were they meeting the workers' essential claims halfway. The non-Communist unions were held back by political pressure from governments in the name of stability. Aid and educational commitments from the American union should change direction and be geared to the promotion of an independent capacity of the "free" unions to exert decisive and fearless negotiating pressure for higher wages. As for the ECA, the CIO repeated its support for the Marshall Plan but in an official statement demanded "bold new policies to encourage improved distribution of national income in the countries receiving aid through the E.R.P."[33]

The Weakness of the Unions: The Italian Case

In the process of critical review which trade union circles close to the ECA started to demand, concern was centered on the lack of power and authority of those "free" unions that represented an essential aspect of the liberal strategy for political realignment of Europe. One of the components of that parity at the negotiating table which would replace class conflict was unable to carry out its role; the whole programming structure was therefore thrown out of balance and ran the risk of turning in on itself with dramatically counterproductive results. The problem seemed especially difficult in Germany, and also in France and Italy, with their large Communist parties. Here the social consensus was relevant strategically, and ambitions of social recovery entrusted to the productivity campaign were more grandiose and at the same time more urgent. The Italian case, in many respects an extreme one, but not at all exceptional or anomalous as the Americans saw it, clearly brought out the dilemmas which arose for the ECA, especially for the trade unionists.

American diplomats had begun to note, even at the end of 1948, that the atmosphere of industrial relations was changing decisively throughout Italy, parallel with the crisis in the CGIL indicated by its split. The industrialists were becoming intransigent and unwilling to negotiate with unions. The CGIL's tactics of "non collaboration" were taken as a sign of weakness, even though they were a source of concern to some since they were perceived as an attempt to sabotage the ERP. Explosions of labor violence were observed more frequently. The Christian Democratic majority in the government as well as the industrialists were hard and inflexible in the face of labor unrest. The government's capacity to resist conflicts promoted by the CGIL was reassuring as an indication of political stability, but there was great concern at the bitterly hostile and irreconcilable character of labor-management relations. Responsibility was attributed equally "to the ignorance of the workers" about industry's production problems and to "the old world attitude" of management, especially concerning low wages. It was emphasized with regret that there were no places to pool efforts for productivity and to instruct workers in company management issues.[34]

In the course of 1949 the ECA was prominent in showing its concern for the state of industrial relations. More than in other countries, the plans for increasing productivity, which constituted the main ERP goal in Italy, along with reform of the administrative and fiscal apparatus, were deemed essential for promoting immediate peace on the labor front. But the acceleration of productivity, which presupposed technical collaboration between management and labor as well as cooperation at the bargaining table, gave rise to various reservations concerning the Italian situation. The consequences of an intense technological restructuring, accompanied by very high unemployment, were feared. Observers asked if this could be done when "labor is dominated by Communists, and industrial organizations such as CONFINDUSTRIA are dominated by large corporations," in a hostile polarization. But these were just the obstacles that the policy of increased productivity was seeking to remove. The spread of an "effective cooperation between management and labor" was the primary goal of ECA operations in the labor field.[35] If the political and economic picture seemed greatly improved after the first applications of the Marshall Plan, American unease was concentrated on the low level of benefits coming to the workers who had participated in the recovery. The high unemployment and the low consumption level that characterized the Italian economy fed fears that the Communist opposition could find strength and vigor by putting itself at the head of new labor unrest. An economy marked by the devaluations of the summer of 1949 led to fears of a return to wage demands that would be very difficult for the non-Communist unions to oppose on the sole ground of democratic resistance to Communist "subversion." Since the workers' demands had well-founded economic justification and could not be ignored, thus leaving worker representation to the Communists, the labor offices in the ECA deemed it essential that the industrialists and the government be more forthcoming. There had to be concessions and collaborative negotiation with the "free" unions.[36] The unions adhering to the ERP insisted that aid be directed to raising wages and employment, and that the priority given to financial recovery be lowered.[37]

The unions' criticisms reflected more strongly and specifically the ECA's accusations against the Italian government presented in March 1949 in the well-known *Country Study*, which questioned the use of ERP funds by the Italian government. These funds had clearly been diverted to rebuild the foreign currency reserves, which in fact had rapidly increased, rather than to increase investment and production. The prevailing Keynesian viewpoint in the ECA saw in this underutilization of resources a dangerous Italian reluctance to emerge from backwardness and overcome an economic stagnation that the Americans regarded as prejudicial to labor-management consensus and political stability.[38] In this manner the contradiction was coming to light between the expansive model proposed by the ERP, based on the political, strategic, as well as economic value of growth, versus the deflationary economic policy initiated in Italy with the credit squeeze of 1947. The ERP's initial anti-inflationary impulse, due to its concern for monetary stability, had been freely converted into Einaudi's free trade viewpoint, marked by rigid and prolonged financial orthodoxy, guiding Italian economic policy along a deflationary path which, in the European landscape of 1948–49, stood in isolation and drew not only criticism from the unions, but even official reprimands from the ECA.[39]

From the point of view of industrial relations and trade union strategies, the conflict was deep and strident. With the policy shift of 1947 came a drastic reshaping of the power balance between management and labor. The deflationary choice had removed employment from the strategic priorities of reconstruction. The sacrifice of domestic demand, coupled with an industrial growth model based on exports, restored that "low consumption equilibrium" which historically had distinguished the development of Italian capitalism.[40] Italian industry, although internally divided on the future timing of expanding the domestic market, was proceeding in unity to the conquest of markets abroad, thanks to low wage levels, and was on its way to a selectively expansive restructuring of its capacities. With the unfreezing of layoffs, industry rediscovered a freedom of maneuver on the labor market that, in the presence of massive unemployment, made possible a rapid reaffirmation of management's full technical and official control within the factories. The anarchic multiplicity of powers that grew up in production areas at the end of the war was dissolved between 1947 and the early 1950s and replaced by the nearly unopposed power of management. With the departure of the leftist political parties from the government, the representation of the workers' interests was relegated to the sidelines of the political arena, while their bargaining power eroded. This caused an exclusion of the workers' economic demands and aspirations for social reform from Italy's political life that became deeper as the Cold War conflict intensified. The simultaneous relegation to the political sidelines, lack of stimulus from domestic demand, and a newly discovered flexibility in a labor market dominated by an excess of supply were thus leading, at the end of the 1940s, to a collapse of workers' bargaining power, a progressive weakening of every union's capacity to represent them, and a historic reshaping of labor's influence as an organized interest.[41] If the economic effects of the 1947 policy shift were only partially and selectively recessive, the results in the labor-management area were unequivocal. There was a sudden large shrinkage in the workers' bargaining strength and of *all* the union organizations.

In 1949 the modernizing ambitions of the Americans were faced with the obvious contrast that had arisen between their own "anti-Communist Keynesianism" and the measures taken by the Italian forces with which they had to ally between 1947 and 1949 due to the necessities of anticommunism. The paths chosen to arrive at political stabilization were different. Acting in comparative freedom on the domestic scene, and protected by the umbrella of American aid and the 1948 electoral victory, the coalition of moderate and conservative interests led by the Christian Democratic majority and CONFINDUSTRIA conducted its anti-Communist struggle by weakening the main social interest represented by the left—that of the industrial workers—organizationally, economically, and at the bargaining table. The crucial difficulty presented by the union question—the convergence point for economic revival, political stabilization, and, at least according to the Americans, modernization—indicated the relative impossibility for the United States to impose sudden changes in historically rooted behavior on its allies. The threat of unemployment and repression of worker power remained the preferred weapons of Italian industrial and political circles. The ECA had hoped that there would be a strategy of demand stimulation and pluralistic negotiation among the interests to accompany the aid. "De Gasperi committed his government to a rather different formula—orthodox financial management combined with the breakup and isolation of the organized working class."[42]

This blocking of their aspirations to modernize was interpreted by the ECA as the result of a backward cast of mind in the business world. Seen as anachronistic manifestations of conservatism, the attitudes of the Italian government and industrialists were compared to the "restrictive" activities with which ECA operations were greeted throughout Europe. Protective measures, oligopolistic divisions of the market, little propensity to mass production or low-price mass consumption, and reluctance of management to collaborate with labor for the sake of productivity were all seen by ERP planners as obstacles to growth which should be removed and overcome in Italy as elsewhere. But in Italy, as in France, the organizational and ideological regeneration of "old world" capitalism seemed much more urgent for political and strategic reasons. The Communists had been relegated to the sidelines but not defeated, social cohesion was precarious, and political stability seemed to be hanging by extremely thin threads. The problem of industrial relations, whose improvement was essential for the productivity campaign's success, embodied these deeper values and appeared in anything but an encouraging light. Labor Attaché Lane fully agreed with the criticisms made by the CISL of "the regressive and shortsighted vision of industrial relations which, on the basis of absolute freedom of management, attempts to place workers secondary to production."[43] The possible political consequences of an antiunion atmosphere then spreading through industry caused special apprehension: "Unionism as such in fact appears to be losing ground and the morale of both the CGIL and CISL is felt to be low. . . . Industry seems to be taking heart from the general loss of ground of unionism and might well attempt to revert to an attitude which would aggravate the very conditions which led to support of the Communist union in the first instance."[44]

In the ECA, wage levels were judged "unbelievably low," especially because they discouraged the workers from using "their own resources to increase technical productivity." But more surprising and regrettable was the lack of consideration by management for the non-Communist unions: "Industry, generally, does nothing to encourage the development of the free trade unions."[45] The unilateral attitude of management, who refused to consider the workers' representatives as possible partners in negotiations for increasing efficiency, scandalized those who looked on the productivity campaign chiefly as a stimulus for management and labor to collaborate and for a convergence of interests on the part of the participants in the productive process. The difference in mindset, more than strategy, was deep. At a CONFINDUSTRIA conference on production costs, Lane asked in astonishment why no trade unionists had been invited. He was told that "industrialists and professors should be compared to surgeons and the workers to patients, and that surgeons did not ask patients how the operation should be performed."[46]

The government's passivity was an equal cause for concern. It did not appear to be looking ahead to forestall an uncontrolled fresh outburst of labor conflict. According to the ECA, it should have opened up to the workers with corrections of its economic policy, with agrarian reform and a greater receptiveness to requests from non-Communist unions. The perception that labor tensions were increasing without the government attempting to bring the workers and lower classes into a true pluralistic dialogue was causing serious concern among American officials. They appreciated the anti-Communist stability and the solidarity of the majority, but they feared that inactivity in the labor field would give dangerous opportunities to the Communist opposition. After the incidents at Modena of 9 January 1950, when the police fired on some strikers and killed several workers, Ambassador Dunn reported that the government should have mitigated the intransigence of management and mediated the dispute earlier, instead of allowing it to come to open conflict.[47] Two months later, in the province of Catanzaro, the LCGIL participated in an occupation of farm land, together with the CGIL and the UIL. Pastore explained to the embassy that the LCGIL could not grant a monopoly of labor protest to the Communists: "Neither government nor CD party is principal counterweight to communists," and therefore that role belonged to the "free" union. Dunn feared that the occupation would diminish the government's authority, but he took seriously the union's frustration "over government's slowness in answering workers' needs." "Pastore's action may have a salubrious effect. . . . As labor organization which hopes to win recognition as not only the equal but the superior of CGIL, the LCGIL must be expected to bring benefits to its members, and to do this is obliged on occasion to act tough."[48]

Lane, who was proud of the LCGIL as his own creation, commented enthusiastically, "The Communists were planning to occupy those same lands and our boys beat them to the jump."[49] The labor offices of the ECA, with the enthusiasm that accompanied the birth of the CISL, had confidence in the non-Communists' capacity to exert pressure for the creation in Italy of "a progressive economic and social program." Since there was not much Social Democratic reformist power, "the only way to solve the problems, in my opinion, is through a free united trade union with the backing of American labor. That is the only hope I have for dear old Italy."[50] But this was only an optimistic desire that was opposed both by economic reality and by the reasons for the internal solidarity of the anti-Communist formation. The contradictions in the American attitude, especially that of the unionists in the ECA, were laid bare by open labor conflicts, when the goal of anti-Communist stabilization of Italian society was seen to be irreconcilable with the ambitions for a pluralistic modernization. In the face of CONFINDUSTRIA's intransigence, did the CISL have to adhere to the strikes and compete openly by the CGIL's side for the sake of labor victories or abstain in the name of labor peace, political stability, and the necessity of isolating the CGIL to take away its legitimacy?

In the summer of 1950 nationwide negotiations on layoff procedures and wage revisions were broken off. Pastore, arguing that industry had to make concessions because productivity had increased, threatened a general strike. He told Lane he was concerned at "the deterioration in the labor situation," which the government could no longer ignore "at a time when the nation is engaging in a strong fight to achieve national solidarity."[51] The CISL adhered "reluctantly," and with much subtle reasoning, to a kind of unity of action pact with the CGIL and the UIL. It believed that a wage increase could be postponed no longer and desired a victory at the negotiating table. But it was afraid of a return to a feeling of unity among the workers and did not want to encourage a relaunching of the CGIL. Pastore insistently asked for the American view, hoping that the embassy and the ECA would press the Italian government for a speedy solution of the problem. The CONFINDUSTRIA was inflexible, "taking advantage of the international situation," according to Lane, "to declare that this is merely a Communist demand and should not be listened to." Irving Brown arrived in Italy and, together with Lane, pressured Pastore to give up the unity of action pact, fearing that CISL collaboration with the CGIL would jeopardize its anti-Communist campaign. But Pastore believed as well that the union demands absolutely had to be satisfied, mainly to strengthen the CISL with a visible success. The embassy was embarrassed and asked Washington for instructions. It feared the inflationary effects of any wage increase and emphasized the danger of the CGIL and the PCI winning back the allegiance of some, to the detriment of the government. On the other hand, the embassy believed it was important for the workers to obtain a concession and for the CISL to affirm itself.[52] The fear of a Communist revival, based on economic demands whose reasonableness was hard to deny, had become especially strong when the CGIL had tried to break out of isolation with the "Piano del lavoro," a plan for an increase in internal demand that in several ways reflected the Keynesian tones of the ERP.[53] In the following weeks, the Ministry of Labor mediated between the parties and the dispute was concluded. Tension eased and the embassy breathed a sigh of relief as it noted that the pact had been terminated and that Pastore was hastening to launch a propaganda campaign to claim credit for the victory for the CISL.[54] The government's intervention was also appreciated in Washington, especially because it made it possible for the American officials to evade the difficult questions that had arisen with the issue. American trade union policy was not able to reconcile its often contradictory ambitions: to reinforce the CISL without endangering peace on the labor front or political stability and to encourage an increase in the workers' bargaining power without giving more scope to the CGIL. For the moment, Irving Brown was given the unpleasant task of urging the CISL through Pastore not to abandon its rigid anti-Communist stance and to avoid joining the CGIL in battle. Characteristically, the reply gave a technical solution that did not solve the political problem. The ECA was to organize a mission to the United States to teach trade unionists and government officials the most current procedures for mediating labor disputes.[55]

However, the dilemma was anything but solved. In fact, it came up again in the same form a year later, with the dispute and the strikes in the civil service which brought back the thorny question of unity of action. It reignited fears that the conflict situation would work against the government's prestige and power. The overall result of these American concerns was to lower still further the already very low inclination of the CISL to take the route of aggressive bargaining. It subordinated this possibility to its fidelity to the anti-Communist commitment. In January 1953, when the CGIL and the UIL arranged a strike of the railroad workers because the government refused wage increases, De Gasperi himself intervened energetically with the CISL, which then ordered its members not to strike, as it was just before the electoral campaign and the DC was attacking the strike as a political maneuver. The strike succeeded, however, and in the subsequent union elections for railway workers the CISL was handily defeated. The need for moderation thus brought the CISL to "give up even a normal commitment to make demands when it feared that could cause serious difficulties for the government." This seriously prejudiced the status of "free" unions as a strong and authoritative force in the labor field.[56]

The political imperatives of the Cold War, together with the unfavorable conditions in the labor market that subjugated any worker representation, put many and repeated obstacles in the way of a struggle for workers' demands, without which the "free" trade union movement was unable to emerge from its status as a simple political and ideological rival of the CGIL, without any effect on the labor market. The modernization of industrial relations through bargaining, caught between the unilateral antiunion intransigence of management and the virtual absence of a dynamic and aggressive trade union movement, could find neither sufficient energy nor appropriate issues with which to get off the ground. It had been abandoned because of the same anti-Communist premises that gave ECA and American union projects their most urgent and fundamental political motivations. In a logic that rigidly gave priority to political stability and sidelined the opposition because it was Communist, every hint of labor conflict appeared negative because it could reopen the door to a role for the CGIL, which still had an ample majority in all manufacturing sectors in spite of the 1948 split. But with no possibility of conflict in the industrial sphere, the non-Communist trade union movement was condemned to remain nearly impotent in the face of these obstacles.[57] The intrinsic incoherence of the American anxiety for reform was nevertheless insufficient to cause an effective change of course. The influence of trade unionists within the ECA was limited, after all. Furthermore, Lane's ironclad anticommunism, and behind him that of the AFL, gave priority to the marginalization of the CGIL over any other objective. In the American foreign policy structure, sensitivity to trade union issues was not great and could not even remotely rival the priority accorded to political stability. Any long-term suggestions for modernizing the fundamental structures of Italian society inevitably took second place behind the immediate requirements of solid order in the government. The ECA could well argue against the propensity of Italian industry to remain anchored in a low-consumption economy, to prefer the competitive advantage of low wages over the promise of social integration contained in the American model of widespread prosperity, and to reject collaboration in negotiations with "free" trade unions to pursue an overall antiunion policy in industrial relations.[58] However, except for considering an unimaginable break with Italian moderate forces, the reformist aspirations had to bow to the traditionalist path taken by stabilization in Italy.

The ECA and the Mutual Security Agency (MSA) that succeeded it promoted a prolonged productivity campaign geared to increase industrial efficiency in Italy and France. The campaign aimed specifically to associate non-Communist unions in tripartite mechanisms for collaboration with government and industry, with the formation of a National Productivity Committee (CNP). It also tried to extend the unions' role in bargaining by launching an experiment in some pilot firms where credits and consultation for increasing productivity were tied to agreements for cooperation between management and union representatives from the CISL and the UIL. An enormous amount of information was heaped on the firms and unions about productive techniques, methods of bargaining, personnel management criteria, and systems of founding and organizing unions that in the United States had progressively established a system of industrial relations that institutionalized collaboration between labor and management and regulated disputes, integrating the most organized groups of the working class into the expansive flow of a high consumption economy. The CISL, which was looking for a "positive identity" beyond anti-Communist ideology around which it could base its activities, gradually linked its strategy to models of growth and social integration proposed by the productivity campaign, and its ideology was profoundly changed by issues deriving from the American experience.[59]

In spite of this, the modernization of industrial relations along bargaining lines remained more a frustrated aspiration than a concrete accomplishment during the 1950s. The CNP, established at the end of 1951, was actually only a governmental consulting commission, where the union leaders participated in a notably subordinate fashion. It was concerned with updating the technical knowledge of the industrial managers in order to distribute new, highly productive techniques in industry. Neither the government, which regarded the "free" unions as no more

than a political and organizational weapon against the CGIL, nor the industrialists, who were all intent on deriving the greatest possible advantage from a labor
market that threatened the base of any union power, had any real interest in giving
the workers' organizations any political or negotiating role and hence a power
whose function was so clear in the American productivist strategy and so hard to
see in the framework of industrial relations in Italian firms. The interaction
between policies of discriminating against the CGIL and the influence of unemployment on worker behavior gave management an almost uncontested dominance. To ensure social discipline and productive efficiency, a strong union partner
did not appear necessary; management's authority and the hierarchy of the firm
were more than enough. In the pilot firms the experiment on productivity increases had good results in efficiency and political impact (the level of CGIL
representation went down). But neither wage levels nor the amount of consultation with the unions increased, as both the CISL and the American agencies had
expected. For a good part of the 1950s, industry obtained notable advantages from
the innovative stimuli coming from America, without having to adapt to genuine
dialogue with the union side. The structural weaknesses and the built-in restraints
imposed by fidelity to the center's political balances hemmed in the CISL's modernizing strategy so much that its choice for development was reduced to "dis-
armed productivism" and its ambition for democratic integration of the workers
to "strategic acquiescence."[60] In a situation of social disequilibrium such as Italy's,
the American model of industrial relations, inspired by collaboration for productivity, remained an inapplicable and disappointing abstraction. Throughout the
decade, productivity increased rapidly, but wages did not keep up. Only a part of
Italian industry was completely in favor of expanding internal demand and promoting mass consumption. Exports and the demand for consumer goods by the
middle class were enough to absorb a rapidly increasing production. Mass consumption for the workers was to come later, at the end of the decade, and more so
in the 1960s, when the labor surplus was much smaller and productive capacity
much greater. Until the years of the "economic miracle," of the reabsorption of the
unemployed, and the advent of the "center-left" alliance of Christian Democrats
and Socialists, the obstacles to a dialogue between labor and management on an
equal footing remained in place. From the New Deal utopia of modernization all
that filtered into Italy were political and economic suggestions for "a greatly
reduced Americanization" which was socially imbalanced.[61]

The affirmation of the geopolitical paradigms of American strategy had taken
place within a political and social order that denied the purpose of profound
transformation of Italian society on which the American vision was based in the

long run. "What the cold warriors of 1947–48 conceived as an alliance for progress with the Italian people was only the latest marriage of convenience for the predominant political class."[62] That it was a marriage of convenience for the moderate and conservative Italian forces is beyond doubt. It is equally obvious that, in assessing the Marshall Plan's effects on Italian reconstruction, considerable weight must be given to the absence of a reformist force inspired by modern economic ideas and with the influence necessary to collaborate efficiently with the expansive and modernizing processes unleashed by the ERP, such as took place at the same time in several countries in northern Europe.[63] The lack of a Social Democratic and reformist interlocutor left the progressive American sectors without an Italian counterpart, which would be indispensable in order to exploit the socially innovative potential of the Marshall Plan, and made inoperable from the start the projects for industrial democratization conceived especially by the CIO. Faced with the exclusion of the left not only from the government but from the entire area of political mediation, with the sidelining of the CGIL and its loss of legitimacy as a representative of the workers' interests, and therefore as a potential agent of social reform, and with a political order that from 1947 on denied any substantial meeting of management and labor on an equal footing, the aspiration for reforming industrial relations and for the social integration of the workers cultivated by the heirs of the New Deal had no concrete basis.[64] The fact that these conditions were desired and pursued by Washington's foreign policy originated from the contradictions and diversities present in the vast array of American forces committed to the postwar reconstruction of Europe. But as a contemporary observer noted in an analysis of the ECA's *Country Study*, a program of economic growth and the spread of prosperity and social equilibrium required a domestic political grouping endowed with the power and the will to carry it out, at the cost of failure.[65] With all its power, neither the America of the 1930s nor, even more so, that of the Cold War period would be able to bring an economic New Deal to life without a corresponding political and social one.

Rearmament and the "Productivity Drive"

The discussion that opened in the ECA in the spring and summer of 1950, with the assessment of the first two years of the ERP, was given a rude shock by the outbreak of the war in Korea. The international confrontation had reached the threshold of a military clash. The American perception of the East-West conflict was deeply influenced by fear of an overall Soviet expansionist threat, and this led

American planners to review the timing and goals of their operations in Europe. The unsolved problems of growth and stability in the West—the social inequalities, the problems of consensus and political consolidation, as well as actual productive goals—took on the dramatic tension of a crisis preceding the outbreak of war. The difficulties brought to light by the state of industrial relations in Italy, though extreme, were not regarded as anomalous or unique, but rather as comparable to the obstacles the ERP was encountering in other countries, in a continental view of productivist modernization.

In August 1950 the report drafted by three American trade unionists after a long trip to France inspired the ECA to a more radical and incisive analysis of the social and trade union problems that came to light in the first two years of the program. The consensus about the Marshall Plan was evaporating, they wrote, because of the "small trickle of benefits which seeped down to the workers. . . . A drastic change in emphasis in the ECA program is imperative." The government should be forced to raise wages, carry out fiscal reform, and change labor law to encourage collective bargaining. The American managers should be mobilized to illustrate "a more enlightened social and economic viewpoint" to the French industrialists, who were to learn "a new type of economic thinking" based on low unit profits multiplied by an ample volume of production and sales. The non-Communist unions should achieve a greater role in the economy; American aid to French industry was to be subordinated to adoption of productivity contracts and to consideration of wage increases and price reductions in relation to increased productivity.[66] The report made a strong impression not only among officials with trade union background and sympathy; in the technical assistance division, which was responsible for the productivity drive, the emphasis fell on the responsibilities of management, which was accused of inefficiency and backwardness. Industry was not being stimulated by open competition, and cartel agreements were an obstacle to the adoption of mass production techniques. The educational activities undertaken with the study trips to the United States should have the ambitious goal of teaching different social groups the importance of pluralistic interaction in a society open to competition: "The sight to see in the U.S. is how an interplay of free forces (including strong and militant labor unions), many of them conflicting, creates instead of chaos, an order, which offers more material satisfactions than any other in the world."[67]

With great pedagogical abstraction, learning American techniques was put forth as a way to reverse not only the traditions but also the power balances in social and trade union relations: "Better management means higher living standards. It is quite apparent that good industrial management is usually the result of outside pressure. In the U.S. that pressure is provided by competition. Since competition is not a powerful force in the French economy, the pressure should come from labor. By familiarizing French labor leaders with good U.S. management techniques we give them a powerful weapon to use at the bargaining table." In bargaining, the union representative could rebut the French manager by showing him "how the wage rise can be made non-inflationary by the introduction of better production techniques."[68]

The labor division converted some of the suggestions in the report on France into a demonstration project illustrating simultaneous intervention in productivity and industrial relations in some pilot firms. The division wanted to show how traditional economic behavior that prevented the start of mass production, reductions in consumer prices, and simultaneous increases in wages could be overcome to everyone's advantage. The experiment in the pilot firms, which was later extended to Italy as well, concentrated technical assistance resources on some large-scale producers of consumer goods. The ECA would supply new machinery, organizational know-how, and American consultants for a rapid increase in productivity. Management and the "free" unions that had exclusive bargaining rights, under the supervision of American experts, were to negotiate a table of wage increases tied to productivity increases, a plan to reabsorb redundant workers, and an agreement to reduce final prices in relation with the fall in the unit production cost. The ECA also committed itself to a vast publicity drive to praise the successes of the pilot firms.[69] Beginning with its plan to educate management in collaboration with the non-Communist unions, the ECA's ambition was to fill what it thought was the principal gap in the Monnet plan for modernizing French industry: the scant attention to industrial relations and to "the human factor" in business management. With the experiment in the pilot firms, the productivity drive evolved totally into an effort to radically change the political and trade union dialogue in the French, Italian, and eventually European societies. "The job, as I see it, has three fronts: 1) to put more starch in the non-Communist labor people, show them that they can bargain, democratically, to win a better deal, that Communism is not the only alternative; 2) to awaken the French Government to active siding with the non-Communist labor people; 3) to bring French owners to their senses."[70]

Clashes of vested interests and priority conflicts were hidden at first, but in such an all-inclusive program as the Marshall Plan they were inevitable. The more these conflicts came to light, the more the trade union structure of the ECA and the two American federations that backed it up reacted. They proposed a bold program of American aid that was an exercise in large-scale social engineering. In what proportions and with what timing would the benefits of reconstruction be divided among social classes? How would negotiating and political power be distributed among the different protagonists of the growth coalition which the ERP had assembled? The recovery of production and investment supported by aid did not bring with it an automatic rise in wages; workers' incomes did not keep up with productivity increases. Unemployment, in Germany and more so in Italy, was not falling as rapidly as hoped. The Communists retained their representative character with their unions in France and Italy, and the "free" unions had not been able to establish themselves as strong bargaining agents. As the limits of American ability to impose on its allies the full adoption of modernization plans emerged, and as the costs of anti-Communist stabilization became apparent, the American trade union forces involved in the ERP pressured the organization with an increasingly ambitious, but scarcely realistic, urge to become the instrument for a profound restructuring of European society. Paradoxically, it was the most progressive of the liberal forces which requested ECA interference in participating nations through putting conditions on aid. The feverish attention to security and defense problems following the war in Korea revived the fear of a "Communist comeback" in Western Europe after the defeat of 1947–48. This offered a telling argument: if the working classes were not fully integrated into the growth process, it would not be difficult to foresee a resurgence of social conflict that would endanger the recent political stability and the effort to rearm. The unhappiness of the union officials, especially from the CIO, in feeling themselves participants in a reconstruction program that at least in some countries obviously sacrificed their reformist aspirations, was mixed with the conviction that the American side had not done enough. After having opened the way to an expansive stabilization of the economy, the American program also had to solve the social problems—always interpreted as backwardness—which accompanied the recovery of productivity. The problem was that the American model of pluralistic settlement of social conflict by negotiation gave priority to development and democratic solidarity, but it did not exclude conflict, especially as the unions interpreted it. This was a conflict free of ideological overtones, which was regulated and directed for the growth of a market economy more than for its transformation. It meant a continuing conflict between organized interests, not a final clash between social classes, but it was still a conflict. This was what was lacking in the experience of the new "free" unions in France and Italy. They were too subjected to the dogma of political and economic stability.

Robert Oliver, one of the senior trade union officials of the ECA and a representative of the CIO, saw the question very clearly. We repeat continuously, he wrote, "that labor is the no. 1 target that we must reach" and that we want democratic unions. For this reason, ECA indicates the American social model as example and hope. But this cannot suffice for the workers: "The best way to offer this hope is to show visible evidence in terms of a better deal for *them*, not in showing them how well off American workers are." Could the growth of unions and the modernization of the social scene, in the name of long-run stability, be achieved without conflict? "We must bear in mind that to be strong a union must be successful. It must have some victories under its belt. . . . In most instances they will be over the custodians of industrial, economic and usually political power in a nation. If achieving these victories requires our help, we must be prepared to give it if we want seriously to have strong unions as a democratic force in a free world. . . . You can't establish a propaganda substitute for a decent standard of living and simple justice."[71]

But in this case it would have meant conflict *within* the coalition of forces that had gathered around the Marshall Plan, Atlanticism, productivity, and anticommunism. Economic aid, propaganda, and suggestions on fundamentals could not replace a union's capacity to operate independently at the bargaining table. But aggressive pursuit of its claims and firmness in negotiations were as necessary as they were specifically renounced in the name of political stability. On the basis of these assumptions the CIO, while it was stepping up the pressure on the ECA for decisive action, sent an autonomous mission to study the situation in France, Italy, Germany, and Austria. Two months later the CIO delegation, led by Victor Reuther, brother of President Walter Reuther of the UAW, drafted a report that recommended opening a permanent CIO office in Europe, to operate independently in support of the non-Communist unions. Europe, according to Victor Reuther, could not be defended solely with more money and more production. The ECA's trade union program was positive but in any case insufficient. Neither the American political leaders nor the governments of those countries demonstrated an adequate awareness of the "free" trade unions' importance. Outdated models of antiunionism prevailed in industrial relations. The benefits of increasing growth were not distributed throughout society; this explained the persistence of Communist strength in France and Italy. The workers had not obtained substantial advantages from the Marshall Plan in large measure because of the weakness of the "free" unions, which were excessively subordinated to governments, lacking in aggressiveness, and incapable of freeing themselves from "a sterile anti-Communism" in their programming. The ECA might multiply its consulting activities, and the ICFTU might be in favor of more intense unionization, but most important was that the American trade unionists should directly stimulate their European colleagues to more effective bargaining pressure on firms and governments. With a line of reasoning based on the Italian example, but whose meaning was to be extended to other countries as well, Reuther stated: "American policy is paying a rather heavy price for the electoral victory won against Communism . . . in April of 1948. We too are the victims of a negative anti-Communism." Inefficient and protected industries and markedly conservative political groupings were blocking every step toward reform. Because of the "political preoccupations" of leaders too sensitive to governmental power balances, the non-Communist unions "have had some marked success in frustrating Communist political strikes, but have lost their own ability to use the strike weapon for further economic demands." The "Communist predominance" derived from the absence of a "militant working-class organization" to challenge it. The only solution was to integrate the workers, democratically but aggressively, into a high consumption economy, thus opening the way to independent and militant trade union operations. "It is obvious that if the union were less loyal and more militant, the economic position of its adherents would improve. . . . The healthiest thing that could happen in Italy today, in our opinion, is the growth of a trade-union movement geared to the satisfaction of the wage-earners' demands and uninhibited by either political or religious alliances."[72]

The report was approved by the CIO executive board, and Victor Reuther returned to Paris on 13 March 1951 to direct a permanent CIO office, which was to attempt, in conjunction with the ICFTU and the main international federations, to reinvigorate non-Communist trade union operations in France, Germany, and Italy, financing recruitment campaigns in key industries and organizing training schools for members to endow such organizations as the UIL, the French Force Ouvrière and the German Deutscher Gewerkschaftsbund (DGB) with greater aggressiveness in pursuing their demands. This independent move of the CIO supplemented ECA operations, with which Reuther maintained close contact, as a spur to convert the productivity programs of the technical assistance division into more incisive industrial relations programs, opening up more space for the unions and accelerating wage increases.[73]

At the beginning of 1951 the ECA's operations were fully concentrated on the productivity drive. The importance of its strategic goal of consolidating Western Europe as a compact and integrated area was accentuated by the choice of Atlantic rearmament followed by the Korean War. American industry was put on a war footing. Officials of the ECA believed that a military conflict with the USSR was "probably an inevitability." To the commitment for productivity was added not only the desire to rebalance the social effects of the Marshall Plan, but the impelling necessity of developing European defense production without reducing civilian manufactures, maximizing output levels without alienating a working class still widely excluded from the benefits of postwar recovery. The most urgent objective was specified to be overcoming "the European sense of weakness," both economic and psychological. A productivity increase then appeared to be the only way to avoid a hard choice between "guns and bread" and to open up the possibility, or at least the hope, of "a program which gives both." The defense commitment should not further limit consumption and low-level incomes, since they were already dangerously low in key countries such as France, Italy, and Germany. Only greater productivity seemed to meet the simultaneous needs of rearmament and the political consolidation of European societies on the basis of the anti-Communist consensus, offering the key to the solution of the economic and political equations in such a way that the workers' movement could feel that it was "an integral part of Europe's future."[74]

Robert Oliver, who became the principal adviser on trade union affairs at ECA headquarters, presented a project which expanded the idea of the pilot firms and called for special aid for the rapid modernization of plants and workers' organizations in industries deemed essential for military and civilian production. The granting of aid, however, was to be subjected to a commitment not only to greater efficiency, but also to "reasonable prices," "proper wage standards" and good labor relations. "Underlying the whole suggestion is the strong conviction that to superimpose an armaments program upon the economy of certain European countries without adequate safeguards against exorbitant profits, low wage standards, and deterioration of the standard of living, could be disastrous."[75] The publicity section also redefined its operating goals and methods for guiding the leading social sectors to full mobilization for economic efficiency: "Productivity is the key and to achieve any substantial improvement in productivity we must (a) educate management, (b) create a supporting atmosphere of demand on the part of the general public, (c) generate enthusiasm among workers."[76] The labor division, summing up the trade union issue that had to be taken into consideration in light of the new, security oriented priorities for American policy in Europe, insisted that economic conditions constituted a central factor in stability. Industrial relations on the continent overall had been "harmonious throughout the postwar period," but "only partial success" could be recorded for the anti-Communist trade union movement in France and Italy, because of poverty and unemployment. The existence of the ICFTU allowed for greater hopes in political and organizational terms, but the prospect for good labor relations and therefore political peace depended a good deal on improvement in wages and working conditions. "Any important inroads of defense on already low living standards in these countries will probably lead to political losses and economic disorganization outweighing the possible contribution to Western European security."[77]

Concerns about trade union matters interacted with a renewed anxiety to undermine the strong social presence of the Communist parties in Italy and France. They were considered dangerous to rearmament and security, and the American government was updating the guidelines for its aid to Europe. A year before the termination of the ERP, the entire aid plan was revised in the light of NATO defense policies by the Mutual Security Act, voted by Congress on 31 October 1951. American appropriations and plans for imports from the dollar area were now geared to defense production and reinforcement of strategic sectors. The ambitious design of reshaping the European economic order, conceived by the ECA to promote the continent's economic development and independence, received a new stimulus from the compelling defense priority. Beginning on 1 January 1952, the ECA was converted into the Mutual Security Agency, a new agency which was explicitly charged by Congress with guiding aid policy toward the goals of European unity and productivist modernization. "The MSA program is based principally on decisive economic and social measures to improve *productivity* in member countries and in this way to face the new requirements, at the same time increasing the purchasing power of the masses and improving their standard of living. . . . The full realization of the productivity program calls for the following aims: a single market for all Europe, an increase in production, a rise in consumption, a division of profits between the three groups concerned, capital, labor, and consumers, and steadily increasing employment."[78] The American model of an open economy, stimulated by competition and self-regulated by negotiation among organized interests, explicitly inspired the new law; the Benton amendment required that American aid be administered in such a way as "to discourage cartel and monopolistic business practices, and to encourage the development and strengthening of the free labor movement."[79]

From 1951 on, the productivity drive developed to the maximum extent and intensity, coupling an energetic publicity campaign with a large number of study trips, technical education courses, conferences, and experiments in the efficiency field. An enormous quantity of technical and organizational know-how of American origin was piled on European managers and union leaders. The new promise to redirect American aid to the benefit of the workers and to sensitize management to the human and trade union sides of industrial operations renewed the consensus of the American and European trade union organizations, who could foresee a better scenario for their bargaining activities and a head-on attack against the CGIL and the CGT. The prevailing attitude of the non-Communist unions was mostly positive, sometimes even enthusiastic, and always in agreement with the productivist principle that inspired the MSA. At the end of 1951 the ICFTU regional organization for Europe officially declared its adherence to the priority of rearmament and the productivity drive, provided there was a guarantee for "the maintenance of social justice" through price controls and a serious political commitment to full employment.[80]

The approval of the Mutual Security Act, with its specific mandate to encourage "free" unions, gave new vigor, at least temporarily, to the trade union interpretation of the productivity drive as the promotion of the role of unions, an attempt to reform industrial relations, and an effort to improve wage income. But no matter how much attention was given to the problems of social equilibrium, the criterion inspiring the productivity drive and all the MSA's activities was to increase industrial efficiency, especially war production. The reformist overtones and union pressures could perhaps partially condition the way the program was carried out, but they certainly could not replace its fundamental priorities. The new emphasis on social modernization did not remove from the scene the totality of conditions which up to that time had frustrated American expectations of a profound restructuring of the European economic and social order through the leverage of aid. Furthermore, the directive from Congress was subject to interpretations within the MSA that were anything but unequivocal. While the antimonopoly overtones were unanimously agreed upon by all American officials, who prized competitiveness, the choice favoring "free" unions produced reactions that varied with people's official functions as well as their cultural and political origins. For the diplomats, management personnel, and most of the officials charged with stimulating the efficiency of industry and services, the Benton amendment represented only one more detail in the anti-Communist set of goals. Operationally it meant that in allocating offshore contracts and in distributing credits and technology, preference was given to the firms which gave assurances that they would discriminate against Communist unions. Beyond the propagandistic statements, the amendment became only one more incentive for repressing unions that were against the ERP, and this is how it was implemented in most cases.[81] On the other hand, the American unions tied to the MSA, especially the CIO unions, once again insisted with greater energy and conviction that the agency take steps to condition the policies of those European governments which were hardly inclined to social reform measures or increasing wages and consumption. However, they did not achieve significant results.[82]

Between 1952 and 1955 the productivity drive in eleven countries received appropriations for $94 million, of which $30 million was for France and $22 million for Italy; more than 50 percent of the sum was therefore earmarked for the two nations where a strong Communist opposition remained, testifying to the eminently political relevance the United States attributed to the productivity drive. Industrial production increased and productivity indexes rose by 16 percent in the five-year period from 1951 to 1955. But even ten years after the start of the Marshall Plan, the usually rather triumphal official review of the program had to admit disappointedly that in Italy, on the eve of the "economic miracle," "two fundamental problems—unemployment and low per-capita income—remain to be solved."[83] MSA operations contributed in numerous cases to intensifying repression of Communist unions, but it was not of great assistance in the growth of the "free" unions except in terms of ideals and publicity. Where the majority of worker representation remained in the hands of unions inspired by the class struggle, like the CGIL and the CGT, neither the national productivity committees nor the experiments in the demonstration firms were able to change the situation and bring the workers into a bargaining system of industrial relations. On the contrary, the actual management of productivist improvements was often the source of difficulty for the unions that were more inclined to reproduce the American organizational and negotiating models, because their adherence to the productivity drive clashed with its implementation within the firms, which was unilaterally to management's advantage and generally against the unions. The "free" unions in fact remained practically disarmed and substantially passive, even if the MSA's propagandistic message tended to give value to their role. Deprived of the possibility of open recourse to conflict, they could only endure the inferior status dictated by industrial interests who were economically stronger and unwilling to give up their antiunion strategies for the sole purpose of bowing to the New Deal notions of the American ally. In Italy, the entire course of the productivity drive was accompanied by continuous but weak and ineffective polemics of Pastore, and even of Walter Reuther, against CONFINDUSTRIA's refusal of an explicit partnership with the anti-Communist unions, or a more expansive economic policy. In the middle of the 1950s the intense American effort had not succeeded at all in breaking the economic and political conditions that relegated the idea of a union movement based on negotiation to the realm of frustrated conjectures and hopes. One of the technicians who closely followed the productivity drive in Italy bitterly summed up its results, accusing the CNP of having operated "like a technical consulting firm for management, entirely to management's advantage and fundamentally detrimental to free unions." He concluded: "Continuing the present program will only serve to weaken the free unions morally and organizationally."[84] The final balance on the productivity drive was amply positive on the economic and industrial side. Efficiency levels rose rapidly throughout Europe, managers and technicians became familiar with American management systems, and modernization of plants proceeded at a good pace. But there were no comparable results for the political and trade union aspects of the productivity drive. In just those countries where there was greater expectation of expanding mass production and consumption and of innovations in economic behavior and modernization of industrial relations, the drive did not obtain the results hoped for either in wage growth—well below what was achieved in productivity—or in the introduction of American-style labor relations based on bargaining, which was unable in Europe to supplant either the traditional political and conflictual models or the new neocorporatist schemes developed by the social democracies.[85]

With its promise of prosperity in democracy, the Marshall Plan initially had provided a strong political drive for forestalling the breakup of European society into conflict, involving the workers' organizations in a policy of capitalistic stabilization and achieving a clear-cut anti-Communist realignment of Western trade unionism. But its capacity to attract and integrate the trade union movement turned out to be rather narrow. The effort to reshape labor-management relations and economic dynamics according to an American model of prosperous and consensual productivism demonstrated substantial limitations early on. America's aid policy was not successful in overcoming the challenge of modernization launched at Europe, especially in those countries such as France and Italy where a precarious political and social order had inspired the most ambitious American plans. Stabilization took place without reform, the benefits of recovery did not accrue to the workers, and unions were excluded from the economic establishment. The ECA's operations were not successful in changing the hostile behavior inherent in labor-management relations, the antiunion traditions of industry, or the social conservatism of the governments. Only in countries led by Social Democratic governments such as Great Britain and the Scandinavian countries did the New Deal values of the ERP find relatively fertile ground, blending in as they did with national reform policies that gave the unions a significant role. But on a good part of the continent, unions remained a neglected and marginal partner in the growth coalition formed by the ERP. The Benton amendment was seen to be a symbol without real influence. The fact that encouraging "free" trade unionism had become a matter of law testified to the difficulties encountered by American international operations much more than to their capacity to resolve them. Adhering to the ERP, the "free" unions were given a place in a political, national, and international movement that offered them a political standing but compromised their capacity to make demands, that guaranteed them solid legitimacy but postponed the growth of their economic and bargaining power in the future. Even the mechanism of aid, although it stimulated growth by concentrating resources on

investments, did not contemplate any procedures to transmit its benefits immediately to consumers; the increase here was postponed. Prosperity and a pluralistic
mechanism for its social distribution were ERP's promise, but not its short-term
realization. The increase in wages and mass consumption was a goal to which ERP
aid had given political and cultural legitimacy and some indispensable economic
bases, but no guarantee of fulfillment. The ambivalent nature of the relationship
between the ECA and the participating governments, the bias toward private
business that governed the agency's operations, and the flow of investment resources into industry's hands were all factors that reinforced the administrators
and recipients of aid, who saw their power increase and with it the possibility of
relative independence from the economic and social philosophies that ECA would
have liked to see received along with its aid. The ideology of growth and the
productivity mindset seduced the non-Communist unions, but American financing multiplied the economic vigor and social influence of industry, which was
especially useful "to European politicians hoping to back a central political position with a suitable economic programme which could be presented as quite
neutral."[86]

European unions could accept the ERP's economic priorities and participate in
revitalizing capitalistic power in Western Europe in anticipation of future economic advantages and immediate political ones. If they were solidly involved in
national governing mechanisms and in the Atlantic community that was coming
into being, they would achieve legitimacy, security, and, at least in anticipation, an
important role in drafting social and economic policies. But at the same time they
were weighed down by the temporary but decisive renunciation of the use of
contractual force and conflictual pressures. From this came a loss of autonomy, a
status of dependence and, finally, of substantial weakness that worked against the
possibility of their influencing decisions on national economic matters or on ERP
operations. Only in countries with a Social Democratic government was the
renunciation of conflict offset by the unions' influence on government circles. This
made it possible to safeguard some fundamental trade union priorities, starting
with full employment.[87] But unions which had been recently founded and were in
a minority position, such as the CISL and the Force Ouvrière, which needed the
legitimation and identity that ERP adherence offered, could only try to convert
their extreme dependence into a card in their favor, requesting American pressure
to approach those political and economic goals which their weakness did not allow
them to achieve. But there was nothing in the ERP program that could convert
such an illusion, whose nature was not made less delusory by the fact that American trade unionists also nourished it, into reality. This was due chiefly to the fact

that the ECA's capacity to condition national political and economic forces was limited; in the second place, the productivity drive, linchpin of the effort to modernize social relations, did not have that potential to assist unions which the workers' organizations tried in vain to attribute to it. The productivity drive advertised a pluralistic equilibrium among social interests, but it had neither the means nor the coherent will to overturn, from one day to the next, the balance of power between industry and labor. Primarily it supplied technical contributions and knowledge for increasing industrial efficiency, and those who could benefit directly and immediately from this were the industrial firms. Any disposition they might have to receive the New Deal social message from the productivity drive depended not on any hypothetical pressures from the ECA, but on the effective use of negotiation and political power by the national unions. Where they were weak and the dialectic of negotiation out of balance, especially for the marginalization of the Communist-led unions which retained the representation of a majority of workers, the productivity drive could not get away from an implementation unilaterally dominated by management. The ECA's educational efforts could criticize but certainly not redesign the geography of labor-management power, and neither could the moderation chosen by the "free" unions in the interest of anti-Communist stability. In the countries on the frontier of the Cold War—where the international conflict was reflected in a lacerating political and social conflict— the productivity drive, even though the integration of the workers in economic concert was one of its goals, wound up perpetuating the disequilibrium in labor-management relationships, and with it that shrinking of workers' interests which led to the danger of destabilization from the Communist presence. The trade union policy of the ERP did not succeed in having a profound effect on those situations where its modernizing impact was deemed more urgent and politically indispensable.[88]

CONCLUSION

In 1950 the political picture of the trade union movement in Western Europe appeared so different from what it had been barely five years before that it was nearly unrecognizable. The passage from the anti-Fascist alliance to the Cold War had completely redrawn international alignments and, in many cases, domestic alignments as well. The coalitions inherited from the resistance had broken up, and with them went the policy of wide structural reforms that had inspired them. The unity of the trade union movement was replaced by a violent frontal encounter, between Communists on one side and Christian and Social Democrats on the other, which undermined the possibility of making organized labor a central factor in the political life of each nation. The ambitious postwar plans for nationalization, labor's control over economic policy, and a strong public role for the unions were succeeded by a frustrating return to mere negotiations with industry over economic matters. The breakup of the WFTU, the French CGT, and the Italian CGIL, together with anti-Communist purges in other countries, marked a historic step in the worldwide trade union movement, whose manner and timing were dictated by the onset of the Cold War. The main catalyst of this transformation was the Marshall Plan, which linked purely union matters with the economic and political dynamics of postwar reconstruction and reorganization of the international system.

The ERP, originating as a strategic move of the United States in the Cold War and as a project for international economic coordination, was soon presented much more ambitiously as a social philosophy for all of European society, especially industry and the workers. It was the exportation of a new economic and social system—the "American way of life"—that promised prosperity even to the lower classes. It was this social aspect that summoned the principal currents and institutions of American society to participate actively in the development and application of the ERP. The American unions, in particular, could best illustrate and legitimize the ERP's Keynesian message of productivity to European workers. This new interventionist role had a strong fascination for American union leaders.

For the AFL the Marshall Plan was the best vehicle for its own anti-Communist crusade, while for the CIO it was an area in which to reforge a strong, useful alliance with the Truman administration. Furthermore, the ERP furnished both with a solid political and economic platform for establishing their leadership of the trade union movement in the West. Above all, the philosophy of the plan presented American unions as a new triumphant historical model for the representation of the workers' social interests in the postwar world.

With the launching of the Marshall Plan and its rejection by the Soviets, the divisiveness of the Cold War directly penetrated the European trade union movement, reversing its most important strategic decisions. The economic and social character of the American proposal translated apparently remote international issues into crucial, inevitable, and immediate choices on economic policy, social alliances, political alignments, and negotiating strategy. The political struggle within European trade unions led to a final clash on growth prospects and economic strategies of labor. The Christian and Social Democratic trade unionists gave up any hesitation at breaking the unity of the trade union movement. In addition to moral, political, and material support from American unionists, they found in the Marshall Plan a new system of alliances, an economic logic, and a strategic posture to oppose to Communist insistence on structural reform. The prospect that finally opened up through the American aid of prosperous capitalism, with high employment and a high consumption level, could be presented to the workers as a concrete way to a better future. Allying themselves with government and industry in potent centrist coalitions, the trade unionists of Europe would push the Communists into indefensible "subversive" isolation.

For the Truman administration and the American unions this was a conspicuous and clear-cut political success. The anti-Communist shift of the European trade union movement, aided and accelerated by the Marshall Plan, contributed decisively to the political stabilization of Western European nations and provided a wide basis of consensus for American international strategy. The chances for the ERP's economic and political success were multiplied. The realignment of the European unions and the firm commitment of their American counterparts gave the ERP an essential legitimacy as a vehicle of, or at least a hope for, social progress. In particular, the contribution of the American trade union movement—more than any other sector of American society—was the determining factor in the European working classes' understanding of the ERP's fundamental message as a promise of greater well-being and democracy. By the beginning of 1949, American intervention in the world of trade unions had achieved its main political objectives. Most of the European trade union movement had been freed from its

Communist associations and actively supported the ERP. The Communist opposition everywhere was isolated, weakened, and vulnerable. The work of reconstruction based on ERP aid could now go forward in an atmosphere of widespread and solid agreement. It seemed possible at that point to proceed to restructuring the European system of industrial relations according to the American model of industrial democracy, which was at the center of the Marshall Plan's socioeconomic planning.

For the New Dealers and trade unionists in the ECA, the growth cycle stimulated by Marshall Plan aid called for an almost simultaneous rise in all components of national income. Investment was clearly the key to future growth, but wages also had to rise to allow workers to buy and appreciate the benefits of the capitalistic prosperity promised by the ERP. The improvement of employment rates and income levels was deemed urgent and crucial, especially in countries such as France, Germany, and Italy, whose political stability still seemed precarious. In the priority scale dictated by the Cold War, these nations, in addition to being essential factors in the continent's economic revival, were also the front line of the conflict between East and West. It was here that the new non-Communist unions needed to be reinforced, to achieve conspicuous successes, and to win the confidence of the workers in order to bring them effectively into the economic and political mechanisms of the growth process.

Walter Reuther, David Dubinsky, and many officials of the ECA proudly maintained that the American model of industrial democracy offered a response to these simultaneous necessities and therefore indicated to European workers an effective alternative to the dilemma between conservatism and totalitarianism. The ERP was to provide a plan for the democratic resolution of social conflict through prosperity as well as financial aid. The continuous growth of productivity and the creation of an efficient, pluralistic, and consensual negotiating system was to make for an equitable distribution of the benefits of growth in all sectors of society. A constant redistribution of an ever greater pie would constitute the foundation on which to establish political and social stability in Western Europe. For Europe as a whole, the plan looked to continental integration, freeing up trade, intensification of competition, and growth of production. But for the countries on the frontiers of the anti-Communist struggle, the ECA looked directly at a radical restructuring of the economic and institutional outlines of the social contract.

At least at first, the abstract grandiosity of this vision did not appear to impede or intimidate the American planners. But carrying out the "productivity drive" soon dashed many of their hopes, or rather their illusions. The political reality of many European nations was marked by the fact that the political and contractual role of the unions was very much a marginal one, and the power of labor in society was reduced. Rather than initiating reform, the politics of recovery and stabilization activated by the ERP consolidated social structures that were conservative or, in any case, decisively favorable to industry. Furnishing aid did not guarantee that American supremacy would involve the automatic diffusion of American ways of arranging society. Neither the ECA nor the American trade unionists had the power to give to the "free" unions the victories in wage and employment issues that they could not achieve on their own.

Business had no need to make binding compromises with the unions so long as the contractual strength of the workers was reduced to a minimum because of vast unemployment, as in the case of Italy or Germany, or the divisions among the unions, as in France and Italy. The Communist unions were isolated and substantially delegitimized, while the "free" unions had neither the political will nor the necessary strength for an open resort to labor conflict. The "productivity drive" then became a tool for the firms to cut their costs, speed up plant restructuring, and increase profits, while nothing obliged them to divide the benefits with the workers. In most cases, labor received no immediate perceptible advantages from increased industrial efficiency, and the effort to modernize even resulted at times in a fall in employment. To the protests of the American officials, the French and Italian managers usually answered that they did not need to draw up new agreements with the "free" unions, but rather had to confront the Communist ones, which were usually stronger in the manufacturing sectors. Now they were able to do this from a position of strength, and so the circle closed, entirely to industry's advantage.[1] As a result, union membership fell rapidly. In Germany, in spite of the overall growth of the labor force, the principal industrial unions barely held on to their membership. In Italy membership in manufacturing unions fell throughout the 1950s, and in France between 1950 and 1955 the overall number of union members was reduced by half. Even strikes, most being defensive measures against firings and layoffs, declined drastically throughout the decade, picking up again only in 1958–59.[2] For most of the 1950s, union activity was defensive in character and produced few results.

The tripartite productivity committees organized in each country were important centers for dissemination of new managerial methods and technology, and they carried out an important task of educating managers and engineers. Their activities notably increased the familiarity of many European firms with low-cost mass production systems, while the credits, machinery, and know-how furnished through American aid accelerated factory modernization. In a way that varied from country to country, the campaign for productivity led many union leaders to

take on a new managerial mentality. It facilitated their passage from the antagonistic mindset of the prewar period to the ideas of a classless society elaborated by
American liberalism. The campaign favored a modernizing revision of the culture
of industrial relations, the results of which matured over the following decades.[3]

As far as the most directly political level of the national macroeconomic concert
was concerned, the productivity drive met with scant success. In no case did overall
negotiation among organized interests result from the tripartite collaboration in
national productivity committees that was set in motion with so much trouble.
The committees themselves were never charged with the function of consulting on
economic policy, as the European and American trade unionists would have
wished, nor did they become vehicles for the regulation of industrial conflicts. This
was not because the committees could not evolve into clearinghouses for cooperation between state and social interests; rather, it was because neither industry nor
governments had any need to do so. For accelerated modernization and competitive restructuring of each national economy to occur, wage stability and labor
elasticity were much more useful and appreciated than any politically determined
concession to the unions. As long as Cold War anticommunism and the wide
availability of a labor force kept any union pressure under control, even the "free"
unions were bereft of leverage with which to enforce their wage demands and a
recognition of their own role in negotiations. In most cases the unionists left the
productivity committees after several vain attempts to oblige government and
industry to grant political or economic concessions they did not have the strength
to win themselves.

In fact, the "free" unions in France and Italy achieved important successes in
negotiations only on the rare occasions when they allied with the Communist
unions in temporary and politically embarrassing united fronts. Even the stronger
German federation, the DGB, had little power to enforce its demands. The flood
of refugees from the East provided the labor market with great flexibility. In
individual firms, management could outflank the union and reach good agreements with the work councils. And after its defeat in the fight to extend codeter-
mination outside the iron and coal sector, the DGB was forced to renounce an
institutional role as an equal partner of industry and government.[4] The boom in
major European economies took place in a framework of temporary sidelining, if
not exclusion, of labor as an important and influential actor on the social scene.

The American trade unionists were caught between their sincere support of the
anti-Soviet struggle, the necessity of solidarity with their government, and the
weakening of the liberal assumptions during the years of McCarthyism. They were
forced to adapt, albeit with some bitterness, to the fading of their hopes and of

their influence on aid policy. Faced with the risk of destroying the still precarious stability of the political arrangements reached in Western Europe, they finally accepted the priority of the anti-Communist struggle and the sacrifice of their own ambitions for restructuring the social order. This subordinate status did not cause many difficulties for the leaders of the AFL, who looked on the ERP mainly as an arm of the anti-Soviet struggle and attributed to their own international activities a role that was much more political than unionist. The success of anti-Communist containment was an absolute value for them, the historical importance of which was not diminished by delays or stoppages in the progress of the trade union movement. But it was certainly a bitter failure for the New Deal reformism of the CIO leaders, who had left for Europe with the conviction that they would use the Marshall Plan to offer the workers of the Old World a prosperous and democratic alternative to the dilemma of conservatism versus totalitarianism.[5]

The political and socioeconomic objectives of the "politics of productivity" seemed incompatible for this reason, at least in the short term. The American plans constituted a social engineering exercise that was theoretically coherent but too abstract and ambitious to be attainable over just a few years. The impossibility of implanting in Europe a system of balanced social pluralism derived from New Deal doctrine showed that the American international strategy, however incisive and suggestive, was not omnipotent. Economic policy ideas and industrial relations models continued to be dominated for the most part by traditions and conditions peculiar to each country. The internationalization of trade union policy, which was so important in obtaining initial agreement with the ERP and winning one of the great battles of the Cold War, did not, however, change the power relationships between unions, industry, and government in individual countries. Even at the time of strongest dependence on the United States, and of increasing interdependence in the West, the bases of economic and social power, especially in the union field, were essentially national. The factors that defined how much power each party to labor-management negotiations had were rooted in the national framework much more than in the transnational dynamics stimulated by American policy.

In American assistance in the postwar reconstruction of Western Europe, the vigorous exercise of a strategically and politically successful leadership was accompanied by a relative incapacity to shape and guide the internal, national dynamics of the Allied nations. For the liberal currents, which had created the grandiose vision of reform and social pacification and entrusted it to the ERP, these limitations became suffocating and constricting. The "politics of productivity" had met the same ambiguous fate as the other pillar of the American vision of a Europe in the image of the American experience, the idea of continental unification. Both of these conceptions supported the strategy of containment and strongly legitimized American supremacy, but they also brought out its limits, marked by the persistence of national peculiarities in Europe.

The American vision gathered a solid alignment of Western forces and stimulated the creation of new paths to reconstruction, but the solutions drawn up by the Europeans, although strongly in an Atlantic framework, differed markedly from the American models. The principal organizer of national recovery was and remained the national state, which was the pivotal point of competitive modernization of the economy by means of industrial policy, controlled liberalization of trade, establishment of the welfare state, and organization of the agricultural market. European integration, though partial and limited, took the form of intergovernmental agreements that coordinated and reinforced the economic strategies of each nation. The mechanisms for regulating social conflicts and the new framework for industrial relations were reshaped by peculiarly national combinations of corporatist traditions and new electoral-coalition politics. Although politically functional for the strategic plans of the United States, the New Deal ideals of a socioeconomic reconstruction of Europe were shown to be "long-run dreams, which had only an impossible short term to be turned into realities."[6]

The historical reconstruction of the conceptual roots and the political origins of the New Deal vision promoted by the ERP has given us both the essential background of postwar American international policy and a valuable framework for interpreting its motivations, its overall reach, and its intellectual parameters.[7] My own analysis of the international activities of the American unions and, at greater length, of the American effort to reshape industrial relations in postwar Europe reflects and validates many elements of that reinterpretation of American diplomatic history that has taken the name of "corporatist synthesis."[8] But a reconstruction of the goals, motivations, and programs of the United States cannot automatically provide an analysis of their effects and impact on the foreign countries where they were carried out. This is because the consequences were often very different from those foreseen, and in the interaction with external reality the model of American neocapitalism displayed serious limitations and constrictions, as has been seen. Diplomatic history that analyzes the causes without considering their effects and ignores or undervalues the players—in this case the Europeans—runs the risk of reproducing that same flawed idea of American power that characterized the makers of the Marshall Plan.[9] In effect, the most important interpretive work of that school, although it is intensely focused on the force and extent of the impact of the American neocapitalistic model, agrees that the European economic structures and social institutions were only "half-Americanized." This confirms the conclusion to which the officials responsible for aid policy sadly had to come in the latter part of the 1950s. Although they emphasized the success of the "productivity drive" in industrial efficiency, they had to concede that its effects on social institutions and behavior were almost negligible.[10]

From a longer historical perspective, however, the attempt to export an apolitical productivist system of industrial relations based on business unionism gives rise to reservations not only because of its practical failure, but also because of the intrinsic domestic weakness of the model itself. In the Marshall Plan years, in fact, the overall influence of unions in American society began to decrease, commencing a historical phase of deep and steady decline. In the 1950s the principal unions were still able to maintain a relatively privileged status, especially in terms of wages for workers in large unionized firms. But they could no longer extend the area of collective bargaining and broaden union representation in the extensive non-unionized areas. They also had to give up any hope of stimulating the creation of public social welfare institutions. The role of unions in setting economic policy and in influencing major national decisions eroded rapidly, and the influence of labor in political life fell to drastically lower levels compared to those of Western Europe. With the bitter social and political conflict of the immediate postwar period, the unionist ambitions that arose in the New Deal were severely restructured and the workers' movement underwent a historic metamorphosis "from a Social Democratic insurgency into a mere interest group."[11] Forced into a few compartments of a deeply segmented labor market, and without any resources beyond its power of negotiating with firms, the American labor movement would experience a fall from power to comparatively low levels before the crisis of the 1970s and deindustrialization began a new era of structural difficulties for the trade union movement worldwide.

But the American liberals and union leaders, persuaded that the traditional European labor movement with its political base was now only a throwback to the past, had no idea of the coming decline. At the beginning of the Cold War, they thought that the American experience of the 1940s indicated the triumphal affirmation of prosperous capitalism, whose social inequalities would be effectively tempered by unions' negotiating activity. Industrial democracy and the connection of wages to productivity seemed to them a formula that could defeat stagnation and class conflict everywhere, raising business unionism to the status of a protagonist of economic growth.[12] Such a flawed perception of present and future challenges to the American trade union movement originated not only from the intoxication of power to which American leaders of the postwar period were naturally subjected. It was in some manner justified by the exceptional economic conditions of the period, and especially by the privileged position of American industry in world markets. At a time when the American economy turned out 40 percent of the world's production and all its competitors were beset with the task of reconstruction, even the leaders of the CIO could reasonably believe in the historical efficiency of a union model geared to obtaining significant economic benefits for limited sectors of the work force by industrial negotiations. This strategy could hold only so long as American industry enjoyed greater advantages in productivity levels, that is, as long as its uncontested domination of fairly extensive markets allowed it large economies of scale and permitted it to pay very high salaries, and as long as the absence of foreign competitors allowed mass production industries to increase output by expanding operations rather than by improving productivity. Only under these conditions could business unionism succeed in exchanging its own commitment to productivity for increasing wages and benefits. The inflationary consequence would not have immediately damaged the market positions of the major producers, but, as it dramatically came out at the beginning of the 1960s, this union strategy was to be seriously threatened as soon as German machinery and Japanese cars began to penetrate the American market.

The golden age of economic success for contractual American trade unions—the 1940s and 1950s, with their high wages in unionized sectors—did not indicate a universal historical model for improving social conditions by means of collective bargaining. This was only the illusion cultivated by American union leaders and vigorously projected to Europe by way of the Marshall Plan. In reality it was the reflection of a unique historical situation—not repeatable, much less exportable—of America's splendid isolation from the constraints of interdependence. The dislocation of the world's economy brought on by the Depression and the Second World War had provided the United States with two decades of a position so unique as to nourish a confidence—understandable in terms of the moment, but historically blind—not only in America's exceptionality but even in the universal validity of American solutions and characteristics.

The European experience obviously was quite different. In the first decade after the war, the intense restructuring that fed the boom of European economies was shaped and guided by each nation's obsessive concern for its ability to compete—and even to survive—in international markets. Historically oriented more to foreign trade, the countries in Europe—not to mention Japan—committed themselves to battle for exports and foreign currency with a long-term goal of diminishing the vulnerability of their national economies and expanding their presence in world trade. Foreign competition was the factor that determined investment strategies, guided government policy for increased production, and established standards of industrial efficiency.

The urgency of assuring their economy's viability in an interdependent world pushed European nations to modernize industry and take advantage of the extensive availability of labor and the weakness of the unions to keep wages stable and impose strong managerial control on workers. While the pillars of class-oriented trade unionism were being undermined, the severity of industrial restructuring did not allow room for wage increases sufficient to support a new contractualist trade union and productivity-oriented movement. For several years the European unions remained highly vulnerable to the process of competitive modernization of the economy, and no American plan for a productivist partnership with industry could remove the constrictions imposed on them by interdependence. It is on the basis of these deeply differing conditions that the diverging courses of the trade union movements in Europe and America should be interpreted. For the European organizations there was no realistic possibility of entrenching themselves in unassailable sectors of industry whose success in a large domestic market would not have been seriously damaged by a near parallel growth of productivity and wages.

If the weakness in industry prevented the European trade unionists from victoriously playing the contractualist role suggested by the Marshall Plan's New Deal idealism, their skepticism about this should also be considered. In their eyes, the American model appeared not only impracticable, but also intrinsically limited and not very promising. Because of their history and their need to forge solid alliances with political parties and to compensate for their inefficiency in a flexible labor market, European unions looked to a more ambitious and influential integration on the political level. Because industrial restructuring weakened their contractual power, many European unions looked on the investment boom as a process to be corrected and balanced by an increase in social spending to augment the income of the poorest groups. Throughout the 1950s they defined themselves more as a pressure group to increase employment and internal demand than as contract agents for their members.[13]

In effect, the American model proposed by the Marshall Plan suggested objectives both too difficult for the resources of the European unions in the early 1950s and too unsatisfactory for their future ambitions. It was difficult to apply to the present and insufficient in the long run. The American project contemplated a constructive interaction between industry and unions on a technical plane in a private rather than public setting. Labor and industry were supposed to negotiate on the basis of a common commitment to growth, a progressive acceleration of

productivity, and an equitable and timely division of its benefits. This was supposed to take place against a macroeconomic background determined by the
interaction of market forces and government policies that in theory were not to be
negotiated among organized interests. The placement of unions in contract mechanisms was supposed to be at the company level or, at most, at the industrial sector
level. But this was just where workers' organizations, in the first years of the 1950s,
could bring but little pressure to bear and therefore had not much influence. Their
long-run strategies were geared to sharing in the management of welfare state
institutions and formulating macroeconomic policies. In the 1950s this approach
responded to the need to distance themselves from the weakness and vulnerability
of labor in industry. But when increases in employment brought the unions to a
position of relative strength, these strategies drove them to play a political and
social role much more extensive than the one suggested by the trade union policies
of the ECA. After a decade on the sidelines when the wage dynamic was slow, the
European trade union movement acquired new strength, power, and social influence in the 1960s. With the onset of full employment and the end of the paralyzing
internal divisions of the Cold War, the labor organizations expanded their activities well beyond industry, attaining a wide and explicit role in public and
macroeconomic affairs. While the movement in America declined precipitously
and was made virtually impotent strategically, the European unions managed to
erect new systems of neocorporatist collaboration, whose scope of action was
incomparably vaster than the industrial cooperation pacts envisaged by the ECA.

In point of fact, the Marshall Plan's activities in the field of industrial relations
and union policy showed an unequal mixture of political success and ideological
frustration, of powerful geopolitical affirmations and unrealistically grandiose
projects. In this respect the American strategy for hegemony in Europe, in addition to revealing the inner workings of its vision, showed the characteristics of its
later evolution as a global policy. The intrinsic weaknesses of the theory of
modernization that sustained the containment doctrine were to emerge conspicuously in the following twenty years in many areas of the Third World, but they
were already present and working in the formative and victorious phase of that
strategy. The key ideas presiding over the expansion of American hegemony
clearly showed, in spite of the formidable success of postwar stabilization in
Europe, some of the congenital flaws that were later to vitiate their claims to
universal validity.

NOTES

Abbreviations Used in the Notes

AFL-CILR	AFL Committee on International Labor Relations
ALHUA	Archives of Labor History and Urban Affairs, Wayne State University, Detroit, Michigan
CG	Clinton S. Golden Letters, Pennsylvania State University Libraries, University Park, Pennsylvania
CIO-ST	Documents of the CIO, Secretary-Treasurer Collection
CIO-WPR	Documents of the CIO, Walter P. Reuther Collection
DD	David Dubinsky Letters, Archives of the International Ladies' Garment Workers' Union, New York, New York
ECA-W	Economic Cooperation Administration Central Offices, Washington, D.C.
ERP-*Hearings*	U.S. Congress. Senate. *Hearings before the Committee on Foreign Relations.* 80th Cong., 2d sess. Vols. 157–58, *Hearings on the European Recovery Program Bill.*
FRUS	*Foreign Relations of the United States,* 1944–54. Washington, D.C., 1959–77.
FT	Florence Thorne Papers, State Historical Society of Wisconsin, Madison, Wisconsin
LA	Luigi Antonini Letters, Archives of the International Ladies' Garment Workers' Union, New York, New York
OSR	Office of the Special Representative (Paris), Economic Cooperation Administration
PRO-FO	Public Record Office (Great Britain), Archives of the Foreign Office
RG 59 DS-NA	Record Group 59, General Records of the Department of State, National Archives, Washington, D.C.
RG 84 Post-NA	Record Group 84, Records of Foreign Service Posts of the Department of State, National Archives, Washington, D.C.
RG 169 FEA-NA	Record Group 169, Records of the Foreign Economic Administration, National Archives, Washington, D.C.
RG 174 DL-NA	Record Group 174, General Records of the Department of Labor, National Archives, Washington, D.C.

RG 226 OSS-NA   Record Group 226, Records of the Office of Strategic Services, Na-
                   tional Archives, Washington, D.C.
RG 286 ECA-NA   Record Group 286, Records of the Economic Cooperation Admin-
                   istration (within the Records of the Agency for International De-
                   velopment), National Archives, Washington, D.C.
RG 331 ACC-NA   Record Group 331, Records of the Allied Control Commission (within
                   the Records of Allied Operational and Occupation Headquarters,
                   World War II), National Archives, Washington, D.C.
ROWE   Records of the (Department of State) Office of Western European
                   Affairs Relating to Italy, National Archives, Washington, D.C.
VM   Vanni Montana Papers, Archives of the UIL, Rome

Chapter 1

1. "Address by the Secretary of State (Stettinius) before the Council on Foreign Relations, Chicago, April 4, 1945," in *Documents on American Foreign Relations, 1944–45*, 2:28–39.

2. Dean Acheson, *Department of State Bulletin* 22 (22 April 1945): 738.

3. See William A. Williams, *The Tragedy of American Diplomacy* (1959; reprint, New York, 1972), pp. 23–90; N. Gordon Levin, *Woodrow Wilson and World Politics: America's Response to War and Revolution* (New York, 1970). On Franklin D. Roosevelt's foreign policy, see Jean Baptiste Duroselle, *De Wilson à Roosevelt: Politique extérieure des Etats-Unis, 1913–1945* (Paris, 1960). On the influence of the more recent historical experience, see Ernest R. May, *"Lessons" of the Past* (New York, 1973), pp. 3–51. Further, Carlo M. Santoro, *La perla e l'ostrica: Alle fonti della politica globale degli Stati Uniti* (Milan, 1987).

4. See Cordell Hull, *Memoirs*, 2 vols. (New York, 1948); David P. Calleo and Benjamin M. Rowland, *America and the World Political Economy: Atlantic Dreams and National Realities* (Bloomington, Ind., 1973), pp. 35ff.; Gabriel Kolko, *The Politics of War: The World and U.S. Foreign Policy, 1943–45* (New York, 1968), pp. 244ff.; Richard Gardner, *Sterling-Dollar Diplomacy in Current Perspective* (1956; reprint, New York, 1980), pp. 12ff. For a discussion of the contradictory American attitude on the problem of spheres of influence in the final phase of the war, see Thomas G. Paterson, *On Every Front: The Making of the Cold War* (New York, 1979), pp. 33–68.

5. In addition to the work already mentioned by Williams, *Tragedy of American Diplomacy*, and Denna Fleming, *The Cold War and Its Origins (1917–1960)* (London, 1961), which constitute the progenitors of a vast store of revisionist writings, see Joyce and Gabriel Kolko, *The Limits of American Power* (New York, 1972); G. Kolko, *Politics of War*; Walter LaFeber, *America, Russia, and the Cold War, 1945–1966* (New York, 1967); Lloyd Gardner, *Architects of Illusion: Men and Ideas in American Foreign Policy, 1941–1949* (Chicago, 1970); Gar Alperowitz, *Atomic Diplomacy: Hiroshima and Potsdam* (New York, 1965); and Richard Freeland, *The Truman Doctrine and the Origins of McCarthyism* (1970; reprint, New York, 1972), p. 21, from which the quotation was taken. For a criticism of the revisionist approach, see Charles S. Maier, "Revisionism and the Interpretation of Cold War Origins," *Perspectives in American History* 4 (1970): 313–47, and Stanley Hoffman, "Revisionism Revisited," in

Reflections on the Cold War, ed. Ronald W. Preussen and Lynn H. Miller (Philadelphia, 1974), pp. 3–26. Among the principal standard histories of the Cold War, see Herbert Feis, *From Trust to Terror: The Outset of the Cold War, 1945–1950* (London, 1970), and Louis J. Halle, *The Cold War as History* (New York, 1967).

6. The quotation is from John L. Gaddis, "The Emerging Post-Revisionist Synthesis on the Origins of the Cold War," *Diplomatic History* 7, no. 3 (Summer 1983): 173. The main syntheses offered by postrevisionist historians are John L. Gaddis, *The United States and the Origins of the Cold War, 1941–1947* (New York, 1972); Daniel Yergin, *Shattered Peace: The Origins of the Cold War and the National Security State* (Boston, 1977); Robert A. Pollard, *Economic Security and the Origins of the Cold War, 1945–1950* (New York, 1985). The most enlightening specialized studies are Geir Lundestad, *America, Scandinavia, and the Cold War, 1945–1949* (New York, 1980); Bruce R. Kuniholm, *The Origins of the Cold War in the Near East* (Princeton, 1979); Michael S. Sherry, *Preparing for the Next War: American Plans for Postwar Defense, 1941–1945* (New Haven, 1977); Eduard Mark, "American Policy towards Eastern Europe and the Origins of the Cold War, 1941–1946: An Alternative Interpretation," *Journal of American History* 68, no. 2 (1981): 313–36. On the fear of appeasement in public opinion, see Michael Leigh, *Mobilizing Consent: Public Opinion and American Foreign Policy, 1937–1947* (Westport, Conn., 1976), p. 167, and Ralph B. Levering, *American Opinion and the Russian Alliance, 1939–1945* (Chapel Hill, N.C., 1976), p. 93.

7. Truman's phrase is cited in Paterson, *On Every Front*, p. 79. On the Lend-Lease agreements and the Bretton Woods negotiations, see the classic study of R. Gardner, *Sterling-Dollar Diplomacy*. On the connection between peace and prosperity, see the essay of Thomas G. Paterson, "The Quest for Peace and Prosperity: International Trade, Communism, and the Marshall Plan," in *Politics and Policies of the Truman Administration*, ed. Barton J. Bernstein (Chicago, 1970), pp. 78–112.

8. John Morton Blum, *V Was for Victory: Politics and American Culture during World War II* (New York, 1976), p. 9. The following statistical data were also taken from this work. On American society during the war, see also Richard Polenberg, *War and Society: The United States, 1941–1945* (Philadelphia, 1972); Richard E. Lingerman, *Don't You Know There's a War On?* (New York, 1970); James Gilbert, *Another Chance: Postwar America, 1945–1968* (New York, 1981), pp. 3–53; Harold G. Vatter, *The U.S. Economy in World War II* (New York, 1985).

9. For a detailed treatment of industrial relations in the period of postwar reconversion in the United States, see the end of this chapter.

10. Blum, *V Was for Victory*, pp. 245–332. On liberal proposals for the postwar world, see also Alonzo L. Hamby, *Beyond the New Deal: Harry S. Truman and American Liberalism* (New York, 1973), pp. 3ff. For an analysis of the economic and social transformations brought on by wartime mobilization, especially in Great Britain and the United States, and the political conditioning they caused, see Alan S. Milward, *War, Economy, and Society, 1939–1945* (Berkeley, 1977), pp. 339ff.

11. Charles S. Maier, "The Politics of Productivity: Foundations of American International Economic Policy after World War II," *International Organization* 31, no. 4 (1977), the quotations on p. 613 and p. 609, respectively. See also, by the same author, "The Two Postwar Eras and the Conditions for Stability in Twentieth Century Western Europe," *American Historical Review* 86, no. 2 (April 1981): 327–52.

12. On the "continuist" and neocorporatist views of the CIO leaders toward the postwar period, see esp. Nelson Lichtenstein, *Labor's War at Home: The CIO in World War II* (New York, 1982), pp. 216–21.

13. See Minutes of the CIO Executive Board, 16 June 1944, Documents of the CIO, Archives of Labor History and Urban Affairs, Wayne State University, Detroit (hereafter ALHUA), pp. 24–27; *CIO News* 7, no. 48 (25 November 1944) and no. 51 (18 December 1944).

14. On Reuther and the conflict in the UAW, see Harvey A. Levenstein, *Communism, Anticommunism, and the CIO* (Westport, Conn., 1981), pp. 184–206; Roger Keeran, *The Communist Party and the Auto Workers Union* (Bloomington, Ind., 1980), pp. 226–49. On Walter Reuther, see John Barnard, *Walter Reuther and the Rise of the Auto Workers* (Boston, 1983); Victor G. Reuther, *The Brothers Reuther and the Story of the UAW* (Boston, 1976); Henry M. Christman, ed., *Walter Reuther: Selected Papers* (New York, 1961); Irving Howe and Brian J. Widick, *The UAW and Walter Reuther* (New York, 1949); Frank Cormier and William J. Eaton, *Reuther* (Englewood Cliffs, N.J., 1970). On the history of the CIO in general, see Thomas R. Brooks, *Toil and Trouble: A History of American Labor* (New York, 1964); Bert Cochran, *Labor and Communism: The Conflict That Shaped American Unions* (Princeton, 1977); James R. Green, *The World of the Worker: Labor in Twentieth Century America* (New York, 1980); Robert Zieger, "Toward the History of the CIO: A Bibliographical Report," *Labor History* 26, no. 4 (Fall 1985): 485–516; Art Preis, *Labor's Giant Steps: Twenty Years of the CIO* (New York, 1964); and the interpretive essays of David Brody, *Workers in Industrial America: Essays on the Twentieth Century Struggle* (New York, 1980). Finally, on the relations between the CIO and the liberal forces at the end of the war, see Hamby, *Beyond the New Deal*, pp. 5–119, and James C. Foster, *The Union Politic: The CIO Political Action Committee* (Columbia, Mo., 1975), pp. 3–48.

15. On the importance of ethnic groups in the diffusion of anti-Soviet feelings, see in general Gaddis, *United States and the Origins*, pp. 44–53. On the importance of Catholic anticommunism in the CIO, and especially for the ACTU, see Keeran, *Communist Party*, p. 253; Leroy J. Lenburg, "The CIO and American Foreign Policy, 1935–1955" (Ph.D. dissertation, Pennsylvania State University, 1973), pp. 149ff.; Philip Taft, "The Association of Catholic Trade Unionists," *Industrial and Labor Relations Review* 2, no. 2 (January 1949): 210–18; Wilson D. Miscamble, "Catholics and American Foreign Policy from McKinley to McCarthy: A Historiographical Survey," *Diplomatic History* 4, no. 3 (Summer 1980): 236ff.; Michael Harrington, "Catholics in the Labor Movement: A Case History," *Labor History* 1, no. 3 (Fall 1960): 231–63; Ronald W. Schatz, "American Labor and the Catholic Church, 1919–1950," *International Labor and Working Class History* 20 (Fall 1981): 46–53.

16. See Lenburg, "CIO and American Foreign Policy," p. 132; Keeran, *Communist Party*, pp. 226–49; Levenstein, *Communism*, p. 193. For the comments on Yalta, see "CIO Hails Big Three Unity," *CIO News* 8, no. 8 (19 February 1945).

17. Testimony of James Carey, a CIO leader and among the most important protagonists of the federation's foreign policy in the postwar period, before the U.S. House Committee on Ways and Means, 1945, reported in Henry W. Berger, "Union Diplomacy: American Labor's Foreign Policy in Latin America, 1932–1955" (Ph.D. dissertation, University of Wisconsin, 1966), p. 251.

18. See *CIO News* 7, no. 33 (14 August 1944), and 8, no. 3 (14 January 1945).

19. For a historical view of the AFL's foreign policy, see Ronald Radosh, *American Labor and United States Foreign Policy* (New York, 1969), pp. 5–193; William C. Hamilton, "The Development of Foreign Policy Attitudes in Certain American Pressure Groups" (Ph.D. dissertation, Yale University, 1955), pp. 277–334; Michael Rogin, "Voluntarism: The Political Function of an Antipolitical Doctrine," *Industrial and Labor Relations Review* 15, no. 4 (July 1962); Berger, "Union Diplomacy," p. 269 and, for the CIO's international vision, esp. pp. 251–67 and 340–41. Also on the CIO, see Lenburg, "CIO and American Foreign Policy," pp. 104–10, 220–30.

20. See AFL, *Postwar Program* (Washington, D.C., 1944), p. 6; Joseph C. Goulden, *Meany* (New York, 1972), pp. 125–26.

21. AFL, *Postwar Program*, p. 6. On the concept of free trade unions and its importance in the construction of international relations, see Roy Godson, *American Labor and European Politics: The AFL as a Transnational Force* (New York, 1976), pp. 55–57; John P. Windmuller, *American Labor and the International Labor Movement, 1940–1953* (Ithaca, N.Y., 1954), p. 35; Goulden, *Meany*, p. 122.

22. Memorandum from Raphael Abramovich (American Labor Conference on International Affairs) to David Dubinsky, New York, 13 March 1945, David Dubinsky Letters, Archives of the International Ladies' Garment Workers' Union, New York, N.Y. (hereafter DD), box 2-173, folder 3B, p. 3. On George Meany and his anti-Communist development, see Goulden, *Meany*; Archie Robinson, *George Meany and His Times* (New York, 1981), p. 124. On David Dubinsky, see David Dubinsky and Abe H. Raskin, *David Dubinsky: A Life with Labor* (New York, 1977); Max Danish, *The World of David Dubinsky* (Cleveland, 1957); and "David Dubinsky, the ILGWU, and the American Labor Movement," a special issue of *Labor History* 9 (1968).

23. "The Labor Section of the OSS," memorandum from Arthur J. Goldberg to General William J. Donovan, OSS, Archives of the Central Intelligence Agency; see also, on the ILGWU's international activities, Dubinsky and Raskin, *David Dubinsky*, pp. 243–50, and Goulden, *Meany*, pp. 119–20. The influence of the network composed of the ILGWU, the OSS, and the European resistance to the AFL's political formulations was specially emphasized by Victor Reuther, interview with the author, Washington, D.C., 14 August 1984.

24. See American Federation of Labor, *Report of the Proceedings of the Sixty-fourth Annual Convention of the AFL* (Washington, D.C., 1944), pp. 556–57; see also Godson, *American Labor and European Politics*, pp. 36–47; Philip Taft, *Defending Freedom: American Labor and Foreign Affairs* (Los Angeles, 1973), pp. 69–71; Radosh, *American Labor*, pp. 198ff.

25. On Lovestone, see Keeran, *Communist Party*, pp. 188ff.; Radosh, *American Labor*, pp. 200–201. On his subsequent career (he was to become director of international relations of the AFL), see Dan Kurzman, "Labor's Cold Warrior," a series of articles in the *Washington Post*, 30 and 31 December 1965 and 1 and 2 January 1966; and Sidney Lens, "Lovestone Diplomacy," *Nation*, 5 July 1965.

26. Irving Brown, interview with the author, Washington, D.C., 14 August 1984; see also Goulden, *Meany*, p. 123.

27. Confidential memorandum, "To Help the Free and Democratic Labor Movements in Liberated Europe," Varian Fry to David Dubinsky and other members of the FTUC, New

York, 6 April 1945, DD, box 2-173, folder 3B. For the first year of operations in Europe, and for assistance to European union leaders, a total expenditure of $275,000 was estimated.

28. The centralized nature of the AFL's international relations is analyzed in Hamilton, "Development of Foreign Policy Attitudes," pp. 244–62.

29. See the Minutes of the AFL Committee on International Labor Relations (hereafter AFL-CILR), 11 June 1945, Florence Thorne Papers, State Historical Society of Wisconsin, Madison (hereafter FT). On developments of AFL and, more generally, U.S. operations in the German labor movement, see Horst Lademacher, "Konfrontation an der Nahstelle des Ost-West-Konflikts Aktivitäten in den westlichen Besatzungszonen," in *Gewerkschaften im Ost-West Konflikt*, ed. Horst Lademacher (Melsungen, 1982), pp. 13–76; Michael Fichter, *Besatzungsmacht und Gewerkschaften* (Opladen, 1982); Werner Link, *Deutsche und amerikanische Gewerkschaften und Geschäftsleute, 1945–1975* (Dusseldorf, 1978); Carolyn Eisenberg, "Working-Class Politics and the Cold War: American Intervention in the German Labor Movement, 1945–1949," *Diplomatic History* 7, no. 4 (Fall 1983): 283–306. On the case of Japan, see Howard Schoenberg, "American Labor's Cold War in Japan," *Diplomatic History* 3, no. 3 (Summer 1979): 249–72.

30. See Peter Weiler, "The U.S., International Labor, and the Cold War: The Breakup of the World Federation of Trade Unions," *Diplomatic History* 5, no. 1 (Winter 1981): 1–4; David Lasser, "Labor and World Affairs," *Foreign Policy Reports* 25, no. 13 (15 November 1949): 150–52; George E. Lichtblau, "The World Federation of Trade Unions," *Social Research* 25, no. 1 (Spring 1958): 1–11.

31. "New World Labor Setup to Guarantee Unity, Postwar Jobs," *CIO News* 7, no. 50 (11 December 1944). For the AFL's tendency to a privileged relationship with the TUC, see Joseph Carwell, "The International Role of American Labor" (Ph.D. dissertation, Columbia University, 1956), p. 142, and Robinson, *George Meany*, p. 131.

32. Minutes of the CIO Executive Board, 16 November 1944, Documents of the CIO, ALHUA, p. 29, and, on the question of the ILO, 28 January 1944, pp. 335–48; Matthew Josephson, *Sidney Hillman, Statesman of American Labor* (Garden City, N.Y., 1952), pp. 637–45.

33. Minutes of the AFL-CILR, 20 December 1944, FT.

34. See Public Record Office, Archives of the Foreign Office (hereafter PRO-FO), General Correspondence 371, ZM356/66/22, 14 January 1945, and ZM 524/66/22, 22 January 1945. In order not to reinforce the pro-Soviet left, both the TUC and the British government pushed for excluding the CGIL from the conference, in spite of the opposing views of the ambassador in Italy, Sir Noel Charles, who was concerned at the predictable anti-British reaction of the Italians. The CGIL was admitted later, but only at the last stage of the proceedings when the CIO's insistence won out over the opposition of the TUC. See also David Ellwood, *L'alleato nemico: La politica dell'occupazione anglo-americana in Italia, 1943–46* (Milan, 1977), p. 393, and Umberto Scalia, "La Federazione Sindacale Mondiale e i rapporti con la CGIL (1945–1973)," *Quaderni di rassegna sindacale*, no. 66/67 (May–August 1977): 191ff.

35. Minutes of the CIO Executive Board, 10 March 1945, Documents of the CIO, ALHUA, pp. 28–66; CIO, *Report of the CIO Delegates to the World Trade Union Conference*,

London, February 1945 (Washington, D.C., 1945); *CIO News* 8, no. 9 (26 February 1945); Josephson, *Sidney Hillman*, pp. 640–50.

36. See Windmuller, *American Labor*, p. 53; Lenburg, "CIO and American Foreign Policy," pp. 134–35.

37. William Green (president of the AFL), *The AFL and World Labor Unity* (Washington, D.C., August 1945), pp. 2–4; see also AFL Executive Council, *Position of the AFL on International Labor Cooperation* (Washington, D.C., 8 May 1945).

38. "Address by George Meany, Fraternal Delegate from the AFL to the British Trade Union Congress, Blackpool, England, September 1945," FT.

39. See "Report of a Trip to Italy by George Baldanzi, Member Executive Council CIO, August 19–September 24, 1944," Documents of the CIO, Secretary-Treasurer Collection (hereafter CIO-ST), ALHUA, box 132. Baldanzi's report from Italy and on his mission to the CGIL as a member of an Anglo-American trade union delegation will be discussed extensively in the next chapter.

40. See Windmuller, *American Labor*, pp. 223–24. Concerning the USSR, enthusiastic comments are noted from a CIO delegation after a visit in the spring of 1946, when the tension between the two superpowers was already rather high. The delegation seems to have been divided, and within its ranks there was no lack of more skeptical or even critical views, but the public statements of James Carey, even though he was decidedly anti-Communist, were completely positive. See *CIO News* 9, no. 13 (25 March 1946); see also Lenburg, "CIO and American Foreign Policy," p. 134.

41. See WFTU, *Resolution of the World Trade Union Congress* (London, 6–17 February 1945); "Report of the CIO Delegates to the World Trade Union Conference, Paris, Sept. 1945," in the Minutes of the CIO Executive Board, 1 November 1945, Documents of the CIO, ALHUA; "World Labor Unity," *CIO News* 8, no. 41 (8 October 1945); for the CGIL's comments, see *Il Lavoro*, 10 October 1945.

42. For an analysis of the unitary nature of the European unions at the end of the war, their strategy for reconstruction, and their political leanings, see the excellent overall interpretation by Lutz Niethammer, "Structural Reform and a Compact for Growth: Conditions for a United Labor Union Movement in Western Europe after the Collapse of Fascism," in *The Origins of the Cold War and Contemporary Europe*, ed. Charles S. Maier (New York, 1978), pp. 201–43. For a comparison between the trade union situations in Europe and the United States that presents interesting analogies for what concerns the CIO, see Federico Romero, "I sindacati nella Ricostruzione: Europa e Stati Uniti," *Rivista di storia contemporanea* 4 (1986): 527–55.

43. "Report of the Special Committee on Labor Standards and Social Security of the Inter-Departmental Committee on Postwar Foreign Economic Policy," Washington, D.C., April 1944, pp. 2–5, Record Group 59, General Records of the Department of State, National Archives, Washington, D.C. (hereafter RG 59 DS-NA), "Records of Harley Notter, 1939–1945," box 47.

44. "Declaration of Aim and Purposes of ILO," 26th General Conference, Philadelphia, 10 May 1944, in *Documents on American Foreign Relations, 1943–44*, 6:457–60.

45. Weiler, "U.S., International Labor," pp. 10–11, reports a telegram by George Kennan

from Moscow, dated 3 February 1945 (RG 59 DS-NA, 800.5043/2-345), from which this definition was taken.

46. See Radosh, *American Labor*, pp. 314–30; Godson, *American Labor and European Politics*, esp. pp. 131ff., and, by the same author, "The AFL Foreign Policy Making Process from the End of World War II to the Merger," *Labor History* 16, no. 3 (Summer 1975): 325–37; Taft, *Defending Freedom*, pp. 251ff.

47. Lichtenstein, *Labor's War at Home*, pp. 80 and 177. Lichtenstein's book offers the best account of industrial trade union affairs during the war. See also Joel Seidman, *American Labor from Defense to Reconversion* (Chicago, 1953); Patrick Renshaw, "Organized Labour and the United States War Economy, 1939–1945," *Journal of Contemporary History* 21 (1986): 3–22; James A. Gross, *The Reshaping of the National Labor Relations Board: National Labor Policy in Transition, 1937–1947* (Albany, N.Y., 1981).

48. Barton J. Bernstein, "The Truman Administration and Its Reconversion Wage Policy," *Labor History* 6, no. 3 (1965): 222ff.; Barton J. Bernstein and Alan J. Matusow, *The Truman Administration: A Documentary History* (New York, 1966), p. 47. On the liberal vision and priorities in postwar politics, see Hamby, *Beyond the New Deal*, pp. 5ff.

49. Nelson Lichtenstein, "Labor in the Truman Era: Origins of the 'Private Welfare State,'" in *The Truman Presidency*, ed. Michael J. Lacey (Cambridge, 1989), pp. 128–54; Reuther, *Brothers Reuther*, p. 247; Barnard, *Walter Reuther*, pp. 88ff.

50. Niethammer, "Structural Reform," pp. 203–6.

51. Howell Harris, *The Right to Manage: Industrial Relations Policies of American Business in the 1940s* (Madison, Wis., 1982); Hugh Rockoff, "The Response of the Giant Corporations to Wage and Price Controls in World War II," *Journal of Economic History* 41 (1981): 123–28.

52. On the strike at General Motors, see Lichtenstein, *Labor's War at Home*, pp. 224–30; Reuther, *Brothers Reuther*, pp. 248ff.; Brody, *Workers in Industrial America*, pp. 173ff.; Barnard, *Walter Reuther*, p. 102.

53. Harris, *Right to Manage*, p. 88; Neil Chamberlein, *The Union Challenge to Management Control* (New York, 1948).

54. Lichtenstein, *Labor's War at Home*, pp. 227–28; Seidman, *American Labor*, p. 229; Arthur F. McClure, *The Truman Administration and the Problems of Postwar Labor, 1945–1948* (Rutherford, 1969); Robert Donovan, *Conflict and Crisis* (New York, 1977), pp. 208–18; Hamby, *Beyond the New Deal*, pp. 5ff.; Blum, *V Was for Victory*, pp. 329–32.

55. Mary McAuliffe, *Crisis on the Left: Cold War Politics and American Liberals, 1947–1954* (Amherst, Mass., 1978), p. 10; Donovan, *Conflict and Crisis*, pp. 219ff.; Hamby, *Beyond the New Deal*, p. 140.

56. Barnard, *Walter Reuther*, pp. 109–16; Reuther, *Brothers Reuther*, pp. 257ff.; Keeran, *Communist Party*, pp. 250, 257; Ronald Schatz, *The Electrical Workers: A History of Labor at General Electric and Westinghouse, 1923–1960* (Urbana, Ill., 1983), pp. 183ff.; Martin Halpern, "Taft-Hartley and the Defeat of the Progressive Alternative in the U.A.W.," *Labor History* 27, no. 2 (1986): 204–26; Harrington, "Catholics in the Labor Movement," pp. 231–63; Levenstein, *Communism*, pp. 196–233.

57. Brody, *Workers in Industrial America*, p. 224; Foster, *Union Politic*, pp. 67–76; Hamby, *Beyond the New Deal*, pp. 148–68; McAuliffe, *Crisis on the Left*, pp. 7–14; Leon De Caux,

Labor Radical: From the Wobblies to the CIO, a Personal History (Boston, 1987), pp. 471–76; Cochran, *Labor and Communism*, pp. 260–77.

58. James B. Atleson, *Values and Assumptions in American Labor Law* (Amherst, Mass., 1983); Harris, *Right to Manage*, pp. 126–27; Lichtenstein, "Labor in the Truman Era."

59. Brody, *Workers in Industrial America*, pp. 173ff.; Lichtenstein, "Labor in the Truman Era." See also James O'Connor, *The Fiscal Crisis of the State* (New York, 1973), pp. 18–22.

60. Maier, "Politics of Productivity," p. 629.

Chapter 2

1. On the history of the Allied military administration, see Ellwood, *L'alleato nemico*; Harry L. Coles and Albert K. Weinberg, eds., *Civil Affairs: Soldiers Become Governors* (Washington, D.C., 1964); C. R. S. Harris, *Allied Military Administration of Italy, 1943–1945* (London, 1957); Elena Aga Rossi, *L'Italia nella sconfitta: Politica interna e situazione internazionale durante la seconda guerra mondiale* (Naples, 1985); Nicola Gallerano, "L'influenza dell'amministrazione militare alleata sulla riorganizzazione dello Stato italiano (1943–1945)," *Italia contemporanea*, no. 115 (April–June 1974): 4–22; Norman Kogan, *Italy and the Allies* (Cambridge, Mass., 1956). On the economic and financial aspects, see esp. Andrew M. Kamarck, *La politica finanziaria degli Alleati in Italia (luglio 1943–febbraio 1947)* (1951; reprint, Rome, 1977); Elena Aga Rossi, *Il Rapporto Stevenson: Documenti sull'economia italiana e sulle direttive della politica americana in Italia nel 1943–44* (Rome, 1979).

2. See "The Treatment of Italy," 31 August 1944, State Department document cited in Ellwood, *L'alleato nemico*, p. 94. For a discussion of the Hyde Park declaration, see ibid., pp. 97–124 and 317ff. See also John L. Harper, *America and the Reconstruction of Italy, 1945–1948* (Cambridge, 1986), pp. 22–36. The connection of Roosevelt's announcement with the political campaign is specially emphasized by James Miller, "The Politics of Relief: The Roosevelt Administration and the Reconstruction of Italy, 1943–1944," *Prologue* 13, no. 3 (Fall 1981): 193–208. See also Miller's *The United States and Italy, 1940–1950: The Politics and Diplomacy of Stabilization* (Chapel Hill, N.C., 1986), esp. chaps. 2 and 4. On the importance of the Communist problem from March 1944 on, see Ennio Di Nolfo, "The United States and Italian Communism, 1942–1946: World War II to Cold War," *Journal of Italian History* 1, no. 1 (Spring 1978): 74–94, and also Di Nolfo's *Le paure e le speranze degli italiani (1943–1953)* (Milan, 1986), pp. 99–105, as well as Ellwood, *L'alleato nemico*, pp. 77–79.

3. Telegram from Wilson to the Department of State, 2 January 1944, RG 59 DS-NA, 865.5043. For local violations, see Record Group 226, Records of the Office of Strategic Services, National Archives, Washington, D.C. (hereafter RG 226 OSS-NA), report 70757 of 10 May 1944.

4. See Paolo De Marco, "Il difficile esordio del governo militare e la politica sindacale," *Italia contemporanea*, 1979, no. 136:39–66; Bruno Bezza, "La ricostruzione del sindacato nel Sud," in *Problemi del movimento sindacale in Italia, 1943–1973*, Annali della Fondazione Feltrinelli, vol. 16, ed. Aris Accornero (Milan, 1976), pp. 109–33; Maria Teresa Di Paola, "La

politica del lavoro della amministrazione alleata in Sicilia," *Italia contemporanea*, 1977, no. 127:31–51; and Ellwood, *L'alleato nemico*.

5. See reports 56944 of 9 February 1944 and 71333 of 3 April 1944, RG 226 OSS-NA; and Bezza, "La ricostruzione del sindacato," pp. 114–15.

6. CIC memorandum, "Labor Organization," signed by W. Gordon, 11 March 1944, Record Group 331, Records of the Allied Control Commission, Allied Operational and Occupational Headquarters, National Archives, Washington, D.C. (hereafter RG 331 ACC-NA), 10260-146-107. On the stages of the rebirth of the trade unions in the south, see Sergio Turone, *Storia del sindacato in Italia dal 1943 ad oggi* (1973; reprint, Bari, 1984), pp. 69ff. On the CGL in Naples, see Antonio Alosco, *Alle radici del sindacalismo: La ricostruzione della CGL nell'Italia liberata (1943–1944)* (Milan, 1979); Bezza, "Le ricostruzione del sindacato," pp. 125–26; Clara De Marco, "La constituzione della Confederazione Generale del Lavoro e la scissione di Montesanto (1943–1944)," *Giovane critica*, no. 27 (1971): 52–74; Margherita Zander, "Die Schwächen der unvollendeten Einheit Italien," in *Gewerkschaften im Ost-West Konflikt*, ed. Horst Lademacher, pp. 83–87; and Giovanni De Luna, *Storia del Partito d'Azione: La rivoluzione democratica (1942–1947)* (Milan, 1982), p. 141.

7. See the comments of subcommission chairman Bain, in the minutes of the monthly meeting, 30 May 1944, RG 331 ACC-NA, 1000-136-163, pp. 19–20. On the structural inadequacy of the subcommission, see Maurice F. Neufeld, "The Failure of the Allied Military Government in Italy," *Public Administration Review*, April 1946, pp. 137–47.

8. Noel M. MacFarlane to Pietro Badoglio, 19 May 1944, RG 331 ACC-NA, 10000-136-437. The text of General Order No. 28 is in PRO-FO 371, R 17919/1133/22, report no. 1 of Labour Attaché W. Braine.

9. See "Memorandum to Mr. Braine: Draft Decree Dealing with Trade Unions and Associations," 11 July 1945, 10000/146/49; Harland Cleveland to W. H. Braine, 9 February 1945, 10000/146/31; Junius R. Smith to W. H. Braine, 29 January 1945, 10000/146/49, all in RG 331 ACC-NA.

10. Memorandum of E. Scicluna, "General Observations on the Major Issues Raised in the Analysis and Criticism of the May Draft Decree," enclosure to the letter from Junius R. Smith to W. H. Braine, 29 January 1945, cited in n. 9 above.

11. See ibid., p. 14. Further, see A. G. Antolini to the Acting Chief Commissioner, 13 October 1944, 10000/136/438; for the intervention of the State Department, Alexander Kirk to Commodore Stone, 6 October 1944, 10000/136/438, both documents in RG 331 ACC-NA.

12. See "The Government's Draft for Basic Labor Legislation," report of John C. Adams, Rome, 23 April 1945, Record Group 84, Post-Consular Files, Records of the Foreign Service Posts of the Department of State, National Archives, Washington, D.C. (hereafter RG 84 Post-NA), 850.4-Italy.

13. Report of the OSS attached to Alexander Kirk's message to the Department of State, RG 59 DS-NA, 865.5043/8-2144. For the historiographical interpretations of the pact of Rome, on which most agree in emphasizing its political character, see Turone's synthesis, *Storia del sindacato*, pp. 31–82, and, in addition, Sandro Zaninelli, "Politica e organizzazione sindacale dal 1943 al 1948," in *Il sindacato nuovo*, ed. Sandro Zaninelli (Milan, 1981), p. 281; Bianca Beccalli, "La ricostruzione del sindacalismo italiano, 1943–1950," in *Italia, 1943–1950:*

La ricostruzione, ed. Stuart J. Woolf (Bari, 1974), pp. 330–37; Daniel Horowitz, *Storia del movimento sindacale in Italia* (Bologna, 1966), pp. 300–308.

14. For a discussion of the crisis brought on by the request for cost of living allowances, and its many implications, see PRO-FO 371, R 17853/1133/22, where the necessity of an overall review of Allied trade union policy and a change in the myopic and mistrustful attitude of the military administration was explicit and supported by Labour Attaché W. H. Braine. See also Ellwood, *L'alleato nemico*, pp. 388–89.

15. See PRO-FO 371, R 7109/1133/22, for the Department of State's opinion, and PRO-FO 371, R 3045/1133/22, for Bevin's hesitation, in a letter of 30 March 1944.

16. Telegram from Macmillan to the Foreign Office, 12 April 1944, PRO-FO 371, R 5901/1133/22, and A. Eden to Sir W. Citrine, 7 April 1944, PRO-FO 371, R 5424/687/4.

17. In this connection, see the references in n. 2 above.

18. *New York Times*, 3 June 1944.

19. See Luigi Criscuolo to the Secretary of State, New York, 3 June 1944, and Joseph Masci (president of UPWA-CIO Local 11) to the Secretary of State, Boston, 6 June 1944, RG 59 DS-NA, 865.5043; and *New York Times*, 17 June 1944.

20. See Vanni Montana, *Amarostico: Testimonianze euro-americane* (Leghorn, 1975), pp. 171–202. On the center abroad in Switzerland, see Francesca Taddei, *Il socialismo italiano nel dopoguerra* (Milan, 1984), pp. 26–36. On the career of Antonini, see John S. Crawford, *Luigi Antonini: His Influence on Italian American Relations* (New York, 1950).

21. See Ronald L. Filippelli, *American Labor and Postwar Italy, 1943–1954* (Stanford, 1989), pp. 20–32; Miller, "Politics of Relief," and, by the same author, "La politica dei 'prominenti' italo-americani nei rapporti dell'OSS," *Italia contemporanea*, 1980, no. 139:51–70, and *United States and Italy*, chaps. 2 and 4. On the political activities and influence of the Italian Americans as a pressure group, see Elena Aga Rossi, "La politica estera americana e l'Italia nella Seconda Guerra Mondiale," in *Italia e America dalla grande guerra ad oggi*, ed. Giorgio Spini, Gian Giacomo Migone, and Massimo Teodori (Venice, 1976), pp. 159–77, and Nadia Venturini, "Italian American Political Leadership, 1943–1948," *Storia nordamericana* 2, no. 1 (1985): 5–12. On the "fuoruscti" and the Mazzini Society, see Antonio Varsori, *Gli alleati e l'emigrazione democratica antifascista (1940–43)* (Florence, 1982); Maddalena Tirabassi, "La Mazzini Society (1940–1946): Una associazione degli antifascisti italiani negli Stati Uniti," in *Italia e America dalla grande guerra ad oggi*, ed. Giorgio Spini, Gian Giacomo Migone, and Massimo Teodori, pp. 141–58; James Miller, "Carlo Sforza e l'evoluzione della politica americana verso l'Italia," *Storia contemporanea* 7 (December 1976): 825–53. On the IALC in particular, see IALC, *Annual Report of 18 December 1943* (New York, 1944); Serafino Romualdi, *Presidents and Peons* (New York, 1967), pp. 19ff.; Montana, *Amarostico*, pp. 228ff.

22. Two memoranda of Otis Mulliken, RG 59 DS-NA, 865.504/6-2644 and 865.504/7-144; memorandum of telephone conversation, W. Green and B. Long, RG 59 DS-NA, 865.504/7-1344; James Carey to George Baldanzi, 11 July 1944, CIO-ST, ALHUA, box 132.

23. Cunard (Acting Regional Director, Italy) to Scarlett, 15 June 1944, and comments by Ross, 19 June 1944, both in PRO-FO 371, R 9333/1133/22.

24. See the discussion and the Foreign Office telegram to Washington of 21 June 1944, PRO-FO 371, R 9692/1133/22.

25. Telegram from the Foreign Office to Washington, 3 July 1944; the opinion of the Department of State is in the telegram from the British embassy in Washington to the Foreign Office, 25 June 1944; that of the TUC is in the notes dated 29 June 1944; all in PRO-FO 371, R 10002/1133/22. Apparently, the Soviets did not make any request to participate; instead, they sent their own trade union delegation to Italy a few months later.

26. Joint AFL-IALC document, "Italian Labor Is Traditionally Non-partisan in Politics," unpublished, n.d. (but probably May/June 1944), in the Vanni Montana Papers, Archives of the UIL, Rome (hereafter VM).

27. "IALC Warns US against Support of Communists in Italian Coalition Government," *New York Times*, 15 April 1944; Montana, *Amarostico*, pp. 250–51; IALC, "Statement of the Executive Committee," 18 July 1944, RG 59 DS-NA, 865.5043.

28. George Baldanzi to James Carey, 31 July 1944. Baldanzi was trying to obtain an appointment for Philip Murray with Father Luigi Sturzo, and later with President Roosevelt, to promote a drastic change in the American attitude to Italy, emphasizing that the forecasts on the Italian American vote were discouraging for the president, to whose reelection the CIO was deeply committed. Enclosed with the letter was a petition to Roosevelt that had been voted in a mass meeting of the FIALC in New York on 25 July 1944, in which a long message from Father Sturzo had solicited Italy's rehabilitation. For comments on anti-Fascist unity, see Rev. R. A. McGowan to James Carey, "Memorandum on the Catholic Social Movement in Europe," 25 July 1944. All these documents are in CIO-ST, ALHUA, box 132.

29. Memorandum of Otis Mulliken, 865.504/6-2644, cited in note 22 above.

30. PRO-FO 371, R 1314/1133/22 and R 14267/1133/22.

31. "Report on Labor Delegates' Tour of Certain Areas in Liberated Italy," RG 59 DS-NA, 865.504/10-244. Written by the American official B. Di Venuti, who, together with Scicluna of the Labour Sub-Commission, accompanied the delegation, the report contains in an appendix the minutes of nearly all the meetings the five Anglo-American trade unionists had.

32. Ibid.

33. Letters of Luigi Antonini to William Green and David Dubinsky, 1 September 1944, DD, box 2-395, folder 1A.

34. On the conference in Rome, see CGIL, *I Congressi della CGIL*, vol. 1 (Rome, 1970), pp. 17ff., and "Report on Labor Delegates' Tour," enclosures 9 and 10.

35. Walter Schevenels, "Report on Trade Union Visit to Italy, Aug.–Sept. 1944," p. 51, PRO-FO 371, R/17449/1133/22.

36. Notations by A. Ross, 1 November 1944, concerning the Schevenels report, PRO-FO 371, R/17449/1133/22.

37. Major E. Scicluna, "Memorandum on the Soviet Labour Delegation to Italy," p. 34, RG 331 ACC-NA, 10000/132/327. See also Scicluna's reports of 9 and 15 October, in ibid., and Ellwood, *L'alleato nemico*, p. 393.

38. George Baldanzi, "Report of a Trip to Italy to Investigate the Labor Movement of That Country on Behalf of the CIO, Aug. 19–Sept. 24, 1944," CIO-ST, ALHUA, box 132, quotations on pp. 32 and 33.

39. See n. 34 to chap. 1.

40. "Rapporto supplementare di Luigi Antonini sulla missione sindacale in Italia," November 1944, Luigi Antonini Letters, Archives of the International Ladies' Garment Workers' Union, New York, N.Y. (hereafter LA), box 45, folder 2.

41. S. Romualdi to E. Brennan, 30 October 1944; S. Romualdi to L. Antonini, 28 October 1944; L. Antonini to E. Brennan, 12 December 1944; L. Antonini to S. Romualdi, 12 December 1944; all in LA, box 41, folder 4; "IALC Financial Report," 31 December 1944, LA, box 2-256, folder 2B.

42. L. Antonini to S. Romualdi, 18 January 1945, and S. Romualdi to L. Antonini, 25 January 1945, LA, box 41, folder 4; Montana, *Amarostico*, pp. 263–84. Serafino Romualdi, an official of the ILGWU and OSS agent, became the AFL representative in Latin America after the war. Earl Brennan, an OSS official, served during those months as a go-between for the transmission of IALC aid. See Romualdi, *Presidents and Peons*, pp. 22ff.; A. E. Jolis, "The O.S.S. and the Labor Movement," *New Leader*, 31 August 1946; and Roberto Faenza and Marco Fini, *Gli americani in Italia* (Milan, 1976), p. 17.

43. P. Nenni to L. Antonini, 10 March 1945, LA, box 36, folder 6; I. Silone to L. Antonini, 28 March 1945, LA, box 44, folder 1; L. Antonini to S. Romualdi, 1 March 1945, and S. Romualdi to L. Antonini, 15 and 21 February 1945, LA, box 41, folder 4. For the controversy in the newspapers, see *Italia nuova*, 11 February 1945, *l'Unità* and *Italia libera*, 13 February 1945, *Avanti!* and *Il Popolo*, 14 February 1945.

44. S. Romualdi to L. Antonini, 1 April 1945, LA, box 41, folder 4; G. E. Modigliani to L. Antonini, 15, 18, and 27 March 1945, LA, box 35, folder 5.

45. L. Antonini to P. Nenni, 24 May 1945, LA, box 36, folder 6; S. Romualdi to L. Antonini, 21 February 1945, and L. Antonini to S. Romualdi, 1 March 1945, LA, box 41, folder 4. On the decision to use IALC funds for the Socialist party's trade union activities, see also RG 226 OSS-NA, report no. L53265 of 1 February 1945, probably written by Romualdi, and Filippelli, *American Labor*, pp. 33–50.

46. PRO-FO 371, R 10731/1133/22, 7 July 1944.

47. W. H. Braine, "Memorandum on Industrial and Labour Problems in Italy," 14 October 1944; D. F. Howard to Noel Charles, 24 November 1944; both in PRO-FO 371, R 17853/1133/22. Report no. 1 from Braine in PRO-FO 371, R 17919/1133/22.

48. W. H. Braine to Col. Densmore, 29 January 1945, RG 331 ACC-NA, 10000/132/327; "Report on the Naples Congress of the CGIL," written by Scicluna and annexed to A. Kirk to the Secretary of State, RG 59 DS-NA, 865–5043/2-1045; RG 226 OSS-NA, report no. 116087 of 8 February 1945, probably by Romualdi. On the proceedings, see CGIL, *I Congressi*, vol. 1, and *Il Lavoro*, from 30 January 1945 to 2 February 1945.

49. W. H. Braine to Col. Densmore, 14 February 1945, RG 331 ACC-NA, 10000/146/40.

50. W. H. Braine to Economic Section, 25 January 1945, RG 331 ACC-NA, 10000/146/49.

51. W. H. Braine to Economic Section, 8 February 1945, and memorandum of J. Di Fede for Braine, 15 March 1945, both in RG 331 ACC-NA, 10000/146/40.

52. For the application to the CGIL's experience of a similar analytic model constructed on a comparative basis, see Niethammer, "Structural Reform."

53. Adolfo Pepe, "La CGIL dalla ricostruzione alla scissione (1944–1948)," *Storia contemporanea* 5 (1974): 593–611; Vittorio Foa, "Sindacati e lotte sociali," in *Storia d'Italia*, vol. 5, pt. 2 (Turin, 1973), pp. 1815–23.

54. Laura Pennacchi, "La concezione del ruolo del sindacato nella CGIL dal Patto di Roma alla rottura dell'Unità," in *Problemi del movimento sindacale*, ed. Aris Accornero, pp. 257–86; Maurizio Vannicelli, "A Labor Movement in Search of a Role" (Ph.D. dissertation, Harvard University, 1983), chap. 1.

55. "Statement of Labor Sub-Commission Policy," of W. H. Braine, 23 March 1945, enclosure to A. Kirk to the Secretary of State, RG 59 DS-NA, 865.504/3-2345. Actually, historical analysis has pointed out the CGIL's political nature as one of the factors working against the development of Italian labor organizations in the direction of trade unions in the postwar period. See Foa, "Sindacati e lotte sociali," p. 1823, and Piero Craveri, *Sindacato e istituzioni nel dopoguerra* (Bologna, 1977), pp. 38–41.

56. Beccalli, "La Ricostruzione," p. 364.

57. Account of the meeting with Lizzadri and Grandi in "Memorandum for Mr. Braine," by J. Di Fede, 15 March 1945, RG 331 ACC-NA, 10000/146/40; subsequent instructions in "Statement of Labour Sub-Commission Policy," and in W. H. Braine to Col. Densmore, 20 March 1945, RG 331 ACC-NA, 10000/146/49.

58. Secretary of State to A. Kirk, 23 February 1945, RG 59 DS-NA, 865.504/2-2345.

59. "Unsigned Memorandum of Mons. Domenico Tardini," 22 March 1945, enclosure to M. Taylor to the Secretary of State, RG 59 DS-NA, 865.5043/3-2245, and Taylor's comments in this document. To better understand the meaning of Taylor's views, it should be recalled that in his long mission at the Vatican he presented in extensive conversations with the pope and Monsignor Tardini a political vision based on the anti-Communist imperative, the convergence of the liberal and moderate forces with the Christian Democrats, and a greater American presence in Italy and the Mediterranean, which anticipated the groupings that formed later in the frontal clash of the Cold War. In 1944–45 Taylor was already a firm supporter of postwar stability in Italy based on De Gasperi's Christian Democratic party and on the role of the Catholics, as well as the monarchy, in which his views corresponded to those of the Vatican. See Ennio Di Nolfo, *Vaticano e Stati Uniti 1939–1952 (dalle carte di Myron Taylor)* (Milan, 1978).

60. Report of J. C. Adams, "Formation of the Italian Workers Christian Association," 23 March 1945, RG 84 Post-NA, 850.4-ACLI.

61. S. Romualdi to L. Antonini, 21 February 1945, LA, box 41, folder 4.

62. Report of Adams on the ACLI cited in note 60. On the ACLI and the trade union movement, see Giuseppe Pasini, *Le ACLI dalle origini, 1944–1948* (Rome, 1974), pp. 37ff., and the preface by Pietro Scoppola, pp. 6–8; Sandro Fontana, *I cattolici e l'unità sindacale, 1943–1947* (Bologna, 1978), pp. 49–51; Achille Grandi, *Scritti e discorsi, 1944–1946: I cattolici e l'unità sindacale* (Rome, 1976), p. 53 of the introduction by Walter Tobagi.

63. Report of J. C. Adams, "The Italian General Confederation of Labor (CGIL)," 12 April 1945, RG 84 Post-NA, 850.4-Italy (CGIL).

64. W. H. Braine, "Labour and Employment in Northern Italy," 21 May 1945, RG 331 ACC-NA, 10000/146/37; see also "Report of Meeting of Labour Officers for Northern Italy," 26 June 1945, RG 331 ACC-NA, 10000/146/221.

65. Enzo Collotti, "La collocazione internazionale dell'Italia dall'armistizio alle premesse dell'alleanza atlantica (1943–1947)," in *L'Italia dalla Liberazione alla Repubblica*, by Enzo Collotti et al. (Milan, 1976), pp. 50ff.; and Ellwood, *L'alleato nemico*, pp. 297–301 and 396–99.

66. Memorandum of Robert E. Murphy, Assistant to the Director of European Affairs, "Possible Resurrection of Communist International. Resumption of Extreme Leftist Activities, Possible Effect on U.S.," 2 June 1945, in *Foreign Relations of the United States* (hereafter *FRUS*), 1945, 1:267–80.

67. Gaddis, *United States and the Origins*, pp. 198–243; Yergin, *Shattered Peace*, pp. 110ff.; Paterson, *On Every Front*, pp. 39–40.

68. Memorandum of E. W. Stone, "Future Policy toward Italy, 23 June 1945," *FRUS*, 1945, 1:688–94. The commentary is in the accompanying note to the memorandum of W. E. Dowling to J. Grew, 11 July 1945, RG 59 DS-NA, Records of the Office of Western European Affairs Relating to Italy, 1943–51 (hereafter ROWE), box 3. There is a useful discussion on the political implications of this document in Ellwood, *L'alleato nemico*, p. 148.

69. Egidio Ortona, *Anni d'America: La ricostruzione, 1944–1951* (Bologna, 1984), p. 113. This is a particularly significant account because Ortona, recently arrived in Washington as a member of the Italian economic mission to the United States, was then the diplomatic official in charge of the aid negotiations. On the activities and the role of Ambassador Tarchiani, see also Collotti, "La collocazione internazionale," p. 72; Harper, *America and the Reconstruction*, p. 39; and Ellwood, *L'alleato nemico*, p. 150.

70. Harper, *America and the Reconstruction*, pp. 39–42 and 50–57; and Ennio Di Nolfo, "Stati Uniti e Italia tra la seconda guerra mondiale e il sorgere della guerra fredda," in *Italia e USA dall'Indipendenza americana ad oggi, 1776–1976*, by Ennio Di Nolfo et al. (Genoa, 1978), pp. 123–35. On the British attitude, see Ellwood, *L'alleato nemico*, pp. 155–64.

71. Harper, *America and the Reconstruction*, pp. 40ff. William L. Clayton, assistant secretary of state for economic affairs, was the principal supporter of a free trade policy in the immediate postwar period, and of the use of American resources to promote it. For the economic reconstruction of Italy, he proposed measures to liberalize foreign trade, the abolition of trade barriers, and the liquidation of autarchic production. On several occasions, the adoption of such a policy was suggested to Italy as a condition for obtaining financial aid. But in 1945, whatever the Italian decisions might have been, the Department of State was not in a position to obtain significant credits for Italy from Congress. See W. Clayton to A. Kirk, 10 July 1945, RG 59 DS-NA, 865.50/7-1045, and "Memorandum of Conversation" between Clayton and Ambassador Tarchiani, Washington, D.C., 14 September 1945, copy in RG 84 Post-NA, 850.4-Italy.

72. The definition is by Craveri, *Sindacato e istituzioni*, p. 152; on the situation in the main industrial areas, see Liliana Lanzardo, *Classe operaia e partito comunista alla Fiat, 1945–1948* (Turin, 1971), pp. 41–263; Paride Rugafiori, Fabio Levi, and Salvatore Vento, *Il triangolo industriale tra ricostruzione e lotta di classe, 1945–1948* (Milan, 1975). For a different point of view, see Zaninelli, *Il sindacato nuovo*, p. 286; Piero Bairati, *Vittorio Valletta* (Turin, 1983), pp. 130ff.

73. "Summary of Developments in the Labour Field up to June 1945," report of W. H. Braine, PRO-FO 371, ZM 4372/66/22, p. 3.

74. See, for example, the telegram from Secretary of State Byrnes to the ambassador in Rome, 29 August 1945, which requested prompt information on the tendency toward "socialization of corporations," RG 84 Post-NA, 850.4-Italy; Liliana Lanzardo, "I consigli di Gestione nella strategia della collaborazione," in *Problemi del movimento sindacale*, ed. Aris Accornero, pp. 325–30; and Craveri, *Sindacato e istituzioni*, pp. 156–64.

75. "Confidential Monthly Labor Report, Feb. 1946," of J. C. Adams, RG 84 Post-NA, 850.4-Italy. There is a similar British view in N. Charles to E. Stone, 11 March 1946, RG 331 ACC-NA, 10000/136/438.

76. E. Stone to A. Kirk, 26 February 1945, RG Post-NA, 850.4-Italy. On the FIAT agreement and its significance as a turning point in the history of the worker-management councils, see Lanzardo, *Classe operaia*, pp. 203–63; Craveri, *Sindacato e istituzioni*, pp. 176–80. See Bairati, *Vittorio Valletta*, pp. 139–69, for the very close relations between Valletta and the Allies.

77. "Summary of Developments in the Labour Field," pp. 2–4.

78. "Report of Labour Sub-Commission for the Month of May 1945," PRO-FO 371, ZM3640/225/22.

79. "Labour Problem in Italy—August 1945," report of W. H. Braine, PRO-FO 371, ZM 4884/225/22.

80. "The Problem of Unemployment in Northern Italy after Sept. 30, 1945," report of H. G. Ainsworth, 17 September 1945, RG 84 Post-NA, 850.4-Italy. On the views of the industrialists, see Massimo Legnani, "'L'utopia grande-borghese': L'associazionismo padronale tra ricostruzione e repubblica," in *Gli anni della costituente: Strategie dei governi e delle classi sociali*, by Marcello Flores et al. (Milan, 1983), pp. 154–57.

81. "Labour Problem in Italy."

82. Noel Charles to Ernest Bevin, 10 September 1945, PRO-FO 371, ZM 4884/225/22.

83. See, for example, the reports of Scicluna from Piedmont, "Monthly Report for July 1945," 2 August 1945, RG 84 Post-NA, 850.4-Italy, and "Monthly Report for August 1945," 30 August 1945, RG 331 ACC-NA, 10000/146/221. See also two reports of J. C. Adams, "Italian Labor Leaders," 18 June 1945, and "The Position of the Action Party within the Labor Movement," 3 August 1945, both in RG 84 Post-NA, 850.4-Italy.

84. Claudio Dellavalle, "Occupazione e salario: Conflitto e mediazione al nord," in *Gli anni della costituente*, by Marcello Flores et al., pp. 319–23.

85. Noel Charles to Ernest Bevin, Rome, 7 September 1945, PRO-FO 371, ZM 4882/225/22.

86. Report of W. H. Braine, "British Trade Union Delegation—Visit to Northern Italy," 20 December 1945, RG 331 ACC-NA, 10000/146/244. For an account of the visit, see *Il lavoro*, 20 December 1945.

87. "Final Report of Regional Labor Officer, Lombardy Region," 3 October 1945, RG 84 Post-NA, 850.4-Italy.

88. For a detailed analysis of this ambiguity in the nature of the CGIL, see the essays of Pepe, "La CGIL dalla ricostruzione," Beccalli, "La ricostruzione," and Aris Accornero, "Per una nuova fase di studi sul movimento sindacale," in *Problemi del movimento sindacale*, ed. Aris Accornero, pp. 1–105.

89. Vannicelli, "Labor Movement," pp. 1–88. The author sums up these fundamental characteristics of the CGIL in the immediate postwar period with the formulas "ideological globalism" and "tribune role."

90. J. C. Adams, "Confidential Monthly Labor Report, October 1945," 5 November 1945, RG 84 Post-NA, 850.4-Italy.

91. J. C. Adams, "Confidential Judgements on Italian Labor Leaders," 9 November 1945, RG 84 Post-NA, 850.4-Italy, and RG 226 OSS-NA, report no. L15002 of 15 August 1945. See

also J. C. Adams, "Confidential Monthly Labor Report, October 1945," cited in n. 90. Adams mentions the views expressed by Major Fisher, an American who was stationed in Genoa.

92. E. Scicluna to the Director, Labor Sub-Commission, 10 October 1945, RG 331 ACC-NA, 10000/149/49. For Grandi's initiative, see Grandi, *Scritti e discorsi*, pp. 70–73.

93. Report of W. H. Braine, "The Roman Catholic Church and the Italian Worker," 12 September 1945, PRO-FO 371, ZM 4947/66/22.

94. Camillo Daneo, *La politica economica della ricostruzione, 1945–1949* (Turin, 1975), pp. 178–81; Dellavalle, "Occupazione e Salario," pp. 342–54. Craveri, *Sindacato e istituzioni*, p. 210, sees in the industrial agreements the moment of the subordination of the union's bargaining strategies to the restoration of capitalism. Similar views are presented in Vittorio Foa, *Sindacato e lotte operaie, 1943–1973* (Turin, 1975), pp. 29–31.

95. "The Communist Party and the Labor Movement in Italy," report of J. C. Adams, 17 January 1946, RG 84 Post-NA, 850.4-Italy; Filippelli, *American Labor*, pp. 77–80.

96. "Communist Party and the Labor Movement in Italy."

97. "The Christian Democracy and the Labor Movement," report of J. C. Adams, 5 January 1946, RG 84 Post-NA, 850.4-Italy.

98. L. Antonini to P. Nenni, 14 September 1945. Nenni's answer (P. Nenni to L. Antonini, Rome, 24 October 1945) is a demonstration of strong and sincere political and personal dignity: "On the problem of fusion I think now exactly what I thought when we last spoke. I hope for it, that is, I want it. I feel that it would give increased strength to the workers' movement in Italy just as it would in France and Spain, to mention the countries I know best. But this is faced with many objective and subjective difficulties which I must take into account. For this reason, this fusion, or better unity, is for me a hope, a goal, rather than a problem for today. I have read of an IALC decision that states that it wants to assist only the Faravelli-Modigliani group in Italy. (As to Modigliani, his health is not good and that is causing concern.) You of course have the right to do as you wish, but with the approach of the electoral struggle that will have decisive consequences for the future of democracy in Italy, I would submit that it is appropriate to assist the party in the most positive fashion, which would be to send us paper for our election posters. If you cannot, we are facing a Communist organization that is much better equipped than ours and therefore we are in a state of inferiority." Both letters are in LA, box 36, folder 6.

99. P. Nenni, *Tempi di guerra fredda: Diari, 1943–1956* (Milan, 1981), pp. 150–52; Taddei, *Il socialismo italiano*, pp. 153–72.

100. L. Antonini to G. Modigliani, 25 September 1945, LA, box 35, folder 5. Montana, in *New Leader*, 30 June 1945 and 15 September 1945, hoped for Nenni's removal and the transformation of the party into a "Partito socialista indipendente" led by Faravelli, Modigliani, Saragat, and Silone. This party would be the basis of a coalition of democratic forces excluding the PCI.

101. L. Antonini to Alberto Cianca, 16 November 1945, and L. Antonini to G. Modigliani, 16 November 1945, both letters in LA, box 14, folder 2. Faravelli answered Antonini that he wanted to earmark the funds for the "Critica Sociale," to "trade union organizations that follow our line in the labor confederation," and to "official party organizations (federations and sections) that are in our hands." G. Faravelli to L. Antonini, Milan, 19 December 1945, LA, box 17, folder 5. Valiani wrote that he had devoted Antonini's money to a fund for Parri's

election campaign and to preparing a union newspaper, *Secolo* (L. Valiani to L. Antonini, Milan, 31 December 1945, LA, box 48, folder 9). The IALC's contributions were not very large in 1945. The fund entitled "Liberation and Free Trade Union Movement," composed of contributions from Italian American sections and from ILGWU headquarters, amounted to $47,000. Of this amount, up to May 1945, $16,500 was for the Socialist party, $5,000 for the cooperative movement, a few thousand to contributions to individuals, and, from September on, a total of $18,500 went to the three fiduciary committees of the actionist and autonomist factions. See IALC, "Annual Report 1945," LA, box 12, folder 1, and L. Antonini to P. Nenni, 15 February 1946, LA, box 36, folder 6.

102. L. Antonini to L. Valiani, 22 January 1946, LA, box 48, folder 9; Filippelli, *American Labor*, pp. 63–68.

103. IALC, "Resolution for a Just and Early Peace with Italy," New York, 25 January 1946; on the entire campaign and Antonini's activities in Paris, see IALC, "Summary Report, 1946," both in LA, box 12, folder 1.

104. L. Antonini to G. Faravelli, 16 March 1946, LA, box 17, folder 5; L. Antonini to P. Nenni, 16 March 1946, LA, box 36, folder 6; L. Antonini to R. Morandi, 16 March 1946, LA, box 44, folder 5.

105. L. Antonini to G. Saragat, 18 March 1946, LA, box 43, folder 4.

106. L. Antonini to G. Faravelli, 22 May 1946, in answer to a letter from Faravelli dated 6 May 1946, both in LA, box 17, folder 5/6/7. For the sending of funds to the new Socialist secretary Lombardo, see L. Antonini to John Gelo, 8 and 15 May 1946, LA, box 46, folder 6. On the Socialist party congress, see Taddei, *Il socialismo italiano*, pp. 256–88. The author emphasizes how, in addition to the temporary unity achieved in Florence, both the right—Faravelli, in particular—and the left of Basso left the congress convinced that a breakup in the immediate future was inevitable.

107. G. Faravelli to L. Antonini, 8 June 1946, and V. Montana to G. Faravelli, 9 July 1946, both in LA, box 17, folder 5/6/7.

108. Report of J. Gelo to L. Antonini, July 1946, pp. 7–8, LA, box 46, folder 6; Filippelli, *American Labor*, pp. 81–86.

109. J. C. Adams, "Confidential Monthly Labor Report—February 1946," 1 March 1946, and the report for the following month, dated 1 April 1946, both in RG 84 Post-NA, 850.4-Italy. See also Turone, *Storia del sindacato*, pp. 104–26.

110. Foa, *Sindacati e lotte operaie*, pp. 30–31; Pepe, "La CGIL dalla ricostruzione," pp. 622–32; Daneo, *La politica economica*, p. 180; Augusto Graziani, *L'economia italiana dal 1945 ad oggi: Introduzione* (1972; reprint, Bologna, 1979), p. 36.

111. Piero Barucci, *Ricostruzione, pianificazione, Mezzogiorno: La politica economica in Italia, 1943–1955* (Bologna, 1978); by the same author, "Il dibattito sulla politica economica della ricostruzione (1943–1947)," in *L'Italia dalla Liberazione alla Repubblica*, by Enzo Collotti et al., pp. 391–412; Marcello De Cecco, "La politica economica durante la ricostruzione, 1945–1951," in *Italia, 1943–1950*, ed. Stuart J. Woolf, pp. 283–318; Valerio Castronovo, "Storia economica," in *Storia d'Italia*, vol. 4, pt. 1 (Turin, 1975), pp. 354–67; Giuliano Amato, ed., *Il governo dell'industria in Italia* (Bologna, 1972), pp. 16–20 of the introduction; Graziani, *L'economia italiana*, pp. 13–35; Pasquale Saraceno, *Intervista sulla ricostruzione* (Bari, 1977); Daneo, *La politica economica*, pp. 100–169; Mariuccia Salvati, *Stato e industria nella rico-*

struzione (Milan, 1982), pp. 23–169; Legnani, "'L'utopia grande-borghese,'" p. 180; Vittorio Foa, "La ricostruzione capitalistica nel secondo dopoguerra," *Rivista di storia contemporanea* 4 (1973): 433–55; Enzo Piscitelli, *Da Parri a De Gasperi: Storia del dopoguerra, 1945–1948* (Milan, 1975), pp. 129–67; Cesare Pillon, *I comunisti e il sindacato* (Milan, 1972), pp. 374–76; Luciano Cafagna, "Note in margine alla Ricostruzione," *Giovane critica* 37 (Summer 1973); Beccalli, "La ricostruzione," pp. 347–69.

112. Grandi, *Scritti e discorsi*, pp. 90–95 of the introduction by Tobagi; Luciano Lama, *La CGIL di Di Vittorio, 1944–1957* (Bari, 1977).

113. "Inflazione, investimenti, e unità sindacale: Il Direttivo CGIL del 15–19 luglio 1946," *Quaderni di rassegna sindacale*, no. 59/60 (March–June 1976): 198–232. The quotation is from p. 211.

114. Barucci, *Ricostruzione, pianificazione*, pp. 125–26.

115. Daneo, *La politica economica*, pp. 183–84.

116. Di Nolfo, *Le paure e le speranze*, p. 226; Salvati, *Stato e industria*, pp. 172–74 and 269; Foa, "La ricostruzione capitalistica," pp. 40–46; Valerio Castronovo, "Le sinistre e la ricostruzione economica," in *La sinistra europea nel secondo dopoguerra (1943–1948)*, ed. Maria Petricioli (Florence, 1981), pp. 16–20; Daneo, *La politica economica*, p. 322.

117. J. C. Adams, "Confidential Monthly Labor Report—July and August 1946," 23 August 1946, RG Post-NA, 850.4-Italy.

118. Gaddis, *United States and the Origins*, pp. 284–341; Yergin, *Shattered Peace*, pp. 178–255.

119. Harper, *America and the Reconstruction*, p. 103.

120. Ibid., pp. 99–104. On the "new course" proposed by the PCI, see Daneo, *La politica economica*, pp. 115–25.

121. Pietro Merli Brandini, "Evoluzione del sistema contrattuale italiano nel dopoguerra," *Economia e lavoro*, no. 2 (1967), and Daneo, *La politica economica*, pp. 179–80.

122. Dellavalle, "Occupazione e Salario," p. 370.

123. On the atmosphere, see Di Nolfo, *Le paure e le speranze*, pp. 228ff., and Piscitelli, *Da Parri a De Gasperi*, p. 176.

124. Pasini, *Le ACLI dalle origini*, pp. 104–40; Grandi, *Scritti e discorsi*, pp. 75ff. of the introduction by Tobagi; Vincenzo Saba, *Giulio Pastore: Sindacalista* (Rome, 1983), pp. 64ff.; Turone, *Storia del sindacato*, pp. 109–16.

125. Craveri, *Sindacato e istituzioni*, p. 66; Dellavalle, "Occupazione e Salario," pp. 369–70.

126. Transcript of the RAI broadcast "Attualità da Roma," 10 October 1946, LA, box 46, folder 5.

127. L. Antonini, "Risposta al Segretario in terzo grado della CGIL," October 1946, LA, box 38, folder 9; interview with Lizzadri in *L'Unità*, 12 October 1946.

128. Taddei, *Il socialismo italiano*, pp. 303ff., and Piero Boni, *I socialisti e l'unità sindacale* (Venice, 1981), p. 25.

129. L. Antonini to C. Spinelli, 30 October 1946, LA, box 44, folder 5.

130. L. Antonini to G. Favarelli, 7 November 1946, LA, box 17, folder 5/6/7.

131. G. Faravelli to L. Antonini, Milan, 17 December 1946, LA, box 17, folder 5/6/7. On preparation of the Socialist congress and the break under Saragat's leadership, see Taddei, *Il socialismo italiano*, pp. 331–60.

132. L. Antonini to G. Faravelli, 24 December 1946 and 4 December 1946, LA, box 17, folder 5/6/7; Jacob Pat to L. Antonini, New York, 27 December 1946, LA, box 29, folder 11.

133. IALC, "Messaggio ai socialisti d'Italia," 14 December 1946, LA, box 12, folder 1.

134. L. Antonini to G. Faravelli, 7 November 1946, LA, box 17, folder 5/6/7; R. Filippelli, *American Labor*, pp. 86–89.

135. R. Abramovitch to D. Dubinsky, "Memorandum on the Work to Be Done by the AFL in Europe," New York, 9 June 1946, DD, box 2-173, folder 3A; and AFL, "Minutes of Meeting of the International Labor Relations Committee," 13 November 1946, FT.

136. IALC, "Summary Report 1946," 14 December 1946, LA, box 12, folder 1.

137. Harper, *America and the Reconstruction*, p. 116; Miller, *United States and Italy*, pp. 213–49; Faenza and Fini, *Gli americani in Italia*, pp. 174–79.

138. L. Antonini to G. Saragat, 22 January 1947, LA, box 43, folder 4.

139. L. Antonini to G. Faravelli, 8 February 1947, LA, box 17, folder 5/6/7.

140. Di Nolfo, *Vaticano e Stati Uniti*.

141. Collotti, "La collocazione internazionale," pp. 75ff.; Piscitelli, *Da Parri a De Gasperi*, p. 132; Ellwood, *L'alleato nemico*, pp. 190–91; James Miller, "The Search for Stability: An Interpretation of American Policy in Italy, 1943–1946," *Journal of Italian History* 1, no. 2 (1978): 273–74.

142. Harper, *America and the Reconstruction*, pp. 20–21 and 58; Di Nolfo, "United States and Italian Communism," pp. 92–93; Agostino Giovagnoli, *Le premesse della ricostruzione: Tradizione e modernità nella classe dirigente cattolica del dopoguerra* (Milan, 1982), pp. 218ff.

143. Mario G. Rossi, "Le radici del potere democristiano," *Passato e presente*, no. 6 (July–December 1984): 89; Harper, *America and the Reconstruction*, pp. 189–97.

144. *FRUS*, 1946, 5:935; Antonio Gambino, "La situazione politica interna," in *Il Piano Marshall e l'Europa*, ed. Elena Aga Rossi (Rome, 1983), p. 123; Harper, *America and the Reconstruction*, pp. 109ff.

145. Severino Galante, "La Scelta americana della DC," in *La Democrazia Cristiana dal fascismo al 18 aprile*, ed. Mario Isnenghi and Silvio Lanaro (Venice, 1978), p. 120.

146. On De Gasperi's trip to the United States, see *FRUS*, 1947, 3:835–61; Harper, *America and the Reconstruction*, pp. 111ff.; Ortona, *Anni d'America*, pp. 173–85; Alberto Tarchiani, *America-Italia: Le dieci giornate di De Gasperi negli Stati Uniti* (Milan, 1947).

147. Craveri, *Sindacato e istituzioni*, p. 40 and pp. 184ff.; Salvati, *Stato e industria*, pp. 173–74; Castronovo, "Le sinistre e la ricostruzione."

Chapter 3

1. Harry S. Truman, *Public Papers of the Presidents: Harry S. Truman*, 1947 (Washington, D.C., 1961–66), 8:178. The containment policy was explained theoretically a few months later by George Kennan in the famous article published under the pseudonym of X, "The Sources of Soviet Conduct," in *Foreign Affairs* 25 (July 1947).

2. Arthur S. Vandenberg, ed., *The Private Papers of Senator Vandenberg* (Boston, 1952), p. 344. On the unanimity of perception within the government, see Yergin, *Shattered Peace*, pp. 275ff.

3. Testimony on the meeting with congressional leaders, 25 February 1947, in Dean Acheson, *Present at the Creation: My Years at the State Department* (New York, 1969), p. 219.

4. Joseph Jones, *The Fifteen Weeks* (New York, 1955), pp. 139ff.; Leigh, *Mobilizing Consent*, pp. 144–67; LaFeber, *America, Russia, and the Cold War*, pp. 44–46. In the relevant historiography, there is a clear divergence of opinion concerning the intensification of the crisis by the administration's propaganda. Some, like Gaddis, *United States and the Origins*, pp. 348ff., hold that public opinion and Congress were more than willing to follow the government on an anti-Soviet crusade, while others, a bit too abstractly to be fully convincing, have argued that the theme of anticommunism served to frighten the public so much as to push it to support foreign policy objectives with which it did not agree for their own sake. See Freeland, *Truman Doctrine*, pp. 82ff.; Thomas G. Paterson, "Presidential Foreign Policy, Public Opinion, and Congress: The Truman Years," *Diplomatic History* 3, no. 1 (Winter 1979): 1–18.

5. McAuliffe, *Crisis on the Left*. On the level of international politics, the most lucid criticism of the containment strategy was expressed by Walter Lippman, *The Cold War: A Study in United States Foreign Policy* (New York, 1947).

6. *International Free Trade Union News* 2, no. 7 (June 1947) and no. 8 (August 1947); L. Antonini to Harry S. Truman, 17 March 1947, LA, box 47, folder 8; IALC, "Resolution on American Foreign Policy and the Peace Treaty with Italy," 26 April 1947, LA, box 12, folder 2. The new course of the American government was defined as the abandonment of a failed appeasement policy, to which was imputed, among other things, the drafting of the peace with Italy, whose revision in an anti-Soviet sense was therefore requested.

7. James Carey, "Labor Wants Voice in Foreign Policy," *CIO News* 10, no. 15 (14 April 1947); Preis, *Labor's Giant Steps*, p. 377.

8. Statement of P. Murray, *CIO News* 10, no. 16 (21 April 1947).

9. Trade Union Advisory Committee on International Affairs, memorandum of M. Ross on the meeting of 18 March 1947, reported in Thomas R. Brooks, *Clint: A Biography of a Labor Intellectual* (New York, 1978), pp. 251–52.

10. Department of State, "Memorandum of Conversation, 19 May 1947," between the under secretary of state and the representatives of the CIO (Carey and Ross), RG 59 DS-NA, 800.5043/5-1947. Barely ten days before, a speech of Acheson's at the Delta Council in Missouri had for the first time placed public emphasis on the danger of economic collapse in Europe and the necessity for the United States to face the problem with the greatest urgency. See Acheson, *Present at the Creation*, p. 228, and Jones, *Fifteen Weeks*, pp. 24–30. On the appointment of Clinton Golden as labor adviser, see Trade Union Advisory Committee on International Affairs, "Minutes of Fourth Meeting," 13 May 1947, copy in DD, box 2-393, folder 3D.

11. "US Aims to Help Greeks Help Themselves," *CIO News* 10, no. 32 (11 August 1947).

12. Brooks, *Clint*. Golden had published *The Dynamics of Industrial Democracy* (New York, 1942) with Harold Ruttenberg. The book achieved great success as a manifestation of "responsible" trade unionism based on the criterion of efficiency.

13. "Statement of the Labor Division of the American Mission for Aid to Greece," 24 September 1947, copy in DD, box 2-393, folder 3C. On the overall outlook of the American mission, see Lawrence S. Wittner, *American Intervention in Greece, 1943–1949* (New York, 1982), pp. 135–85; Brooks, *Clint*, p. 254.

14. Wittner, *American Intervention in Greece*, pp. 208ff.

15. C. Golden to William Batt, 5 January 1948, cited in Brooks, *Clint*, pp. 307–8.

16. Brooks, *Clint*, pp. 309–16, and Wittner, *American Intervention in Greece*, p. 210.

17. Telegrams from the Secretary of State to the embassy in Italy, 20 May and 6 June 1947, *FRUS*, 1947, 3:909 and 919.

18. Department of State, "The USSR and the World Federation of Trade Unions," RG 59 DS-NA, 800.5043/6–2347.

19. T. W. Hollan to D. Acheson and P. Nitze, 16 May 1947, memorandum in preparation for the meeting with the CIO leaders, RG 59 DS-NA, 800.5043/5-1647.

20. Department of State, "Memorandum of Conversation, 19 May 1947."

21. *CIO News* 10, no. 26 (7 July 1947) and no. 25 (30 June 1947).

22. Lawrence A. Steinhardt to the Secretary of State, "Report on WFTU Meeting in Prague, June 2–14, 1947," RG 59 DS-NA, 800.5043/7-1947.

23. "Carey Likens WFTU to UN," *CIO News* 10, no. 31 (4 August 1947).

24. R. Abramovitch, "Memorandum on the Work to Be Done by the AFL in Europe," 9 June 1946, p. 1, DD, box 2-173, folder 3A.

25. Minutes of the AFL-CILR, 19 July 1946; see also the minutes of the subsequent meeting, 8 August 1946, still dedicated largely to Germany, and that of 13 November 1946, all in FT. For the history of American attitudes to reconstructing German trade unions, see the references in n. 29 to chap. 1.

26. George Meany, "We Back America," *American Federationist* 53, no. 7 (July 1946): 3–6; Lenburg, "CIO and American Foreign Policy," pp. 136–37.

27. Berger, "Union Diplomacy," p. 272; Minutes of the AFL-CILR, 2 August 1946, FT.

28. AFL, "Memorandum of Meeting Held in M. Woll Office, re: London Conference of ITWF," 10 December 1945, and Minutes of the AFL-CILR, 19 July 1946, both in FT; Windmuller, *American Labor*, pp. 104–16; Godson, *American Labor and European Politics*, pp. 88–111; Weiler, "U.S., International Labor," p. 7.

29. L. B. Schwellenbach, Secretary of Labor, to W. Green, 28 October 1946, copy in DD, box 2-393, folder 3E; U.S. Department of Labor, *35th Annual Report of the Secretary of Labor* (Washington, D.C., 1947). The consultative committee was composed of George Meany, Matthew Woll, David Dubinsky, and Robert Watt for the AFL, and Frank Rosenblum, Clinton Golden, James Carey, and Michael Ross for the CIO; there were also T. Barkins and A. Lyon representing the independent railway unions, which were frequently near the AFL in international questions. See also Trade Union Advisory Committee on International Affairs, Department of Labor, "Minutes of Meeting," 27 January, 24 February, 18–19 March, 22 April 1947, copies in DD, box 2-393, folder 3D, and Berger, "Union Diplomacy," pp. 280–90.

30. See, for example, Trade Union Advisory Committee on International Affairs, "Minutes of the Fourth Meeting," 13 May 1947, and David Morse to George Meany, 17 October 1947, copies of both documents in DD, box 2-393, folder 3C-D.

31. Lens, "Lovestone Diplomacy"; Dan Kurzman, "Lovestone's Cold War," *New Republic*, 25 June 1966, and "Labor's Cold Warrior (I)," *Washington Post*, 30 December 1965; Goulden, *Meany*, p. 134; Anthony Carew, "The British and American Trade Union Movement in the Marshall Plan" (Paper delivered at the workshop of the European University Institute,

"Trade Unions and Labour Movements in Western European Reconstruction, 1945–1954," Florence, February 1985).

32. William M. Leary, ed., *The Central Intelligence Agency: History and Documents* (Birmingham, Ala., 1984), p. 40; Trevor Barnes, "The Secret Cold War: The CIA and American Foreign Policy in Europe, 1946–1956," pt. 2, *Historical Journal* 25, no. 3 (1982): 669–70.

33. Trevor Barnes, "The Secret Cold War," pt. 1, *Historical Journal* 24, no. 2 (1981): 404–13.

34. NSC Report no. 7, 30 March 1948, cited in Weiler, "U.S., International Labor," p. 14; Barnes, "Secret Cold War," pt. 1, pp. 412–13. On the Italian electoral campaign of 18 April 1948, see James Miller, "Taking Off the Gloves: The U.S. and the Italian Elections of 1948," *Diplomatic History* 7, no. 1 (Winter 1983): 35–55.

35. See the statement by Thomas Braden, the CIA official responsible for these operations, "I'm Glad the CIA Is Immoral," *Saturday Evening Post*, 20 May 1967; the statement was never repudiated. See also Goulden, *Meany*, pp. 128–30, and Weiler, "U.S., International Labor," p. 14.

36. Dan Kurzman, "Labor's Cold Warrior (II)," *Washington Post*, 31 December 1965; Lens, "Lovestone Diplomacy"; Philip Agee, *Inside the Company: CIA Diary* (New York, 1975), pp. 68–69.

37. Braden, "I'm Glad the CIA Is Immoral"; Reuther, *Brothers Reuther*, pp. 424–27.

38. For the conspiracy theory, see Radosh, *American Labor*, p. 314. The AFL's leaders of that period and their defenders insist on its independence, but the attempt to deny any collaboration with the CIA is neither well-founded nor credible. See Dubinsky and Raskin, *David Dubinsky*, p. 48; Taft, *Defending Freedom*.

39. "Certain Aspects of the European Recovery Problem from the U.S. Standpoint (Preliminary Report)," Policy Planning Staff 4 (Department of State), 23 July 1947, reported in Thomas H. Etzold and John Lewis Gaddis, eds., *Containment: Documents on American Policy and Strategy: 1945–1950* (New York, 1978), pp. 108–9; and Jones, *Fifteen Weeks*, p. 80.

40. For the apologetic interpretations of the Marshall Plan, see, for example, Jones, *Fifteen Weeks*. For the revisionist historiography, see J. and G. Kolko, *Limits of American Power*, and, especially for the exploitation of anticommunism, Freeland, *Truman Doctrine*.

41. John Gimbel, *The Origins of the Marshall Plan* (Stanford, Calif., 1976).

42. Scott Jackson, "Prologue to the Marshall Plan: The Origins of American Commitment for a European Recovery Program," *Journal of American History* 65, no. 4 (March 1979): 1043–68; Thomas G. Paterson, *Soviet-American Confrontation: Postwar Reconstruction and the Origins of the Cold War* (Baltimore, 1973), esp. chap. 10; Yergin, *Shattered Peace*, pp. 308–9. The most recent discussion on these issues is in Charles S. Maier's introduction to *The Marshall Plan and Germany*, ed. Charles S. Maier (New York, 1991), pp. 12–17.

43. Alan S. Milward, *The Reconstruction of Western Europe, 1945–1951* (London, 1984), esp. the first and concluding chapters. The quotation is from p. 54.

44. "Policy with Respect to American Aid to Western Europe," Policy Planning Staff (Department of State), 23 May 1947, *FRUS*, 1947, 3:224.

45. Michael J. Hogan, "The Search for a 'Creative Peace': The United States, European Unity, and the Origins of the Marshall Plan," *Diplomatic History* 6 (1982): 268. On the issue of integration, and on its disputed development in the Marshall Plan years, see esp. Milward, *Reconstruction of Western Europe*, pp. 56ff.

46. Hogan, "Search for a 'Creative Peace,'" p. 283; Jones, *Fifteen Weeks*, pp. 253ff. On the original nature of the Marshall Plan and on its beginnings, in addition to works already cited, see Harry B. Price, *The Marshall Plan and Its Meaning* (Ithaca, N.Y., 1955); Pollard, *Economic Security*, esp. pp. 133–67; Hadley Arkes, *Bureaucracy, the Marshall Plan, and the National Interest* (Princeton, 1972); Immanuel Wexler, *The Marshall Plan Revisited: The European Recovery Program in Economic Perspective* (Westport, Conn., 1983). The memoirs of some of its principal architects are of interest: Acheson, *Present at the Creation*; Charles Bohlen, *Witness to History: 1929–1969* (New York, 1973); George Kennan, *Memoirs, 1925–1950* (Boston, 1967).

47. Price, *Marshall Plan*, pp. 47–52; Gaddis, *United States and the Origins*, p. 328; Freeland, *Truman Doctrine*, p. 189; Paterson, "Quest for Peace and Prosperity," p. 98.

48. Price, *Marshall Plan*, pp. 40–56; Wexler, *Marshall Plan Revisited*, pp. 26–31; and esp. Arkes, *Bureaucracy*. For a discussion of the positions taken concerning the Marshall Plan by various organized interests, see Gabriel A. Almond, *The American People and Foreign Policy* (1950; reprint, Westport, Conn., 1977), pp. 160ff.; William F. Sanford, "The American Business Community and the European Recovery Program" (Ph.D. dissertation, University of Texas, Austin, 1980).

49. John Hickerson to H. Freeman Matthews, 25 June 1947, RG 59 DS-NA, ROWE, box 3.

50. Charles S. Maier, "The Two Postwar Eras and the Conditions for Stability in Twentieth Century Western Europe," *American Historical Review* 86, no. 2 (April 1981): 341–48. On the political effects of the Marshall Plan, see Lutz Niethammer, "La nascita e la caduta delle prospettive socialiste nell'Europa del secondo dopoguerra," in *Il Piano Marshall e l'Europa*, ed. Elena Aga Rossi, p. 104: "The attractiveness of the Marshall Plan was not the project in itself, but its intrinsic capacity to involve the European left in its administration."

51. Maier, "Politics of Productivity," p. 630.

52. Telegram from the embassy in Czechoslovakia to the Secretary of State, 1 July 1947, cited in Weiler, "U.S., International Labor," pp. 219–20; and Eleanor Finger, "Labor and European Recovery," in *The House of Labor*, ed. John B. S. Hardman and Maurice F. Neufeld (New York, 1951), pp. 159–67.

53. "Memo on Misconception of Our Capitalistic System in Europe," 24 October 1947, RG 59 DS-NA, 840.00R/10-2947. This document, which circulated at the highest levels of the Department of State, was written by Richard Allen, in charge of American assistance in Europe after the termination of UNRRA, following a trip to Italy, Greece, and Austria.

54. Telegram from the embassy in Belgium to the Secretary of State, RG 59 DS-NA, 800.504/9-547; *International Free Trade Union News* 2, no. 9 (September 1947).

55. "Harriman Admits That the ERP Is Vulnerable to Sabotage by Communist-led Unions," *New York Times*, 13 November 1947; Barnes "Secret Cold War," pt. 1, p. 407.

56. Notes on a talk by Irving Brown at the Department of State, 9 November 1948, RG 59 DS-NA, 840.504; Godson, *American Labor and European Politics*, pp. 60–61. Irving Brown (interview with the author, Washington, D.C., 14 August 1984) argued that the Soviet leaders would have opted, in conducting the Cold War, for a policy of destabilizing Europe after considering the historical lessons of the 1920s, when the Bolshevik revolution had been

isolated and defeated on the international scene by the failure of the revolution in Germany following economic stabilization there.

57. On the split in the Force Ouvrière, see Alain Bergounioux, *Force Ouvrière* (Paris, 1975); on the American view, especially AFL support, see Godson, *American Labor and European Politics*; Weiler, "U.S., International Labor," pp. 12–15; Radosh, *American Labor*, pp. 201ff.; and Taft, *Defending Freedom*. Several years later, George Meany was to proudly claim the role played by the AFL in the FO's split, which he said was "primarily due to our efforts. We financed a split in the Communist-controlled union in France—we paid for it. We sent them American trade union money, we set up their offices, we sent them supplies and everything else so we could weaken the Communist front." Speech of 1964, cited in Goulden, *Meany*, p. 129. Irving Brown's pressure seems to have played a not unimportant role at the moment of the decision, in persuading the group of FO leaders, where there was reservation and indecisiveness, to make the break from the unified CGT. Notes on a talk by Brown, cited in note 56; Victor Reuther, interview with the author, Washington, D.C., 14 August 1984.

58. "Memorandum to the President: AFL Program for World Recovery and Lasting Peace," 19 December 1947, in *International Free Trade Union News* 3, no. 1 (January 1948).

59. See "Statement of William Green, AFL President," U.S. Congress, Senate, *Hearings before the Committee on Foreign Relations*, 80th Cong., 2d sess. (hereafter ERP-*Hearings*), 157:835: "American labor can best convince the workers of Europe of the integrity of Government's purposes and guarantee that no aggression or domination will follow."

60. "Cominform and the WFTU," *International Free Trade Union News* 2, no. 11 (November 1947).

61. Windmuller, *American Labor*, pp. 40 and 123–24.

62. Report of I. Brown, 10 November 1947, and Minutes of the AFL-CILR, 11 November 1947, both in FT.

63. In addition to the Minutes of the AFL-CILR, 5 January 1948, FT, see Godson, *American Labor*, pp. 108–12, and, on Bevin's activities, Anthony Carew, *Labour under the Marshall Plan: The Politics of Productivity and the Marketing of Management Science* (Manchester, 1987), pp. 73–76.

64. Telegram from the embassy in France to the Secretary of State, RG 59 DS-NA, 800.5043/1-2848.

65. Price, *Marshall Plan*, pp. 40–66.

66. E. Cope to C. Golden, Paris, 29 October 1947, Clinton S. Golden Letters, Pennsylvania State University Libraries (hereafter CG).

67. Victor Reuther, interview with the author, Washington, D.C., 14 August 1984. E. Cope (letter to C. Golden, 8 December 1947, CG) wrote from Paris: "The Communists . . . for over two weeks prosecuted a general strike of the CGT that was doomed to failure. . . . They have all but wrecked the trade unions as a unified force in French social and economic life. . . . From the very beginning the unions were split wide open in response to the strike call. . . . For a time early in the strike it looked to me like the Communists were really bent on armed insurrection. That was the only explanation that made sense. . . . Perhaps much good will come of the strike. The Communist leadership has been pretty well discredited. There is a chance that L. Jouhaux will be able to take over the badly battered CGT." The letter was

written a few days before the FO split. From Greece, Clinton Golden wrote (letter to J. Carey, 12 December 1947, CG): "The enactment of antistrike legislation last week was quite unnecessary and ill advised but it was induced largely by reports of what the Commies are up to in France. After all a civil war is in progress in this poor country and if the government gets a bit panicky at times it can be understood."

68. Cochran, *Labor and Communism*, pp. 272ff.; Lenburg, "CIO and American Foreign Policy," p. 151; Levenstein, *Communism*; Carwell, "International Role of American Labor," p. 471.

69. Jonathan Stout, "State Department Seeks Labor Aid," *New Leader*, 18 October 1947.

70. Account of the discussion in *CIO News* 10, no. 42 (20 October 1947); on Murray's mediation, see Preis, *Labor's Giant Steps*, pp. 339–40.

71. E. Cope to C. Golden, Paris, 8 December 1947, CG; *CIO News* 10, no. 49 (8 December 1947).

72. Levenstein, *Communism*, p. 337.

73. "CIO Opposes 3rd Party," *CIO News* 11, no. 4 (28 January 1948).

74. For the right wing, this was a long-awaited opportunity, a battle that finally came with no more compromises or accommodations. See, for example, Van A. Bittner to C. Golden, Atlanta, 4 February 1948, CG: "It was really the first open fight between trade unionists and the Communists and in the end I am sure it will do the CIO a lot of good."

75. *CIO News* 11, no. 4 (28 January 1948).

76. International Longshoremen's and Warehousemen's Union, "Statement on European Recovery Program," ERP-*Hearings*, 158:2002–9. On criticism of the American Communist left on the Marshall Plan, see also William Z. Foster, *Labor and the Marshall Plan* (New York, 1948).

77. "Statement Offered by Phil Murray," ERP-*Hearings*, 158:1289–90.

78. "Statement of Walter Reuther," ERP-*Hearings*, 158:1386–95. On the problem of anti-inflationary controls, see also Paterson, "Quest for Peace and Prosperity," pp. 95–97.

79. Brody, *Workers in Industrial America*, p. 228.

Chapter 4

1. Telegram from the embassy in London to the Secretary of State, RG 59 DS-NA, 840.5043/1-1248.

2. Telegram from the embassy in London to the Secretary of State, RG 59 DS-NA, 840.5043/2-1148.

3. Telegrams to the Secretary of State from the embassy in London (840.5043/2-1948 and 800.5043/3-348) and from the mission in Berlin (800.5043/3-248), all in RG 59 DS-NA; *CIO News* 11, no. 6 (9 February 1948), and Windmuller, *American Labor*, p. 129.

4. Telegram from Caffery in Paris to Lovett, RG 59 DS-NA, 811.5043/2-2248; for the angry reaction of the AFL, see Dubinsky to G. Meany, 20 February 1948, and Press Release of the AFL, n.d., both in DD, box 2-203, folder 5.

5. J. H. Oldenbroek to D. Dubinsky, 22 February 1948, DD, box 2-173, folder 2A.

6. Niethammer, "Structural Reform," p. 231. For reactions in the United States to the

coup in Prague, see Freeland, *Truman Doctrine*, p. 275, and, for trade union circles, Godson, *America Labor and European Politics*, p. 63.

7. Windmuller, *American Labor*, p. 131.

8. ERP-International Trade Union Conference, "Declaration," London, 10 March 1948, copy in DD, box 2-261, folder 3B.

9. Report of F. Fenton, I. Brown, B. Jewell, 15 March 1948, copy in DD, box 2-261, folder 3A.

10. Director of European Affairs, "Policy Memo to the Secretary of State," 23 March 1948, RG 59 DS-NA, ROWE, box 3.

11. Telegram from the Secretary of State to the embassy in London, 10 March 1948, and to the embassy in Rome, 24 March 1948, *FRUS*, 1948, 3:847, 867; for a detailed analysis of the affair, see the following chapter.

12. S. Berger, "Memorandum of Conversation," with Murray, Carey, and Golden, Washington, D.C., RG 59 DS-NA, 800.5043/3-2348.

13. Telegram from the embassy in Rome to the Secretary of State, RG 59 DS-NA, 865.5043/4-2248.

14. Telegram from the embassy in London to the Secretary of State, RG 59 DS-NA, 840.5043/4-2648. In a letter to Jay Lovestone, dated 26 April (copy in DD, box 2-261, folder 3B), Irving Brown reported on the ERP-TUAC meeting: "The London meeting was a washout. . . . I fought hard for some action and for an early reconvening of the ERP Conference but Tewson is an old grandmother and scared stiff. . . . The British seem very reluctant to move on an international or overall basis in relationship to OEEC. They keep stressing the importance of national trade union centers playing a role in relationship to their respective governments as the most decisive thing to be done. . . . No ideas, nothing new, complete 'wait and see' policy, scared over WFTU etc. . . . We were the only ones with ideas and programs of action." The clash between a supranational and integrationist approach and a nationalistic one concerning the implementation of the ERP was always a sore point between the AFL and the TUC, corresponding exactly to the differences between their respective governments.

15. Telegram from the embassy in Rome to the Secretary of State, RG 59 DS-NA, 865.5043/4-348, and from the embassy in London to that in Rome, 6 April 1948, RG 84 Post-NA, 850.4-Italy/CGIL; Carew, *Labour under the Marshall Plan*, pp. 4–5 and 76–79; Weiler, "U.S., International Labor," p. 19.

16. Telegram from the Secretary of State to the embassy in Rome, RG DS-NA, 865.5043/4-2248 (but actually 7 May 1948).

17. Telegram from the embassy in Rome to the Secretary of State, RG 59 DS-NA, 865.5043/4-3048.

18. WFTU, "Session du Comité Executif, 5–10 Mai 1948 à Rome," in "FSM Comitati Esecutivi—1948," Archives of the CGIL, Rome; Windmuller, *American Labor*, pp. 135–39.

19. *CIO News* 11, no. 19 (10 May 1948) and no. 23 (14 June 1948); *International Free Trade Union News* 3, no. 6 (June 1948), and Matthew Woll, "The CIO Role in WFTU," *New Leader*, 3 July 1948.

20. Telegram from Ambassador Dunn to the Secretary of State, RG 59 DS-NA, 800.5043/5-1348.

21. Homer M. Byington to the Secretary of State, Rome, 13 May 1948, RG 59 DS-NA, 800.5043/5-1348.

22. Eisenberg, "Working-Class Politics," p. 299.

23. Greetings by Averell Harriman reported in *CIO News* 11, no. 32 (16 August 1948); see also "Report by Jay Lovestone, Secretary, in Behalf of A.F. of L. Delegation to ERP Trade Union Conference—London, July 29–30, 1948," copy in DD, box 2-33, folder 6.

24. "Report by Jay Lovestone"; *CIO News* 11, no. 32 (16 August 1948). Brown's comment is reported in Carwell, "International Role of American Labor," p. 521.

25. "Report by Jay Lovestone."

26. "Memorandum of Conversation on European Labor Participation in ECA," Washington, D.C., RG 59 DS-NA, 840.5043/8-2048. During the meeting it was Clinton Golden especially who bitterly criticized the TUC for its national, rather than continental, outlook. According to Golden, this lessened the ERP's political impact in the anti-Communist struggle.

27. Telegram from the embassy in London to the Secretary of State, RG 59 DS-NA, 800.5043/8-1348; telegram from the Secretary of State to the embassy in Rome, RG 59 DS-NA, 865.5043/8-1248.

28. Minutes of the AFL-CILR, 9 September 1948, FT; *International Free Trade Union News* 3, no. 9 (September 1948); telegram no. 5011 from the embassy in Paris to the Secretary of State, 23 September 1948 (a copy of this message is to be found, curiously enough, among the AFL papers in FT).

29. Telegram from the embassy in London to the Secretary of State, RG 59 DS-NA, 800.5043/9-1648.

30. Telegram from the Secretary of State to the embassy in London, RG 59 DS-NA, 811.5043/9-1848.

31. David Dubinsky, "Rift and Realignment in World Labor," *Foreign Affairs* 27 (January 1949): 235.

32. The TUC's decision was made in close consultation with the Foreign Office; see Weiler, "U.S., International Labor," p. 19; Lewis Lorwin, *The International Labor Movement* (New York, 1953), p. 260.

33. Hamby, *Beyond the New Deal*, pp. 283ff.; Lichtenstein, *Labor's War at Home*, p. 287; Levenstein, *Communism*, p. 333; Lenburg, "CIO and American Foreign Policy," pp. 175–80.

34. On the anti-Communist purge in the CIO, see Preis, *Labor's Giant Steps*, pp. 397ff.; Schatz, *Electrical Workers*, pp. 184ff.; Cochran, *Labor and Communism*, pp. 310ff.; David Caute, *The Great Fear: The Anti-Communist Purge under Truman and Eisenhower* (New York, 1978), pp. 349ff.

35. *CIO News* 11, no. 47 (29 November 1948).

36. AFL, 67th Annual Convention, "World Labor, the Key to World Peace," in *American Labor Looks at the World*, vol. 3 (Washington, D.C., 1949); notes on a talk by Irving Brown at the Department of State, 9 November 1948, RG 59 DS-NA, 840.504.

37. Memorandum from Boris Shishkin, director of the Labor Division of the ECA in Europe, to Averell Harriman, ECA Special Representative, 15 January 1949, in Record Group 286, Records of the Economic Cooperation Administration, Office of the Special Representative, National Archives, Washington, D.C. (hereafter RG 286 ECA-NA, OSR),

Labor Information Div., General Subject File 1949–51, box 6. See also telegram from the embassy in London to the Secretary of State in RG 59 DS-NA, 800.5043/1-1349.

38. Statement by James Carey in *CIO News* 12, no. 5 (31 January 1949).

39. Horst Lademacher et al., "Der Weltgewerkschaftsbund in Spannungsfeld des Ost-West Konflikts," *Archiv für Sozialgeschichte* 18 (1978): 119–25; Weiler, "U.S., International Labor," pp. 19ff.; Niethammer, "Structural Reform," pp. 229ff.; Windmuller, *American Labor*, pp. 131ff.

40. ERP-TUAC, "Summary Record of the Fifth Meeting," Berne, 22 January 1949, copy in CIO-ST, ALHUA, box 132; telegram from the embassy in Berne to the Secretary of State, RG 59 DS-NA, 800.5043/1-2349; "Declaration on the Schevenels Case by the International Committee of the AFL," 31 January 1949, FT; Lincoln Evans, president of the British Iron and Steel Trades Confederation, to D. Dubinsky, London, 19 January 1949, and J. Green to D. Dubinsky, Washington, D.C., 27 January 1949, both in DD, box 2-173, folder 2A.

41. "Declaration of the Executive Council of the AFL on the Break-up of the WFTU," Miami, 31 January 1949; Minutes of the AFL-CILR, 31 January 1949, both in FT.

42. Memorandum from S. Saposs to B. Shishkin, 28 January 1949, RG 286 ECA-NA, OSR, Labor Information Div., Office of the Economic Advisor, GSF 1949–51, box 7, ERP-TUAC.

43. Memorandum of C. Swayzee to Secretary of State Dean Acheson, "AFL International Affairs Committee Conference with the Secretary," 8 March 1949, RG 59 DS-NA, 800.5043/3-1449. The meeting of the AFL leaders with Acheson brought out the federation's full support for the establishment of NATO and the project to unify the West German occupation zones into the Federal Republic of Germany. An account of the meeting is in RG 59 DS-NA, 811.5043/3-949.

44. "Statement by the International Labor Relations Committee of the AFL," 7 April 1949, and Minutes of the AFL-CILR, 7 April 1949, FT; memorandum from Fraleigh, 11 March 1949, RG 59 DS-NA, 811.5043/3-1149; memorandum from C. Swayzee to the Secretary of State, "Secretary's Conference with J. Carey and M. Ross—CIO," RG DS-NA, 811.5043/3-2949; memorandum from Brown, "White House Intervention in CIO-AFL Discussions," RG 59 DS-NA, 811.5043/5-349.

45. Circular from the Secretary of State to American embassies, "International Labor Movements after the WFTU Split," RG 59 DS-NA, 800.5043 FTUI/5-1249. Weiler, "U.S., International Labor," pp. 20–21, emphasizes the sharp contrast with the claim of the American trade unionists to be moving toward an apolitical organization of unions, "free" from any government interference. For the conclusion of the negotiations between the AFL, CIO, and TUC, see B. Shishkin to M. Woll, Paris, 24 May 1949, and B. Shishkin to F. Thorne, Paris, 31 May 1949, both in FT; circular airgram from the Secretary of State to American embassies, "Steps toward Formation of Free Trade Union International," RG 59 DS-NA, 800.5043 FTUI/5-1149.

46. Circular from the Secretary of State to American embassies, RG 59 DS-NA, 800.5043 FTUI/7-449; *CIO News* 12, no. 27 (4 July 1949) and no. 28 (18 July 1949); Windmuller, *American Labor*, pp. 156–57.

47. Memorandum of C. H. Humelsine, "Formation of a Free Trade Union International," 1 June 1949, RG DS-NA, 800.5043 FTUI/6-149; in an accompanying letter from Mrs. Carter

to Mr. Russel, 7 July 1949, was added the recommendation to make every effort "to prevent the impression growing that this new organization is a State Dept. sponsored body."

48. Harry Martin to A. Harriman, 1 August 1949, RG 286 ECA-NA, OSR, Labor Information Div., CSF 1948–51, box 11, Italy.

49. "Memorandum of Conversation," with G. Delaney, AFL, RG DS-NA, 800.5043/10-2049; Reuther, *Brothers Reuther*, pp. 403ff.; *CIO News* 12, no. 43 (13 October 1949).

50. Editorial in the *CIO News* 12, no. 47 (28 November 1949): 4.

51. "Constitution of the ICFTU," pp. 1–2, in ICFTU, *Official Report of the Free World Labour Conference and of the First Congress of the ICFTU* (London, 1949).

52. D. Dubinsky to H. Haskel, London, 9 December 1949, DD, box 2-33, folder 5; Carwell, "International Role of American Labor," p. 622, and William J. Handley, "American Labor and World Affairs," *Annals of the American Academy of Political and Social Science* 274 (July 1951): 131–38.

53. "Constitution of the ICFTU," pp. 5–6. The definition is from David McDonald in his report to the CIO executive board; see the Minutes of the CIO Executive Board, 14 February 1950, Documents of the CIO, ALHUA, p. 87.

54. J. Lovestone to L. Antonini, London, 4 December 1949, LA, box 24, folder 2; David Dubinsky, "World Labor's New Weapon," *Foreign Affairs* 28 (April 1950): 452.

55. The statement of Reuther is in *CIO News* 12, no. 50 (19 December 1949); that of McDonald is in the following issue, no. 51 (26 December 1949).

56. "Constitution of the ICFTU," p. 1; see also "AFL Amendments Adopted Illustrating Its Influence on Basic Issues," a list with no indications of date or author, DD, box 2-261, folder 6C.

57. Dubinsky, "World Labor's New Weapon," pp. 455–60; Windmuller, *American Labor*, pp. 160–74; Carwell, "International Role of American Labor," p. 548; Val R. Lorwin, "Labor's Own 'Cold War,'" *Labor and Nation* 6, no. 1 (Winter 1950): 8–9. For the positions of the British TUC, see Arthur Deakin, "The International Trade Union Movement," *International Affairs* 26, no. 2 (April 1950): 167–71.

58. Circular airgram from the Secretary of State to the American embassies, RG 59 DS-NA, 800.5043 ICFTU/12-1249.

59. Memorandum of H. Martin to A. Harriman, "New International Confederation of Free Trade Unions," Paris, 15 December 1949, RG 286 ECA-NA, OSR, Labor Information Div., GSF 1949–51, box 6.

60. L. Lorwin, *International Labor Movement*, pp. 262ff.

61. G. Meany, "Report on ICFTU Executive Board Meeting," 29 May 1950, copy in DD, box 2-261, folder 6D; D. J. Saposs to John E. Lawyer, "Report on ICFTU Emergency Committee Meeting," 21 September 1950, RG 286 ECA-NA, OSR, Labor Information Div., GSF 1949–51, box 7; Minutes of the AFL-CILR, 14 December 1950, FT; Trade Union Advisory Committee on International Affairs (Department of Labor), "Minutes of the Standing Committee Meeting," 1 September 1950, and "Minutes of the Fourteenth Meeting," 19 December 1950, copies of both in DD, box 2-393, folder 3A. See also Windmuller, *American Labor*, pp. 174ff.

62. For the trade union difficulties of the ERP, see chap. 6. On the Milan congress, see ICFTU, *Report on the Second World Congress Held at Milan, Italy, 4–12 July 1951* (Brussels,

1951); for the address by George Meany, see esp. pp. 405–12. For the positions with which the American delegations arrived at the congress, see *CIO News* 14, no. 20 (14 May 1951) and no. 26 (25 June 1951). For a fuller analysis of the history of the ICFTU and the American presence there, see Windmuller, *American Labor*, pp. 184ff.; Adolf Sturmthal, *Left of Center: European Labor since World War II* (Urbana, Ill., 1983); Jack Kantrowitz, "Le Rôle des Syndicats Américains dans le monde syndical international libre" (Ph.D. dissertation, Paris X-Nanterre, 1977), esp. pp. 240–57; W. E. Goldman, "ICFTU: History of an Organization, 1949–1962" (Ph.D. dissertation, University of Southern California, 1967).

Chapter 5

1. Miller, *United States and Italy*, p. 213.

2. Dispatches of Ambassador Dunn to the Secretary of State, 1, 12, and 15 April 1947, *FRUS*, 1947, 3:877, 880, and 882.

3. Miller, *United States and Italy*, pp. 226–27; on the central role played by modernization criteria in extending American aid, see also David Ellwood, "Il Piano Marshall e il processo di modernizzazione in Italia," in *Il Piano Marshall e l'Europa*, ed. Elena Aga Rossi, pp. 149–54, and, for Europe as a whole, Hogan, "Search for a 'Creative Peace,'" pp. 277–79.

4. Dispatches from Washington to the embassy in Rome, 25 April and 1 May 1947, *FRUS*, 1947, 3:886 and 889.

5. Embassy in Rome to Secretary of State, 3 and 6 May 1947, *FRUS*, 1947, 3:889–91 and 894. On the crisis atmosphere of the spring of 1947, see Di Nolfo, *Le paure e le speranze*, esp. chap. 7.

6. Embassy in Rome to Secretary of State, 7 May 1947, *FRUS*, 1947, 3:895–97; Harper, *America and the Reconstruction*, pp. 117–33.

7. *FRUS*, 1947, 3:902–16. For an account of various stages in the crisis, especially relations between Rome and Washington, and for the historical interpretation of that crucial moment in postwar Italy, see Miller, *United States and Italy*, pp. 223ff.; Galante, "La Scelta americana della DC," and, by the same author, *La fine di un compromesso storico: PCI e DC nella crisi del 1947* (Milan, 1980); Collotti, "La collocazione internazionale," pp. 90ff.; Gambino, "La situazione politica interna," pp. 121–27; Simon Serfaty, "Gli Stati Uniti, l'Italia, e la guerra fredda: L'anno della decisione, 1947," in *America-Europa: La circolazione delle idee*, ed. Tiziano Bonazzi (Bologna, 1976), pp. 146ff.; Eric S. Edelman, "Incremental Involvement: Italy and United States Foreign Policy, 1943–1948" (Ph.D. dissertation, Yale University, 1981), pp. 465ff. For a different view, which emphasizes the realism of De Gasperi's actions given the weight of his international ties and contends that the left excluded itself from political responsibility in order to support recovery and stabilization, see Pietro Scoppola, *La proposta politica di De Gasperi* (Bologna, 1977), esp. pp. 307ff., and Giovagnoli, *Le premesse della ricostruzione*, pp. 367ff.

8. Telegram from the embassy in Rome to Secretary of State, 8 June 1947, *FRUS*, 1947, 3:920; and Price, *Marshall Plan*, p. 50.

9. Embassy in Rome to Secretary of State, 17 June 1947, *FRUS*, 1947, 3:922–23; for the State Department's opinion on the PSLI, see ibid., p. 919, telegram of 6 June 1947.

10. On the premises, implementations, and consequences of the anti-inflationary policy, see De Cecco, "La politica economica"; Barucci, *Ricostruzione, pianificazione, Mezzogiorno*; Graziani, *L'economia italiana dal 1945 ad oggi: Introduzione*, pp. 37–41; Salvati, *Stato e industria nella ricostruzione*, pp. 214ff.; Milward, *Reconstruction of Western Europe*, pp. 11–15. A full discussion of the industrialization model used in the reconstruction is in Castronovo, "Storia economica," pp. 339ff.

11. Harper, *America and the Reconstruction*, chap. 9; Miller, *United States and Italy*, pp. 213–49.

12. J. C. Adams, "The First Two Years of the CGIL," report of 3 March 1947, RG 84 Post-NA, 850.4-Italy/CGIL.

13. Beccalli, "La ricostruzione," pp. 347–69; Vannicelli, "Labor Movement," chap. 1.

14. G. Faravelli to L. Antonini, 8 February 1947; see also Faravelli's letter of 5 March and Antonini's reply of 18 March, all in LA, box 17, folder 5/6/7.

15. G. Faravelli to L. Antonini, 31 March 1947; G. Faravelli and G. Vassalli to L. Antonini, 31 March 1947; L. Antonini to G. Faravelli, 8 April 1947; L. Antonini to G. Faravelli and G. Vassali, 7 May 1947, all in LA, box 17, folder 5/6/7; and "Declaration of Guarantee," signed by Giuseppe Saragat and Matteo Matteotti, New York, 7 July 1947, LA, box 44, folder 7, in which the PSLI representatives committed themselves to pay back a fiftieth of the sum within ten years. See also Montana, *Amarostico*, pp. 333–37; Valerio Agostinone, "Una testimonianza: Sindacati americani e italiani al tempo delle scissioni," in *Italia e America dalla grande guerra ad oggi*, ed. Giorgio Spini, Gian Giacomo Migone, and Massimo Teodori, p. 226; Filippelli, *American Labor*, pp. 95–102.

16. J. C. Adams, "Preparations for the CGIL Congress," report of 22 May 1947, RG 84 Post-NA, 850.4-Italy/CGIL.

17. Turone, *Storia del sindacato*, pp. 127–30; Galante, "La scelta americana della DC," pp. 186–87; Boni, *I socialisti e l'unità sindicale*, pp. 31–33.

18. Pepe, "La CGIL dalla ricostruzione," p. 635; Gianni Baget-Bozzo, *Il partito cristiano al potere: La DC di De Gasperi e di Dossetti, 1945–1954* (Florence, 1974), pp. 173–74; Saba, *Giulio Pastore*, pp. 74–77; Pasini, *Le ACLI dalle origini*, pp. 149–70. For a discussion of Article 9, see Foa, *Sindacati e lotte operaie*, pp. 72–73.

19. Embassy in Rome to Secretary of State, dispatch of 12 June 1947, and "Confidential Labor Report" of 2 July 1947, from J. C. Adams; both in RG 84 Post-NA, 850.4-Italy.

20. Pasini, *Le ACLI dalle origini*, pp. 143–49. Within the ACLI, at that point it was thought that the necessity of forming a new union was quite likely to arise.

21. Daneo, *La politica economica*, p. 242; Dellavalle, "Occupazione e salario," pp. 378–82; Antonio Gibelli, "La ricostruzione organizzativa della CGIL, 1945–1947," in *Gli anni della costituente*, by Marcello Flores et al., p. 298; Craveri, *Sindacato e istituzioni*, pp. 212ff.

22. Accornero, "Per una nuova fase di studi," p. 16; Saba, *Giulio Pastore*, pp. 77ff.; Craveri, *Sindacato e istituzioni*, p. 221; Pillon, *I comunisti e il sindacato*, pp. 429–31; Zaninelli, *Il Sindacato Nuovo*, pp. 313–15 and 323.

23. Baget-Bozzo, *Il partito cristiano al potere*, p. 175; Turone, *Storia del sindacato*, p. 131; Pasini, *Le ACLI dalle origini*, p. 177.

24. *New York Times*, 5 and 22 September 1947, and telegram from the embassy in Moscow to the Secretary of State, RG 59 DS-NA, 865.5043/9-2347.

25. *FRUS*, 1947, 3:976–1001; Miller, *United States and Italy*, pp. 231ff., and Di Nolfo, *Le paure e le speranze*, pp. 245ff.

26. *FRUS*, 1947, 3:965, and 1948, 3:753.

27. *International Free Trade Union News* 2, no. 2 (February 1947) and no. 12 (December 1947); *New Leader*, 6 December 1947 and 20 December 1947; "IALC Summary Report—1947," LA, box 12, folder 2.

28. Report of Irving Brown, 10 November 1947, and Minutes of the AFL-CILR, 11 November 1947, both in FT.

29. D. Dubinsky to L. Antonini, 29 November 1947, LA, box 34, folder 4: "During Irving Brown's brief visit with us here, he kept hammering away at the fact that despite all our activities in Italy, nothing is being done as far as the trade union movement is concerned, and that so long as the labor movement in Italy continues to be dominated by the Communists, he felt, and I do too, that the money we are spending there is, in the main, wasted. It should have been our primary function to strengthen the trade union movement. Since you have overlooked this up until now, it would be most advisable that you call this matter to the attention of your friend Sarragat [*sic*] and ask him to see to it that part of the funds being sent to him should be used on activity in the trade union movement." See also Filippelli, *American Labor*, pp. 116–17.

30. Saba, *Giulio Pastore*, p. 84; Baget-Bozzo, *Il partito cristiano al potere*, p. 180.

31. "The Communist Party and the Labor Movement," report of J. C. Adams, 6 December 1947, RG 84 Post-NA, 850.4-Italy/CGIL. After this report, the activities of this acute and refined analyst seem to conclude. From the papers in the Department of State, it has not been possible to ascertain the reason for the end of his assignment. It could have been normal rotation, voluntary departure, or abolition of the position. It is striking, however, that Adams, a Roosevelt Democrat, finished his job as labor attaché just when his obvious sympathies for the Socialists, especially Santi, the secretary of the CGIL, his mistrust of the Catholics, and even a stated personal admiration for Di Vittorio became decidedly extraneous to, if not incompatible with, the line followed by American diplomacy in Italy and, more generally, the violent acrimony of the Cold War.

32. Miller, *United States and Italy*, pp. 264–65.

33. NSC 1/1, "The Position of the United States with Respect to Italy," 14 November 1947, *FRUS*, 1948, 3:724–26; for the clandestine operations, see Leary, *Central Intelligence Agency*, p. 40, and Miller, "Taking Off the Gloves."

34. Telegram from the embassy in Rome to Secretary of State, 7 February 1948, *FRUS*, 1948, 3:827–30.

35. See the National Security Council resolutions of 10 February and 8 March 1948, NSC 1/2 and NSC 1/3, *FRUS*, 1948, 3:765 and 775; for the support to government forces, see the documents published in ibid., pp. 816ff., and in Faenza and Fini, *Gli Americani in Italia*, pp. 267–304; on the clandestine operations, see Barnes, "Secret Cold War," pts. 1 and 2; and Leary, *Central Intelligence Agency*, p. 40. On the propaganda campaign, see Robert T. Holt and Robert W. Van de Velde, *Strategic Psychological Operations and American Foreign Policy* (Chicago, 1960); Lester Markel et al., *Public Opinion and Foreign Policy* (New York, 1949). On the role of the Italian American communities, see Venturini, "Italian American Political Leadership," p. 1. On the activation of American unions, see Minutes of the AFL-CILR, 19

February 1948, FT; D. Dubinsky to Morgan Phillips, Secretary of the British Labour Party, 16 March 1948, DD, box 2-173, folder 2A; L. Antonini to G. Faravelli, 31 March and 6 April 1948, LA, box 17, folder 5/6/7; "IALC Summary Report—1948," LA, box 12, folder 2; *CIO News* 11, no. 13 (29 March 1948); Montana, *Amarostico*, p. 338; Filippelli, *American Labor*, pp. 130–34.

36. On the elections of 1948, see Antonio Gambino, *Storia del dopoguerra dalla Liberazione al potere DC* (Bari, 1974), pp. 44ff., and Di Nolfo, *Le paure e le speranze*, pp. 245ff.; on the American intervention, Miller, "Taking Off the Gloves," and, by the same author, "L'ERP come fattore determinante nelle elezioni italiane del 1948," in *Il Piano Marshall e l'Europa*, ed. Elena Aga Rossi, pp. 139–48; on the American domestic aspects of this preelectoral tension, see Freeland, *Truman Doctrine*, p. 275, and Paterson, "Presidential Foreign Policy."

37. Gambino, "La situazione politica interna"; and Franco Rodano, "Il Piano Marshall e l'Italia," *Rinascita* 3 (March 1948): 103–7. For the government statements, see *FRUS*, 1948, 3:835–60.

38. *New York Times*, 1 January 1948; Radar, "Il Piano Marshall," *Lavoro* 1, no. 8 (7 April 1948); Turone, *Storia del sindacato*, p. 138; Saba, *Giulio Pastore*, p. 86; Boni, *I socialisti e l'unità sindacale*, p. 41.

39. See chapter 3. For the importance of the Marshall Plan in the parallel crisis of trade union unity in France and Italy, see Horst Lademacher, "Possibilità e limiti d'azione del movimento operaio europeo nel primo dopoguerra," in *La sinistra europea*, ed. Maria Petricioli, pp. 49–96; Zander, "Die Schwächen der unvollendeten Einheit Italien," pp. 109ff.; Agostinone, "Una testimonianza," p. 227.

40. Telegram from the embassy in Brussels to Secretary of State, RG 59 DS-NA, 800.5043/2-1148.

41. *Notiziario della CGIL* 2, no. 6 (March 1948), and Turone, *Storia del sindacato*, pp. 131–37.

42. Dispatch from the embassy in Rome to the Secretary of State, RG 59 DS-NA, 865.5043/3-848; see also telegram sent on 10 March, *FRUS*, 1948, 3:846.

43. See chapter 4; "Memorandum of Conversation with Enrico Parri," dispatch from the embassy in Rome to the Secretary of State, RG 59 DS-NA, 865.5043/3-1648; *CIO News* 11, no. 13 (29 March 1948); see also Zaninelli, *Il Sindacato Nuovo*, pp. 306–8.

44. Giuseppe Faravelli, "New Trends in Italian Trade Unionism," *International Free Trade Union News* 3, no. 3 (March 1948).

45. Telegram from Secretary of State for the labor attaché (Berger) at the embassy in London, 10 March 1948, *FRUS*, 1948, 3:847–48; telegram from Secretary of State for Berger, 8 March 1948, RG 84 Post-NA, 850.4-Italy/CGIL, and the account of a conversation with Santi, the Socialist leader of the CGIL, in telegram from the embassy in Rome to Secretary of State, 3 March 1948, *FRUS*, 1948, 3:841.

46. "Text of Conversation between James B. Carey, Secretary-Treasurer CIO, and Giuseppe Di Vittorio, Secretary General, CGIL, and Fernando Santi, also of CGIL, on March 12, 1948, London," copy of report drafted by the CIO in DD, box 2-173, folder 2A; Filippelli, *American Labor*, pp. 128–29.

47. *Lavoro* 1, no. 4 (21 March 1948); telegram from the embassy in Rome to the embassy in London and Secretary of State, 12 March 1948, RG 84 Post-NA, 850.4-Italy/CGIL; S.

Berger, "Memorandum of Conversation" with Murray, Carey, and Golden, RG 59 DS-NA, 800.5043/3-2348; telegram from the embassy in Rome to the Secretary of State, RG 59 DS-NA, 840.50 Recovery/3-2748.

48. Director of European Affairs, "Policy Memo to the Secretary of State: Proposed Joint Interview with President Green and Secretary Meany of AFL and President Murray and Secretary Carey of CIO," 23 March 1948, RG 59 DS-NA, ROWE, box 3; S. Berger, "Memorandum of Conversation" cited in note 47.

49. Telegram from Secretary of State to the embassy in Rome, 24 March 1948, *FRUS*, 1948, 3:867. On Washington's decision for the breakup of the CGIL, see also Miller, *United States and Italy*, pp. 255–62, and Zander, "Die Schwächen der unvollendeten Einheit Italien," p. 113. The CIA was also beginning to take an interest in European trade unions, asking the American embassies for detailed information on officials and on the structure of all the unions. See memorandum of Stauffer and Horowitz, RG 59 DS-NA, 811.5043/4-548.

50. Telegram from the embassy in Rome to Secretary of State, RG 59 DS-NA, 865.5043/4-248.

51. Report of the embassy in Rome on the ACLI, RG 59 DS-NA, 865.5043/3-3048.

52. Miller, *United States and Italy*, p. 249.

53. *CIO News* 11, no. 17 (26 April 1948); telegram from M. Woll to G. Pastore, G. Canini, and E. Parri, 21 April 1948, copy in FT.

54. Telegram from the embassy in London to Secretary of State and the embassy in Rome, 5 April 1948, RG 84 Post-NA, 850.4 Italy/CGIL; telegram from the embassy in Rome to Secretary of State, RG 59 DS-NA, 865.5043/4-348 and 865.5043/4-2648.

55. L. Antonini to G. Faravelli, 6 May 1948, and L. Antonini to S. Romualdi, 14 May 1948, LA, box 17, folder 5/6/7, and box 41, folder 4, respectively.

56. Telegram from the embassy in Rome to Secretary of State, RG 59 DS-NA, 865.5043/4-2248.

57. I. Brown to J. Lovestone, Geneva, 26 April 1948, copy in DD, box 2-261, folder 3B.

58. Colonel Lane had been sent to Rome from Trieste (where he was in charge of trade union policy in the Allied military government) to reinforce the staff at the embassy in the crucial months before 18 April. He was later assigned to the position of labor attaché at the end of April, when the delicate trade union situation called for an expert, capable official for the months to come. Lane, who had belonged in the past to the AFL and later became an official of the Department of Labor, had important trade union experience and knew Italy. He arrived there in 1944 as an official in the labor division of the military government, working in Florence for a long time and then in Trieste. Lane was well known in the Italian trade union movement and had good contacts. His arrival in Rome coincided with the American decision to intervene directly in trade union matters. His own way of interpreting the labor attaché role was the rash, conspiratorial, and sectarian view of one who—like Irving Brown and other AFL leaders, to whom the extremely anti-Communist Lane was closely tied—interpreted the Cold War as a crusade. From 1948 on, his personal interpretation of the policy dictated by the State Department—and also the ECA, since Lane for a long time was labor officer at that mission too—always coincided with the tactics and extremist ways of the AFL, so much as to often make it difficult to distinguish whether he was working for the government or the labor federation.

59. Telegrams from the embassy in Rome to the Secretary of State, RG 59 DS-NA, 800.5043/4-3048 and 800.5043/5-1348. See also the discussion of the consequences of the WFTU meeting in chapter 4.

60. Telegram from Secretary of State to the embassy in Rome, RG 59 DS-NA, 865.5043/4-2248 (but actually dated 7 May 1948).

61. Telegram from Secretary of State to the embassy in Rome, RG 59 DS-NA, 865.5043/4-2248 (but actually dated 20 May), where the CIO comments were also reported; telegram from the embassy in London to Secretary of State, RG DS-NA, 800.5043/5-2848; *Lavoro* 1, no. 12 (18 May 1948).

62. Pasini, *Le ACLI dalle origini*, pp. 188–200; Saba, *Giulio Pastore*, p. 89; Davide La Valle, "Dalla corrente sindacale cristiana alla CISL: Il dibattito tra i dirigenti cattolici," in *Itinerari sindacali*, ed. Emilio Santi and Antonio Varni (Rome, 1982), pp. 545–99.

63. Turone, *Storia del sindacato*, pp. 143–44; Horowitz, *Storia del movimento sindacale*, p. 344; La Valle, "Dalla corrente sindacale cristiana alla CISL"; Saba, *Giulio Pastore*, p. 92.

64. See, for example, the long analysis of the advantages and potential problems of the alliance written by G. Faravelli in a letter of 22 June 1948 to L. Antonini, LA, box 17, folder 5/6/7.

65. Telegram from the embassy in Rome to Secretary of State, RG 59 DS-NA, 865.5043/6-2548; "Memorandum of Conversation with Luigi Gedda, President of Comitati Civici," and "Memorandum of Conversation with Professor Storchi, President of ACLI," both dated 16 June 1948, RG 84 Post-NA, 850.4 Italy/CGIL.

66. G. Baldanzi, president of the Italian-American Trade Union Committee of the CIO, to Harry S. Truman, 28 June 1948, RG 59 DS-NA, 811.5043/6-2848; G. Baldanzi to J. Carey, 21 May 1948, and J. Carey to G. Baldanzi, 7 June 1948, CIO-ST, ALHUA, box 83.

67. W. C. Dowling to Ambassador J. Dunn, 7 July 1948, RG 59 DS-NA, ROWE, box 3.

68. "Policy Memorandum: The United States Policy with Regard to Italy," 9 July 1948, RG 59 DS-NA, ROWE, box 3. Here Dowling recommended maintaining constant pressure on the De Gasperi government to carry out fiscal and social reforms to strengthen the democratic consensus. Both the political use of the union by the PCI, against the ERP, and the conservative instinct of the industrialists in defense of their privileges had to be reined in.

69. Turone, *Storia del sindacato*, pp. 145–49.

70. Telegram from the embassy in Rome (Byington) to Secretary of State, 17 July 1947, RG 84 Post-NA, 850.4 Italy/CGIL. The message reported that the leaders of CONFIN-DUSTRIA, through Vice-President De Micheli, had confided to the embassy that they thought a break "undesirable at present time," since it would have obliged them to continue to deal with the CGIL.

71. Turone, *Storia del sindacato*, pp. 153–54; Saba, *Giulio Pastore*, pp. 95ff.; Horowitz, *Storia del movimento sindacale*, pp. 349ff.; Baget-Bozzo, *Il partito cristiano al potere*, p. 238; *Lavoro* 1, no. 21 (1 July 1948).

72. Telegram from the embassy in Rome (Byington) to Secretary of State, 25 July 1948, RG 84 Post-NA, 850.4 Italy/CGIL. The CGIL violently attacked the presence in Rome of the American trade unionists, whom they defined as "specialists in breakups." *Lavoro* 1, no. 22 (28 July 1948). Dubinsky recounted his meeting with the pope in these terms: "I broke the ice by saying: 'Father, you did a great job in the elections.' His aides looked scandalized. Not so the

Pope. He smiled, clasped the hands in front of his chest and turned his eyes heavenward: 'When the truth is attacked, one must rise to the occasion and defend the truth,' he said." Dubinsky and Raskin, *David Dubinsky*, p. 258.

73. Telegram from Secretary of State to the embassy in Rome, RG 59 DS-NA, 865.5043/ 8-1248; telegram from the embassy in Rome to Secretary of State, 3 August 1948, RG 84 Post-NA, 850.4 Italy/CGIL.

74. Telegram from the embassy in Rome to Secretary of State, RG 59 DS-NA, 865.5043/ 8-2748 and 865.5043/9-948; for Antonini's attitude, see his letter to G. Faravelli, 10 May 1949, LA, box 17, folder 5/6/7.

75. Telegram from Secretary of State to the embassy in Rome ("Ambassador's eyes only"), RG 59 DS-NA, 865.5043/9-148.

76. Minutes of the AFL-CILR, 9 September 1948, FT; telegram from the embassy in Rome to Secretary of State, RG DS-NA, 865.5043/9-648.

77. Telegram from Secretary of State to the embassy in Rome, RG 59 DS-NA, 865.5043/ 9-1348; F. Thorne to Matthew Woll, Washington, D.C., 15 September 1948, FT.

78. Telegram from Secretary of State to the embassy in Rome, RG 59 DS-NA, 865.5043/ 9-1648. See, for example, the article from Rome in the *New York Times*, 14 September 1948, which spoke of the Vatican's plan to break the Communist domination of the trade union movement with Luigi Gedda's Civic Committees.

79. Baget-Bozzo, *Il partito cristiano al potere*, p. 241; Pasini, *Le ACLI dalle origini*, pp. 200–214; Saba, *Giulio Pastore*, p. 108; Turone, *Storia del sindacato*, pp. 159ff. For a defense of the defeated plan for a religiously oriented trade union movement, see the essay of Giuseppe Rapelli in *I sindacati in Italia*, by Giuseppe Di Vittorio et al. (Bari, 1955), pp. 231–71, and his account of the break in Walter Tobagi, "I sindacati nella ricostruzione, 1945–1950," *Il Mulino* 23, no. 235 (November–December 1974): 944ff.

80. Telegram from the embassy in Rome to Secretary of State, 21 September 1948, RG 84 Post-NA, 850.4 Italy/ACLI; memorandum from W. L. Munger to J. D. Zellerbach ("Conference with Messrs. Parri—PRI—and Villani—PSLI"), 17 September 1948, RG 84 Post-NA, 850.4 Italy; W. E. Knight, "Memorandum of Conversation with On. Giulio Pastore," 22 September 1948, RG 84 Post-NA, 850.4 Italy.

81. Telegram from Secretary of State to the embassy in Rome, RG DS-NA, 865.5043/ 9-1748 (but actually dated 4 October 1948).

82. Telegram from the embassy in Rome to Secretary of State ("for the acting secretary eyes only"), RG 59 DS-NA, 865.5043/9-2148. Dunn reported that he had discussed using counterpart funds for Pastore with Zellerbach, head of the ECA mission, and assured the State Department that he could guarantee the maximum discretion in managing these and other American funds.

83. L. Antonini to G. Faravelli, 5 October 1948, LA, box 17, folder 5/6/7.

84. J. Carey, "We've Got the Reds on the Run," *CIO News* 11, no. 36 (6 September 1948). Subsequent negative opinions came from A. Bellanca (see Carwell, "International Role of American Labor," p. 560n) and especially from Victor and Walter Reuther. See Reuther, *Brothers Reuther*, p. 350, and author's interview with Victor Reuther, Washington, D.C., 14 August 1984.

85. See, for example, Giorgio Candeloro, *Il movimento sindacale in Italia* (Bari, 1950), pp.

169ff., and Renato Mieli, "Le scissioni sindacali in Italia e gli aiuti degli esperti americani," *Rinascita*, June 1949. For a minimizing view, see Horowitz, *Storia del movimento sindacale*, pp. 138ff.; a more balanced judgment is in Turone, *Storia del sindacato*, pp. 148–53.

86. Particularly convincing in that direction is the interpretation suggested by Craveri, *Sindacato e istituzioni*, pp. 233ff.

87. "Memorandum of Conversation" with A. Simonini, 20 October 1948, RG DS-NA, ROWE, box 3; G. Faravelli to L. Antonini, 7 October 1948, LA, box 17, folder 5/6/7.

88. "Memorandum of Conversation" with L. Morelli and R. Cappugi, 21 October 1948, RG 59 DS-NA, ROWE, box 3; "Memorandum of Conversation" with G. Pastore, 5 November 1948, RG 84 Post-NA, 850.4 Italy.

89. Memorandum, n.d. (but early in October 1948, presumably by T. Lane), "United States Policy toward the Non-Communist Labor Movement in Italy," RG 84 Post-NA, 850.4 Italy.

90. *International Free Trade Union News* 3, no. 10 (October 1948); telegram from the embassy in Rome to Secretary of State, RG 59 DS-NA, 865.5043/10-2948, and Washington's reply of 3 November 1948, RG 84 Post-NA, 850.4 Italy-Pastore.

91. Press conference of Giulio Pastore, 14 November 1948, reported in Saba, *Giulio Pastore*, p. 116.

92. Ibid., pp. 122–23.

93. Telegram from ECA-Rome to ECA-Washington, 6 July 1949, RG 286 ECA-NA, OSR, Labor Information Div., GSF 1949–51, box 1; circular from the consultative committee on union affairs of the ERP to the provincial representatives of LCGIL, Rome, 13 April 1949, Archives of the CISL Confederal Secretariat, Giulio Pastore Foundation, Rome. At the same time, a committee was formed for publicizing the Marshall Plan, made up of Italian public figures and directed by government and ECA officials. It had the task of propagandizing the advantages of the ERP, first of all among industrial workers and farmers, who were perceived as the most important elements in the Communist electorate. Newspapers, films, radio programs, comic strips, and exhibitions were distributed in enormous quantities for the purpose of producing "direct effects on mass thinking." See F. R. Shea to A. Bearding, Paris, 24 February 1949; memorandum of A. Friendly to Foster, Paris, 14 December 1948; and memorandum of A. Bearding to J. Zellerbach, Rome, 24 February 1949, all in RG 286 ECA-NA, OSR, Labor Information Div., CSF 1948–50, box 6, Italy. Telegram from the embassy in Rome to Secretary of State, 18 February 1949, RG 84 Post-NA, 560.1 Italy/LCGIL.

94. Carwell, "International Role of American Labor," p. 581; D. Saposs to B. Shishkin, Paris, 28 January 1949, RG 286 ECA-NA, OSR, Labor Information Div., Office of Economic Advisor, GSF 1949–51, box 7, ERP-TUAC; *Bollettino d'informazione sindacale* 2, no. 2 (30 January 1949); Saba, *Giulio Pastore*, p. 121.

95. Telegram from the embassy in Rome to Secretary of State, 12 February 1949, RG 84 Post-NA, 560.1 Italy, and "Memorandum of Conversation" with Simonini, 8 March 1949, RG 59 DS-NA, ROWE, box 3.

96. "Policy Statement and Background Data on Unification of Italian Non-Communist Trade Unions," 22 November 1949, *FRUS*, 1949, 4:710. One of the ECA officials who went on the trip insisted especially on political-psychological pressure exerted by American trade

unionists: "Our own labor leaders would invariably . . . ask them whom they were fighting, the reds or each other." J. Toughill to J. Hutchinson, Rome, 19 April 1949, RG 286 ECA-NA, OSR, Labor Information Div., GSF 1949–50, Policy Planning Section, box 7; telegram from Secretary of State to the embassy in Rome, RG 59 DS-NA, 865.5043/3-449, and Dunn's reply from Rome, 7 March 1949, RG 84 Post-NA, 560.1 ICFTU.

97. *Abbiamo visto: Tre sindacalisti italiani tra i lavoratori d'America* (Rome, 1949), p. 32; *Bollettino d'informazione sindacale* 2, no. 8 (1 May 1949): 58.

98. Telegram from Secretary of State to the embassy in Rome, RG 59 DS-NA, 865.5043/4-1249.

99. Memorandum from Fraleigh to Dowling, 31 March 1949, RG 59 DS-NA, ROWE, box 3; Pastore, Rocchi, and Canini to L. Antonini, 16 April 1949, LA, box 37, folder 3; L. Antonini to T. Lane, 3 May 1949, and L. Antonini to G. Canini, 3 June 1949, both in LA, box 28, folder 1. See also Montana, *Amarostico*, p. 346, and the testimony of Rocchi and Parri in Tobagi, "I sindacati nella ricostruzione," pp. 938–40.

100. L. Antonini to G. Canini, 3 June 1949, LA, box 28, folder 1; telegram from the embassy in Rome to Secretary of State, 13 June 1949, RG Post-NA, 560.1 Italy/FIL; *FRUS*, 1949, 4:704–5; see also Turone, *Storia del sindacato*, p. 162, and Aldo Forbice, *Scissioni sindacali e origini della UIL* (Rome, 1981), pp. 58–65; *Conquiste del lavoro* 2, no. 23 (12 June 1949); *Lavoro* 2, no. 24 (12–18 June 1949).

101. Telegram from the embassy in Rome to Secretary of State, RG 59 DS-NA, 865.5043/6-2349 (see also 865.5043/6-2049); Forbice, *Scissioni sindacali e origini*, pp. 83–96.

102. Enrico Parri to L. Antonini, 28 July 1949, and also Parri's letter of 9 July and Antonini's reply of 13 July 1949, all in LA, box 24, folder 3. See also G. Canini to L. Antonini, 25 and 30 June 1949, and Antonini's replies of 1 and 6 July 1949, all in LA, box 28, folder 1; D. Dubinsky to Averell Harriman (in charge of the ECA in Europe), 1 July 1949, DD, box 2-255, folder 3B.

103. "Notes on Labor," of T. Lane, RG 59 DS-NA, 865.5043/7-2249, and two circulars from Secretary of State to embassies, "International Labor Movement after the WFTU Split," RG 59 DS-NA, 800.5043 FTUI/5-1249 and 800.5043 FTUI/7-449.

104. A highly critical description of Lane's activities and methods was given by a direct, well-informed witness, Joseph La Palombara, in "Democratic Trade Unionism in Postwar Italy" (Ph.D. dissertation, Princeton University, 1954), chap. 7. For Irving Brown (interview with the author, Washington, D.C., 14 August 1984), Pastore was an outstanding figure and an excellent leader, devoted to the idea of trade union independence, unlike other Italian union leaders, whom Brown considered to be inspired primarily by party interests, ideological prejudices, and sectarian animosities.

105. I. Brown to L. Antonini, Brussels, 20 August 1949, LA, box 24, folder 2; J. Lovestone to V. Montana, 2 August and 27 July 1949, both in VM; V. Montana to J. Lovestone, 27 July and 22 August 1949, and V. Montana to D. Dubinsky, 22 August 1949, all in VM; I. Brown to D. Dubinsky, Rome, 4 September 1949, DD, box 2-255, folder 3B; telegram from the embassy in Rome to Secretary of State, RG 59 DS-NA, 865.5043/8-1649; *Conquiste del lavoro* 2, no. 33 (28 August 1949). For the situation within the FIL, see Forbice, *Scissioni sindacali e origini*, pp. 97–99.

106. "Notes on Labor," T. Lane, RG 59 DS-NA, 865.5043/9-1249, and Lane's report of 13

September 1949 on the autonomist current, RG 84 Post-NA, 560 Italy/Labor; *Il lavoro italiano* 1, no. 5 (16 September 1949); Forbice, *Scissioni sindacali e origini*, pp. 98–106.

107. Text of Thomas's telegram, *FRUS*, 1949, 4:706; "Memorandum on the Unity of Non-Communist Labor Groups in Italy, from Norman Thomas," n.d. (but September 1949), DD, box 2-255, folder 3B. On Norman Thomas, see William Swanberg, *Norman Thomas: The Last Idealist* (New York, 1976); *L'Umanità*, 20 September 1949; Montana, *Amarostico*, pp. 347–48; *Lavoro* 2, no. 39 (23 September 1949); *Il lavoro italiano* 1, no. 17 (30 September 1949); telegram from the embassy in Rome to Secretary of State, 23 September 1949, RG 84 Post-NA, 560.1 Italy.

108. Telegram from Secretary of State to the embassies in London and Rome, 9 October 1949, and telegram from the embassy in Rome to Secretary of State, 4 October 1949, RG 84 Post-NA, 560.1 Italy; memorandum from Unger to Thompson, "Italian Non-Communist Labor Movement," RG 59 DS-NA, 865.5043/10-449; Saba, *Giulio Pastore*, pp. 133ff. For the controversies in the Italian press, see Forbice, *Scissioni sindacali e origini*, pp. 110ff.; J. N. Greene to E. Page, Washington, D.C., 27 September 1949, and E. Page to J. N. Greene, Rome, 5 October 1949, RG 59 DS-NA, ROWE, box 3.

109. L. Antonini to G. Saragat, 29 September 1949, LA, box 43, folder 5; M. Woll to V. Montana, 5 October 1949, VM; press release of N. Thomas, 10 October 1949, and letter of L. Antonini, 18 October 1949, LA, box 24, folder 3.

110. "Memorandum of Conversation" with J. Lovestone and A. Bellanca, 25 October 1949, RG 59 DS-NA, ROWE, box 3; *FRUS*, 1949, 4:707–11; Filippelli, *American Labor*, pp. 162–76.

111. Telegram from the embassy in Rome to Secretary of State, 25 October 1949, RG 84 Post-NA, 560.1 Italy/LCGIL.

112. Telegram from the embassy in Rome to Secretary of State, RG 59 DS-NA, 865.5043/11-2949; *Conquiste del lavoro* 2, no. 45 (6 November 1949); on the proceedings and resolutions of the congress, see *Bollettino d'informazione sindacale* 3, no. 42 (15 January 1950), and Saba, *Giulio Pastore*, pp. 141ff.

113. Circular airgram from Secretary of State to embassies, RG 59 DS-NA, 800.5043 ICFTU/12-1249; *New York Times*, 10 December 1949; memorandum of H. Martin to A. Harriman, "New International Confederation of Free Trade Unions," 15 December 1949, RG 286 ECA-NA, OSR, Labor Information Div., GSF 1949–51, box 6; "Memorandum of Conversation with G. Pastore," RG 59 DS-NA, 800.5043 ICFTU/12-1649; Saba, *Giulio Pastore*, pp. 149ff.

114. Turone, *Storia del sindacato*, pp. 163–64; Forbice, *Scissioni sindacali e origini*, pp. 143–50; *Il lavoro italiano* 2, no. 3–4 (20–27 January 1950). D. Dubinsky to Hannah Haskel, London, 9 December 1949, DD, box 2-33, folder 5; "Memorandum of Conversation" with G. Pastore and M. Woll, Rome, n.d. (but 16 December 1949), RG 59 DS-NA, ROWE, box 3; telegram from the embassy in Rome to Secretary of State, RG 59 DS-NA, 865.5043/12-1649; "Progetto Unificazione," approved on 15 December 1949 by the Unification Committee, in the Lamberto Giannittelli Letters, Giulio Pastore Foundation, Rome.

115. J. C. Dunn to George Perkins (Assistant Secretary of State), Rome, 27 January 1950, RG 59 DS-NA, ROWE, box 7; *Conquiste del lavoro* 3, no. 6 (12 February 1950) and no. 8 (26 February 1950); Saba, *Giulio Pastore*, pp. 152ff.

116. On the founding congress of the CISL, see *Conquiste del lavoro* 3, no. 18 (7 May 1950); *Bollettino d'informazione sindacale* 3, no. 9 (15 May 1950); Saba, *Giulio Pastore*, pp. 171ff. On the establishment of the UIL, see *Il lavoro italiano* 2, no. 9–10 (10 March 1950), and Forbice, *Scissioni sindacali e origini*, pp. 166–90; Boni, *I socialisti e l'unità sindacale*, pp. 45ff.; Alberto Bonifazi and Gianni Salvarani, *Dalla parte dei lavoratori: Storia del movimento sindacale italiano* (Milan, 1976), 3:69ff.; also Turone, *Storia del sindacato*, pp. 164–68, and Horowitz, *Storia del movimento sindacale*, pp. 359ff.

117. Minutes of the AFL-CILR, 26 April 1950, FT; telegram from L. Antonini to G. Pastore and G. Canini, 25 April 1950, LA, box 28, folder 2; T. Lane, "Unification of Non-Communist Trade Unions" and "CISL Executive Committee Meeting," reports of 8 May and 21 June 1950, and also by Lane, "Notes on Labor," 29 May and 13 June 1950, all in RG 84 Post-NA, 560.1 Italy. On the CISL's economic and political leanings, and on its union program, the clearest and most exhaustive document remains the essay by Giulio Pastore in *I sindacati in Italia*, by Giuseppe De Vittorio et al., pp. 121–94; *CIO News* 13, no. 23 (5 June 1950) and no. 32 (7 August 1950).

118. Forbice, *Scissioni sindacali e origini*, pp. 201ff.; Turone, *Storia del sindacato*; Filippelli, *American Labor*, pp. 182ff. The debate in the U.S. diplomatic establishment, the activities of the embassy in Rome, and the attitude of both the AFL and the CIO are amply documented in the State Department's archives for the period 1950–54: RG 59 DS-NA, series 865.06, and RG 84 Post-NA, series 560. On the Italian policy of the AFL, see esp. report from L. Antonini to W. Green, G. Meany, M. Woll, D. Dubinsky, J. Lovestone, I. Brown, T. Lane, 7 September 1951, LA, box 47, folder 1; report of I. Brown to J. Lovestone, Brussels, 2 December 1951, DD, box 2-262, folder 6A; and "Report on the Italian Labor Situation," from I. Brown, 15 January 1952, DD, box 2-255, folder 2B; AFL Executive Council, "Resolution on ICFTU Executive Council Meeting," 2 February 1952, DD, box 2-261, folder 6. On the CIO's attitude, see Reuther, *Brothers Reuther*, pp. 328ff.; Victor Reuther, interview with the author, Washington, D.C., 14 August 1984; "Report of Special CIO Committee to Europe to CIO Committee on International Affairs," Washington, D.C., 1 March 1951, in Documents of the CIO, Walter P. Reuther Collection (hereafter CIO-WPR), ALHUA, box 64; "Memorandum of Conversation: U.S. Policy toward Italian Trade Unions," Washington, D.C., 18 December 1951, RG 59 DS-NA, ROWE, box 7.

119. "Memorandum of Conversation with G. Pastore," RG 59 DS-NA, 800.5043 ICFTU/12-1649; telegram from the embassy in Rome to Secretary of State, RG 84 Post-NA, 560.2 Italy/Strikes; *FRUS*, 1950, 3:1484.

120. See, for example, the memorandum on the Italian trade union situation prepared by the ECA Mission in Rome, presumably by Lane, and circulated by the OSR on 19 December 1949 to all the other missions, RG 286 ECA-NA, OSR, Information Div., CSF 1948–50, box 6, Italy. There was a nearly apocalyptic vision of the CGIL, which was supposed to be on the point of taking power the day after the attempt on Togliatti's life. This was opposed by an exaggerated confidence in the possibility that "free" trade unions, thanks to the breakup Pastore engineered, "broke the back of the near-revolution" and, as soon as they were united, would have such an impact that "the power of the CGIL, now sharply reduced, will completely vanish."

Chapter 6

1. *Foreign Assistance Act of 1948*, 80th Cong., 2d sess., 1948, in *U.S. Statutes at Large*, vol. 62, pt. 1, p. 137. On the plan's economic aspects, see, among the more recent discussions, Wexler, *Marshall Plan Revisited*.

2. Milward, *Reconstruction of Western Europe*, pp. 98–99; Michael J. Hogan, "American Marshall Planners and the Search for a European Neocapitalism," *American Historical Review* 90, no. 1 (February 1985): 47–48; for an opposing view, see J. and G. Kolko, *Limits of American Power*, pp. 428–29.

3. Arkes, *Bureaucracy*, p. 301.

4. Hogan, "American Marshall Planners," p. 72; Milward, *Reconstruction of Western Europe*, pp. 466–67.

5. The most representative figure from this point of view is Walter Reuther. At the International Trade Union Conference on the ERP in London in March 1948, AFL representative Frank Fenton, recalling the necessity that the unions be given a role in the management of ERP, stated: "The production expansion which is envisaged by 1951 is similar in general scale to that adhered to by the U.S. in the mobilization years 1940–1944. Where would Americans have been in those trying war years if the trade union movement were not enthusiastically supporting and participating in that production effort?" "International Trade Union Conference on the ERP," report by F. Fenton, I. Brown, B. Jewell, 15 March 1948, copy in DD, box 2-261, folder 3A. From the side of the industrialists, the analogy with wartime experience was especially evident in the activities of Paul Hoffman, president of the automobile manufacturer Studebaker, champion of particularly advanced industrial relations with the UAW, and, from 1948 to 1950, administrator of the ERP. His book, significantly entitled *Peace Can Be Won* (New York, 1951), is one of the most representative expositions of a philosophy of social prosperity in postwar Europe.

6. *Foreign Assistance Act*, pp. 139ff.; Hogan, "American Marshall Planners," pp. 54–60; Harris, *Right to Manage*, pp. 135–39; see esp. the detailed analysis of Arkes, *Bureaucracy*.

7. Director of European Affairs, "Policy Memo to the Secretary of State," 23 March 1948, RG 59 DS-NA, ROWE, box 3; Eleanor Finger, "Labor's Role in ECA," *Labor and Nation*, July 1949, pp. 13–14.

8. See in particular the testimony of Walter Reuther at the congressional hearings on the ERP, quoted in chap. 3 at n. 78. Also see the presentation by James Carey—whose theme was "to sell democracy and prosperity" to the European workers—at the Council on Foreign Relations, in "Labor Movement in Europe: Digest of Meeting," New York, 8 April 1948, Archives of the Council on Foreign Relations, New York, N.Y., Records of Meetings, vol. 13, 1947–48. The official request to be represented in the ECA is repeated in every union document from the beginning of 1948; see, for example, "AFL Program for World Recovery and Lasting Peace: Memorandum to the President of the United States," in AFL, *American Labor Looks at the World*, 1948, 2:5–8; "Statement Offered by Phil Murray," in ERP-*Hearings*, 158:1289–90. The idea that the ECA should directly support "free" trade unions with financial contributions was frequently brought forward by American trade unionists; see memorandum from Fraleigh to Swayzee on a talk given by J. Carey at the Department of State, 11 March 1949, RG 59 DS-NA, 811.5043.3-1149.

9. Trade Union Advisory Committee on International Affairs (Department of Labor), "Minutes of the Ninth Meeting," 9 April 1948, and "Minutes of the Tenth Meeting," 9 September 1948, copies in DD, box 2-393, folders 3B and 3C. J. Green to Charles J. Kersten, Washington, D.C., 2 April 1948, FT; Matthew Woll to J. Green, New York, 27 April 1948, copy in DD, box 2-261, folder 3B; Brooks, *Clint*, pp. 315–17.

10. D. Morse (Acting Secretary of Labor) to George V. Allen (Assistant Secretary of State), 12 May 1948, Record Group 174, General Records of the Department of Labor, National Archives, Washington, D.C. (hereafter RG 174 DL-NA), Office of the Secretary, box 221; report of W. G. Patterson (director of the apprenticeship office of the Department of Labor), "The Feasibility of Establishing with European Countries an Interchange of Persons, Knowledge, and Skills in the Labor Field," 1 July 1948, copy in RG 84 Post-NA, 850.4 Italy, misc. 1948. Also, Finger, "Labor's Role in ECA"; Price, *Marshall Plan*, pp. 110–11.

11. I. Brown, M. Ross, H. Rutz, A. Steinbach, "Report to the Labor Department's Trade Union Advisory Committee on International Affairs Concerning Observations and Recommendations of Its Sub-Committee Sent to Germany," Paris, 30 June 1948, copy in DD, box 2-393, folder 3B.

12. Final resolution, in "Report by Jay Lovestone, Secretary. In Behalf of A.F. of L. Delegation to the ERP Trade Union Conference—London, July 29–30, 1948," copy in DD, box 2-33, folder 6.

13. "European Labor Participation in ECA, Memorandum of Conversation with C. Golden," RG 59 DS-NA, 840.5043/8-2048; Brooks, *Clint*, pp. 318ff. On the Anglo-American Council on Productivity, see esp. Carew, *Labour under the Marshall Plan*, pp. 131–57. Golden defined the establishment of the joint Anglo-American committee by the union and industrial organizations as "a landmark of the new order" which the ERP should promote in Europe. *CIO News* 11, no. 33 (23 August 1948).

14. Wexler, *Marshall Plan Revisited*, pp. 89ff.

15. A foretaste of these future problems could already be discerned in the ERP-TUAC discussions at the beginning of 1949, especially in relation to unemployment and the fact that in some countries (Italy, Germany, Austria) the trade unions belonging to the ERP were neither consulted by the governments concerned nor involved in administering the aid; see ERP-TUAC, "Summary Record of the Fifth Meeting," Berne, 22 January 1949, copy in CIO-ST, ALHUA, box 132. When the technical assistance program was just getting started, the trade union consultant to the mission in Greece noted with concern that its activities might benefit only the industrialists if the unions were not able to control its application closely. See Joe Heath to G. Delaney (international representative of the AFL), Athens, 12 March 1949, copy in FT.

16. "Summary of ECA European Labor Staff Conference, July 6–8, 1949, Paris," RG 286 ECA-NA, OSR, Labor Information Div., GSF 1949–51, box 5.

17. Pierre Melandri, *Les Etats-Unis face à l'unification de l'Europe, 1945–54* (Paris, 1980); Milward, *Reconstruction of Western Europe*; Hogan, "American Marshall Planners"; Pier Paolo D'Attorre, "Anche noi possiamo essere prosperi: Aiuti ERP e politiche della produttività negli anni '50," *Quaderni storici* 20, no. 58 (April 1985): 59–62, and, by the same author, "Il Piano Marshall: Politica, economia, relazioni internazionali nella ricostruzione italiana," *Passato e presente* 7 (1985): 52ff.

18. "Summary of ECA European Labor Staff Conference."

19. "Manual of Operations: Labor Policies of ECA," directive from Deputy Administrator William Foster to all the ECA offices, 18 August 1949, RG 286 ECA-NA, OSR, Labor Information Div., GSF 1949–51, box 5.

20. "Confidential Memorandum: Prospective Trade Union Attitude in Western Europe," 31 August 1949, RG 286 ECA-NA, OSR, Labor Information Div., GSF 1949–51, box 5.

21. "The AFL Fight for World Peace," resolution of the annual convention of the AFL, 1949, in AFL, *American Labor Looks at the World*, 1950, 4:17.

22. ERP-TUAC, "Seventh Meeting, Paris, 19–20 January 1950," minutes by the CIO, CIO-ST, ALHUA, box 132; memorandum of D. J. Saposs to B. Shishkin, "Relationship of ERP-TUAC with OEEC," Paris, 18 November 1949, and J. Stern to B. Jewell and C. Golden, Paris, 20 January 1950, both in RG 286 ECA-NA, OSR, Labor Information Div., GSF 1949–51, respectively in box 1 and box 11, productivity.

23. Memorandum of Robert Mullen, director of the ECA Information Office, to P. Hoffman and W. Foster, 30 December 1949, copy in FT.

24. Circular from A. Harriman to all the ECA missions, Paris, 8 February 1950, RG 286 ECA-NA, OSR, Labor Information Div., GSF 1949–51, box 11, productivity; "Manual of Operations: Labor Participation in Arrangements for T. A. Productivity Teams," directive from W. Foster to all ECA offices, 31 January 1950, RG 286 ECA-NA, ECA/W, Productivity and Technical Assistance Div., SF 1950–51, box 3.

25. H. Martin to Ambassador Katz, Rome, 21 March 1950, RG 286 ECA-NA, OSR, Labor Information Div., GSF 1949–51, box 1; J. Stern to K. Douty, Paris, 17 February 1950, and H. Martin to B. Shishkin, Paris, 16 March 1950, both in RG 286 ECA-NA, OSR, Labor Information Div., GSF 1949–51, box 11, productivity.

26. "Summary of Labor Staff Presentation at the Industrial Productivity Conference," 31 March 1950; "Abbreviated Transcription of Industrial Production Conference at OSR," Paris, 27–28 March 1950; and S. Freeland to W. Auman, 30 March 1950, all in RG 286 ECA-NA, OSR, Labor Information Div., GSF 1949–51, box 11, Productivity Conference. Memorandum from D. Saposs to B. Shishkin, "Salient Decisions of ERP—International Trade Union Conference, Rome, April 18–20, 1950," 25 April 1950, RG 286 ECA-NA, OSR, Labor Information Div., GSF 1949–51, box 1.

27. "ECA Labor Conference—Working Paper," Washington, D.C., 28 April 1950, RG 286 ECA-NA, ECA/W, Assist. Admin. for Programs, GSF box 33, Labor; B. Jewell to B. Shishkin, Washington, D.C., 12 April 1950, and the minutes of the conference held in Washington on 5 May 1950, both in RG 286 ECA-NA, OSR, Labor Information Div., GSF 1949, box 4.

28. "Proceedings of ECA Labor Officers Conference, May 22–24, 1950," Paris, quotation from p. 8, and also K. Douty to B. Jewell, Paris, 1 May 1950, both in RG 286 ECA-NA, OSR, Labor Information Div., GSF 1949–51, box 4.

29. "Some Comments on Future ECA Programming by Labor Staff of ECA Country Missions," Paris, 24 May 1950, and also A. Harriman to the Secretary of State, Paris, 27 May 1950, both in RG 286 ECA-NA, OSR, Labor Information Div., GSF 1949–51, box 5 and box 4, respectively.

30. National Security Council Resolution NSC/68, *FRUS*, 1950, 1:234–92; Yergin, *Shat-*

tered Peace, pp. 394–410; Timothy Smith, *The United States, Italy, and NATO, 1947–1952* (New York, 1991).

31. H. Martin to C. Golden, B. Jewell, R. Mullen, Paris, 26 July 1950, RG 286 ECA-NA, ECA/W, Office of Information, GSF 1949–52, box 11.

32. M. Katz to W. Reuther, Paris, 9 June 1950, RG 286 ECA-NA, OSR, Labor Information Div., GSF 1949–51, box 11, productivity; *New York Times*, 6 August 1950; "ECA Labor Resume II," August 1950, and B. Kornby to H. Martin, 7 August 1950, both in RG 286 ECA-NA, OSR, Labor Information Div., GSF 1949–51, respectively box 5 and box 11, productivity.

33. Minutes of the CIO Executive Board and "Foreign Policy Statement," Documents of the CIO, ALHUA, 29 August 1950, p. 90. The issue of a more equitable distribution of income in Italy and France, in the name of anticommunism, became a recurring subject in CIO publicity from then on: *CIO News* 13, no. 47 (20 November 1950) and no. 48 (27 November 1950).

34. "Memorandum of Conversation" with W. H. Braine, 23 November 1948, RG 59 DS-NA, ROWE, box 3; telegram from the embassy in Rome to the Secretary of State, 29 November 1948, RG 84 Post-NA, 850.4 Italy; W. Barbour to Mr. Matlock, "Policy Memorandum," 24 January 1949, RG 59 DS-NA, ROWE, box 3; Leslie L. Rood to the embassy in Rome, "Consigli di Gestione," Milan, 14 March 1949, RG 84 Post-NA, 560.1 Italy-Cdg.

35. J. D. Walker to B. Shishkin, "Technical Assistance Program for Italy," 18 July 1949, RG 286 ECA-NA, OSR, Labor Information Div., Office of the Economic Advisor, CSF 1949–50, box 12, Italy; Production Specialist to B. Shishkin, 11 August 1949, RG 286 ECA-NA, OSR, Labor Information Div., GSF 1949–51, box 11, productivity; "Manual of Operations: Labor Policies of ECA," directive from Deputy Administrator William Foster to all ECA offices, 18 August 1949, RG 286 ECA-NA, OSR, Labor Information Div., GSF 1949–51, box 5.

36. "Confidential Memorandum: Prospective Trade Union Attitude in Western Europe," 31 August 1949, RG 286 ECA-NA, OSR, Labor Information Div., GSF 1949–51, box 5; Trade Union Advisory Committee on International Affairs (Department of Labor), "Report on Recent Developments in the Labor Situation Abroad," 26 September 1949, DD, box 2-393, folder 3B.

37. See, for example, the issues and conclusions reached at the LCGIL congress, where the choice for freeing trade for Europe's progressive economic integration was accompanied by criticism of the tight financial policy pursued by the government, in *Conquiste del lavoro* 2, no. 45 (6 November 1949), and in *Bollettino d'informazione sindacale* 3, no. 1/2 (15 January 1950); see also "Italy Must Break Tradition to End Poverty," *CIO News* 12, no. 36 (12 September 1949).

38. U.S. Economic Cooperation Administration, *Italy—Country Study*, by Paul Hoffman (Washington, D.C., 1949); for an analysis of the background of the *Country Study*, see D'Attorre, "Il Piano Marshall," pp. 38–48.

39. Milward, *Reconstruction of Western Europe*, pp. 98 and 197–98; D'Attorre, "Il Piano Marshall," pp. 32–34. On the controversy on economic policy between the De Gasperi government and the United States, see Rosaria Quartararo, "L'Italia e il Piano Marshall (1947–1950)," *Storia contemporanea* 16, no. 4 (August 1984): 647–722. In the historical

discussion, the traditional negative view of the deflation promoted by the restrictive economic measures of 1947 (see De Cecco's standard treatment, "La politica economica") has recently been revised and criticized. Other scholars, emphasizing that investments were not lacking, put the recessive effects in a different light and have ascribed the origin of these measures to Italian industry's lack of competitiveness. See Giuseppe Maione, *Tecnocrati e mercanti: L'Industria italiana tra dirigismo e concorrenza internazionale, 1945–1950* (Milan, 1986); Bruno Bottiglieri, *La politica economica dell'Italia centrista, 1948–1950* (Milan, 1984). Two works by Vera Zamagni, "Betting on the Future: The Reconstruction of Italian Industry, 1946–1952," in *Power in Europe?*, ed. Joseph Becker and Franz Knipping (Berlin and New York, 1986), pp. 283–302, and "A Mass Market for Italian Industry: Reconstruction and American Models of Production and Consumption" (Paper delivered at the European University Institute workshop, "The Reconstruction and Re-integration in the World Economy of West Germany and Italy in the Postwar Period," Florence, 30–31 October 1986), show the limited and protected, if not backward, nature of the Italian industrial system in the 1940s. They criticize the feasibility of applying the Keynesian model proposed by the ECA to an economy like Italy's, which was not prepared to respond to the mass demand that was to develop only in the 1950s. All these contributions underestimate the social and political significance of an economic policy that was only selectively deflationary: economic and power relationships among the various social groups altered drastically between 1947 and the early 1950s.

40. Franco Bonelli, "Il capitalismo italiano: Linee generali d'interpretazione," in *Storia d'Italia, Annali I, Dal feudalesimo al capitalismo* (Turin, 1978), pp. 1193–1255.

41. Legnani, "'L'utopia grande-borghese,'" pp. 174–93; Salvati, *Stato e industria*, pp. 282–83 and 385–410; Craveri, *Sindacato e istituzioni*, p. 214 and pp. 260ff.; Beccalli, "La ricostruzione," pp. 369ff.; Vannicelli, "Labor Movement"; Turone, *Storia del sindacato*, pp. 181ff.

42. Harper, *America and the Reconstruction*, p. 163.

43. Report by T. Lane, "CISL Executive Committee Meeting," 21 June 1950, RG 84 Post-NA, 560.1 Italy; *Conquiste del lavoro* 3, no. 23 (11 June 1950).

44. Report by Consul Joel C. Hudson, "Increasing Apathy in Milan Labor Field," RG 59 DS-NA, 865.06/7-2750.

45. Lem Graves, Jr., to H. Martin, "General Report on Italian Tour," 6 March 1950, RG 286 ECA-NA, OSR, Labor Information Div., GSF 1948–51, box 11, Italy Reports.

46. T. Lane, "Required Labor Report—May 1950," RG 59 DS-NA, 865.06/6-1450.

47. Telegram from the embassy in Rome to Secretary of State, 11 January 1950, RG 84 Post-NA, 560.2 Italy/Strikes.

48. Telegram from the embassy in Rome to Secretary of State, RG 59 DS-NA, 865.062/3-450.

49. "Proceedings of ECA Labor Officers Conference, May 22–24, 1950, Paris," RG 286 ECA-NA, OSR, Labor Information Div., GSF 1949–51, box 4, p. 104, address by Thomas Lane.

50. Ibid., p. 105.

51. T. Lane, "Labor Roundup," RG 59 DS-NA, 865.06/3-3150; on the course of this affair, its implications for the state of bargaining in Italy, and its consequences for the political and trade union world, see Craveri, *Sindacato e istituzioni*, pp. 261–72.

52. Report from the embassy in Rome to Secretary of State, "Discussion of Implications of Fall Campaign for Wage Increases," 23 August 1950, and report of 30 August, "Fall Campaign of National Labor Organizations," both in RG 84 Post-NA, 560.2 Italy/Wages. Also see T. Lane, "Notes on Labor," 31 August 1950, RG 84 Post-NA, 560 Italy.

53. Telegram from the embassy in Rome to Secretary of State, 31 August 1950, and, for commentary on the "Piano del lavoro," the report "CGIL National Economic Conference," 2 March 1950, both in RG 84 Post-NA, respectively 560.2 Italy/Strikes and 560.1 Italy/CGIL. On the plan as a growth proposal of internal demand based on imperfect and politically late Keynesianism after the breakup of 1947–48, see *Il Piano del Lavoro della CGIL, 1949–1950*, by Paolo Santi et al. (Milan, 1978); Renzo Razzano, "I modelli di sviluppo della CGIL e della CISL," in *Problemi del movimento sindacale*, ed. Aris Accornero, pp. 527–42.

54. T. Lane, "Notes on Labor," 11 September 1950, RG 84 Post-NA, 560 Italy; telegram from the embassy in Rome to Secretary of State, 29 September 1950, RG 84 Post-NA, 560.2 Italy. On the conclusion of the dispute, see *Conquiste del lavoro* 3, no. 41 (22 October 1950).

55. Memorandum from Greene to Fraleigh in RG 59 DS-NA, 865.062/8-2350 (but actually 9 October 1950); T. Lane, "Notes on Labor," 8 November 1950, RG 84 Post-NA, 560 Italy.

56. Turone, *Storia del sindacato*, p. 192; on the CISL's renunciation of conflict, see Vannicelli, "Labor Movement," pp. 152–53; Guido Baglioni, *Il Sindacato dell'autonomia* (Bari, 1975), pp. 18–22; Vittorio Foa, "Sindacati e classe operaia," in *L'Italia contemporanea*, ed. Valerio Castronova (Turin, 1976), pp. 253–55; Tiziano Treu, "I governi centristi e la regolamentazione dell'attività sindacale," in *Problemi del movimento sindacale*, ed. Aris Accornero, pp. 571–75; *Conquiste del lavoro* 4, no. 36 (30 September 1951). On the railway strike, see *Bollettino d'informazione sindacale* 6, no. 3 (15 February 1953); telegram from the embassy in Rome to Secretary of State, RG 59 DS-NA, 865.062/1-853.

57. Accornero, "Per una nuova fase di studi," p. 61; Mario Ricciardi, "Conflitto ideologico e pluralismo sindacale," in *Problemi del movimento sindacale*, ed. Aris Accornero, pp. 589–608. Acute observations were already being made by several observers to the effect that the American model developed at the end of the war could not be applied in a noncontroversial way. This model of industrial relations was founded on pluralistic bargaining between organized interests and was anything but peaceful. See the analysis by Enrico Levi in CNP, *Primo convegno dei sindacalisti democratici reduci da missioni negli USA* (Rome, 1953), pp. 27–31, and by Joseph La Palombara in "Trade-Union Education as an Anti-Communist Weapon in Italy," *Southwestern Social Science Quarterly* 27, no. 1 (June 1956): 29–42; Filippelli, *American Labor*, pp. 198–203.

58. See especially the controversy that arose at the end of 1950 between the new head of the ECA mission (Dayton) and the CONFINDUSTRIA, which, through its chairman, Angelo Costa, decisively rejected both the ECA criticisms of the excessively low consumption levels and the implications of social manipulation contained in the program for increasing productivity. See D'Attorre, "Anche noi possiamo essere prosperi," pp. 67–68, and, by the same author, "Il Piano Marshall," pp. 159–60; Legnani, "'L'utopia grande-borghese,'" pp. 183–84. In the controversy, the ECA obviously enjoyed the full support of the CISL and the UIL; see *Conquiste del lavoro* 3, no. 42 (29 October 1950); "OK Mr. Dayton," *Il lavoro italiano* 2, no. 41 (27 October 1950).

59. Giuseppe Berta, *Lavoro, solidarietà, conflitti: Studi di storia delle politiche e delle relazioni*

del lavoro (Rome, 1985), p. 95. On the ECA's campaigns, see *L'ERP in Italia*, ed. by the MSA Special Mission in Italy (Rome, 1952); the collection by the review *Nel Mondo del lavoro*, published from 1950 on by the ECA's Information Division and later by the MSA; Ellwood, "La propaganda del Piano Marshall in Italia," *Passato e presente* 9 (September–December 1985): 153–71. On the experiments with the pilot firms, see *Produttività* 3, no. 9 (September 1952). On the productivist line of the CISL, see CISL, *Memoria sulla congiuntura economica presentata al Consiglio Generale di Bari, 4–6 gennaio 1951* (Rome, 1952); CISL, *Documenti Ufficiali (1950–1958)* (Rome, 1959), esp. pp. 31, 73–76; Giulio Pastore, "I sindacati operai e la produttività," *Produttività* 3, no. 4 (April 1952): 299–301; Mario Romani, *Appunti sulla evoluzione del sindacato* (1951; reprint, Rome, 1981); Ada Becchi Collidà, "Il rapporto tra salario e produttività nella teoria e nella prassi della CISL," in *Analisi della CISL*, ed. Guido Baglioni (Rome, 1980), pp. 517–47. On the influence of the theoretical and practical lore of the American trade unions on the development of the union outlook of the CISL in the 1950s, see Silvana Sciarra, "L'influenza del sindacalismo americano sulla CISL," in *Analisi della CISL*, ed. Guido Baglioni, pp. 283–307; Enzo Bartocci, "La CISL e il modello sindacale nord-americano," *Economia e lavoro* 13, no. 1 (January–March 1979): 167–84; Benedetto De Cesaris, "La scuola CISL di Firenze negli anni 50," *Rassegna sindacale: Quaderni* 37 (1972): 80–94. For contemporary criticism by the CGIL, see Piero Boni, "La CISL: Un'aiuola del sindacalismo americano," *Mondo operaio*, 20 January 1952; and Emilio Rienzi, "Produttività americana," *Il Lavoro* 52 (December 1951).

60. The two formulations are, respectively, by Accornero ("Per una nuova fase di studi," p. 61) and Vannicelli ("Labor Movement," p. 160).

61. D'Attorre, "Anche noi possiamo essere prosperi," p. 80. On the experience with the pilot firms and the CNP, see *Produttività* 4, no. 5 (5 May 1953); UIL, *Il lavoro italiano* 6, no. 14 (12 April 1954), and 7, no. 8 (21 February 1955) and no. 38 (27 June 1955); CISL, *Bollettino di studi e statistiche* 1, no. 1 (10 November 1953), and 2, no. 1 (January 1954) and no. 7 (July 1954); the collection by the review *Cronache della produttività* 1, no. 1 (25 February 1953), and following issues. See also Federico Romero, "Gli Stati Uniti e la 'modernizzazione' del sindacalismo italiano (1950–1955)," *Italia contemporanea*, no. 170 (March 1988): 72–96. On the relation between productivity and wages, see Franco Momigliano, *Sindacati, progresso tecnico, programmazione economica* (Turin, 1966), esp. pp. 63–69.

62. Harper, *America and the Reconstruction*, p. 166.

63. On the inability of postwar Italian society to reform, see Barucci, *Ricostruzione, pianificazione, Mezzogiorno*, pp. 377ff.; Castronovo, "Le sinistre e la ricostruzione economica," and Ennio Di Nolfo, "La sinistra europea dalla guerra contro il fascismo alla guerra fredda," both in *La sinistra europea*, ed. Maria Petricioli, pp. 3–24 and 297–314, respectively; Giuliano Amato, introduction to *Il governo dell'industria in Italia*, pp. 13–75.

64. On the exclusion of labor from the political and economic establishment, see Craveri, *Sindacato e istituzioni*, p. 327; Salvati, *Stato e industria*, pp. 171–74; Treu, "I governi centristi," pp. 553–87. For a differing opinion, see Scoppola, *La proposta politica*, pp. 307ff., who blames the exclusion of the working classes on the leftist forces, whose maximalism and pro-Soviet attitudes led to a kind of autoexclusion, in this way driving away the representatives of the workers' interests from an active political role in governing Italy.

65. Ruggero Amaduzzi, "Un suggerimento inattuabile," *Mondo operaio* 19 (April 1949).

66. Report of W. Bellanger, H. Gibbons, C. Lucia, 24 August 1950, enclosure to "Memorandum" by B. Jewell and R. Oliver, 1 October 1950, RG 286 ECA-NA, ECA/W, Productivity and Technical Assistance Div., SF 1950–1, box 3.

67. H. Lennon to J. Fobes, 24 August 1950, RG 286 ECA-NA, ECA/W, Productivity and Technical Assistance Div., SF 1950–1, box 3.

68. H. Lennon to J. Fobes, 25 September 1950, RG 286 ECA-NA, ECA/W, Productivity and Technical Assistance Div., SF 1950–1, box 3.

69. "A Recommended Program for France," 27 September 1950, RG 286 ECA-NA, ECA/W, Productivity and Technical Assistance Div., SF 1950–1, box 3.

70. Robert Mullen, director of the Office of Information, to William Joyce, "French Labor Report," 16 October 1950, RG 286 ECA-NA, ECA/W, Office of Information, GSF 1949–52, box 11; for observations on the Monnet plan, see C. W. Jeffers to W. Joyce, "Labor Relations and Communism in France," 18 October 1950, RG 286 ECA-NA, ECA/W, Productivity and Technical Assistance Div., SF 1950–1, box 3.

71. Robert Oliver to W. Foster, 20 October 1950, RG 286 ECA-NA, ECA/W, Productivity and Technical Assistance Div., SF 1950–1, box 3. Oliver, Clinton Golden's assistant in Washington, took Golden's place at the end of 1950, becoming the principal labor adviser at ECA headquarters.

72. V. Reuther, E. De Lasalle, and F. Bellanca, "Report of Special CIO Committee to Europe to CIO Committee on International Affairs," Washington, D.C., 1 March 1951, CIO-WPR, ALHUA, box 64.

73. M. Ross, "Memorandum of Members of CIO International Committee," 28 March 1951, CIO-ST, ALHUA, box 83. On the work of the CIO office in Europe, see also the autobiographical report of Victor Reuther, *Brothers Reuther*, pp. 332ff.

74. Svend A. Godfredsen to N. Cruikshank, "Report on ECA European Labor Staff Conference," 18 January 1951; also, "Agenda for European Labor Staff Conference—Paris, January 10–12, 1951," and McCloy to OSR, Paris, 20 December 1950, all in RG 286 ECA-NA, OSR, Labor Information Div., GSF 1949–51, box 3.

75. R. Oliver to W. Foster, R. H. Bissel, P. Porter, and W. H. Joyce, "Productivity Program for Meeting Armament Requirements Maintaining Essential Civilian Economy of NATO Countries," 6 February 1951, RG 286 ECA-NA, ECA/W, Productivity and Technical Assistance Div., SF 1950–1, box 3.

76. R. Mullen to W. Foster and D. Stone, 12 March 1951, RG ECA-NA, ECA/W, Office of Information, GSF 1949–52, box 11.

77. Memorandum by Nelson Cruikshank, new director of the labor division in Paris, "The Labor Situation in the ERP Countries," 17 April 1951, RG 286 ECA-NA, OSR, Labor Information Div., GSF 1949–51, box 3.

78. *L'ERP in Italia*, ed. MSA Special Mission in Italy, p. 7.

79. *FRUS*, 1951, 1:427; MSA, *European Effort for Productivity* (Paris, 1953); U.S. Department of Labor, *Mobilizing for Defense: 39th Annual Report of the Secretary of Labor* (Washington, D.C., 1952), pp. 177–78.

80. E. Kocher, "Report on ICFTU European Regional Organization Meeting," Brussels, 14 November 1951, RG 286 ECA-NA, OSR, Labor Information Div., GSF 1949–51, box 7; "Labor Reaction to New Productivity Campaign," 21 August 1951, RG 286 ECA-NA,

ECA/W, Productivity and Technical Assistance Div., SF 1950–1, box 3. For the AFL, see AFL, *American Labor Looks at the World*, 5 (1951): 75–77, and 6 (1952): 7–9; for the positions of the CIO, see *CIO News* 14, no. 32 (6 August 1951) and no. 35 (27 August 1951), and esp. V. Reuther to J. Potofsky, Paris, 22 August 1951, CIO-WPR, ALHUA, box 1.

81. For illuminating documentation on Italy, see Gian Giacomo Migone, "Stati Uniti, FIAT, e repressione antioperaia negli anni 50," *Rivista di storia contemporanea* 2 (1974): 232–81.

82. See, for example, H. Martin to Paul Porter, "Implementation of Benton Amendment, Section 3," 17 January 1952, RG 286 ECA-NA, ECA/W, Office of Information, GSF 1949–52, box 11; "Memorandum of CIO International Committee to Averell Harriman, MSA," *CIO and World Affairs* 3 (April 1952): 15.

83. International Cooperation Administration, *European Productivity and Technical Assistance Programs: A Summing Up, 1948–1958* (Paris, 1958), pp. 3–23 and, for the quotation on Italy, p. 207. See also MSA, *European Effort*.

84. "Productivity Survey," report from labor adviser Shapiro, Productivity and Technical Assistance Div., to R. M. Cabot, 3 June 1955, copy in CIO Washington Office Collection, Documents of the CIO, ALHUA, box 67f. On the controversy with CONFINDUSTRIA, see CISL, *Gli atti di una polemica* (Rome, 1953); "Il CNP al lavoro," *Bollettino di studi e statistiche CISL* 2, no. 7 (July 1954): 11–18; Saba, *Giulio Pastore*, pp. 246–48; *New York Times*, 18 and 28 July 1953; W. Reuther to A. Costa, Washington, D.C., 2 February 1954, and W. Reuther to V. Agostinone, 5 February 1954, both in CIO-WPR, ALHUA, box 67, folders 13 and 14; see also the interesting article by Adriano Olivetti, "How U.S. Aid Boomeranged in Italy," *World*, November 1953. For a more detailed analysis of the effects of the productivity drive in Italy, see D'Attorre, "Anche noi possiamo essere prosperi," and Romero, "Gli Stati Uniti e la 'modernizzazione.'"

85. For an evaluation of the economic impact of the productivity drive, see Wexler, *Marshall Plan Revisited*, pp. 89–96. For a comparison of productivity dynamics with wage dynamics to the disadvantage of the latter, see, on Italy, Momigliano, *Sindacati, progresso tecnico*, pp. 63–67; on France and Germany, see Walter Galenson, "The Labour Force and Labour Problems," in *The Fontana Economic History of Europe: The 20th Century, Part One*, ed. Carlo M. Cipolla (London, 1976), pp. 171–74; Sima Lieberman, *The Growth of European Mixed Economies* (Cambridge, Mass., 1977), pp. 15 and 19. See also Walter Kendall, *The Labour Movement in Europe* (London, 1975); Peter Lange, George Ross, Maurizio Vannicelli, *Unions, Change, and Crisis: French and Italian Union Strategy and the Political Economy, 1945–1980* (London, 1982); Philip Armstrong, Andrew Glyn, John Harrison, *Capitalism since World War II: The Making and the Breakup of the Great Boom* (London, 1984).

86. Milward, *Reconstruction of Western Europe*, p. 124.

87. See Arkes, *Bureaucracy*, p. 319, and Leo Panitch, "Trade Unions and the Capitalist State," *New Left Review* 125 (1981): 30–34.

88. See the analysis of one of the most committed of the American trade union technicians, who served as an ECA consultant in trade union training connected with the productivity drive: William Gomberg, "Labor's Participation in the European Productivity Program: A Study of Frustration," *Political Science Quarterly* 74, no. 2 (June 1959): 240–55. David Heaps reached similar conclusions in "Union Participation in Foreign Aid Programs," *Industrial*

and Labor Relations Review 9, no. 1 (October 1955): 100–108; Joseph La Palombara, "The Political Role of Organized Labor in Western Europe," *Journal of Politics* 17, no. 1 (February 1955): 78–81; Murray Edelman, "Labor's Influence in Foreign Policy," *Labor Law Journal* 5, no. 5 (May 1943): 323–29.

Conclusion

1. Romero, "Gli Stati Uniti e la 'modernizzazione,'" pp. 71–96; Stephen Burwood, "American Labor, French Labor, and the Marshall Plan: Battleground and Crossroads" (Paper presented at the Ninth Annual North American Labor History Conference, Detroit, 22–24 October 1987).

2. Michael Shalev, "Lies, Damned Lies, and Strike Statistics: The Measurement of Trends in Industrial Conflict," in *The Resurgence of Class Conflict in Western Europe since 1968*, ed. Colin Crouch and Alessandro Pizzorno (London, 1978), 1:1–19.

3. See Carew, *Labour under the Marshall Plan*; Volcker R. Berghahan, *The Americanization of West German Industry, 1945–1973* (New York, 1986); D'Attorre, "Anche noi possiamo essere prosperi," pp. 55–93.

4. Walter Muller Jentsch and Hans Joachim Sperling, "Economic Development, Labour Conflict, and the Industrial Relations System in West Germany," in *The Resurgence of Class Conflict*, ed. Colin Crouch and Alessandro Pizzorno, pp. 287–306; Michael Fichter, *Besatzungsmacht und Gewerkschaften* (Opladen, 1982).

5. Irving Brown, interview with the author, Washington, D.C., 14 August 1984; Victor Reuther, interview with the author, Washington, D.C., 14 August 1984.

6. Milward, *Reconstruction of Western Europe*, p. 501; see also Alan S. Milward, "Was the Marshall Plan Necessary?," *Diplomatic History* 13, no. 2 (1989): 231–53; Federico Romero, ed., "Americanizzazione e modernizzazione nell'Europa postbellica," a discussion with Michael Hogan, Leonardo Paggi, Vibeke Sorensen, *Passato e presente* 9, no. 23 (1990): 19–46.

7. See esp. Michael Hogan, *The Marshall Plan: America, Britain, and the Reconstruction of Western Europe, 1947–1952* (New York, 1987); Maier, "Politics of Productivity," pp. 607–33.

8. In addition to the works of Hogan cited above, see the attempt at theoretical definition by Thomas J. McCormick, "Drift or Mastery? A Corporatist Synthesis for American Diplomatic History," *Reviews in American History* 10 (1982): 318–30; and esp. Michael Hogan, "Corporatism: A Positive Appraisal," *Diplomatic History* 10, no. 4 (1986): 363–72. However, I am in complete disagreement with the use of the term "corporatist" to indicate American neocapitalism, whose organizational principles are quite far from those forms of centralized collaboration between the state and organized social interests that the neocorporatism of societies in northern Europe connotes. Even though the term is now established in American historiography, the concept runs too much risk of confusion. In particular, if it is applied to the system of industrial relations, the term "corporatist" is totally inapplicable to the American case, whose pluralistic and privatistic model is all the further from any corporatist scheme. See also the discussion on the following pages.

9. In this sense, I find salutary the criticism of the excessive concentration by the "corpora-

tist synthesis" on the internal origins of American foreign policy presented by John Lewis Gaddis in "The Corporatist Synthesis: A Skeptical View," *Diplomatic History* 10, no. 4 (1986): 360–61.

10. Hogan, *Marshall Plan*, p. 436; International Cooperation Administration, *European Productivity and Technical Assistance Programs*.

11. Steven Fraser and Gary Gerstle, eds., *The Rise and Fall of the New Deal Order, 1930–1980* (Princeton, 1989), p. xix.

12. See "Statement of Walter P. Reuther, President of the U.A.W. (CIO)," ERP-*Hearings*, 158:1386–95; and Dubinsky, "World Labor's New Weapon," pp. 451–62.

13. See Peter Lange, George Ross, and Maurizio Vannicelli, *Unions, Changes, and Crisis: French and Italian Union Strategy and the Political Economy, 1945–1980* (London, 1982); Andrei S. Markovits, *The Politics of the West German Trade Unions* (Cambridge, 1986); Christian Deubner, "Change and Internationalization in Industry: Toward a Sectoral Interpretation of West German Politics," *International Organization* 28, no. 3 (1984): 501–35; Turone, *Storia del sindacato*.

SELECTED SOURCES

Archival Sources

Italy

Rome
  Archives of the CGIL
  Archives of the UIL
    Vanni Montana Papers
  Giulio Pastore Foundation
    Archives of the CISL Confederal Secretariat
    Lamberto Giannittelli Letters
    Giulio Pastore Letters

Great Britain

London
  Public Record Office
    Archives of the Foreign Office
      General Correspondence 371

United States

Detroit, Michigan
  Archives of Labor History and Urban Affairs, Wayne State University
    Documents of the Congress of Industrial Organizations
      CIO Washington Office Collection
      Minutes of the CIO Executive Board
      Walter P. Reuther Collection
      Secretary-Treasurer Collection
      UAW President Collection
Madison, Wisconsin
  State Historical Society of Wisconsin
    Florence Thorne Papers
New York, New York
  Archives of the Council on Foreign Relations

Archives of the International Ladies' Garment Workers' Union
    Luigi Antonini Letters
    David Dubinsky Letters
University Park, Pennsylvania
  Pennsylvania State University Libraries
    Clinton S. Golden Letters
Washington, D.C.
  Archives of the American Federation of Labor
  Archives of the Central Intelligence Agency
  Catholic University of America
    Joseph Brophy Letters
    Richard Deverall Letters
    Philip Murray Letters
  National Archives
    Record Group 59: General Records of the Department of State
    Record Group 84: Records of the Foreign Service Posts of the Department of State (Rome)
    Record Group 169: Records of the Foreign Economic Administration
    Record Group 174: General Records of the Department of Labor
    Record Group 218: Records of the U.S. Joint Chiefs of Staff
    Record Group 226: Records of the Office of Strategic Services
    Record Group 286: Records of the Agency for International Development (Economic Cooperation Administration)
    Record Group 319: Records of the (U.S.) Army Staff
    Record Group 331: Records of Allied Operational and Occupation Headquarters, World War II (Allied Control Commission in Italy)

Interviews with the Author

Irving Brown, Washington, D.C., 14 August 1984.
Victor Reuther, Washington, D.C., 14 August 1984.

Newspapers and Periodicals

AFL Weekly News Service, 1946–51
American Federationist, 1944–54
Bollettino d'informazioni sindacali, 1948–55
CIO and World Affairs, 1950–54
CIO News, 1944–55
Conquiste del lavoro, 1948–55
Cronache della produttività, 1953–55
International Free Trade Union News, 1946–54

Lavoro, 1948–54
Il lavoro italiano, 1949–54
Monthly Labor Review, 1944–45
Nel mondo del lavoro, 1951–52
New Leader, 1944–54
New York Times, 1943–55
Notes on Labor Abroad, 1947–53
Notiziario CGIL, 1947–55
Produttività, 1950–55

Official Documents, Published Sources, and Testimony

Abbiamo visto: tre sindacalisti italiani tra i lavoratori d'America. Rome, 1949.
AFL. *AFL and Reconversion*, by William Green. Washington, D.C., 1944.
———. *American Labor and the World Crisis*. New York, 1952.
———. *American Labor Looks at the World*. Vols. 1–9. Washington, D.C., 1947–55.
———. *Democracy and the Free Labor Movement*. Washington, D.C., n.d.
———. *Italian Labor Today*, by Luigi Antonini. Washington, D.C., 1944.
———. *Postwar Program*. Washington, D.C., 1944.
———. *Report of the Proceedings of the Sixty-fourth Annual Convention of the AFL*. Washington, D.C, 1944.
Carey, James. "Why the CIO Bowed Out." *Saturday Evening Post*, 11 June 1949.
CIO. *Report of the CIO Delegates to the World Trade Union Conference, London, February 1945*. Washington D.C., 1945.
CISL. *Gli atti di una polemica*. Rome, 1953.
———. *Azione sindacale e speculazione politica. Le direttive della CISL*. Rome, 1951.
———. *Il centro di studi sindacali*. Rome, 1953.
———. *Documenti ufficiali (1950–1958)*. Rome, 1959.
———. *Un'economia forte per un sindacato forte*. Rome, n.d.
———. *I lavoratori difendono l'Italia; l'Italia difenda i lavoratori*. Rome, 1951.
———. *Memoria sulla congiuntura economica presentata al Consiglio Generale, Bari, 4–6 gennaio 1951*. Rome, 1952.
———. *Primo Congresso Nazionale. I lavori e gli atti (Relazione della Segreteria Confederale)*. Rome, 1952.
———. *Secondo Congresso Nazionale. Relazione della Segreteria Confederale. I lavori e gli atti*. Rome, 1956.
CISL Ufficio Studi. *Per una storia della CISL (1950–1962)*. Rome, 1962.
Clifford, Clark M. *American Relations with the Soviet Union: A Report to the President by the Special Counsel to the President, September 1946*. In *Memoirs: Sixty Years on the Firing Line*, by A. Krock. New York, 1968.
CNP. *Primo convegno sindacalisti democratici reduci da missioni negli USA*. Rome, 1953.
Documents on American Foreign Relations, 1944–52. Edited by the World Peace Foundation. New York, 1944–52.

Dubinsky, David, "Isolate Communist Aggression." *Labor and Nation* 5, no. 4 (1949): 20–22.

———. "Labor Internationalism Is Part of Progressivism at Home." *Labor and Nation* 5, no. 5 (1949): 75–77.

———. "Rift and Realignment in World Labor." *Foreign Affairs* 27 (January 1949): 232–45.

———. "World Labor's New Weapon." *Foreign Affairs* 28 (April 1950): 451–62.

L'ERP in Italia (1952). Edited by Mutual Security Agency Special Mission in Italy. Rome, 1952.

ERP Mission in Italy. *Il Piano Marshall in Italia.* Milan, 1950.

Etzold, T. H., and J. L. Gaddis, eds. *Containment: Documents on American Policy and Strategy, 1945–1950.* New York, 1978.

Finger, Eleanor. "Labor's Role in ECA." *Labor and Nation* 5, no. 4 (1949): 13–14.

Foreign Assistance Act of 1948 (ERP). In *U.S. Statutes at Large,* vol. 62, pt. 1. 80th Cong., 2d sess., 1948.

Foreign Relations of the United States. 1944–54. Washington, D.C., 1959–77.

IFCTU. *Official Report of the Free World Labour Conference and of the First Congress of the ICFTU.* London, 1949.

———. *Report of the Second World Congress Held at Milan, Italy, 4–12 July 1951.* Brussels, 1951.

"Inflazione, investimenti e unità sindacale: Il Direttivo della CGIL del 15–19 luglio 1946." In *Quaderni di rassegna sindacale,* no. 59/60 (March–June 1976): 198–232.

International Cooperation Administration. *European Productivity and Technical Assistance Programs: A Summing Up, 1948–1958.* Paris, 1958.

Kaiser, Philip M. "American Labor in International Affairs." In *Proceedings of the Fourth Annual Meeting of the Industrial Relations Research Association.* Vol 4. Madison, Wis., 1952.

LCGIL. *Primo anno. Relazione della Segreteria Confederale al 1 Congresso Nazionale.* Rome, 1949.

Lorwin, Val L. "Labor's Own 'Cold War.'" *Labor and Nation* 6, no. 1 (1950): 8–10.

Meany, George. *The Last Five Years: How the AFL Fights Communism Around the World.* Washington, D.C., 1951.

Morse, David A. "Labor and American Foreign Policy." *Industrial and Labor Relations Review* 1, no. 1 (October 1947): 18–28.

Mutual Security Agency. *European Effort for Productivity.* Edited by Productivity and Technical Assistance Division, OSR in Europe. Paris, 1953.

NATO Information Service. *The Trade Unions and NATO.* Paris, 1957.

Reuther, Walter. "How to Beat the Communists." *Collier's,* 28 February 1948.

———. *Selected Papers.* Edited by Henry M. Christman. New York, 1961.

Ross, Michael. "American Labor's World Responsibilities." *Foreign Affairs* 30 (October 1951): 112–22.

———. "American Unions and West European Recovery." In *Proceedings of the Fourth Annual Meeting of the Industrial Relations Research Association.* Vol. 4. Madison, Wis., 1952.

Truman, Harry S. *Public Papers of the Presidents: Harry S. Truman*. Vols. 1–8. Washington, D.C., 1961–66.

UIL. *La UIL dall'Atto Costitutivo 1950 al Congresso di Bologna 1977*. Rome, n.d.

U.S. Congress. Senate. *Hearings before the Committee on Foreign Relations*. 80th Cong., 2d sess. Vols. 157–58, *Hearings on the European Recovery Program Bill*.

U.S. Council of Economic Advisers. *The Impact of Foreign Aid upon the Domestic Economy*. Washington, D.C., 1947.

U.S. Department of Labor. *Annual Reports of the Secretary of Labor*. Washington, D.C., 1944–54.

U.S. Economic Cooperation Administration. *Italy—Country Study. European Recovery Program*, by Paul Hoffmann. Washington, D.C., 1949.

U.S. Information Service. *Cooperazione Economica Italia–Stati Uniti, 1944–1954*. Rome, n.d.

U.S. President's Committee on Foreign Aid. *European Recovery and American Aid*. Washington, D.C., 1947.

WFTU. *Report of Activity of the World Federation of Trade Unions, 15 Oct. 1945–30 April 1949*. Paris, 1949.

———. *Report of the Proceedings of the Second World Trade Union Congress*. Paris, 1949.

———. *Resolution of the World Trade Union Congress*. London, 1945.

INDEX